T0222272

Foundation Flex
for Developers

Data-Driven Applications with
PHP, ASP.NET, ColdFusion, and LCDS

Sas Jacobs with Koen De Weggheleire

friendsof

DESIGNER TO DESIGNER™

an Apress® company

Foundation Flex for Developers
Data-Driven Applications with PHP, ASP.NET, ColdFusion, and LCDS

Credits

For my partner David, who has supported and loved me while writing this book. And for our son, whose birth interrupted the writing process. I love you both.

Sas Jacobs

CONTENTS AT A GLANCE

CONTENTS

Chapter 6 **Working with Data in Flex Applications** **147**

Chapter 8 **Using XML in Flex Builder** **227**

PART 2 DATA-DRIVEN APPLICATIONS

PART 3 LIVECYCLE DATA SERVICES

ABOUT THE AUTHORS

Sas Jacobs is a web developer who set up her own business, Anything Is Possible, in 1994, working in the areas of web development, IT training, and technical writing. The business works with large and small clients building web applications with .NET, Flash, XML, and databases.

Sas has spoken at such conferences as Flashforward, webDU (previously known as MXDU), and FlashKit on topics related to XML and dynamic content in Flash. She is also the author of books about Flash and XML.

In her spare time, Sas is passionate about traveling, photography, running, and enjoying life.

Koen De Weggheleire is a faculty member of the Technical University of West-Flanders (HOWEST), department PIH-Multimedia and Communication Technology (MCT) in Belgium, where he teaches Flash Platform Solutions (Flash, Flex, AIR) with a smile. As the Adobe User Group Manager for Belgium (www.adobeusergroup.be), Koen is heavily addicted to the community and inspires the community by his blog (www.newmovieclip.com) and by speaking at national and international industry events. Koen also coordinates the yearly Belgian multimedia conference, Multi-Mania (www.multi-mania.be), where 800 people come together to learn from industry experts and to share knowledge.

When he has time, you can find Koen doing freelance Flash platform consultancy on advanced award-winning Rich Internet Applications.

Sometimes it happens that Koen is not talking ActionScript. Then you can find him producing music, collecting Adobe gadgets, eating pizza, or renovating his 100-year-old house.

ABOUT THE TECHNICAL REVIEWER

 **Charles E. Brown** is one of the most noted authors and teachers in the computer industry today. His first two books, *Beginning Dreamweaver MX* and *Fireworks MX Zero to Hero*, have received critical acclaim and are consistent bestsellers. In early 2004, Charles coauthored a book on VBA for Microsoft Access: *VBA Access Programming*. His latest book, *The Essential Guide to Flex 2 with ActionScript 3.0*, continues to be a best seller, and is used as a textbook at several international universities. In the spring of 2008, the book will be updated for Flex 3.

In addition to his busy writing schedule, Charles conducts frequent seminars as an Adobe Certified Trainer. His topics include Flex, Flash, Dreamweaver, and ActionScript programming. He is also frequently called in as a consultant for major web sites involving Adobe technologies.

Charles is also a noted classical organist, pianist, and guitarist; and studied with such notables as Vladimir Horowitz, Virgil Fox, and Igor Stravinsky. It was because of his association with Stravinsky that he got to meet and develop a friendship with famed artist Pablo Picasso. Charles can be contacted through his web site at www.charlesebrown.net.

ABOUT THE COVER IMAGE DESIGNER

 **Corné van Dooren** designed the front cover image for this book. After taking a brief vacation from friends of ED to create a new design for the *Foundation* series, he worked at combining technological and organic forms, with the results now appearing on this and other books' covers.

Corné spent his childhood drawing on everything at hand and then began exploring the infinite world of multimedia—and his journey of discovery hasn't stopped since. His mantra has always been "The only limit to multimedia is the imagination," a saying that keeps him moving forward constantly.

Corné works for many international clients, writes features for multimedia magazines, reviews and tests software, authors multimedia studies, and works on many other friends of ED books. You can see more of his work at and contact him through his web site: www. cornevandooren.com.

If you like Corné's work, be sure to check out his chapter in *New Masters of Photoshop: Volume 2* (friends of ED, 2004).

ACKNOWLEDGMENTS

I'd like to acknowledge the hard work from all the people at friends of ED. Chris, Ben, Matt, Beth, Nancy, Liz, and anyone else I've forgotten, thanks for your valuable input. I'd also like to thank Koen for contributing two chapters to this book at short notice. We couldn't have done it without you!

Sas Jacobs

When I started writing this book, it felt like one big interesting adventure. It has been a long adventure because we really wanted to be sure the book contained the latest and greatest information available on Adobe Flex concerning data-driven applications.

I really want to thank the dedicated and patient people at friends of ED: Chris Mills, Beth Christmas, Charles Brown, Matthew Moodie, Elizabeth Berry, Tina Nielsen, and Nancy Sixsmith for their professional help and guidance through this wonderful adventure.

Also my thanks go to my coauthor Sas Jacobs. Sas put an incredible amount of work in this book and with her wealth of knowledge she made sure this book had everything it needed.

Of course, finally, I also want to thank my friends and family for being supportive and for understanding why I sometimes didn't have enough time.

I learned a lot from the community myself, and I still do, but I am very happy that I can give something back. You know, it's all about giving back to the community!

Happy coding!

Koen De Weggheleire

INTRODUCTION

Regardless of which type of application they're building, developers usually have to carry out a range of common tasks: communicating information to a user, displaying pop-up windows, showing repeating information in a tabular or grid layout, providing forms to update an external data source, and so on. Many times, when learning a new programming language I've wanted a book that provided me with a set of building blocks showing me how to achieve one of these tasks. So I wanted to write one about the Flex framework that covered these common developer tasks and then brought the concepts together in a series of case studies. Welcome to this book.

If you've picked up the book, you're probably a designer or developer who has some experience with the Flex 2 or 3 framework. You've probably had some exposure to ActionScript 2.0 and are keen to learn more about ActionScript 3.0.

With this book, you can take your skills to the next level. No book can cover everything, but here you'll learn some of the more useful tools for Flex application development. Most importantly, you'll learn how to include external data within your Flex applications. I'll focus particularly on XML documents and content from databases and show you how to add this information to your Flex interfaces.

The book is purposely simple so you can get the basic concepts right. Each chapter covers a small topic, demonstrating, with some basic examples, how you might achieve specific tasks using Flex. It's not until the second part of the book that we put these concepts together to create four complete applications.

This book started as a book about Flex 2. During the writing process, Adobe announced the release of Flex 3, so I changed the focus halfway through. It was also interrupted by the birth of my son in June 2007, so it's been a long road.

I hope you enjoy reading this book and that you find it useful for demonstrating some of the complexities of Flex 3 and ActionScript 3.0. I find Flex to be a very powerful application development tool and I hope to share my excitement about it with you!

Layout conventions

To keep this book as clear and easy to follow as possible, the following text conventions are used throughout.

Important words or concepts are normally highlighted on the first appearance in **bold type**.

Code is presented in `fixed-width font`.

New or changed code is normally presented in **`bold fixed-width font`**.

Pseudo-code and variable input are written in _`italic fixed-width font`_.

Menu commands are written in the form Menu ➤ Submenu ➤ Submenu.

Where I want to draw your attention to something, I've highlighted it like this:

> _Ahem, don't say I didn't warn you._

Sometimes code won't fit on a single line in a book. Where this happens, I use an arrow like this: ➥.

```
This is a very, very long section of code that should be written all on the same ➥
line without a break.
```

Part 1

FLEX APPLICATION BASICS

In the first part of this book, I introduce the Flex framework and discuss some of the tools that developers need to start building applications. You'll examine how ActionScript 3.0 works with Flex applications and see some of the approaches that you can use to structure these applications. You'll look at common developer tasks such as interacting with the user, communicating with the web browser, working with external data sources, and displaying dynamic data, and you'll see how to use these techniques within Flex Builder 3.

Chapter 1

INTRODUCTION TO FLEX

Flex 3 provides a new approach to building SWF applications that run with Flash Player 9. Like Flash before it, the Flex framework creates SWF files, but there's a world of difference between the two products. If you've worked with version 1 of Flex, versions 2 and 3 are a major revamp, so you'll need to forget what you already know and be prepared to start again.

For developers who've worked with Flash previously, Flex 3 introduces a wide range of new possibilities. It provides a development environment specifically suited to creating SWF-based applications, and it shifts the focus from animation to creating user interfaces and interactions. Developers who've worked with tools such as Visual Studio .NET will find it easy to adapt to the changes because the development environment, Flex Builder 3, uses a very similar approach.

Instead of creating keyframes in a timeline, Flex applications use an XML vocabulary called MXML to describe the components that make up the user interface. Each MXML tag corresponds to an ActionScript 3.0 class, and developers can access the methods, properties, and events of each class through attributes of the tag. Developers can also use ActionScript 3.0 to create and wire up these user interface components to respond to user interactions.

ActionScript 3.0 represents a major overhaul of the ActionScript language to provide a more standards-based and robust approach. The new version is compliant with the ECMAScript Language Specification, Third Edition (ECMA-262). Developers with a solid grounding in ActionScript won't find it too hard to make the transition, but there are some major differences. I'll cover some of the most important changes to the ActionScript language a little later in the chapter.

This chapter introduces you to the role of Flex in web application development and provides you with some of the key concepts you'll need to get started. I'll explain the role of ActionScript 3.0 and of MXML, and provide an introduction to each. I'll give you an overview of the new features in the ActionScript 3.0 language as well as introducing some of the new classes.

I also want to explain the different ways to work with data in Flex applications: the types of data-driven applications, the types of data that you can include in them, and the tools in the Flex framework that are specific to working with data-driven applications. I'll finish up with some useful resources for learning more about Flex.

Let's start by discussing how Flex fits into the world of web applications.

Understanding web applications

Web applications present data within web pages that appear within a web browser. These web pages provide an easy way for users to access and interact with the data.

Web applications typically consist of a number of different layers: the user interface, the data used to populate the user interface, and a third layer that allows the user interface to interact with the data layer. These layers are often called **n-tier** or **multi-tier** architecture.

The user interface provides the means for a user to interact with the data in the web application. It usually consists of web pages that include standard elements such as buttons, text inputs, drop-down lists, images, and hyperlinks. The user interface responds when the user interacts with each element, perhaps clicking a button or hyperlink, or moving the mouse over an image.

In n-tier architecture, the user interface is referred to as the **presentation** tier or layer. In web applications, the presentation layer occurs within the web browser using XHTML or SWF objects, and client-side scripting such as JavaScript or ActionScript.

The user interface displays data from databases, XML and text documents, the file system, and data streams from web services and RSS feeds. Increasingly, web applications rely on XML structures to provide content. The XML content might result from a request to a database or by receiving a response from a web service.

This layer is called the **data** tier in n-tier architecture. The layer is abstracted from the presentation tier and is located separately. A database server provides a good example of the data tier. It exists separately from the web browser and server.

To include data from the data tier within the presentation tier, there's a need for a middle layer between the two. In n-tier architecture, this layer is called the **business logic**, or **application**, tier. This tier exists as an intermediary between the data source and the application interface. It also enforces business rules and other logic required within the web application.

The **business logic** tier exists within an application server and relies on server-side languages such as ColdFusion, ASP.NET, and PHP. This layer is responsible for requesting data from the data tier and providing it to the presentation tier in an appropriate format, often using an XML structure.

There can be a little more to n-tier architecture than I've presented here. However, the idea was to give you an overview of the architecture that typically underpins a web application.

One implication of using n-tier architecture is that this approach separates the presentation layer from the data source. It's not possible for the client software (the web browser, in this case) to communicate directly with a database. Instead, the communication between the two is handled with a server-side language and an application or web server within the business logic tier.

You can see that this approach makes a lot of sense from a security standpoint. Allowing a web page to access a database directly would open up all sorts of possibilities for executing malicious code. It's for this reason that there are so many restrictions on the functionality of XHTML and client-side scripts such as ActionScript.

So how does Flex fit into an n-tier architectural style?

Understanding the role of Flex

In traditional web applications, the user interface is built using XHTML. The user makes a request for a web page and waits until the web server responds and the requested page loads into the web browser. Each time users require new information, they make a request for another web page so that each state in the application responds to a new web page. When a new page loads from the server, the user interface is loaded again. This means that traditional web applications are very stop/start in nature.

Recent years have shown a fundamental change in the way web applications are built, and a new model has evolved: the Rich Internet Application (RIA). RIAs don't rely on the traditional request/response model. Instead, they use requests to the server to populate specific parts of the user interface. As a result, RIAs provide more responsive and media-rich interfaces. Users don't have to wait around for each new page to load from the server. In fact, the concept of pages within a web application has disappeared altogether, replaced by a single page interface in which only parts of the page change in response to user interaction.

As a style of web application, RIAs demand new approaches and tools for web application development. Examples of approaches for building RIAs include both Ajax and SWF-based applications. These applications can be created with a combination of XHTML and JavaScript, or by using Flash or Flex to generate SWF files. One key feature is that data is requested asynchronously so that users don't have to wait for a server response each time they carry out an action.

Flex 3 provides a framework for building RIAs that are compiled to SWF files. Flash does the same, although the Flex framework is targeted more toward the developer community. SWF files represent the presentation tier within an n-tier web application and offer an alternative to XHTML and JavaScript-based approaches.

SWF-based presentation tiers provide functionality that is possible using browser scripting alone. Developers can use SWF files to work with multimedia content and to create more expressive online applications. SWF files can also be deployed to devices such as mobile phones and PDAs.

Within the Flex 3 framework, developers can use an XML vocabulary, MXML, with ActionScript 3.0 to describe user interfaces and capture user interactions. Flex 3 applications are compiled to create ActionScript capable of being viewed in Flash Player 9. The Flash Player can be embedded within a web browser or in a standalone application.

The Flex framework includes a rich class library of components for creating user interfaces for use in web applications. In addition to the range of standard user interface elements, the Flex framework includes advanced controls specifically aimed at displaying data: DataGrid, Tree, and Repeater controls.

The class libraries within the Flex framework also include mechanisms for consuming dynamic content provided by the business logic tier, or server-side files supplying data to a web application. The Flex framework can make requests for text and XML content from external sources, and display the responses in the user interface elements. However, as with any technology involved in the presentation tier, applications built in Flex cannot interact directly with databases or with the server file system.

While there is a small learning curve for developers who want to use the Flex framework to build SWF files, it does leverage existing ActionScript and web application development skills. Flex Builder 3, the dedicated Flex 3 IDE, provides a similar approach to that found in software such as Visual Studio .NET. In addition, developers familiar with web standards such as XML, SOAP, ECMAScript, and E4X will find that they are integrated into the Flex 3 framework.

Developers can use both MXML and ActionScript 3.0 to create Flex 3 applications, so it's worth understanding the role of each.

Understanding the role of MXML and ActionScript 3.0

The two foundations of the Flex framework are MXML and ActionScript 3.0. MXML is an XML vocabulary that allows developers to describe user interfaces. MXML consists of a set of tags or elements that correspond to ActionScript 3.0 classes. The MXML elements are compiled into the relevant ActionScript code when a SWF file is created. The attributes in each MXML tag correspond to either a property or method of the ActionScript class, a style applied to the object created with the tag, or an event listener for the object.

MXML elements describe everything from user interface elements, visual layouts and effects, to data connections. Users add these elements to their applications declaratively, in the same way that they'd add XHTML to generate a web page. They can also add elements by dragging and dropping them in the Design view of Flex Builder 3.

As mentioned, the methods, properties, and events described in ActionScript are represented by attributes in MXML tags. When you view the help content for the Flex framework, you can either see an API for the MXML elements or for the ActionScript equivalent classes.

It's possible to create an application interface using only MXML tags, entirely in ActionScript 3.0, or using a combination of both (the most likely alternative). Let's look a little more closely at the structure of MXML documents.

Understanding MXML

MXML provides the same role in Flex applications as XHTML does in web pages. Both are markup languages describing a user interface. Because MXML is a vocabulary of XML, all the XML construction rules apply. An MXML document must be a well-formed XML document, which means the following:

- The MXML document contains one or more elements or nodes.
- The MXML document contains a single root node, usually the <mx:Application> element that can contain other nested elements.
- Each element closes properly.
- Elements nest correctly.
- Attribute values are contained in either double or single quotes.

All MXML documents start with an XML declaration, as shown here:

```
<?xml version = "1.0" encoding = "utf-8" ?>
```

The root element of an MXML document is usually the <mx:Application> tag, although you can use other elements for the root node. The root element represents the container for all other parts of the MXML document and will enclose all other containers and controls.

The root element also includes a reference to the namespace www.adobe.com/2006/mxml. You can see it here within the <mx:Application> element:

```
<mx:Application xmlns:mx="http://www.adobe.com/2006/mxml">
```

Although the namespace refers to a URI, it doesn't actually reference a page at that location. Instead, using a unique URI provides a reference saying that all tags using the same prefix (in this case, mx:) come from the same XML vocabulary. Each time a Flex element appears in an MXML file, it must use this prefix.

Developers can add other namespaces with their own prefixes to the <mx:Application> element if they develop custom components. For example:

```
<mx:Application xmlns:mx="http://www.adobe.com/2006/mxml"
   xmlns:comp="components.*">
```

In this case, any custom components must use the prefix comp: to distinguish them from built-in Flex components.

The following code block shows a very simple Flex interface written with MXML tags:

```
<?xml version="1.0" encoding="utf-8"?>
<mx:Application xmlns:mx="http://www.adobe.com/2006/mxml">
  <mx:Button id="btnClickMe" label="Click me" />
</mx:Application>
```

The interface contains a single element: a button. The code creates an instance of the Button ActionScript 3.0 class using the <mx:Button> tag. It sets the id and label properties of that instance using attributes within the tag. When you compile the application, the process will create the relevant ActionScript to create the button within the SWF file.

All MXML tags and class names begin with an uppercase letter, and if there is more than one word in the name, each word in the name starts with an uppercase letter (for example, ComboBox).

As mentioned, MXML elements are compiled to create a SWF file. During this process, the MXML tags are parsed, and the compiler generates the corresponding ActionScript classes. The compiler then compiles the ActionScript classes into SWF bytecode contained in a SWF file. This process occurs either by using Flex Builder 3 or through the free command-line compiler included with the Flex SDK. As a bit of a hint, it's much easier to compile SWF files using Flex Builder 3!

MXML works hand in hand with ActionScript 3.0.

Understanding ActionScript 3.0

ActionScript 3.0 is the new version of this scripting language and is at the heart of the Flex framework. It is based on ECMAScript and is fully compliant with the ECMAScript language specification, Third Edition (ECMA-262). You can find a copy of this specification at www.ecma-international.org/publications/standards/Ecma-262.htm.

ActionScript 3.0 is run by the ActionScript Virtual Machine (AVM) inside Flash Player 9. Unlike earlier versions, Flash Player 9 includes two AVMs—one for ActionScript 3.0 (AVM2) and one for earlier language versions (AVM1). Changes to the AVM mean that the new version of ActionScript works much more quickly than ActionScript 2.0 or 1.0. It also means that you can't include different versions of ActionScript in the same application. Flex 3 applications must work with ActionScript 3.0.

The ActionScript 3.0 language is made up of two parts: the core language and the Flash Player API. The core language describes the basic language elements, including data types, expressions, loops, and conditions. This part of the language hasn't changed much. The Flash Player API describes the ActionScript classes that are run by the Flash Player, and this is the area in which you'll find the most changes.

Developers can work with ActionScript 3.0 in Flex applications in the following ways:

- Adding inline ActionScript statements to MXML tags
- Adding code blocks with the <mx:Script> tag in an MXML file
- Working with external ActionScript files, perhaps as the source for an <mx:Script> element or as a custom class

Developers familiar with earlier versions of ActionScript will need to make some adjustments when learning ActionScript 3.0. There are new data types and changes to the way class files are written. You can find out about the main changes to the language a little later in the chapter.

The following code block shows an application that uses ActionScript 3.0 declarations to create the same interface as the preceding application built with MXML tags:

```xml
<?xml version="1.0" encoding="utf-8"?>
<mx:Application xmlns:mx="http://www.adobe.com/2006/mxml"
  creationComplete="buttonCreator(event)">
  <mx:Script>
    <![CDATA[
      import mx.controls.Button;
      import mx.events.FlexEvent;
      private var btnClickMe:Button;
      private function buttonCreator (e:FlexEvent):void {
        btnClickMe = new Button();
        btnClickMe.label = "Click me";
        addChild (btnClickMe);
      }
    ]]>
  </mx:Script>
</mx:Application>
```

Instead of adding an <mx:Button> tag directly in the application, the code block uses a function called buttonCreator to create the button. The function is called when the application finishes creating and, as in the previous example, the interface contains a single button element.

You can see that the ActionScript code is contained within a CDATA block. It includes a constructor for creating the button, new Button(), as well as a new method for displaying the button in the interface (addChild). Don't bother to try this code yourself because it's just an illustration. I've got some much more interesting examples ahead.

As you can see from the previous code block, there are some major changes to the ActionScript language in version 3.0.

Understanding the major changes in ActionScript 3.0

The basic constructs of ActionScript 3.0 haven't changed greatly, although there have been some major changes to the packages and classes within the language. For example, ActionScript 3.0 now provides support for regular expressions that is consistent with the ECMA-262 specification, and the Void keyword has been changed to lowercase: void.

The use of the trace statement has changed. Previously, you could use trace to show messages in an output window. Now, when you use trace you can view messages in the Flex Builder 3 IDE only when you are debugging an application. These messages appear in the Console view, and you can also write them out to a log file.

ActionScript 3.0 includes some new primitive data types. ActionScript 2.0 recognized the Number data type, which handled all numeric data, integer or floating point. ActionScript 3.0 contains the **int** and **uint** types in addition to the Number type, which handles floating-point numbers. An int type is a 32-bit, signed integer that's useful for loop counters and integer variables. The uint type is an unsigned, 32-bit integer type used in RGB color values and byte counts.

One of the big changes is the way that ActionScript 3.0 deals with XML content. The XML class from earlier versions of ActionScript has been renamed to the XMLDocument class for legacy application support. The new and revamped XML class provides support for the ECMAScript for XML standard (ECMA-357), also known as E4X. This standard provides for a more intuitive way to target content in XML documents. It works with the new XMLList class (you'll find out more later on in the book).

Another change is to the way external content is loaded. The XML and LoadVars classes no longer handle the loading of external data. Instead, the URLLoader, HTTPService, and WebService classes access content from external files. The new Loader class loads external assets such as SWF files and images.

ActionScript 3.0 handles visual elements quite differently from previous versions. The MovieClip object is no longer the focal point of a SWF file. Instead of focusing on MovieClip objects stacked at different depths and levels, ActionScript 3.0 introduces the concept of a display list that indicates the relative hierarchy of screen elements. The display list handles depths automatically, so there's no need to manually deal with the stacking order of elements as in earlier versions of ActionScript.

In ActionScript 2.0, each application has a main timeline that corresponds to the stage. The stage includes movie clips that have their own timelines and objects. You can keep adding new layers to the hierarchy as required.

In ActionScript 3.0, the hierarchy operates a little differently. The display list still contains the stage at the top of the hierarchy. The stage contains a single child, the **application**. Instead of relying only on movie clips, the application contains display containers and display objects. Display containers include the new Sprite object, the MovieClip object, and Shape objects. Display objects are visual elements such as MovieClip objects and TextField objects. They must be placed inside display containers before they will appear in the user interface. Each display container can include other containers and display objects in a hierarchy.

Even the way that developers need to write custom ActionScript classes has changed. In ActionScript 3.0, all ActionScript classes must appear inside packages declared with the package statement. Each package corresponds to a hierarchy of folders. If you don't specify a package location, any classes you declare must be included in the top-level package that is the same as the root for the project. This is not the recommended approach, and it's better to create a directory structure for all classes and reference the package path using dot notation.

The new class structure is shown in the following code block:

```
package com.aip {
  //import statements
  public class MyClass extends Sprite {
    //constructor
    public function MyClass() {
    }
  }
}
```

In the preceding code block, the file MyClass.as would appear within the aip folder inside the com folder.

Methods and properties can be declared as private, public, protected, and internal. These declarations modify how visible the code is to other sources. The public modifier means that the content can be accessed from anywhere, while a private statement allows access only inside the current class. The new protected modifier allows access only within a specific class and subclasses, while the internal keyword provides access to classes within the current package. A default value of internal is assumed if no visibility modifier is included when declaring members.

ActionScript 3.0 removes many language elements from previous versions, including createTextField, createEmptyMovieClip, duplicateMovieClip, loadMovie, onClipEvent, removeMovieClip, stopAllSounds, tellTarget, unloadMovie, loadBitmap, setTransform, getTransform, swapDepths, LoadVars, _global, and _level. In addition, many other language elements have been relocated and reorganized into new ActionScript 3.0 classes.

Adobe includes a great article containing tips for working with ActionScript 3.0 at www.adobe.com/devnet/actionscript/articles/actionscript_tips.html.

Now that you understand some of the basics, let's move on to see how Flex works with applications in a general sense.

Working with applications in Flex

Developers can create the following types of applications with the Flex 3 framework:

- Static data applications
- Simple dynamic data-driven applications
- Flex LiveCycle Data Services applications

Static data applications include their data within the application and don't reference external data sources. Each time data changes, you need to modify the Flex application and recompile the SWF file. Examples of this type of application might include calculators or applications that chart fixed data points. Static data applications aren't a very flexible way to include data.

Simple dynamic data-driven applications load external data from a range of sources. The next section of this chapter covers the types of data you're likely to work with in this sort of application. Dynamic applications also often provide mechanisms for updating existing data and adding new data. Changing the external data source is enough to update the content in this type of application; there is no need to recompile the SWF file. This makes dynamic applications more flexible compared with storing data within the application.

Applications that use Flex LiveCycle Data Services are more tightly integrated with server-side logic. These applications facilitate ActionScript classes to talk directly to Java libraries so that they can be called from within the Flex application. If you've worked with Flash Remoting previously, you'll recognize this approach.

In this book, I'll focus on the last two types and show you how to create applications that use different types of data.

Working with data in Flex

One of the great things about Flex is its capability to include dynamic data from external sources. Flex can include the following types of data:

- XML content from static files, server-side files, and calls to SOAP and REST web services
- Text content from static or server-side files
- Text content formatted into name-value variable pairs from static or server-side files
- AMF content through Flex LiveCycle Data Services

Forget what you know about loading data in previous ActionScript versions. The LoadVars class from earlier versions of ActionScript has been removed from the language. The ActionScript 2.0 XML class has also been renamed to the XMLDocument class and replaced with a completely new ActionScript 3.0 XML class.

Flex uses the new HTTPService, URLLoader, URLRequest, and WebService classes to request external XML and text content. You can use the new classes to track a wider range of events and improve error handling.You can also use the MXML <mx:HTTPService> and <mx:WebService> tags to load external content without the need to write ActionScript.

The Flex 3 framework provides many other tools specifically targeted at data-driven applications.

Flex tools for working with data

The Flex framework provides several tools that you'll find useful for working with data-driven applications, including the following:

- Client-side data models
- Data binding
- Validation
- Formatting
- Data-driven components

Let's have a brief look at what each of these tools means for developers. They're covered in more detail in later chapters of the book.

You can store server-side content in client-side objects called Data Models. These objects are represented by the <mx:Model> and <mx:XML> tags, which provide simple representations of your data. For more complicated data structures, you can use custom ActionScript 3.0 class files.

Developers can also take advantage of data binding functionality. Data binding provides a mechanism for you to link the properties of two objects so that an updated value in one of the properties leads to an updating of the related value in the second object. Developers can add bindings using curly braces syntax { }, through the <mx:Binding> tag, or by writing ActionScript to create the bindings. You'll see examples of all these methods later in the book.

The Flex framework includes a range of built-in validation tools to check for appropriate user input. Validators allow developers to check credit card numbers, Social Security numbers, Zip code and telephone numbers, number and currency values, dates, e-mail addresses, and regular expressions. Developers can also build their own custom validators.

Flex includes a range of built-in formatters that can change the way data displays in an application. These controls take raw data and add formatting, such as a currency or date format, before displaying it in the user interface. Again, developers can also create their own formatters.

A number of Flex components are specifically designed for displaying and manipulating data. Components such as List, ComboBox, and DataGrid allow developers to bind their data directly to a data provider. The DataGrid component also provides mechanisms for editing content within the data provider.

You can see that Flex includes a range of tools specifically aimed at working with data, and I'll cover all of them in this book. Before I wind up, it's useful to get an idea of the type of process that you're likely to work through when creating data-driven Flex applications.

The application development process

Flex application development normally follows through a standard range of steps:

1. Create the MXML application in Flex Builder 3 or a text editor.
2. Create the layout for the interface by adding one or more container components.
3. Create the interface by adding user interface controls to the containers.
4. Define a data model for the application.
5. Add a call to external content such as consuming a web service, connecting to an external file, or requesting a remote Java object (Flex Data Services).
6. Add data bindings.
7. Add formatting to display the data.
8. Add validation to user input controls.
9. Write ActionScript to wire up the user interface.
10. Run or debug the application, or use the command-line compiler to create a SWF file.
11. Deploy the application.

You'll see these steps as you start building applications later in the book.

I want to finish by providing you with some resources that you might find useful.

Useful resources

There are lots of web sites providing information about Flex. In this section, I want to show you some of the links that I think you'll find most useful.

The logical starting point for all things Flex is the product section in the Adobe web site (www.adobe.com/products/flex/). The site provides full access to all software downloads as well as Flex quick start tutorials, code samples, demonstration applications, and a Flex developer community.

The following Flex explorers are useful for viewing sample code:

- Flex Component Explorer: http://examples.adobe.com/flex2/inproduct/sdk/explorer/explorer.html
- Flex Style Explorer: http://examples.adobe.com/flex2/consulting/styleexplorer/Flex2StyleExplorer.html

Flex.org is a useful web site for developers coming to grips with Flex Builder 3, Flex Data Services, and the Flex SDK. You can find it at www.flex.org/. Similarly, the community Flex site at www.cflex.net/ might be a good starting point.

The Flexcoders discussion group (http://groups.yahoo.com/group/flexcoders/) is specifically aimed at software developers who focus on Flex. It discusses methods and practices for developing Flex applications as well as best practices. It's a useful discussion group in which developers can share code tips and ask questions.

Summary

That's it for the introduction to the Flex framework. In this chapter, I talked about the role of Flex in building web applications. I explained the role of MXML and ActionScript 3.0 in the Flex framework, and provided an overview of some of the ActionScript 3.0 changes.

I showed you the different types of data that you might want to work with in Flex and introduced the new loading methods. I also explained the different types of applications that you can create in Flex. I finished by listing some resources that you might find useful.

In the next chapter, I want to delve deeper into the world of ActionScript 3.0.

Chapter 2

WORKING WITH ACTIONSCRIPT 3.0 IN FLEX 3

ActionScript 3.0 is the latest version of the ActionScript scripting language for use in Flash Player 9. You can create applications by using this language version in Flex Builder 3, Flash 9, a text editor, or another development environment, but you need to have access to the Flex SDK, which contains the library of ActionScript 3.0 classes.

ActionScript 3.0 includes a major overhaul of the language and introduces a number of new features as well as a reorganization of packages and class files. Chapter 1 provides an overview of the major changes to the language and you'll see examples throughout this chapter.

ActionScript 3.0 and the new Flash Player 9 ActionScript Virtual Machine (AVM2) speed up processing to make SWF files run more quickly. Adobe states that the new version of ActionScript speeds up development time because of features such as improved error reporting, E4X support when working with XML content, and support for regular expressions. You can make up your own mind after you get started with ActionScript 3.0.

Flash Player 9 also provides support for applications built with earlier versions of ActionScript because it includes the relevant virtual machine: AVM1. Even though this is the case, it's not possible to just mix and match different versions. Developers need to take notice of the following rules for working with multiple language versions:

- You can't include earlier versions of ActionScript with applications that use ActionScript 3.0.

- You can load an external SWF file that uses ActionScript 1.0 or ActionScript 2.0, but you won't be able to access the code within the file.

- SWF files that include earlier versions of ActionScript can't load SWF files that include ActionScript 3.0.

In this chapter, I want to get you started with ActionScript 3.0. I'll show you different ways to include ActionScript in your Flex applications, and you'll write some ActionScript 3.0 custom classes so you can compare the approach with that used in ActionScript 3.0. You can download the resources that I refer to in this chapter from the friends of ED web site at www.friendsofed.com.

Note that this chapter does not provide a complete introduction to the ActionScript 3.0 language. It assumes that you understand the basics. If you need to go back and cover some of the introductory concepts, I recommend *The Essential Guide to Flex 3 with ActionScript 3.0*, by Charles E. Brown (friends of ED 2007, ISBN: 1590597338), and *Foundation ActionScript 3.0 for Flash CS3 and Flex 3*, by Steve Webster and Sean McSharry (friends of ED 2007, ISBN: 1590598156).

Throughout this chapter and the rest of the book, I'll be using Flex Builder 3 for all of the examples, but remember that you can use other packages, including a text editor, provided that you have the Flex SDK installed. In this case, you'll have to use the command-line compiler to generate SWF files.

Let's get started.

Working with ActionScript 3.0 in Flex applications

You can work with ActionScript 3.0 in Flex 3 applications in the following ways:

- By writing ActionScript statements inline within Flex elements in an MXML file.

- By including ActionScript statements in an MXML file in an `<mx:Script>` element.

- By writing ActionScript statements in an external ActionScript (.as) file and including a source attribute in an `<mx:Script>` element in an MXML file. This approach has the same effect as if the statements are inside the MXML file itself.

- By using an `include` directive inside an `<mx:Script>` block to copy the contents of the external .as file to an MXML file.

- By creating custom class files and adding and referring to them with `import` statements in an MXML application.

- By creating an ActionScript project that defines all aspects of the application.

We'll look at each of these options in this section of the chapter. I'll work through a simple example, showing you how to use the preceding approaches to work with ActionScript 3.0. To keep things simple, you'll create a calculator in the example that converts distances between miles and kilometers and back again. The first approach is to use inline ActionScript to power the calculator.

Using inline ActionScript statements

The simplest way to include ActionScript 3.0 in an MXML file is to include it within attributes of an MXML element. You might do this because you're implementing simple data binding between two elements or because you want to add an event handler. The approach is very similar to that of writing inline JavaScript inside XHTML elements in a web page.

Let's look an example that uses this method. Start by creating a new Flex project using File ➤ New ➤ Flex Project, and call it LengthConverter. Store the application file in the root directory of the project rather than in the src folder. Create the following interface, which defines the simple calculator:

```
<?xml version="1.0" encoding="utf-8"?>
<mx:Application xmlns:mx="http://www.adobe.com/2006/mxml"
  layout="absolute">
  <mx:VBox x="10" y="10">
    <mx:HBox>
      <mx:Label text="Distance"/>
      <mx:TextInput id="txtDistance"/>
      <mx:ComboBox id="cboUnit">
        <mx:dataProvider>
          <mx:Array>
            <mx:Object label="Kilometers to miles" data="0.621371"/>
            <mx:Object label="Miles to kilometers" data="1.609344"/>
          </mx:Array>
        </mx:dataProvider>
      </mx:ComboBox>
    </mx:HBox>
    <mx:Button label="Convert" id="btnConvert"/>
    <mx:HBox>
      <mx:Label id="txtResult"/>
    </mx:HBox>
  </mx:VBox>
</mx:Application>
```

I created the interface using MXML elements added declaratively in Source view. You could also drag these elements into the application in Design view. VBox and HBox elements control the layout of the interface elements. You can see that these nest inside each other to create a layout that doesn't use x and y placement values.

By default, the <mx:Application> tag adds the layout attribute with a value of absolute. This attribute requires that you have to provide x and y values to lay out the controls in the application. In other words, there is no automatic layout as there would be with an attribute value of vertical or horizontal.

The ComboBox component is populated by using an <mx:dataProvider> element. The element contains an array of objects, and each object contains both a label and data property. The label content will display in the ComboBox while the data contains the conversion figure. I'll multiply the figure by the amount that the user enters in the TextInput control to calculate the converted amount.

Figure 2-1 shows how the interface appears in a web browser.

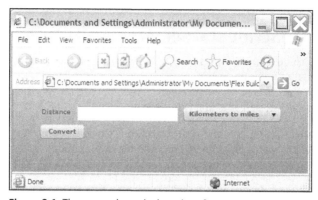

Figure 2-1. The conversion calculator interface

It's a very simple interface, and I haven't bothered to change the default style.

You should catch any errors that the user enters before carrying out the conversion, such as a text or blank value, so this calculator will be a little more robust if it uses an <mx:NumberValidator> element. The <mx:NumberValidator> element will see whether you entered a valid number, and will respond appropriately if you didn't.

To add the validation, I have to bind the validator to the text property of the TextInput; I'll do this by using curly braces { } notation. This notation allows you to add simple data binding between two MXML elements by specifying the id of the bound control as well as the bound property. For example, in the following line of code, the text property of the control txtBoundControl is bound to the text property of the control called txtMyInput:

```
<mx:TextInput id="txtBoundControl" text="{txtMyInput.text}"/>
```

You'll learn more about data binding later in the book.

To create the binding, add the following code below the opening <mx:Application> element:

```
<mx:NumberValidator id="validateDistance" required="true"
    source="{txtDistance}" property="text"
    trigger="{btnConvert}" triggerEvent="click"
    invalid="txtResult.text = 'Enter only numbers for distance'"/>
```

This element ensures that the user has entered a numeric value in the control called txtDistance. The element checks the text property of the TextInput control. Validation normally occurs when the user exits the TextInput control, but in this case, I want it to happen when I click the Convert button. That's why I set the trigger for the validation to the click event of the btnConvert control.

Notice the way I wrote the invalid attribute. The value of this attribute is a simple ActionScript statement that sets the text property of the txtResult control:

```
txtResult.text = 'Enter only numbers for distance'
```

I had to use single quotes around the text value as it appears inside the double quotes used by the invalid attribute.

Run the application to test the validator. Figure 2-2 shows what happens if you enter a text value and click the Convert button. You can see an error message in the txtResult Label control below the Convert button. Again, I haven't bothered with styling the message, but you could easily make that change.

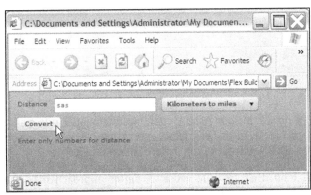

Figure 2-2. The validator displays a message when an invalid value is entered in the TextInput control.

The next step is to configure the Convert button so that when the user clicks it, the converted distance appears in the txtResult label. Modify the <mx:Button> element as shown in bold:

```
<mx:Button label="Convert" id="btnConvert"
  click="txtResult.text= =
  String(cboUnit.selectedItem.data * Number(txtDistance.text))"/>
```

The code adds a click attribute that sets the value of the text property for the txtResults control. The text property uses the value of the data property associated with the selectedItem in the ComboBox multiplied by the number entered in the txtDistance control. The selectedItem property provides access to the item that has been chosen from the data provider for the ComboBox—in this example, the array of objects. The application could then access either the data or label property of the selected object.

Notice that I have to cast the txtDistance.text property as a number and then cast the calculated result as a string before I can display it in the Label control. Flex 3 applications are stricter about enforcing data types than earlier ActionScript 2.0 applications.

Even though this approach provides an easy way to update the interface, you can see that the click attribute is very long and appears to be quite clumsy. I find the inline code a little difficult to read. You'll change this in the next example. In the meantime, run the application again to test it out. Figure 2-3 shows the finished calculator converting a value.

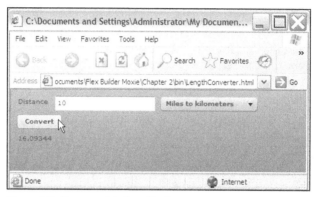

Figure 2-3. The completed application

In this example, you saw how to include ActionScript 3.0 statements inside elements in an MXML file. You can see my finished file saved as LengthConverter1.mxml with your resources. You'll need to import it into a Flex project if you want to run it from within Flex Builder.

This approach doesn't lend itself to code reuse. A better approach may have been to add the ActionScript statements in an <mx:Script> block to the top of the page.

Using the <mx:Script> element

The <mx:Script> element allows you to include blocks of ActionScript 3.0 code within an MXML file. You can't reuse code in this element within other Flex application files, so it's not a good approach for code reuse.

You must add any <mx:Script> block as a child of the root element, which is most likely to be the <mx:Application> tag. The convention is to place the <mx:Script> block just below the opening tag. While you can have more than one <mx:Script> block in the MXML file, your code is likely to be easier to read if you consolidate it into a single block.

When you add an <mx:Script> element in Flex Builder, it is automatically enclosed in a CDATA declaration, as shown here:

```
<mx:Script>
  <![CDATA[
  ]]>
</mx:Script>
```

If you're not using Flex Builder, don't forget to add this declaration around any ActionScript code contained within an MXML file.

The CDATA declaration prevents Flex Builder from parsing the contents of the <mx:Script> element as XML content. Without the CDATA block, ActionScript code would be interpreted as XML elements that aren't well formed, and you'd see a whole lot of errors when you tried to compile the application.

You'll re-create the previous calculator using an ActionScript code block in an MXML file. The application will populate the ComboBox using an ActionScript function. The application will call the function after the interface is created. To avoid adding ActionScript code to the MXML tags, a function will handle the conversion when the user clicks the Convert button. The application also uses an ActionScript function to respond when the user enters an invalid value for conversion in the TextInput control.

Create a new MXML file in the same project by choosing File ➤ New ➤ MXML Application. Give it the name LengthConverter2. You probably wouldn't add multiple application files in practice, but doing so here saves you from having to create a new project each time you want to try something different.

The first step is to add a NumericValidator to the application. This component checks that the user has entered a number. It can also check that the value of the number falls within a specific range, although this example doesn't do that. Notice that in this example the element uses the required attribute to make sure that the user has entered a value for the distance.

Add the following interface including the <mx:NumericValidator> element:

```
<?xml version="1.0" encoding="utf-8"?>
<mx:Application xmlns:mx="http://www.adobe.com/2006/mxml"
  layout="absolute">
  <mx:NumberValidator id="validateDistance" required="true"/>
  <mx:VBox x="10" y="10">
    <mx:HBox>
      <mx:Label text="Distance"/>
      <mx:TextInput id="txtDistance"/>
      <mx:ComboBox id="cboUnit"/>
    </mx:HBox>
    <mx:Button label="Convert" id="btnConvert"/>
    <mx:HBox>
      <mx:Label id="txtResult"/>
    </mx:HBox>
  </mx:VBox>
</mx:Application>
```

I removed the <mx:dataProvider> element from inside the <mx:ComboBox> element because you'll add the data provider programmatically after the application has been created. After the application finishes drawing the interface, it dispatches a CREATION_COMPLETE FlexEvent. The application will use an ActionScript function called populateCombo that runs when this event is dispatched. You'll need to add a creationComplete attribute in the <mx:Application> element referencing this function.

Add an <mx:Script> block below the opening <mx:Application> tag. If you're using Flex Builder, notice that it adds the CDATA declaration automatically. If you're using another development environment, make sure your code block looks like the following:

```
<mx:Script>
  <![CDATA[

  ]]>
</mx:Script>
```

The populateCombo function will create an array containing the values for the ComboBox and assign it to the dataProvider property. Add the following function to the script block:

```
import mx.events.FlexEvent;
private function populateCombo(e:FlexEvent):void {
  var dp:Array = new Array();
  dp.push({label:"Kilometers to miles",data:0.621371});
  dp.push({label:"Miles to kilometers",data:1.609344});
  cboUnit.dataProvider = dp;
}
```

There are a few things to notice in this block of ActionScript. First, the call to the populateCombo function automatically passes a FlexEvent event object as an argument. Remember that this function is called when the FlexEvent is dispatched because it will be referenced in the creationComplete attribute of the <mx:Application> tag.

Second, the first line of code is an import statement that references the mx.events.FlexEvent class. This is no different from the import statement used in ActionScript 2.0. I need to include the import statement so I can refer to the type of event dispatched by creationComplete without writing a fully qualified name. I can use FlexEvent instead of the full package reference mx.events.FlexEvent.

Finally, notice that I declared the function as private. ActionScript 2.0 recognized public and private access modifiers. ActionScript 3.0 recognizes four modifiers: public, protected, private, and internal. Table 2-1 summarizes the difference between these modifiers and shows how they affect members of a class.

Table 2-1. Access modifiers available in ActionScript 3.0

Modifier	Explanation
public	The member can be accessed from anywhere by any other object. Class constructor methods must be declared as public, as should any custom classes that you intend to use in your Flex applications.
protected	Hides access to the member from everything except subclasses. You can't access protected members from other instances and you can't define classes as protected.
private	The member is accessible only from the class in which it is defined. You can't access private members from other instances and you can't define classes as private.

Modifier	Explanation
internal	Similar to public and the default access for items that don't include a specific access modifier. You can access internal members from any class in the same package. There is no access from other packages.

The populateCombo function returns nothing, and you'll notice that the return type of void uses a low-ercase first letter unlike the Void return type in ActionScript 2.0.

The populateCombo function creates a new array and pushes two objects containing the same labels and data as in the previous example. Finally, the function assigns the array to the dataProvider property of the ComboBox.

You need to call this function in the opening <mx:Application> element, as shown in bold in the following code block:

```
<mx:Application xmlns:mx="http://www.adobe.com/2006/mxml"
  layout="absolute" creationComplete="populateCombo(event)">
```

Notice that the function explicitly passes the event object as an argument to the populateCombo function. As discussed, this object will be of the type FlexEvent.

Run the application now and you'll see that the ComboBox populates (refer to Figure 2-1).

This version of the application sets up the NumericValidator using an ActionScript function named setUpValidator. The function identifies the source component and the relevant text property, as well as the trigger and triggerEvent for the validation.

Add the following function to the <mx:Script> block underneath the populateCombo function:

```
private function setUpValidator(e:FlexEvent):void{
   validateDistance.source = txtDistance;
   validateDistance.property = "text";
   validateDistance.trigger = btnConvert;
   validateDistance.triggerEvent = "click";
}
```

This function uses ActionScript to assign values to the properties that were previously set using attributes in the tag. Notice that each attribute equates to a property of the same name.

Again, you need to call this function in the opening <mx:Application> element, so modify it as shown here in bold:

```
<mx:Application xmlns:mx="http://www.adobe.com/2006/mxml"
  layout="absolute" creationComplete="populateCombo(event);
  setUpValidator(event);">
```

If you run the application now, you should see the validator highlight in red if you enter an invalid value in the TextInput.

The last step in this example is to configure the Convert button. Clicking the button will call an ActionScript function called doConversion that will calculate the converted amount and display the result in the txtResult component.

Before you add this function, you need to add two more import statements to the script block:

```
import flash.events.MouseEvent;
import mx.events.ValidationResultEvent;
```

The button click handler dispatches an event object of type MouseEvent so the code needs to include a reference to this class. The validator dispatches an event object of type ValidationResultEvent when it validates the contents of the TextInput. This event object will also be dispatched when the user clicks the Convert button because the validator uses the click triggerEvent.

Add the following doConversion function to the script block:

```
private function doConversion(e:MouseEvent):void {
  if (validateDistance.validate().type==ValidationResultEvent.VALID){
    var convertedAmount:Number = Number(txtDistance.text) ➥
      * cboUnit.selectedItem.data;
    txtResult.text = String(convertedAmount);
  }
  else {
    txtResult.text = "Enter only numbers for distance";
  }
}
```

Note that Flex Builder usually adds any required import statements when you type the class name in your code. If you hadn't already included the import statement for the MouseEvent class, Flex Builder would have automatically added it when you typed e:MouseEvent.

The doConversion function first checks whether the NumberValidator successfully validated the entry in the TextInput. It does this by comparing the outcome of the validation with a VALID response using the following line:

```
if (validateDistance.validate().type==ValidationResultEvent.VALID){
```

If the content is valid, the calculation proceeds and the value displays in the Label control. The previous inline example used the same approach. If the content is invalid, an error message displays in the Label control.

The function is called when the user clicks the Convert button. Add the click handler to the MXML element, as shown in bold:

```
<mx:Button label="Convert" id="btnConvert"
  click="doConversion(event)"/>
```

When the user clicks the button, the application calls the doConversion function, dispatching a MouseEvent.

If you run the application now, you should be able to enter a number, choose a conversion type, and see a converted amount. If you enter an invalid amount, you should see an error message. You can find my completed example saved as LengthConverter2.mxml with your resources.

You can see that the <mx:Script> block quickly adds many lines to the application file. You can reduce the size of the file by storing the ActionScript content in an external .as file.

Using the source attribute in <mx:Script>

The source attribute of the <mx:Script> element allows an external block of script to be treated as if it were included in the current MXML file. The attribute is added to the opening <mx:Script> element and it can include relative paths to the file:

```
<mx:Script source="myCode.as"/>
```

One advantage of this approach is that it allows you to reduce the size of the MXML file. Storing code externally is a better way to organize large blocks of ActionScript code. It's not the same as defining classes in .as files, and you can't use this method to refer to class files.

Note that you can't set the source attribute in the <mx:Script> tag and add ActionScript code inside the same element. You'd need to include any ActionScript stored inside the MXML file in a second <mx:Script> tag.

Let's use the previous example to create an external script file. Create a new ActionScript file by choosing File ➤ New ➤ ActionScript file. Give it the name LengthConverterScript and click Finish.

Save your LengthConverter2.mxml file as LengthConverter3.mxml so you don't accidentally overwrite the original. Copy the content inside the <mx:Script> element to the LengthConverterScript.as file—you don't need to include the CDATA declaration. Remove everything from inside the <mx:Script> block except for the opening tag and modify it as follows (the changes appear in bold):

```
<mx:Script source="LengthConverterScript.as"/>
```

You should be able to save and run the application as before. The only change is that you have two files now instead of just one. You can find the finished files LengthConverter3.mxml and LengthConverterScript.as with the other downloaded resources.

An alternative to using the source attribute is to add an include statement.

Using include inside an <mx:Script> element

You can use the include statement to copy the contents of an ActionScript file into an MXML file. It's written this way inside an <mx:Script> block:

```
<mx:Script>
 <![CDATA[
   include "file.as";
 ]]>
</mx:Script>
```

Each include statement can refer to only one .as file, but you can include more than one include statement in the MXML file. You can also conditionally include files inside if statements.

You could rework the previous example by changing the script block to read as follows:

```
<mx:Script>
  <![CDATA[
    include "LengthConverterScript.as";
  ]]>
</mx:Script>
```

When you run this example, you should see the same results as before. You can see this example saved as LengthConverter4.xml with the other resources.

It's worth noting that Adobe doesn't recommend using include with a large number of external ActionScript files. Instead, it's probably best to rework the code into class files.

Creating custom class files

Storing code inside custom class files is an alternative method to including ActionScript 3.0 logic in a Flex project. You can use the class file to work with an existing MXML file or you can create the application entirely in ActionScript.

Understanding packages

The way that developers need to create custom classes has changed in ActionScript 3.0 compared with ActionScript 2.0. All ActionScript 3.0 class files must appear inside a package, and this wasn't a previous requirement.

Packages allow developers to group related classes together in folders. In fact, a package equates to a directory on the computer. Storing class files inside packages helps developers to avoid name conflicts where different classes use the same name. It's not possible to include two classes of the same name in the same package, so using different folder structures sidesteps this problem.

There is one top-level package in a Flex project that equates to the current folder containing the application. Adobe recommends that you don't use the default package to store your classes. Instead, you can define other packages stored in different locations. If you're using Flex Builder, it will create the folder structure for you when you define the class.

Packages are normally relative to the current project, but you can define a different classpath so the compiler knows where to locate the package. You might do this, for example, if you want to store classes in a central library and reuse them. The default classpath includes the current folder containing the application, but you can add other folders to the classpath. You need to do this for each project in Flex Builder.

Add a new folder to the classpath by right-clicking a project and choosing Properties. Click the Flex Build Path option on the left of the window and choose the Add Folder option on the right. You can then navigate to and select the external folder, as shown in Figure 2-4.

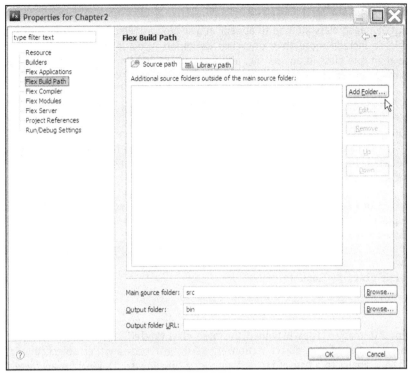

Figure 2-4. Adding to the classpath for a Flex project

If you're not using Flex Builder, you'll need to pass the classpath as an argument to the command-line compiler.

Class files always start with the package name, normally written in lowercase:

```
package myPackage {
}
```

The package name uses dot syntax to indicate the folder structure:

```
package allPackages.myPackage {
}
```

If you're creating libraries of classes, a common convention is to use the name of the owner to name the package. Another is to use the reverse domain name when specifying package structures. For example, if the package creator is myCompany.com, the package names might start with com.myCompany. Using this type of naming convention makes it easier to create unique package names, especially when working in a large company.

You'd specify a folder inside the current project if you weren't likely to reuse the class in other applications. Then you'd probably name the package with the name of the application, for example, myCompany.myApplication.

Understanding custom classes

In ActionScript 2.0, each class file had to appear in a single .as file of the same name as the class. It wasn't possible to include more than one class definition in a file. ActionScript 3.0 allows you to include more than one class in an .as file, although you're still limited to a single public class. The other classes might be helper classes—accessible only to the public class.

Even though you can include multiple classes in the same file, good practice might keep you separating your classes because it's easier to reuse them if you store them in separate files. It can also be confusing to store a class file in an .as file that has a different name, especially if you're used to ActionScript 2.0. For example, it would not be very obvious that the file MyClasses.as includes a class called UserDetails. Adobe actually recommends that you continue to follow the ActionScript 2.0 practice of including each class in its own file of the same name.

As with ActionScript 2.0, classes start with a class declaration. In ActionScript 3.0, the class declaration must be placed inside a package declaration. By convention, developers normally use uppercase names for classes and lowercase for package names:

```
package myPackage {
  public class MyClass {
  {
}
```

In ActionScript 2.0, many classes extended the base class MovieClip so that they could access the methods and properties of that object. ActionScript 3.0 introduces another object: the Sprite. As an object, a Sprite is similar to a MovieClip, but without a timeline, so it's ideal for anything that doesn't need to reference a timeline. It's also more lightweight than a MovieClip.

The class file normally includes a constructor that is called to create a new instance of the class. This function must have the same name as the class file without the .as suffix.

```
package myPackage {
  public class MyClass {
    public function MyClass() {
      //statements
    }
  {
}
```

Constructor functions are always public and don't provide a return value, although you can pass arguments to them. You use the constructor to create a new instance of the class, as follows:

```
var newInstance:MyClass = new MyClass();
```

You need to add an appropriate import statement for any classes that aren't within the default package:

```
import myPackage.MyClass;
```

You can create class files like you did in ActionScript 2.0. One point to remember is that you no longer need to use the mx.utils.Delegate class because ActionScript 3.0 enables a method closure to remember its original object instance automatically. You no longer have to pass a reference to the original object. That's likely to make life a lot easier for developers!

The next section shows a simple custom class example.

Working through an example

Let's work through the same calculator example using a class file to provide the functionality. The application will still use an MXML file for part of the interface, but the other elements will be created in ActionScript. Start by creating a new MXML application called LengthConverter5.mxml.

Add the following code to create the interface:

```
<?xml version="1.0" encoding="utf-8"?>
<mx:Application xmlns:mx="http://www.adobe.com/2006/mxml"
  layout="absolute">
  <mx:VBox x="10" y="10">
    <mx:HBox id="inputs">
      <mx:Label text="Distance"/>
    </mx:HBox>
    <mx:Button label="Convert" id="btnConvert"/>
    <mx:HBox id="outputs"/>
  </mx:VBox>
</mx:Application>
```

If you worked through the previous examples, you'll notice that there are some interface elements missing here. I haven't added a TextInput for the distance or a ComboBox for the conversion type. I also haven't created a Label to display the results. I'll add those controls programmatically; to do this I gave id attributes to the two HBox controls. You might also notice that I didn't include the NumberValidator element. Again, the application will handle validation in ActionScript.

There are probably much better ways to handle interface elements than creating them in a class file. However, I have done so in this example only because I want to introduce the concept of the display list and show you how you can create display elements with ActionScript.

In the first chapter, I introduced you to the new mechanism that ActionScript 3.0 uses for working with visual elements: the display list. Instead of working with movie clips that are dynamically added to and removed from the stage, ActionScript 3.0 recognizes a hierarchy of display containers and display objects. The stage is at the top of the hierarchy and contains the application. The application consists of display containers and display objects that may be nested in a hierarchy.

In the interface for this example, the display list hierarchy looks something like Figure 2-5.

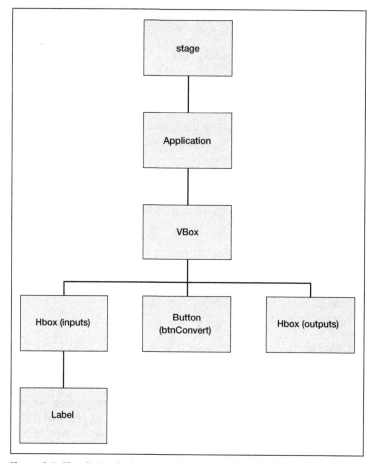

Figure 2-5. The display list hierarchy in the current application

This example uses ActionScript to add controls to two HBox containers: inputs and outputs.

Create a new ActionScript class using File ➤ New ➤ ActionScript Class. Enter the options shown in Figure 2-6 and click Finish.

I entered the package name converters and the name KmMilesConverter for the class. It's a public class based on the flash.display.Sprite class. Unless you're extending another class, it's common to use Sprite as the super class. You can click the Browse button to select the relevant class name from the list. If there's no obvious class to extend, you can leave the Superclass section blank.

When you click Finish, the Navigator view should show a file called KmMilesConverter.as in a folder called converters. If you're not using Flex Builder, you'll need to create this folder structure and the .as file manually.

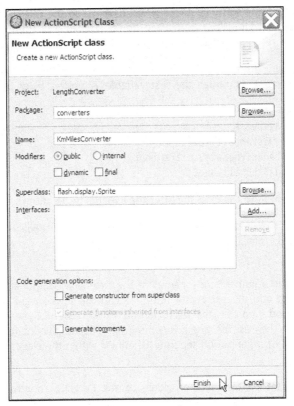

Figure 2-6. Creating a new ActionScript custom class

The class file contains the following code:

```
package converters
{
  import flash.display.Sprite;
  public class KmMilesConverter extends Sprite
  {
  }
}
```

To start, add some import statements for the classes used in the example. Doing this means that the application won't need to use fully qualified names. Add the new import statements underneath the existing one that appears after the package declaration:

```
import mx.containers.HBox;
import mx.controls.TextInput;
import mx.controls.ComboBox;
import mx.controls.Label;
```

If you're using Flex Builder, the software package will usually add the relevant import statements as you add code to your class file. While you often don't need to add these references manually, I included the list here for reference and for readers who aren't using Flex Builder.

The next step involves adding the private variables for the class. These variables refer mainly to the application interface elements, although the first variable, dp, refers to an array that will populate the ComboBox control.

```
private var dp:Array;
private var userDistanceTI:TextInput;
private var distanceTypeSelector:ComboBox;
private var resultsLabel:Label;
```

Add the constructor function to the class file after the variable declarations:

```
public function KmMilesConverter(inputHBox:HBox, outputHBox:HBox) {
  init(inputHBox, outputHBox);
}
```

The constructor takes two arguments: the names of the two HBox components. The application will need these references to add the extra user interface controls in the right place a little later. The KmMilesConverter method then calls the init method. I find it useful to separate functionality into separate functions within the class file, and it is common practice to give the initialization function the name init. This method of organization separates the logic within the class file and makes the code easier to read.

The init function will set up the data provider for the ComboBox control. It will then call the createInterface function to set up the additional interface elements. Add the init function that follows:

```
private function init(inputHBox:HBox, outputHBox:HBox):void{
  dp = new Array();
  dp.push({label:"Kilometers to miles",data:0.621371});
  dp.push({label:"Miles to kilometers",data:1.609344});
  createInterface(inputHBox, outputHBox);
}
```

This function creates the array called dp and adds two elements. The code is identical to the approach in the previous example. When the function finishes creating the array, it calls the createInterface function, passing the reference to the two HBox controls. Add this function now. It will need a little explaining afterward.

```
private function createInterface(inputHBox:HBox, outputHBox:HBox):void {
  userDistanceTI = new TextInput();
  distanceTypeSelector = new ComboBox();
  distanceTypeSelector.dataProvider = dp;
  resultsLabel = new Label();

  inputHBox.addChild(userDistanceTI);
  inputHBox.addChild(distanceTypeSelector);
  outputHBox.addChild(resultsLabel);
}
```

The createInterface function illustrates how easy it is to create interface elements dynamically. If you look through the first few lines, you'll see that the ActionScript can create new controls by calling their constructor functions; for example, new TextInput() or new ComboBox(). Once created, you can then set attributes for the controls.

The function creates three new controls: a TextInput, a ComboBox, and a Label. It sets the dataProvider for the ComboBox. At this point, the controls have no visual appearance in the application, even though they exist.

The addChild method adds the controls to the display list so that they become visible in the interface. Notice that the code must specify the parent for each control to create the correct hierarchy.

Let's test the application at this point by switching to the MXML file and adding a new instance of the class. Add the following script block:

```
<mx:Script>
  <![CDATA[
    import converters.KmMilesConverter;
    import mx.events.FlexEvent;
    private var converter:KmMilesConverter;

    private function initApp(e:FlexEvent):void {
      converter = new KmMilesConverter(inputs, outputs);
    }
  ]]>
</mx:Script>
```

The code block starts by importing the custom class, specifying the package and class names. It also imports the FlexEvent class, which is the type of event object broadcast by the creationComplete event. The code then declares a private variable called converter of the type KmMilesConverter. The code includes a call to the initApp function, which creates a new instance of the class, passing the ids of the two HBox elements to the constructor.

The application needs to call the initApp function in the creationComplete event handler of the <mx:Application> element as shown in bold here:

```
<mx:Application xmlns:mx="http://www.adobe.com/2006/mxml"
  layout="absolute" creationComplete="initApp(event)">
```

Run the application and you should see the same interface that appears in Figure 2-1, complete with the populated ComboBox. The only thing left to do is to add functionality to the Button element so that it carries out the conversation when clicked by the user.

Switch back to the class file and add the following convert public method. The application will call it with the click handler for the button.

```
public function convert():void {
  var convertedAmount:Number = Number(userDistanceTI.text) * ➡
  distanceTypeSelector.selectedItem.data;
  if (isNaN(convertedAmount)) {
    resultsLabel.text = "Enter only numbers for distance";
```

```
    }
    else {
      resultsLabel.text = String(convertedAmount);
    }
  }
```

The function takes no arguments and returns no values. It starts by calculating the converted distance by multiplying the entered number by the appropriate conversion factor. You've seen this code before. Instead of relying on a NumberValidator control, ActionScript tests whether or not the calculator returns a number. If not, the application shows an error message in the results label control; otherwise, it shows the calculated amount.

Switch back to the MXML file and modify the Button control, as shown in bold:

```
<mx:Button label="Convert" id="btnConvert"
  click="doConversion(event)"/>
```

You now need to add this function to the `<mx:Script>` block at the top of the file:

```
private function doConversion(e:MouseEvent):void {
  converter.convert();
}
```

This function calls the convert method of the converter object. If Flex Builder didn't add the following import statement automatically, add it yourself:

```
import flash.events.MouseEvent;
```

You're now ready to test the application. After running it, you should be able to enter a value and see either the converted amount or an error message. You can find the completed files saved with the other resources as LengthConverter5.mxml and KmMilesConverter.as.

The final approach to working with ActionScript is to create an ActionScript-only project. This is a much more difficult proposition as this type of project can't reference Flex user interface components.

Creating ActionScript projects

You don't have to include or reference ActionScript from inside MXML application files. Instead, your SWF application can be constructed entirely from ActionScript. Instead of creating a Flex project, you can use Flex Builder to create a new ActionScript project by choosing File ➤ New ➤ ActionScript Project.

Be aware that if you do take this approach, you can't use any Flex elements, so automatic layouts using the VBox and HBox containers won't be possible. You'll also have to avoid using the Flex components. ActionScript-only projects either have to draw their own elements with the drawing API or rely on simple elements such as the TextField.

If you need access to Flex components, at the bare minimum you'll need to link the ActionScript files to a simple MXML file containing an `<mx:Application>` element and basic container and then write the appropriate ActionScript statements.

Flex components are useful and cut down development time enormously. Given that this book is about Flex development, it's beyond its scope to create projects solely in ActionScript. I'm not going to take you through an ActionScript-only example. Instead, I'll show you an example that creates the interface mostly in ActionScript, but still relies on Flex components for layout and user interaction.

Working with a minimal Flex interface

In this example, you'll re-create the conversion calculator using a minimalist MXML file. You'll embed most of the application code in ActionScript files and create the interface programmatically.

Create a new Flex application file and call it LengthConverter6.mxml. Add the following MXML elements:

```
<?xml version="1.0" encoding="utf-8"?>
<mx:Application xmlns:mx="http://www.adobe.com/2006/mxml"
  layout="absolute">
  <mx:VBox id="appContainer"/>
</mx:Application>
```

That's about as simple as it gets! The application contains only a VBox container. The application will place all controls inside this container programmatically.

Create a new ActionScript class in the converters package and give it the name KmMilesConverter2. The class should extend the Sprite class, and the code looks like the following.

```
package converters
{
  import flash.display.Sprite;

  public class KmMilesConverter2 extends Sprite
  {
  }
}
```

Add the following import statements underneath the initial statement added by Flex Builder. The complete list follows with the new statements shown in bold:

```
import flash.display.Sprite;
import mx.containers.VBox;
import mx.containers.HBox;
import mx.controls.Label;
import mx.controls.TextInput;
import mx.controls.ComboBox;
import mx.controls.Button;
import flash.events.MouseEvent;
```

The application has to reference all these classes for the Flex components in the custom class file. The last import statement references the MouseEvent class.

The application also needs to include some private variables that will control the interface. Add the following variable declarations inside the class declaration:

```
private var dp:Array;
private var container:VBox;
private var inputs:HBox;
private var outputs:HBox;
private var distanceLabel:Label;
private var userDistanceTI:TextInput;
private var distanceTypeSelector:ComboBox;
private var convertButton:Button;
private var resultsLabel:Label;
```

The purpose of each variable is fairly self-explanatory from its name. The first variable, dp, is the data provider for the ComboBox component. The other variables relate to the containers and controls that I'll add programmatically to the initial VBox component.

The class file needs a constructor method and will receive a reference to the VBox container as a parameter. Add the following function:

```
public function KmMilesConverter2(container:VBox) {
  init(container);
}
```

This simple method calls the init function, passing along the VBox reference. Add this private function next:

```
private function init(container:VBox):void{
  dp = new Array();
  dp.push({label:"Kilometers to miles",data:0.621371});
  dp.push({label:"Miles to kilometers",data:1.609344});
  createInterface(container);
}
```

The init method populates the dp array variable with the items that will appear in the ComboBox component. After doing so, it calls the createInterface method, which will do all the work. Add the function now and I'll work through it afterward:

```
private function createInterface(theContainer:VBox):void {
  container = theContainer;
  inputs = new HBox();
  outputs = new HBox();
  distanceLabel = new Label();
  distanceLabel.text = "Distance";
  userDistanceTI = new TextInput();
  distanceTypeSelector = new ComboBox();
  distanceTypeSelector.dataProvider = dp;
  convertButton = new Button();
  convertButton.label = "Convert";
  convertButton.addEventListener(MouseEvent.CLICK, convert);
  resultsLabel = new Label();
```

```
        container.addChild(inputs);
        inputs.addChild(distanceLabel);
        inputs.addChild(userDistanceTI);
        inputs.addChild(distanceTypeSelector);
        container.addChild(convertButton);
        container.addChild(outputs);
        outputs.addChild(resultsLabel);
    }
```

I separated the code into two blocks. The first block creates the containers and controls that will make up the interface. The second block actually adds the elements so they'll display visually. You can see that each component is programmatically created using the new constructor, followed by the component type. You can then set properties for each component where appropriate. For example, the code assigns a text property to the first Label control and a dataProvider to the ComboBox.

The second block adds the components to the interface using the addChild method. It does this in order of how each component will appear. I could also have used addChildAt if I wanted to specify the exact location for each child. The addChildAt method takes an additional parameter that is the position of the component, starting from 0.

One point to notice is that the code adds an event listener to the Button control. The event listener listens for the click event (MouseEvent.CLICK) and calls the convert function in response. Add that method now. Note that it's the same method used in the previous example.

```
    private function convert(e:MouseEvent):void {
      var convertedAmount:Number = Number(userDistanceTI.text) * ➡
      distanceTypeSelector.selectedItem.data;
      if (isNaN(convertedAmount)) {
        resultsLabel.text = "Enter only numbers for distance";
      }
      else {
        resultsLabel.text = String(convertedAmount);
      }
    }
```

And that's all for the class file. You can check my KmMilesConverter2.as file saved with the other resources if you want to compare your class file with mine.

To finish, the MXML application file needs to reference the class file. Switch back to LengthConverter6.mxml and add the following script block:

```
    <mx:Script>
      <![CDATA[
        import converters.KmMilesConverter2;
        import mx.events.FlexEvent;
        private var converter:KmMilesConverter2;
        private function initApp(e:FlexEvent):void {
          converter = new KmMilesConverter2(appContainer);
        }
      ]]>
    </mx:Script>
```

This code block imports the new class file as well as the FlexEvent class. It then creates a variable of type KmMilesConverter2. The code includes a single initApp function, and the application will call this function in the <mx:Application> element. The function has a FlexEvent parameter, passed from the function call, and it creates a new instance of the KmMilesConverter2 class called converter.

Modify the <mx:Application> tag, as shown in bold, so that the application calls the initApp function after it is created:

```
<mx:Application xmlns:mx="http://www.adobe.com/2006/mxml"
    layout="absolute" creationComplete="initApp(event)">
```

That's it! Run the application and you should see the same result as in the previous examples—a simple kilometers- and miles-conversion tool. The resources download includes the two finished files from the example KmMilesConverter2.as and LengthConverter6.mxml.

In this section, I showed you how to create the same application in several different ways. I tried to get these examples to address the main issues that you'll need to know for working with ActionScript 3.0, but there are some additional points that might be useful.

Additional points

There are a couple of additional points that weren't really addressed in the examples that you've worked through so far. These are some basic issues that are important in the understanding of ActionScript 3.0:

- The new event model in ActionScript 3.0
- Data binding and bindable properties
- The trace statement

I want to go through each of these issues, starting with the new event model.

Understanding ActionScript 3.0 events

Event handling has changed quite a bit in ActionScript 3.0, so it's worth exploring the topic in a bit of detail. Events are triggered when something changes in a Flex application, such as clicking a button or creating the application. The new system of event handling is based on the same approach as the Document Object Model (DOM) Level 3 Events Specification, which you can find at www.w3.org/TR/DOM-Level-3-Events/.

In earlier versions of ActionScript, you had a range of choices about how to handle these events. In ActionScript 3.0, you can handle these events in only one way. You can't use the on or onClipEvent event handlers or the addListener method available in earlier ActionScript versions. In ActionScript 3.0, all event detection happens by using listeners. An event listener is a function that responds to the specific event.

Flex components have a set of predetermined events, each represented by an event object. Developers can also create and dispatch their own custom events. The built-in event objects come from one of the Event classes or subclasses. The event object is dispatched when the event fires in the application and the object is passed to the target of the event. For example, when you click a button, the MouseEvent object is dispatched.

Developers can include ActionScript in the MXML component declaration to handle the event. For example, the following MXML tag includes a handler for the click event that passes the event object:

```
<mx:Button id="myButton" label="Click me"
  click="clickHandler(event)"/>
```

You'd then write the clickHandler function, making sure that it includes a MouseEvent argument, the type of the passed event object:

```
function clickHandler(e:MouseEvent):void {
  //do stuff
}
```

Developers can also assign and create the event handler purely in ActionScript. The following line shows ActionScript that adds the same event listener to the myButton instance:

```
myButton.addEventListener(MouseEvent.CLICK, clickHandler);
```

When a user clicks myButton, this listener responds to the click event with a call to the clickHandler method. Notice that instead of passing the string click to represent the event, the application passes the constant MouseEvent.CLICK. This approach is recommended by Adobe, so you don't cause problems by accidentally entering typos when specifying the event. By the way, there's no requirement for you to name the method above clickHandler. It's simply a convention that some developers prefer to use to make it easier to identify the purpose of the function.

The event listener can be removed by using the following:

```
myButton.removeEventListener(MouseEvent.CLICK, clickhandler);
```

Notice that the method required the event type and handler function to remove it from the instance.

Developers can use the event object passed to the handler function to find out information about the event. They can also access properties and methods associated with the event object; for example, it's possible to find out the event type using the type property. Some other useful event properties include the following:

- currentTarget: Refers to the object that is currently processing the event object
- target: Refers to the object that is the target of the event
- toString: Creates a string representation of the event object

The destination point for the event object is the event target. Where the target is an item in the display list, it may need to be passed through the hierarchy of objects in the display list. This process is called the event flow.

One useful side effect of the new event model is that there is no longer a need to delegate the scope of a listener method as in ActionScript 2.0. You can say goodbye to the mx.util.Delegate class!

Another implication is that Flash Player 9 recognizes a series of default behaviors for specific events. An example is that new text displays in a TextInput control as it is entered. Flash Player automatically creates an instance of the TextEvent class to handle this display. You can find out about default behaviors in the Flex documentation. Developers can cancel many of these default events using the preventDefault method.

Creating bindable properties

In an earlier example, you saw that it is possible to use curly braces to specify data binding between two components. I'll discuss this topic in much more detail later in the book, but in the meantime, it's worthwhile mentioning that you can bind properties to components in ActionScript as well.

When you add a variable to a block of ActionScript code, you can use the [Bindable] metatag to indicate that it can be bound to a component; for example:

```
[Bindable]
public var myArray:Array;
```

You can then assign the variable directly to a component using curly braces notation:

```
<mx:ComboBox dataProvider="{myArray}"/>
```

This type of binding is useful because when the value of the variable changes, the bound property will update automatically. Therefore, you can modify the bound property from any number of methods without having to explicitly assign a value using ActionScript.

What happened to trace?

If like me, you were used to using trace statements in earlier versions of ActionScript, you'll notice that the code in this chapter doesn't use a single one. You can include trace statements to display information at various points in your ActionScript code, but they operate a little differently in Flex Builder.

In Flash, when you include a trace statement, you are used to seeing the results display in an Output window. There isn't an Output window in Flex Builder, so don't expect to see the results in the same way when you run an application. Instead, you have to choose the Debug option (to the right of the Run button) to compile the application.

When you debug the application, any trace statements within your code will appear in the Console view within Flex Builder. The application will run in the debug version of Flash Player 9, and you'll have to switch back to Flex Builder to see the results from the trace statements in the Console view. You can also add output from trace statements to a log file. I'll talk about debugging applications in some detail later in the book.

ActionScript 3.0 best practices

To finish this chapter, I want to cover a couple of best practices that will help you make the transition to ActionScript 3.0:

- Declaring data types appropriately
- Importing classes
- Creating appropriate packages

I'm sure that there are plenty of other best practices that you'll come across in your Flex work, but I think that these are some of the most important.

Declaring data types appropriately

Always declare data types for your variables, parameters, and method return values, including a return type of void for functions that don't return anything. ActionScript 3.0 doesn't require that you declare all data types, but doing so will help to track down errors in your application more easily. It will also improve performance as the Flash Player won't need to carry out implicit type conversions.

As an aside, ActionScript 3.0 includes the capability to supply optional arguments to your methods. You can do this by assigning default values as shown here:

```
public myMethod(arg1:String, arg2:Boolean = false):void {
  // do something
}
```

Back to data types. A related recommendation is to use the new int data type for creating loops. You can use this data type anywhere you need a number that doesn't have decimals, and it will improve performance slightly compared with using the Number data type.

You can use the as operator to change the data type of variables. The following example casts the variable strXML to the data type of XML:

```
var myXML:XML = strXML as XML;
```

If you need to create a variable that can be any data type, use the following declaration instead of leaving out the data type:

```
var anything:*;
```

Importing classes

You should import classes so you don't have to use fully qualified names in your code:

```
import import flash.events.MouseEvent;
```

Be aware, however, that you can't leave out the import statement even if you do use fully qualified names when referring to classes.

You'll have better control over your code if you import individual classes instead of entire packages. That way, you can be sure which class is involved in your code in case you strike any problems.

Creating appropriate packages

Don't store class definitions in the default package; that is, the top-level package in your application. This happens when you save your class files in the root directory of the application and define the package without a path, as shown:

```
package {
}
```

Instead, you should create a folder structure to support your classes. If you plan on reusing your classes, add them to an external location and edit the classpath in your Flex application to reference the external folder. You can do this by right-clicking the project in Flex Builder, choosing Properties, selecting the Flex Build Path area, and using Add Folder to locate the external folder.

Summary

In this chapter, I showed you the different ways to work with ActionScript in a Flex application. I set up an example and showed you several different ways to add functionality with ActionScript. The chapter showed how to write inline ActionScript within MXML elements; how to include an <mx:Script> block in an MXML file and use it to add code, reference external ActionScript files with the source attribute, and import external code into the MXML file. I also worked through two examples that showed how to create custom class files and add interface elements.

In the next chapter, I want to look at how you can create your own components for reuse in Flex applications.

Chapter 3

CREATING CUSTOM COMPONENTS

The Flex framework includes a number of built-in components: user interface controls, containers, navigation controls, and even a range of charts. You can use these components to create the interfaces for their Flex applications. Each component corresponds to an ActionScript class contained in the Flex SDK.

Developers can also build their own custom components, often based on one or more prebuilt components. They can do this in one of two ways: by using MXML files or by creating ActionScript classes. Even pure MXML components are likely to include some ActionScript.

Creating custom components allows developers to create reusable functionality in their applications. Why spend time re-creating something that's already built? Building components also allows developers to break their application code into smaller parts. Instead of writing one long MXML file, it might be easier to split the code into smaller, function-specific files. This approach also allows developers in a team to take on different development tasks.

The best components are independent of other code in the application and are what's referred to as **loosely coupled**. This term means that the component doesn't rely on any other components or instances and it operates independently. When you develop components in this way, it's important to make it very clear to other developers what parameters are needed to create the component and what values the component can return. Developers need to be aware of the properties and methods of the component, as well as having an understanding of which events the components can dispatch.

In this chapter, I'll show you how to build custom components that you can reuse. I'll show you three approaches: how to use MXML components, how to use ActionScript components, and how you might use a hybrid approach. We'll work through examples that include prebuilt components as well as supporting ActionScript. You can download the resources for this chapter from the friends of ED web site at www.friendsofed.com.

Let's start by looking at the process involved in creating a simple MXML component based on built-in components.

Creating components using MXML

To build a simple MXML component, developers generally work through the following steps:

1. Create a new MXML file for the component inside a subfolder.
2. Provide a name for the MXML file that will adequately describe the component.
3. Instead of using the <mx:Application> tag as the root node, use a component such as a container or user interface control as the base class for the component.
4. Add the required components inside the root node.
5. Add the ActionScript required for the working of the component.

The component can then be referenced from an application file in the project.

A couple of points are worth noting here. First, in step 1, I mentioned that we should create the component inside a subfolder of the Flex project. While this approach is not necessary, it's certainly a good practice because it organizes the Flex project and allows you to refer to all custom components using a namespace. It also means that you can avoid conflicting names for your components.

The name you give for the component file is the same one that Flex applications will use when creating tags for the component. For example, if you call the file MyNewComponent.mxml, Flex will use the tag name <MyNewComponent> to create the component. It's important that your tag name is descriptive.

You'll notice in step 3 that we can't use the <mx:Application> tag as the root node for a component MXML file. This happens because we'll be referencing the component inside an application file that already uses that root node. It's not possible to have more than one <mx:Application> tag in an application. The root node in the component file will need to declare the namespace www.adobe.com/2006/mxml namespace.

It's also important to note that a custom component can contain other custom components along with the components included with the Flex framework. You might build up a library of components that you can include within your applications.

Developers need to be able to reference custom components in their MXML applications. They do this by adding a new namespace to the <mx:Application> tag with an appropriate short name. You can use any prefix for the namespace, and the following line uses comp:

```
xmlns:comp="components.CountriesCombo"
```

The namespace refers to the directory structure for the component; for example, the previous line adds a namespace referring to the CountriesCombo component in the components folder. I could also use an asterisk (*) to refer to all components.

If you add components at the top level of the Flex project, you'd use the following namespace, although as mentioned, this location isn't recommended:

```
xmlns:comp=" *"
```

To add the component called CountriesCombo in the application, we can reference it using the namespace prefix and file name as follows:

```
<comp:CountriesCombo/>
```

The best way to see this process is to create a simple component in an MXML file. The component will be a ComboBox that displays a list of countries. We'll be able to add this component in an application. If you're an experienced developer, I'm sure you've often needed this type of functionality.

Example: Creating a country ComboBox component

Create a new Flex project using File ➤ New ➤ Flex Project. Give it the name CustomComponents and click the Finish button. You can choose any location for this project. Choose the root folder as the location for application files.

Create a new folder in the project called components by right-clicking the name in Navigator view and choosing New ➤ Folder. Create a new component file in that folder called CountriesCombo. Choose the ComboBox as the base class.

At this point, your component file should look like the following:

```
<?xml version="1.0" encoding="utf-8"?>
<mx:ComboBox xmlns:mx="http://www.adobe.com/2006/mxml">
</mx:ComboBox>
```

We want to display a list of countries, so we'll need to add a data provider to the ComboBox. So it won't take forever, I'll add only a few countries, but you are welcome to add the complete list of all countries if you like. Add the following data provider to the ComboBox control:

```
<mx:dataProvider>
   <mx:Object label="Australia" data="AU"/>
   <mx:Object label="Canada" data="CA"/>
   <mx:Object label="New Zealand" data="NZ"/>
   <mx:Object label="United Kingdom" data="UK"/>
   <mx:Object label="United States of America" data="US"/>
</mx:dataProvider>
```

Unlike the other tags, the <mx:dataProvider> tag is in lowercase because it's a property of the ComboBox control, not a class in its own right. In fact, you're probably aware that there are a number of components (such as the List and charting controls) that can use a dataProvider property.

Notice that we populate the ComboBox from a series of objects, and each contains a label and data property. By using these names, we can automatically populate the corresponding properties in the ComboBox component.

You can switch to Design view to get a preview of how this component will appear. In Figure 3-1, you'll notice that the Design view looks different from that for an application file.

Figure 3-1. The complete
component shown in Design view

We need to switch back to the main application file: CustomComponents.mxml. To add the component, we'll need to add a namespace to the opening <mx:Application> tag, as shown here in bold:

```
<mx:Application xmlns:mx="http://www.adobe.com/2006/mxml"
    layout="absolute" xmlns:comp="components.*">
```

We can now use the prefix comp to refer to any custom components that we want to include. Add the following lines inside the <mx:Application> tag to add the custom component to this application inside a VBox control:

```
<mx:VBox x="10" y="10">
  <comp:CountriesCombo id="countryCBO"/>
</mx:VBox>
```

When you run the application, you should see something similar to Figure 3-2.

Figure 3-2. The application,
including the custom component

The application includes the ComboBox control containing the list of countries.

Because the component uses the ComboBox base class, it inherits all the properties and methods from that class, so you can use any of them in your main application. Let's extend the example so we can extract the label of the selected item from the ComboBox and display it in another control.

Start by adding the following Label control in the application file, underneath the custom component:

```
<mx:Label id="selectedCountry"/>
```

We'll then use the change event of the custom component to change the text displayed in the Label control. Because we based the component on a ComboBox, it inherits the change event, and we can include it as an attribute in the control. Add the following attribute, shown in bold, to the custom component.

```
<comp:CountriesCombo id="countryCBO"
  change="selectedCountry.text=countryCBO.selectedItem.label"/>
```

The line sets the text property of the selectedCountry control to the label of the selected item in the custom component. When you run the application and select a country, you should see the Label control update, as shown in Figure 3-3.

Figure 3-3. Responding to the change event in the custom component

If you want to check the finished code, you can find my files saved in the 3-1 folder with your resources. You'll need to import these into a Flex project to see them work.

One of the reasons for creating custom components is so that developers can create a library of reusable controls that are available to any application. For this reason, it's important to be able to pass property values to components—and we'll look at this topic next.

Passing a value to the component

Loosely coupled components don't rely on specific elements in the main application file. Rather, they have properties that the application can set in the component. The usual way to add properties is by using ActionScript statements to declare them. You can either use setter and getter methods to work with the properties or you can declare them with the public access modifier. Using the public keyword allows an application file using the component to set or get the value of the property directly. You'll see how this works as we modify the previous example.

We could improve on the first example by allowing the main application file to set the selected value in the ComboBox. You'd need to do this if you are presenting a prepopulated form in the application. When the application file adds the component, it will pass in a value that we'll use to set the selected item. We'll call this property country, so we'll need to add a public variable of the same name in the custom component.

I'll also show you what happens if you change the base class for your component from a ComboBox to a VBox container. Modify the starting component file CountriesCombo.mxml so it looks like the following:

```
<?xml version="1.0" encoding="utf-8" ?>
<mx:VBox xmlns:mx="http://www.adobe.com/2006/mxml">
  <mx:ComboBox id="countriesCombo"/>
</mx:VBox>
```

I added the ComboBox control inside a VBox and moved the namespace declaration to the new root element. The code adds an id attribute for the ComboBox and removes the data provider. We'll populate the ComboBox using ActionScript.

You could use any container you like for the ComboBox. I chose the VBox for convenience, but it means that the custom component no longer inherits the properties, methods, and events from the ComboBox. Making these changes in the custom component will cause an error in the main application file because the VBox doesn't have a change event. We can still reference the ComboBox within the custom component from the application file or we can remove the change attribute altogether. We'll do the latter so that the code for CustomComponents.mxml appears as follows:

```
<?xml version="1.0" encoding="utf-8"?>
<mx:Application xmlns:mx="http://www.adobe.com/2006/mxml"
  layout="absolute" xmlns:comp="components.*">
  <mx:VBox>
    <comp:CountriesCombo id="countryCBO"/>
    <mx:Label id="selectedCountry"/>
  </mx:VBox>
</mx:Application>
```

Switch back to the custom component and add the following init function to populate the ComboBox control, inside an <mx:Script> block. Place this block immediately below the opening VBox tag:

```
<mx:Script>
  <![CDATA[
    private var dp:Array = new Array();
    private function init():void {
      dp.push({label:"Australia", data:"AU"});
      dp.push({label:"Canada", data:"CA"});
      dp.push({label:"New Zealand", data:"NZ"});
      dp.push({label:"United Kingdom", data:"UK"});
      dp.push({label:"United States of America", data:"US"});
      countriesCombo.dataProvider = dp;
    }
  ]]>
</mx:Script>
```

The script block creates a private array variable called dp and populates it using the same values as before. It uses the push method to add each new item at the end of the array. It then assigns the array to the dataProvider property of the ComboBox component. Because the variable uses the private modifier, it is not accessible to applications that use the custom component.

We'll need to call the init function when the component is created, so we'll do this in the creationComplete event of the root node, the VBox control. Add the following attribute, shown in bold.

```
<mx:VBox xmlns:mx="http://www.adobe.com/2006/mxml"
  creationComplete="init(event)">
```

Notice that the attribute passes an event object to the init function. We'll need to modify the function declaration as shown in bold so that it recognizes that a FlexEvent object is passed with the function call.

```
private function init(e:FlexEvent):void {
```

Flex Builder should add the following import statement at the top of the script block. If not, add it yourself:

```
import mx.events.FlexEvent;
```

We still haven't dealt with passing a property value to the ComboBox control inside the custom component. As mentioned, we'll create the property as a public variable, so add the following declaration below the import statement.

```
public var country:String = "Australia";
```

We call the public variable country and we can use it as an attribute of the custom component in the main application file. Notice that I've set a default value of Australia for this variable in case the user doesn't pass the value from the main application file.

We then need to use this variable to set the value in the ComboBox and we'll do this in a function called setSelectedCountry. Add a call to the function at the bottom of the init function:

```
private function init(e:FlexEvent):void {
  dp.push({label:"Australia", data:"AU"});
  dp.push({label:"Canada", data:"CA"});
  dp.push({label:"New Zealand", data:"NZ"});
  dp.push({label:"United Kingdom", data:"UK"});
  dp.push({label:"United States of America", data:"US"});
  countriesCombo.dataProvider = dp;
  setSelectedCountry();
}
```

Add this private function to the script block below the init function:

```
private function setSelectedCountry():void {
  if (country.length >0) {
    for (var i:int;i<dp.length;i++) {
      if (country == dp[i].label) {
        countriesCombo.selectedIndex = i;
        break;
      }
    }
  }
}
```

We test if the country variable is longer than 0 characters and, if so, use it to set the value in the ComboBox component. We loop through the data provider to match the selected value and use it to set the selectedIndex property of the ComboBox.

Switch to your CustomComponents.mxml file and modify your custom component line, as shown in bold.

```
<comp:CountriesCombo id="countryCBO" country="Canada"/>
```

The line sets Canada as the selected value in the ComboBox. Run the application and test that you can see that value initially selected. You can find the saved files in the 3-2 folder with your resources.

Note that in this example, we defined a public property using ActionScript. We could also use getter and setter methods to avoid creating public properties. I purposely didn't take this approach to simplify the example. You'll see an example of a setter method later in the chapter.

Let's modify this example so that we can create a public variable that we can then bind to the ComboBox component. Instead of populating the variable in the init function, we'll use the curly braces binding syntax so that the application file can take the same approach.

Binding a property in the component

We could re-create the dp array in the previous example as a bindable property in our application file. This approach would simplify the init function in the custom component. It would also allow us to change the data provider for the ComboBox each time we use it in a new application. You might do this if you want to be able to choose a different set of countries each time.

To make the changes, start by removing the content from the <mx:Script> block in the custom component file CountriesCombo.mxml. You'll also need to remove the creationComplete event from the <mx:VBox> tag.

To be able to populate the ComboBox from external data in an application, we'll create a public array variable called dataSource and bind it to the ComboBox. Add the following public variable to the component:

```
[Bindable]
public var dataSource:Array = new Array();
```

Your <mx:Script> block should look like the following:

```
<mx:Script>
  <![CDATA[
    [Bindable]
    public var dataSource:Array = new Array();
  ]]>
</mx:Script>
```

You can then set the data provider for the ComboBox by making the following change, shown in bold:

```
<mx:ComboBox id="countriesCombo" dataProvider="{dataSource}"/>
```

At this point, the ComboBox doesn't contain any data, but it is bound to an empty public array variable called dataSource. We'll be able to populate this array from the main application file.

Switch to the CustomComponents.mxml application and remove the country attribute from the countryCBO component. We can create a new Bindable variable and bind it to the dataSource public variable in the custom component. Add the following <mx:Script> block below the <mx:Application> tag:

```
<mx:Script>
  [Bindable]
  private var theCountries:Array = new Array({label:"Australia",➡
    data:"AU"},{label:"Canada", data:"CA"},{label:"New Zealand",➡
```

```
            data:"NZ"},{label:"United Kingdom", data:"UK"},➡
            {label:"United States of America", data:"US"});
      </mx:Script>
```

You can then bind this variable to the dataSource property of the ComboBox in the custom component by modifying the <comp:CountriesCombo> tag, as shown in bold:

```
      <comp:CountriesCombo id="countryCBO" dataSource="{theCountries}"/>
```

If you run the application, you should see that the ComboBox component populates as before. To change the countries that display, you can modify the theCountries variable in the application file. You can find the finished files for this example saved in the 3-3 folder.

In addition to being able to set properties, loosely coupled components should be able to call methods and dispatch events so that they can integrate fully with other elements in an application. You'll see an example of a method call a little later, but in the meantime, let's look at how the component can dispatch events to the application.

Dispatching events

It's possible to set up a custom component so that it dispatches events to the application that hosts it. First, you need to declare the event that will be broadcast. You then need to dispatch the event in response to some action within the component. Finally, you can capture and respond to the broadcast event in the main application.

We'll extend the example we've been working on so it dispatches an event whenever a user selects a new value in the ComboBox component. We'll call this the countryChanged event. Because we based our component on the VBox container, we can't simply hook into the change event of the ComboBox.

To add the new event, we need to create an <mx:Metadata> element above the script block in the custom component file. These elements provide additional information to the Flex compiler. This <mx:Metadata> element contains an [Event] tag that specifies the name of the event that the component can dispatch and its type. Add the following code block to the custom component file, above the <mx:Script> block:

```
      <mx:Metadata>
        [Event(name="countryChanged", type="flash.events.Event")]
      </mx:Metadata>
```

The <mx:Metadata> tag inserts meta tags into an MXML file that pass information to the Flex compiler about the application. By convention, this tag is usually placed underneath the opening <mx:Application> tag above the <mx:Script> tag in an application file. You can also place the Event declaration directly within a block of ActionScript code, without the <mx:Metadata> tag.

In the preceding code block, the <mx:Metadata> tag creates a new event called countryChanged that is of the flash.events.Event type. This class is the basis for all events. We need to be able to dispatch this event whenever the value in the ComboBox component changes, so add a change attribute to the ComboBox component, as shown in bold.

```
      <mx:ComboBox id="countriesCombo" dataProvider="{dataSource}"
        change="comboChange()"/>
```

Each time the ComboBox selection changes, we'll call the function comboChange to dispatch the countryChanged event. We'll add this function now in the script block:

```
private function comboChange():void {
  dispatchEvent(new Event("countryChanged"));
}
```

The function dispatches the countryChanged event using dispatchEvent. The dispatchEvent method takes the event object as an argument.

We can respond to the countryChanged event in the main application file by writing it as an attribute of the custom component. Make the following change in the component in the CustomComponents. mxml file:

```
<comp:CountriesCombo id="countryCBO" dataSource="{theCountries}"
  countryChanged="countryChangedHandler(event)"/>
```

The attribute responds to the countryChanged event by calling the countryChangedHandler function, which you now need to add to the script block. Notice that the function passes the event to the handler:

```
private function countryChangedHandler(e:Event):void {
  selectedCountry.text = "Broadcast from the " + e.type + " event";
}
```

The countryChangedHandler function sets the value of the text that displays in the selectedCountry label control. It accesses the type of event using the type property. Run the application to see how the example works. Selecting a value in the ComboBox dispatches an event that is detected in the main application file, and the text in the Label component updates, as shown in Figure 3-4.

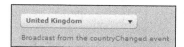

Figure 3-4. The custom component broadcasts an event of countryChanged type to the application.

You can find the finished files saved in the 3-4 folder with the other resources.

While this simple example is a good illustration of custom events, it isn't very useful. It would be more useful if we could access properties about the event such as the selected label and data from the ComboBox. We can do this by creating a custom event class that passes the details of the selected item back to the application.

Creating a custom event class

If we want to pass data with a custom event, we'll need to create a custom event class. This class must extend the flash.event.Event class, which is the base class for all events. The custom class needs to call the super method of the Event class to create a new event object. In our custom class, we will pass the type of the custom event when we call the super method.

We must also override the clone method of the Event class, so we can return a new copy of the event object. The override method replaces the original clone method with a new one, specific to the custom class. The new clone method will return a copy of the custom class, setting the type of the event and any properties that it must pass.

The custom component then needs to create a new instance of this class, passing in any properties required by the event. It can then dispatch this custom event to the application. Let's see how this might work by creating a custom class called CountrySelectedEvent.

We'll need to create a new ActionScript class using File ➤ New ➤ ActionScript Class. Create the class inside the components folder and give it the name CountrySelectedEvent. It should extend flash.events.Event, which means that we'll be able to use all the methods and properties of the Event class. Once created, the custom class file should appear as follows:

```
package components
{
  import flash.events.Event;
  public class CountrySelectedEvent extends Event
  {
  }
}
```

The custom event will pass two properties with the event object: the selected country and the code for the selected country. These properties correspond to the label and data properties of the selected item in the ComboBox component. We'll start by adding these properties inside the class declaration, as shown here. They need to be public properties so we can access them from the custom component file.

```
public var selectedCountry:String;
public var selectedCountryCode:String;
```

We'll be able to access these properties directly from the event object using the previous variable names. We'll also create a constant that references the name of the event that we'll broadcast. Add the following line below the two you just added:

```
public static const COUNTRYSELECTED:String ="countryChanged";
```

This line creates a constant called COUNTRYSELECTED, which will refer to the name of the event: countryChanged. We now need to add the constructor method, as well as overriding the clone method. Add the following code to the class file:

```
public function CountrySelectedEvent(type:String,➥
  theSelection:Object) {
  super(type);
  selectedCountry = theSelection.label;
  selectedCountryCode = theSelection.data;
}
override public function clone():Event{
  return new CountrySelectedEvent(type, selectedCountry);
}
```

The constructor function takes two arguments: the string event type and the selected item from the ComboBox. It calls the super method of the Event class passing the new event type. This method calls the constructor of the base Event class, so we can create an Event object first, before we set the values of our public variables in the custom class.

The CountrySelectedEvent function then sets the values of the two event properties selectedCountry and selectedCountryCode, which are derived from the label and data properties of the selected item object.

The second method overrides the clone method, returning a new event with the relevant event type and selected item. As mentioned earlier, we need to do this to return the correct event object type. The clone method returns a copy of the event object; in our case, a copy of the CountrySelectedEvent. We use the keyword override to replace the original clone method in the Event base class. The override prevents us from returning an Event object and instead returns a CountrySelectedEvent object.

We also need to call the clone method to support event bubbling. By using this method, the event can bubble to any parent containers. This is necessary to inform any other components that are listening for this event. If you don't override the clone method, the event can't bubble.

We need to refer to this custom event in the custom component file, so switch to the CountriesCombo.mxml file. Modify the <mx:Metadata> tag as shown here:

```
<mx:Metadata>
  [Event(name="countryChanged", ➡
    type="components.CountrySelectedEvent")]
</mx:Metadata>
```

This [Event] meta data tag defines a new event for the custom component called countryChanged that is of the type components.CountrySelectedEvent, our new custom event class. We'll need to import this class into the script block with the following line:

```
import components.CountrySelectedEvent;
```

We'll also need to dispatch the new event when a user changes the value in the ComboBox component. We can do this by modifying the existing comboChange function, as shown in bold:

```
private function comboChange():void {
  var eventObj:CountrySelectedEvent = new CountrySelectedEvent ➡
    (CountrySelectedEvent.COUNTRYSELECTED, ➡
    countriesCombo.selectedItem);
  dispatchEvent(eventObj);
}
```

The function starts by creating a new instance of the CountrySelectedEvent in a variable called eventObj. To create the instance, we need to pass the type and selected item from the ComboBox, as defined in the constructor function. We pass the constant CountrySelectedEvent.COUNTRYSELECTED to indicate the event type. The final line in the function dispatches this new event.

Switch to the CustomComponents.mxml file so we can respond to this event. We'll need to import the custom event class with the following statement inside the <mx:Script> block:

```
import components.CountrySelectedEvent;
```

From the previous example, we're already handling the countryChanged event using the countryChangedHandler function so we can simply modify this function to process the new event properties, as shown in bold.

```
private function countryChangedHandler(e:CountrySelectedEvent):void {
  selectedCountry.text = "changed to "  + e.selectedCountry;
}
```

The event type passed to the function has changed to the custom CountrySelectedEvent type. This handler now shows the text changed to with the selectedCountry property from the custom event. When you run the application, Figure 3-5 shows the effect of making a new selection in the ComboBox component.

Figure 3-5. Displaying a property
from a custom event type

This example demonstrated how to pass properties with a custom event type. We created the new event with an ActionScript class that extended the base Event class. You can find the finished files in the 3-5 folder with your other resources.

Flex custom components can include other components, both built-in and custom. We call components that contain this type of structure **composite components**.

Creating a composite component

One advantage of using a modular component structure is that you can include one custom component inside another. We'll work through an example here that includes the countries ComboBox component inside a new custom UserForm component.

Start by creating a new component called UserForm in the components folder and base the component on the Form element. Because we want to include our ComboBox custom component, we'll need to add another namespace declaration to the root element, as shown here in bold:

```
<mx:Form xmlns:mx="http://www.adobe.com/2006/mxml"
  layout="absolute" xmlns:comp="components.*">
```

Add the following form elements to the component, after the opening `<mx:Form>` element:

```
<mx:FormHeading label="Enter user details"/>
<mx:FormItem label="Name">
  <mx:TextInput/>
</mx:FormItem>
<mx:FormItem label="Email address">
  <mx:TextInput/>
</mx:FormItem>
<mx:FormItem>
  <mx:Button label="Update"/>
</mx:FormItem>
```

Figure 3-6 shows how this interface appears in Design view.

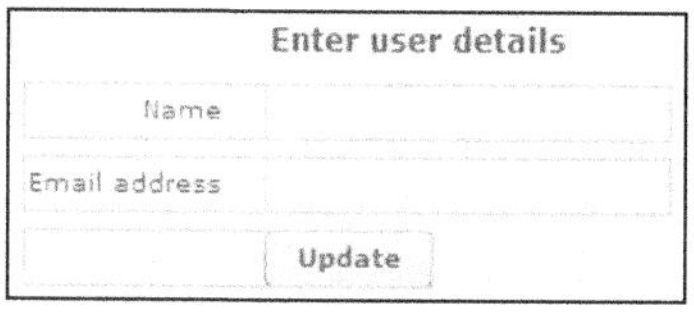

Figure 3-6. The interface shown in Design view

Now we'll add the custom `ComboBox` component from the `CountriesCombo.mxml` file. Add the following tags, shown in bold, before the form button:

```
<mx:FormItem label="Country">
  <comp:CountriesCombo id="countryCBO"/>
</mx:FormItem>
<mx:FormItem>
  <mx:Button label="Update" click="updateHandler(event)"/>
</mx:FormItem>
```

Notice that we use the comp prefix to refer to the component. The `CountriesCombo` component actually contains the `ComboBox` control inside a `VBox`. Strictly speaking, we should probably remove that element, but I won't do that so we can keep things simple and follow straight on from the previous examples.

We'll need to test the `UserForm` component inside a new application. Create a new MXML file called `ComplexComponents.mxml` and add the following namespace to the `<mx:Application>` tag:

```
xmlns:comp="components.*"
```

We'll add the `UserForm` component inside a `VBox` control and we'll also add a label to display messages. Add the following elements to the application:

```
<mx:VBox x="10" y="10" >
  <comp:UserForm id="myForm"/>
  <mx:Label id="txtMessage"/>
</mx:VBox>
```

Run the application and you should see an interface similar to that shown in Figure 3-7.

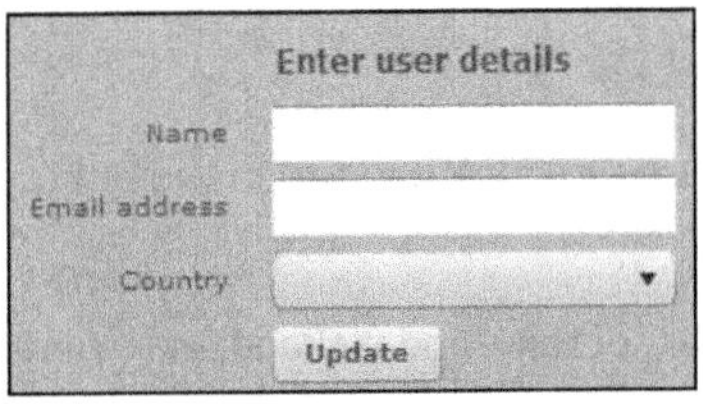

Figure 3-7. The application interface

Notice that the ComboBox component isn't yet populated. We can handle that in the UserForm custom component. Previously, we used data binding to set the dataSource attribute in the application file. Because the ComboBox component is included in the UserForm component, we'll do the binding at that point. By populating the ComboBox from its hosting MXML file, we can reuse it in other situations with different data.

Switch to the UserForm.mxml file and add the following script block:

```
<mx:Script>
  <![CDATA[
    [Bindable]
    private var theCountries:Array = new Array({label:"Australia",➡
        data:"AU"},{label:"Canada", data:"CA"},{label:"New Zealand",➡
        data:"NZ"},{label:"United Kingdom", data:"UK"},➡
        {label:"United States of America", data:"US"});
  ]]>
</mx:Script>
```

This block sets up the data provider for the ComboBox control. You can reference it by changing the <mx:ComboBox> tag, as shown in bold:

```
<comp:CountriesCombo id="countryCBO" dataSource="{theCountries}"/>
```

If you run the ComplexComponents.mxml application now, you'll see that the ComboBox populates with the list of countries from the theCountries array variable.

We could add some validation and error handling to the form, but that's a little beyond the scope of this example. Feel free to do it yourself if you want to extend this example.

As a last step, we'll dispatch an event from the user form to indicate to the application file that the Update button has been clicked. The application can then respond appropriately.

Add the following [Event] metadata tag to the UserForm.mxml component file:

```
<mx:Metadata>
  [Event(name="formUpdated", type="flash.events.Event")]
</mx:Metadata>
```

The declaration indicates that the component will dispatch an event called formUpdated, which is a flash.event.Event type. We'll also need to import that class into the script block with the following line:

```
import flash.events.Event;
```

To capture the event, we must define a change handler in the Button control. Modify it as shown here in bold:

```
<mx:Button label="Update" click="updateHandler(event)"/>
```

We now need to add the following updateHandler function in the <mx:Script> block:

```
private function updateHandler(e:Event):void {
  dispatchEvent(new Event("formUpdated"));
}
```

This function dispatches the formUpdated event to the hosting application, where it can be captured as an attribute of the custom component. Modify the UserForm component in the ComplexComponent.mxml application file, as shown here in bold:

```
<comp:UserForm id="myForm"
  formUpdated="txtMessage.text = 'You updated the form'"/>
```

The component could have responded by calling another function, but for simplicity I used inline ActionScript to display a message in the txtMessage component.

Run the application and click the Update button. Figure 3-8 shows the main application interface responding to the dispatched event.

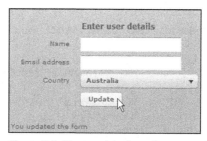

Figure 3-8. The user interface after responding to the formUpdated event

You can find the finished files for this example in the 3-6 folder.

This example shows how easy it is to create applications that use composite components. The UserForm component includes the CountriesCombo component that we created earlier. You can imagine that a ComboBox containing a list of countries is a useful component that we might reuse in a number of different applications.

So far in this chapter, you've seen how to create components using MXML. You can also create components using ActionScript, and that's the topic for the next section.

Creating components using ActionScript

Another approach for developers is to create components using ActionScript classes and refer to them with MXML tags in their applications. Even though we use MXML tags to create the component, it is still an ActionScript class.

These components can be used in much the same way as MXML components, but they can also include more complex content such as nonvisual elements. Again, the name you give to the class file will be the name of the corresponding MXML tag in the application.

Building an ActionScript component is pretty much the same as building any ActionScript class and uses the following steps:

1. Determine whether the component needs to extend an existing class.
2. Create the class and add properties and methods.
3. Determine whether the component needs to override any methods of the base class.
4. Decide whether the component needs to dispatch events.

The best way to get started is by re-creating some of the examples that we worked through earlier in the chapter.

Working through examples

Let's start by creating a new application in the Flex project called CustomComponentsAS.mxml. We'll also create a new ActionScript class in the components folder called CountriesComboAS. To start with, this class will extend the existing ComboBox class and populate the control with a predefined list of countries. Add the following variable declaration containing the list of countries to display:

```
private var dp:Array = new Array({label:"Australia", data:"AU"},
    {label:"Canada", data:"CA"},{label:"New Zealand", data:"NZ"},
    {label:"United Kingdom", data:"UK"},
    {label:"United States of America", data:"US"});
```

As before, for simplicity the code doesn't supply a complete list of all countries in the world, and we pass both a label and data property in the objects within the array.

Add a constructor method to the class file as shown:

```
public function CountriesComboAS() {
    super();
    dataProvider = dp;
}
```

The function calls the super method, so we can create the ComboBox from the base class constructor method. The function sets the dataProvider property to the array stored in the private dp variable. The complete class file follows if you want to check your code to this point:

```
package components {
  import mx.controls.ComboBox;
  public class CountriesComboAS extends ComboBox {
    private var selectedCountry:String;
    private var dp:Array = new Array({label:"Australia", data:"AU"},➡
      {label:"Canada", data:"CA"},{label:"New Zealand", ➡
      data:"NZ"},{label:"United Kingdom", data:"UK"},➡
      {label:"United States of America", data:"US"});
    public function CountriesComboAS() {
      super();
      dataProvider = dp;
    }
  }
}
```

Switch to the new CustomComponentsAS.mxml file and modify the <mx:Application> tag to include a namespace for the components folder:

```
<mx:Application xmlns:mx="http://www.adobe.com/2006/mxml"
  xmlns:comp="components.*">
```

I used the comp prefix for the custom components. We can add the custom component inside a VBox with the following lines. I also included a Label control to display messages:

```
<mx:VBox>
  <comp:CountriesComboAS id="countryCBO"/>
  <mx:Label id="selectedCountry"/>
</mx:VBox>
```

Run the application and you should see a ComboBox control populated with a list of countries. Again, because we extended the ComboBox class when we created the component, we can use all the properties, methods, and events of that class. For example, we could update the text in the Label control with the chosen country as before by using the following:

```
<comp:CountriesComboAS id="countryCBO"
  change="selectedCountry.text=countryCBO.selectedItem.label"/>
```

You can find this simple example saved in folder 3-7 with the other resource files. Let's move on to see how to set the value in the ComboBox control using an attribute in the CountriesComboAS component.

Passing values to ActionScript components

We might want to allow the main application file to set the selected value in the ComboBox component using an attribute. We can do this by adding a public setter method to the ActionScript file that takes a country name and sets the appropriate item in the ComboBox. We'll call this method country and it will set a private variable called selectedCountry. Using a setter method means that we don't have to add a public variable within the class file.

Create the selectedCountry variable now with the following declaration below the dp declaration:

```
private var selectedCountry:String = "Australia";
```

The line creates the private variable, setting a default value of Australia. We now need to add the country public method that follows:

```
public function set country(theCountry:String):void {
  selectedCountry = theCountry;
  setCountry();
}
```

This method takes one argument, the name of the preselected country, and it returns nothing. The first line sets the value of the private variable selectedCountry while the second calls the setCountry private method that will do all the work. Add that function now:

```
private function setCountry():void{
  for (var i:int=0;i<dp.length;i++){
    if (selectedCountry == dp[i].label) {
      selectedIndex = i;
      break;
    }
  }
}
```

The function works in the same way as the code you saw earlier in the chapter. It loops through the data provider array until it finds a match for the selectedCountry variable. When it does so, it sets the selectedIndex of the component and exits with a break statement. Notice that I can access a property of the component directly (in this case, the selectedIndex property). I could also use the statement this.selectedIndex with the same effect.

Switch to the CustomComponentsAS.mxml file and modify the custom component, as shown in bold:

```
<comp:CountriesComboAS id="countryCBO"
  change="selectedCountry.text=countryCBO.selectedItem.label"
  country="Canada"/>
```

The component uses the country attribute to call the corresponding public method. Run the application and you should see that Canada is selected in the ComboBox. The completed example appears within folder 3-8 with the other resources.

Let's move on to dispatching events from an ActionScript custom component.

Dispatching custom events in ActionScript components

In this example, I'll show you how to dispatch a custom event from an ActionScript component. We'll use the custom event that we created earlier, CountrySelectedEvent. You can find a full explanation of this class earlier in the chapter, including the theory behind dispatching custom events.

The approach that we'll use here is similar to the one we used with the MXML custom component. The custom component will dispatch the event whenever the value in the ComboBox control changes, providing the name and code for the country as properties with the event object. If you didn't create the CountrySelectedEvent class earlier, you can use the one from folder 3-5 with the chapter resources.

We need to start in the CountriesComboAS.as file by importing the classes that we'll need. Add the following import statements above the class declaration:

```
import flash.events.Event;
import components.CountrySelectedEvent;
```

These statements import references to the base Event class as well as to the custom class we created earlier. We'll also need to specify the new event that the component will dispatch with the following line:

```
[Event(name="countryChanged",type="components.CountrySelectedEvent")]
```

The [Event] tag specifies that the component will dispatch the countryChanged event to the application and that it is of the type components.CountrySelectedEvent. As mentioned earlier, we don't use a metadata tag in an ActionScript file.

We need to add an event listener to the constructor method so that we can detect when the ComboBox component changes and respond with an appropriate function. Modify the CountriesComboAS constructor method as shown in bold:

```
public function CountriesComboAS() {
  super();
  dataProvider = dp;
  addEventListener("change", comboChange);
}
```

When the change event fires in the ComboBox control, it calls the comboChange function. Add that private function now:

```
private function comboChange(e:Event):void{
  var eventObj:CountrySelectedEvent = new CountrySelectedEvent➥
    (CountrySelectedEvent.COUNTRYSELECTED, selectedItem);
  dispatchEvent(eventObj);
}
```

The function creates a new custom CountrySelectedEvent object and dispatches it so that it can be detected by the application hosting the component. It passes the event type and the item selected in the ComboBox component.

We now need to switch to the CustomComponentsAS.mxml application file so we can capture the custom event and write an appropriate handler to deal with the properties contained within the event object. Start by adding an import statement for the custom event class in the <mx:Script> tag:

```
import components.CountrySelectedEvent;
```

We'll also need to add the handler function to the script block:

```
private function countryChangedHandler(e:CountrySelectedEvent):void {
  selectedCountry.text = "changed to " + e.selectedCountry;
}
```

Finally, we need to add an attribute for the countryChanged event to the custom component tag. Modify the tag as shown here in bold:

```
<comp:CountriesComboAS id="countryCBO"
  countryChanged="countryChangedHandler(event)"/>
```

When you run the application, you should see the same result that you saw in Figure 3-5. You can find the completed files saved in folder 3-9 with the other resources.

This section showed how to use ActionScript to create Flex components. You've also seen how to use MXML files to achieve the same thing. But how do you know which is the better approach to take when creating custom components?

Deciding on MXML or ActionScript

So far in this chapter, you've seen that there are two approaches to creating custom components. The first involves creating an MXML file to define the contents of the component. There is usually a need for some ActionScript in this file to wire up the components and to set properties or to dispatch events. Developers can also write custom components purely in ActionScript by creating a class file that extends a base class. But how do you know which approach is better in your application?

You probably want to consider some of the following questions when making your choice about how to create the component:

- Are you building a simple component?
- Is the component made up of other components?
- Are you creating a nonvisual component?
- Do you need to modify the behavior of an existing component?
- Are you creating a new component?

We'll look at each of these points in turn.

Creating simple components

Simple components contain few built-in components and don't include other custom components. If you're building a simple component, it's usually quicker to create the component using MXML. If you're adding simple properties or binding to the component, it's probably easier to do this using MXML declarations instead of ActionScript.

Creating composite components

Composite components are made up of a number of built-in components and can include custom components. One benefit of creating this type of component in MXML files that you can take advantage of is the built-in containers for layout and positioning of each element. It's generally harder to create these interfaces in pure ActionScript, although it can be done.

Creating nonvisual components

Flex includes a number of nonvisual built-in components such as effects, formatters, and validators. If you need to create a component that extends one of these nonvisual components, your best approach is to use ActionScript.

Modifying component behavior

You'll need to use ActionScript if you want to modify the behavior of an existing component. It will probably be easier to create a new ActionScript class based on an existing class and then either override its methods or extend its behavior with new methods.

If your component needs to dispatch custom events, you'll have to write custom classes for each event, and I've certainly found it easier to implement them in ActionScript.

Creating a new component

If your component isn't based on any of the existing components, but contains completely new functionality, your best bet is to create it as an ActionScript component. If you're creating a new visual component, you'd normally base it on the UIComponent class, which contains the functionality common to all visual components.

Instead of choosing to build either an MXML or an ActionScript component, it's possible to use a hybrid approach that Adobe calls the **code-behind** approach. In this approach, the MXML code lays out the component while the ActionScript appears in a class definition. The ActionScript class is then the root element of the component.

Using the code-behind approach

It's worth mentioning that you can create custom components using an MXML file with an ActionScript class using the code-behind approach. While I don't intend to go through this approach in any detail, the broad steps are as follows.

1. Create an ActionScript class for the component, using an appropriate base class.
2. Create an MXML component that uses the ActionScript class as its root element.

3. Lay out the visual elements using appropriate containers in the MXML component.

4. Use the ActionScript class file to create the properties, methods, and events of the component.

To use this approach with the previous example, I'd create an ActionScript class for the component, extending the CountriesComboClass ComboBox control. I'd use this class to add any functionality associated with the custom component. In this case, I'd add event listeners for the creationComplete event so that I could populate the data provider for the ComboBox. I'd also add a change event listener so I could respond to changes in the selected item of the ComboBox. The class would dispatch the CountrySelectedEvent, as discussed previously.

I could use the existing CountrySelectedEvent class for my custom event. I'd create another class to store the data associated with the component, the selected country. I could access the selected country in this class through the CountriesComboClass using a getter and setter method.

Finally, the component file would extend CountriesComboClass, using the name as the root element. It would include the ComboBox component:

```
<?xml version="1.0" encoding="utf-8"?>
<comp:CountriesComboClass xmlns:mx="http://www.adobe.com/2006/mxml"
  xmlns:comp="components.*">
  <mx:ComboBox id="cboCountries"/>
</comp:CountriesComboClass>
```

I could then include this component in an MXML application file.

Note that if the ActionScript class needs to reference child controls in the component MXML document, you have to create these as public properties of the ActionScript class. Adobe says this is necessary because of a limitation of Flex.

As an area for further study, you might want to give this approach a try. There's a useful example at the Adobe web site: www.adobe.com/devnet/flex/quickstart/building_components_using_code_behind/.

After you build your components, you need to decide how to distribute them in your applications and to other developers.

Sharing components

I mentioned that, for developers, one advantage of working with components is that they can create reusable functionality that you can include in more than one project. The examples in this chapter all refer to components stored in a subdirectory of the current Flex project. However, we could also have stored them in a central location and referenced them in the project.

To do this, create a folder structure for your components outside of the Flex project. If you're using Flex Builder, you can add a reference in the current project by right-clicking the project name in Navigator view and choosing Properties. Select the Flex Build Path option on the left. Click Add Folder to add a reference to the component location and use the Browse button to find the location of the external folder (see Figure 3-9).

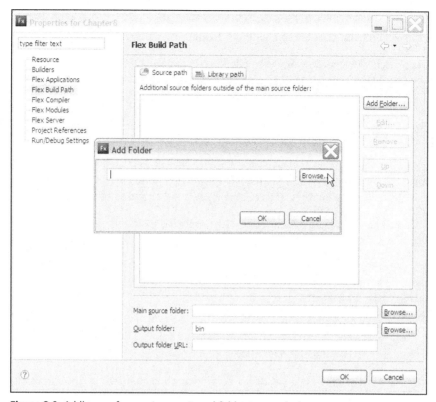

Figure 3-9. Adding a reference to an external folder to a project

If you're not using Flex Builder, you can use the source-path option with the command-line compiler to specify the location of the folder containing the components. Use the compiler file mxmlc.exe in the bin folder of the sdk folder in the Flex installation directory. Run the mxmlc.exe application from the command line and add the library-path option, specifying the path to the external folder, as shown here:

```
mxmlc -library-path+=c:/flexcomponents/
```

You can distribute components by providing the relevant files to other developers. You can also create SWC files and shared libraries.

Distributing SWC files

An SWC file is a compiled archive of components, and you could use one to create a component library to distribute to other developers. The SWC file can contain one or more components and uses the zip archive format. One advantage of these files is that a SWF file inside the SWC is compiled, so it's not easy to extract the code.

If you're using Flex Builder, you can create a library project using File ➤ New ➤ Flex Library Project. You specify the name and location for the project. You can then specify which components to include in the SWC file.

You can also create an SWC file by using the compc command-line utility to compile existing MXML or ActionScript components. You can find the compc utility in the bin folder in the sdk folder in the Flex installation location. Again, you can run the application from the command line, specifying the source-path argument and listing the location for the SWC using the output option:

```
compc -source-path+= c:/flexcomponents/ ➥
    -output bin\ComponentLibrary.swc
```

You can find more about the other arguments in the Flex help documentation. You can reference an existing SWC file using the Flex Build Path.

Using SWC files

You can add an SWC file to your project by specifying the location of the file using the Library path option, as shown in Figure 3-10. In Flex Builder, right-click the project and select the Properties option. Choose the Flex Build Path section and click the Library path tab. You can use the Add SWC button to add references to the SWC files.

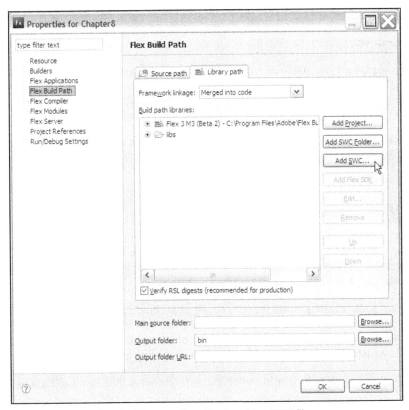

Figure 3-10. Accessing the Library path option to add an SWC file

It's also possible to include the SWC file using the `mxmlc.exe` file with the command-line compiler:

```
mxmlc -library-path+=c:/flexlibrary/FlexComponents.swc
```

An alternative to SWC files is to create shared libraries of components.

Distributing Runtime Shared Libraries

In a SWF application, you can distribute shared assets such as custom components in files that are cached on the client. These are known as Runtime Shared Libraries (RSLs) and using them allows applications to share common components. If you are working with a single application, there's no advantage to creating RSLs, but if you have created several applications that use the same components, you can reduce their overall file size by using this approach.

Create either a SWF or an SWC file containing the assets that you want to use. You can then load them as RSLs using the `mxmlc` tool. You can either load the files at run time or compile time.

Specify the SWF to load as an RSL using the `runtime-shared-libraries` option.

```
mxmlc -runtime-shared-libraries= c:/flexrsl/componentlibrary.swf
```

This option allows you to load the SWF file at run time.

You could also specify an SWC file using the `external-library-path` option. This option allows you to specify a compile-time location:

```
mxmlc -external-library-path= c:/flexcomponents/ComponentLibrary.swc
```

You can find out more from the Flex help documentation. You can reference an existing RSL using the same approaches described earlier in the section.

Summary

In this chapter, I introduced you to creating custom Flex components. I showed you how to build components using both MXML and ActionScript, and you saw how to achieve tasks like setting property values, calling methods, and dispatching custom events. You'll see more about custom components as you progress through this book.

One way to learn about creating components is to see what other developers are doing. flexlib is a site that provides an open source Flex 2 component library. You can find it at http://code.google.com/p/flexlib/. At the time of writing, the site included only components created in ActionScript, but should provide a useful learning resource for developers wanting to extend their skills in the area.

In the next chapter, I want to look at some of the different ways that Flex applications can interact with users.

Chapter 4

INTERACTING WITH USERS

It's common for developers to need to create ways for users to interact with their web applications. The application might need to provide messages or other information to users. It might also be necessary to collect information from users, perhaps to log in or register.

There are many different types of user interactions. The most simple could involve displaying a message to the user for information purposes. The application might also need to ask a question and elicit a yes/no response. The interaction could be more complex, perhaps displaying a form to collect content that is more complicated. The form could appear in a pop-up window or as part of the application itself.

All these types of interactions are possible and often necessary in Flex applications. In this chapter, we'll look at the range of methods that developers can use so that their applications can interact with users. In particular, the chapter will cover the following:

- Creating simple alerts
- Creating pop-up windows
- Displaying forms

Flex alerts are simple components that are somewhat similar to JavaScript alerts. You can use them to display a simple message to a user that includes an OK button.

However, Flex alerts are more complex than JavaScript alerts because they offer additional options such as icons.

Developers who need something a little more sophisticated can use pop-up windows that contain other user interface elements such as TextInput, ComboBox, and CheckBox controls. The main application window can interact with these pop-ups: passing and receiving values, and receiving events.

The final topic for the chapter is Flex forms, which capture user input in a variety of user interface controls, many of which we've already seen. The controls you can add to forms are no different to those you can add to pop-ups and other containers. However, using a Form container allows you to lay them out more easily in the application interface. We'll also see how to bind form elements to a data model and how you can use the built-in validation and formatting controls.

Throughout the chapter, I'll work through a series of examples so you can see different user interaction techniques. You can download the resources for this chapter from the friends of ED web site: www.friendsofed.com.

Let's begin by looking at Alerts.

Working with the Alert control

Alerts display simple pop-up messages to users. In Flex, alerts can include a message; a choice of OK, Yes, No, and Cancel buttons; a title; and an icon. They are modal dialog boxes, so that they will take focus from the rest of the application until the user responds. Because alerts are modal, they stop a user from carrying out any other action in the application until they are processed. The alert closes when the user clicks one of the buttons or presses the Esc key on the keyboard.

Alerts don't exist as controls in MXML. Rather, you need to create and work with them in ActionScript. Before you can do this, you should import the Alert class within the controls package using the following:

```
import mx.controls.Alert;
```

You can display an Alert control using the show static method. The method returns a reference to the alert and it takes the following arguments:

```
Alert.show(text, title, flags, parent, closeHandler, iconClass,➥
  defaultButtonFlag)
```

I'll work through each argument in a bit more detail in the next sections. After that, I'll go through a simple example to tie all these concepts together.

Adding a message and title

The first parameter in the show method, text, is the message that will appear centered inside the Alert. The second parameter, title, appears in the title bar at the top left of the box. For example, you can add these elements using the following:

```
Alert.show("Learn more about Flex?", "Question");
```

If you don't want to set any of the other options, you can create an alert using only these two arguments.

Adding buttons

By default, an alert shows only the OK button. If you need to show additional buttons, you can specify them using the flags argument. You can choose from the following constants:

- Alert.OK
- Alert.YES
- Alert.NO
- Alert.CANCEL

You need to list multiple buttons in brackets separated by the pipe character (|); for example, (Alert.YES | Alert.NO). It doesn't matter in which order you list the buttons, because they'll always appear in the order shown in the preceding list. You can display Yes and No buttons using the following:

```
Alert.show("Learn more about Flex?","Question",(Alert.YES|Alert.NO));
```

Setting the parent

The **parent** for the alert dictates how the control centers on the screen. You can use this to refer to the application:

```
Alert.show("Learn more about Flex?","Question",(Alert.YES|Alert.NO),➡
  this);
```

Adding a closeHandler method

The closeHandler method determines what happens when the alert closes. Regardless of which button the user clicks, the alert calls the same method, passing a CloseEvent event object. You can use the detail property of this object to determine which button the user clicked.

The following code block shows an alert that calls a function named findResponse when the user clicks a button:

```
Alert.show("Learn more about Flex?","Question",(Alert.YES|Alert.NO),➡
  this, findResponse);
```

The findResponse function might look something similar to the following:

```
function findResponse(e:CloseEvent):void{
  if (e.detail == Alert.YES) {
    //the user clicked yes, respond appropriately
  }
  else {
    //the user clicked no, respond appropriately
  }
}
```

Closing the alert passes a CloseEvent object to the handler function findResponse. The detail property of this object indicates which button was clicked and contains one of the button constants: Alert.OK, Alert.CANCEL, Alert.YES, or Alert.NO. In the previous function, we used this property to determine which button the user clicked.

Setting the iconClass argument

The iconClass parameter lists the name of the icon class that appears on the left of the text in the alert box. It normally refers to an embedded image file. Before you can display an icon in the alert, you need to create the icon class with the following code:

```
[Embed(source="assets/icon.jpg")]
public var iconSymbol:Class;
```

This code embeds the image icon.jpg from the assets folder and refers to it with the object iconSymbol. You can then add iconSymbol as an argument in the show method. The following show method works with the previous Embed statement. It uses the embedded icon iconSymbol, which refers to the icon.jpg image in the assets folder.

```
Alert.show("Learn more about Flex?","Question",(Alert.YES|Alert.NO),➥
   this, findResponse, iconSymbol);
```

Setting the defaultButtonFlag argument

Finally, you can set which button appears as default in the alert. The default button is the one that will be triggered when the user presses the Enter key. It appears in the application surrounded by a blue border. The following show method makes the No button the default option:

```
Alert.show("Learn more about Flex?","Question",(Alert.YES|Alert.NO),➥
   this, findResponse, iconSymbol, Alert.NO);
```

In this example, we specify that the alert displays two buttons: Yes and No. The last argument specifies that the No button is the default button for the alert.

If you don't specify a button, the default is Alert.OK.

Let's work through a simple example so you can see how to use the show method in practice.

A simple example

Create a new Flex project using File ➤ New ➤ Flex Project. Give it any name and location and set the project root as the folder for the application files. Create a folder within the project by right-clicking and choosing New ➤ Folder. Name the folder assets. Add the foelogo.jpg file from the downloaded resources to this folder by importing it from the File system. You can choose a different logo if you prefer.

Create the following interface in the application file:

```
<mx:VBox x="10" y="10">
  <mx:HBox>
    <mx:Label text="Enter your name"/>
```

```
      <mx:TextInput id="txtName"/>
    </mx:HBox>
    <mx:Text id="txtMessage"/>
    <mx:Button label="Click me"/>
  </mx:VBox>
```

Figure 4-1 shows how the interface appears when you run the application.

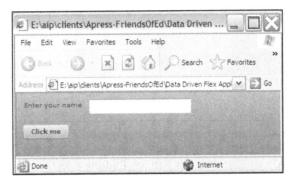

Figure 4-1. The interface for the simple alert example

We'll show an alert when the user clicks the Click me button so we need to add a click handler to the Button control. Modify it as shown here:

```
<mx:Button label="Click me" click="showAlert(event)"/>
```

We need to add the click handler function now. Add an <mx:Script> block below the <mx:Application> tag, as shown here:

```
<mx:Script>
  <![CDATA[
    import flash.events.MouseEvent;
    import mx.controls.Alert;
    private function showAlert(e:MouseEvent):void {
      Alert.show("Click a button","Hello",(Alert.YES|Alert.NO));
    }
  ]]>
</mx:Script>
```

The ActionScript code block starts by importing the MouseEvent class. It also imports the Alert class and creates the showAlert function. This function creates a simple alert with the message Click a button and the title Hello. The alert shows two buttons: Yes and No.

Clicking the Click me button calls the showAlert function, passing a MouseEvent object. This is the type of event object passed with a mouse click. The showAlert function then displays the alert.

Run the application. Figure 4-2 shows the effect of clicking the Click me button.

Figure 4-2. Clicking the button generates an alert

We see a simple message in an alert with two buttons. Clicking either button will close the alert, but there is no code to respond to each button individually.

Let's modify the code so we can detect which button the user clicks. To do this, we'll need to add a closeHandler argument to the alert. We'll display which button the user clicked in the Text control txtMessage in the main application file.

Modify the Alert line in the script block. The changes appear in bold:

```
Alert.show("Click a button","Hello",(Alert.YES|Alert.NO), this, ↪
    findResponse);
```

We added this as the parent for the alert. Using this allows us to center the alert relative to the main application.

The user calls the findResponse function when they click one of the buttons in the alert. The handler function will have a single parameter passed to it: a CloseEvent object. We'll need to import this class with the following line, so add it with the other import statements:

```
import mx.events.CloseEvent;
```

Add the following function to the code block:

```
private function findResponse(e:CloseEvent):void{
  if (e.detail == Alert.YES) {
    txtMessage.text = "You clicked yes";
  }
  else {
    txtMessage.text = "You clicked no";
  }
}
```

The function receives a CloseEvent object from the alert. It uses the detail property to find out which button the user clicked. The function compares this value to the constant Alert.YES to find out whether the user clicked Yes. If so, the Text control shows You clicked yes; otherwise it shows You clicked no.

Run the application and click the Click me button to bring up the alert. Click either button in the alert and you should see the relevant text in the Text control.

Let's add an icon to the alert. We'll use the foelogo.jpg file from the assets folder. First, we'll need to embed the image so we can refer to it with a class name. Add the following code below the import statements:

```
[Embed(source="assets/foelogo.jpg")]
public var iconSymbol:Class;
```

If you used a different image, replace foelogo.jpg with your image name.

We can then use iconSymbol as an argument in the alert as shown here:

```
Alert.show("Click a button","Hello",(Alert.YES|Alert.NO), this,➥
    findResponse, iconSymbol);
```

When you run the application and click the Click me button, you should see the icon inside the alert, as shown in Figure 4-3.

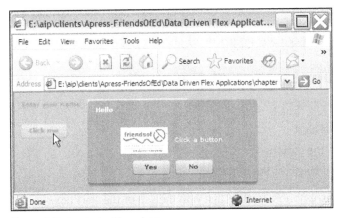

Figure 4-3. An alert with an icon

Let's finish the example by setting a default button and including the name of the user from the main application file in the displayed message. Modify the Alert line as shown in bold here:

```
Alert.show("Hi " + txtName.text + ". Click a button","Hello",➥
    (Alert.YES|Alert.NO), this, findResponse, iconSymbol, Alert.NO);
```

The changes set No as the default button and include the name entered in the main application within the alert message.

Run the application, enter a name, and click the Click me button to see the effect shown in Figure 4-4.

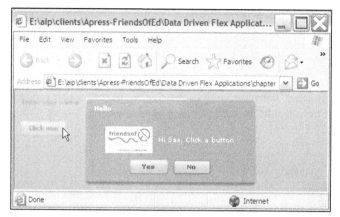

Figure 4-4. The completed example

In this example, I showed you how to set various properties in an Alert control. We showed Yes and No buttons and added a closeHandler so that we could respond appropriately, depending on which button the user clicked.

You can find my completed example saved as SimpleAlert.mxml with your resources. You'll need to import it into a project to run the application.

In this example, we accepted the default size of the Alert control. It's also possible to set the size and other aspects of appearance using properties of the Alert object returned by the show method.

Changing the appearance of the alert

You can change several aspects of the appearance of the alert, including the following:

- The size of the alert
- The labels on the buttons
- The width and height of the buttons

Let's see how you might do this, starting first with the size of the alert box.

Changing the size of the alert

It's easy to resize an alert by using the width and height properties of the returned Alert object. You need to set a reference for the object returned by the show method first:

```
var theAlert:Alert = Alert.show("Learn more about Flex?","Question");
```

You can then set the size of the alert using the reference, as follows:

```
theAlert.width = 400;
theAlert.height = 200;
```

Changing the button labels

The Alert control has several static properties that relate to the button labels okLabel, yesLabel, noLabel, and cancelLabel. As they are static properties, you need to set them before you create the alert, as shown here:

```
Alert.yesLabel = "Absolutely!";
Alert.noLabel = "No way!";
Alert.show("Learn more about Flex?","Question");
```

Changing the button size

You can also change the size of the buttons inside the alert using the static properties buttonHeight and buttonWidth. Again, you need to set these properties before you create the alert:

```
Alert.buttonHeight = 15;
Alert.buttonWidth = 100;
Alert.show("Learn more about Flex?","Question");
```

A simple example

Let's see how to change the appearance of the alert we created earlier in this chapter. We need to start by modifying the code, so we set a reference for the Alert object returned by the show method. Modify the showAlert function as shown here in bold:

```
private function showAlert(e:MouseEvent):void {
    var theAlert:Alert = Alert.show("Hi " + txtName.text + ➥
      "Click a button","Hello", (Alert.YES|Alert.NO), this, ➥
      findResponse, iconSymbol, Alert.NO);
}
```

We'll resize both the alert and the buttons in the alert and change the button labels. Modify the preceding function, as shown in the following code block. Again, the changes appear in bold:

```
private function showAlert(e:MouseEvent):void {
    Alert.buttonHeight = 20;
    Alert.buttonWidth = 120;
    Alert.yesLabel = "Absolutely!";
    Alert.noLabel = "No way!";
    var theAlert:Alert = Alert.show("Hi " + txtName.text + ➥
      "Click a button","Hello", (Alert.YES|Alert.NO), this, ➥
      findResponse, iconSymbol, Alert.NO);
    theAlert.width = 300;
    theAlert.height = 120;
}
```

We resized the buttons in the alert by setting the buttonHeight and buttonWidth properties. Notice that we did this before we created the alert. We also changed the words displayed on the Yes and No buttons using the yesLabel and noLabel properties. We then created the alert, assigning the object theAlert at the same time. Finally, we used this object to set the width and height of the alert.

Running the application produces the screenshot shown in Figure 4-5.

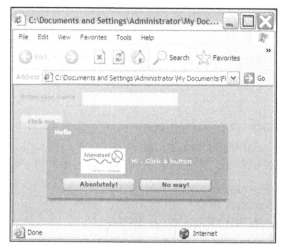

Figure 4-5. Changing the appearance of the alert

You can find the completed SimpleAlert1.mxml file saved with your resources.

Alerts provide a structured way to display messages to users who respond to their interactions. You can choose from four different buttons. If you find that you don't have enough flexibility with the built-in buttons, you can create custom pop-up windows containing any of the user interface controls.

Working with pop-ups

The PopUpManager class allows you to create your own pop-up windows to interact with users. You can use these windows modally so that they halt processing until the user takes an appropriate action.

To create the pop-up content, you'll need to make a custom component or class that contains the controls that you need. You can then refer to the component or class when you create your pop-up window using the createPopUp method. This method takes the following arguments:

```
createPopUp(parent, className, modal, childList)
```

The arguments are as follows:

- The parent determines the parent for the pop-up, and it's common to use a value of this to refer to the main application file.

- The className argument specifies the name of the class to create inside the pop-up.

- You can specify a modal pop-up by setting the modal argument to true.

- Finally, the childList specifies the childList in which to add the pop-up, and it is one of the following values: PopUpManagerChildList.APPLICATION, PopUpManagerChildList.POPUP, or PopUpManagerChildList.PARENT. If you don't specify anything, the default value is PopUpManagerChildList.PARENT.

The createPopUp method returns an IFlexDisplayObject, which represents the pop-up window. This object defines the interface for skin elements and is required so that the pop-up can display. You can create a pop-up window using the LoginForm class, as shown here:

```
myPopUp = createPopUp(this, LoginForm, true);
```

You can then remove the pop-up by referring to the returned pop-up object in the removePopUp method:

```
removePopUp(myPopUp);
```

You can also close a pop-up window from within the custom component or class by using this:

```
removePopUp(this);
```

We'll work through a simple example so you can see how to create and remove a pop-up window.

A simple example

In this example, we'll create a login form component that we'll use to populate a pop-up window. The component won't have any functionality, but it will demonstrate how to work with pop-ups.

Start by creating a new folder called components that we'll use for our LoginForm component. Within this folder, create a new component by choosing the MXML Component option from the New menu. Figure 4-6 shows the settings for this component.

Figure 4-6. Settings for the new component

Notice that the component was based on the TitleWindow control. This control includes a title bar, an automatic close button, and an area for displaying the other controls. It's a common choice as the basis for a pop-up window component.

Add the following user interface controls between the opening and closing <mx:TitleWindow> tags:

```
<mx:VBox x="10" y="10">
  <mx:HBox>
    <mx:Label text="Username" width="100"/>
    <mx:TextInput/>
  </mx:HBox>
  <mx:HBox>
    <mx:Label text="Password" width="100"/>
    <mx:TextInput/>
  </mx:HBox>
  <mx:HBox>
    <mx:Button label="Login"/>
  </mx:HBox>
</mx:VBox>
```

The interface includes VBox and HBox layout containers. Inside these containers, there are two Labels and two TextInput controls for the username and password, respectively. There is also a Login button inside.

We'll add a title to the TitleWindow control as well as a close button. Change the <mx:TitleWindow> tag as shown in bold here. The change also reduces the size of the control to 300 by 150:

```
<mx:TitleWindow xmlns:mx="http://www.adobe.com/2006/mxml"
  layout="absolute" width="300" height="150"
  title="Login" showCloseButton="true"/>
```

When you set the showCloseButton attribute to true, the TitleWindow shows a cross at the top-right corner. The user can click it to close the pop-up. You can add a handler for the close event of the TitleWindow, as shown here in bold:

```
<mx:TitleWindow xmlns:mx="http://www.adobe.com/2006/mxml"
  layout="absolute" width="300" height="150"
  title="Login" showCloseButton="true"
  close="PopUpManager.removePopUp(this)"/>
```

When the close event fires, the pop-up will be removed from the application using the static removePopUp method. Notice that we refer to the pop-up window using this.

To improve the appearance of the pop-up, it's nice to center it when the LoginForm loads. We can do this in the creationComplete event of the LoginForm component by using the static centerPopUp method. Modify the root element as shown in bold:

```
<mx:TitleWindow xmlns:mx="http://www.adobe.com/2006/mxml"
  layout="absolute" width="300" height="150"
  title="Login" showCloseButton="true"
  close="PopUpManager.removePopUp(this)"
  creationComplete="PopUpManager.centerPopUp(this)">
```

When the interface is created, the pop-up will center itself.

Because we referred to the PopUpManager class in the <mx:TitleWindow> tag, we'll need to import the class in an ActionScript block as follows. Add this now under the component's opening tag:

```
<mx:Script>
  <![CDATA[
    import mx.managers.PopUpManager;
  ]]>
</mx:Script>
```

If we were making a fully working component, we'd need to refer to some server-side login logic and respond appropriately. Because this is a simple example, we'll just close the pop-up window when the user clicks the Login button.

Add the following private function to the script block:

```
private function doLogin(e:MouseEvent):void {
  PopUpManager.removePopUp(this);
}
```

You'll also need to import the MouseEvent class:

```
import flash.events.MouseEvent;
```

Finally, you'll need to modify the click attribute for the button, as shown in bold, to call the doLogin handler method:

```
<mx:Button label="Login" click="doLogin(event)"/>
```

The complete code for the LoginForm component follows:

```
<?xml version="1.0" encoding="utf-8"?>
<mx:TitleWindow xmlns:mx="http://www.adobe.com/2006/mxml"
  layout="absolute" width="300" height="150"
  title="Login" showCloseButton="true"
  close="PopUpManager.removePopUp(this)"
  creationComplete="PopUpManager.centerPopUp(this)">
  <mx:Script>
    <![CDATA[
      import mx.managers.PopUpManager;
      import flash.events.MouseEvent;
      private function doLogin(e:MouseEvent):void {
        PopUpManager.removePopUp(this);
      }
    ]]>
  </mx:Script>
  <mx:VBox x="10" y="10">
    <mx:HBox>
      <mx:Label text="Username" width="100"/>
      <mx:TextInput/>
```

```
      </mx:HBox>
      <mx:HBox>
        <mx:Label text="Password" width="100"/>
        <mx:TextInput/>
      </mx:HBox>
      <mx:HBox>
        <mx:Button label="Login" click="doLogin(event)"/>
      </mx:HBox>
    </mx:VBox>
  </mx:TitleWindow>
```

Now that we've finished creating the component, we need to make a new application that displays the pop-up showing the login form. Normally we wouldn't have multiple application files in the same project, but for simplicity, create the application file in the same project using File ➤ New ➤ MXML Application. I called my file PopUpManagerExample.mxml.

Create the following simple interface in the application:

```
<mx:VBox x="10" y="10">
  <mx:Button label="Click me" click="showPopUp(event)"/>
</mx:VBox>
```

You can't get much simpler than a button inside a VBox!

Notice that the button calls the showPopUp function when clicked. We now need to add that function inside a script block. We'll also need to import the relevant classes. Add the following code beneath the opening <mx:Application> tag:

```
<mx:Script>
  <![CDATA[
    import components.*;
    import flash.events.MouseEvent;
    import mx.managers.PopUpManager;
    import mx.core.IFlexDisplayObject;
    private var myLoginForm:IFlexDisplayObject;
    private function showPopUp(e:MouseEvent):void {
      myLoginForm = PopUpManager.createPopUp(this, LoginForm, true);
    }
  ]]>
</mx:Script>
```

The code starts by importing the components package, which will include all custom components and classes inside that package. It imports the MouseEvent, the PopUpManager class, and the IFlexDisplayObject class for the returned pop-up window.

We create a variable called myLoginForm to reference the pop-up window. The variable is of the type IFlexDisplayObject. The code also includes the showPopUp function, which will be called by clicking the Click me button. This function uses the static createPopUp method to show a pop-up based on the LoginForm custom component. We specified that the window is modal by setting the last argument to true.

Run the application and click the Click me button. You should see a pop-up window populated by the LoginForm component, as shown in Figure 4-7.

Figure 4-7. The complete application showing a modal pop-up window

You should be able to close the pop-up by clicking the cross at the top right of the window. You should also be able to close the pop-up by clicking the Login button. It's a simple example but it shows the relationship between a pop-up and a custom component.

You can find my completed files saved as PopUpManagerExample.mxml and LoginForm.mxml with the other chapter resources. If you're going to import them into your project without completing the exercise, make sure you add the LoginForm.mxml file to a components folder.

The example might have been more useful if we could have passed a value from the LoginForm component back to the application; for example, the username. Let's see how we might make this happen by extending the example.

Passing values from the pop-up

We'll extend the previous example so that we can send the entered username back to the main application and display it in a Text control in the interface. We'll need to make some changes to both the LoginForm component and the application file, so save copies of them as LoginForm2.mxml and PopUpManagerExample2.mxml, respectively. Doing this means that you'll have examples of both approaches used so far in this chapter.

We'll start by making changes to the component file. Because we want to reference the Text control in the main application file within the custom component file, we need to import the Text class and create a public variable.

Add the following import statement to the script block inside the LoginForm2.mxml file:

```
import mx.controls.Text;
```

We'll create a public property called username of the type Text that will reference the control in the main application using the following line. Add the line below the import statements:

```
public var username:Text;
```

We can then set the value of the text property of the control to the value the user entered in the pop-up. When we close the pop-up, we want to display the username in the Text control in the main application.

To refer to the first TextInput control programmatically, we need to add an id attribute. Modify the element as shown in bold:

```
<mx:Label text="Username" width="100"/>
<mx:TextInput id="txtUsername"/>
```

Add the following line, shown in bold, to the doLogin function:

```
private function doLogin(e:MouseEvent):void {
  username.text = "Welcome back " + txtUsername.text;
  PopUpManager.removePopUp(this);
}
```

Before we close the pop-up, we set the text property of the Text control username to say Welcome back and include the entered username. You'll see how this works after we make changes to the main application file.

Switch to the application file so that we can change the way we call the pop-up. Before we start, we have to add a Text control with an id of txtMessage below the button. This control will display the username that we pass from the pop-up.

```
<mx:Text id="txtMessage"/>
```

The custom component LoginForm2 contains a public variable username, and the intent is that we'll access this variable from any application using the component. However, before we can do this, we need to set the data type appropriately for the custom component in the application file. If we don't change the data type, the component has the type IFlexDisplayObject. We want it to have the type LoginForm2.

In our example, we need to change the type of myLoginForm to be a LoginForm2 type, so make the alteration in the variable declaration:

```
private var myLoginForm:LoginForm2;
```

We can change the type by casting the component when it is created. The next line shows how to do this, so modify it in the showPopUp function:

```
myLoginForm = LoginForm2(PopUpManager.createPopUp(this, LoginForm2,➥
  true));
```

Note that if you didn't change the name of the custom component at the beginning of this exercise, you'd need to use the type LoginForm.

You can also remove the following import statement from the script block because we changed the data type of the LoginForm2 component:

```
import mx.core.IFlexDisplayObject;
```

We can refer to the public variable username as a property of the component. Modify the showPopUp function as shown here in bold:

```
private function showPopUp(e:MouseEvent):void {
  myLoginForm = LoginForm2(PopUpManager.createPopUp(this, LoginForm2,➡
    true));
  myLoginForm.username = txtMessage;
}
```

Notice that we had to cast the pop-up to the data type LoginForm2 to be able to access the public property username within the custom component. The new line sets this property to reference the txtMessage control. The pop-up can then use the variable username to refer to the txtMessage control in the application file.

The complete code for the application follows:

```
<?xml version="1.0" encoding="utf-8"?>
<mx:Application xmlns:mx="http://www.adobe.com/2006/mxml"
  layout="absolute">
  <mx:Script>
    <![CDATA[
      import flash.events.MouseEvent;
      import mx.managers.PopUpManager;
      import components.*;
      private var myLoginForm:LoginForm2;
      private function showPopUp(e:MouseEvent):void {
        myLoginForm = LoginForm2(PopUpManager.createPopUp(this,➡
          LoginForm2, true));
        myLoginForm.username = txtMessage;
      }
    ]]>
  </mx:Script>
  <mx:VBox x="10" y="10">
    <mx:Button label="Click me" click="showPopUp(event)"/>
    <mx:Text id="txtMessage"/>
  </mx:VBox>
</mx:Application>
```

Run the application and click the button to bring up the pop-up window. Enter a username and click Login. You should see the text Welcome back with the name you entered displaying in the main application.

You can find the completed files LoginForm2.mxml and PopUpManagerExample2.mxml with the other resources for the chapter.

The final extension of this example is to show how we can pass values to fields in the LoginForm custom component from the application file.

Passing values to the pop-up

It's sometimes useful to be able to set values in a pop-up window from the main application. We'll extend the previous example so that the username is already populated when the LoginForm component opens in the pop-up. You might do this if you had already accessed the username in the application, perhaps through a SharedObject or a JavaScript cookie.

In the custom component, we need to set a bindable public property for each value that we want to set from the main application. We can then bind the public property to the relevant property in a control in the custom component. In our case, we'll create a public string variable for the username and bind it to the text property of the TextInput control txtUsername.

Start in the custom component file and save a copy under the name LoginForm3.mxml. Add the following bindable public variable to the new file:

```
[Bindable]
public var user:String;
```

We'll bind this variable to the txtUsername control, as shown in the following line:

```
<mx:TextInput id="txtUsername" text="{user}"/>
```

When we set the value of the public variable from the application, it will appear in the text of the txtUsername control.

Switch to the application file and modify the showPopUp function, as shown here in bold:

```
private function showPopUp(e:MouseEvent):void {
  myLoginForm = LoginForm2(PopUpManager.createPopUp(this, LoginForm2,➥
    true));
  myLoginForm.user = "Sas";
  myLoginForm.username = txtMessage;
}
```

The new line sets the public variable user within the custom component to the value Sas (feel free to use your own name if you prefer). Because we bound the public variable to the TextInput control, the value will appear when the pop-up displays.

Run the application and click the Click me button. As in Figure 4-8, you should see the Username value populated with the name entered in the main application; Sas in this case. Obviously, we set the value in code. You could equally set the value from a TextInput in the application.

To set any other values in controls in the custom component, you just need to bind them to public bindable variables. You can then set these values from the main application file. You can also write ActionScript to set the properties of the custom component directly from the application; for example, the title property of the TitleWindow control.

I saved the resource files for this example as PopUpManagerExample3.mxml and LoginForm3.mxml. They contain examples in which the application sets the label property of the button and the title property of the TitleWindow control.

Figure 4-8. The Username value is populated from the main application.

As you can see, it's possible to control many aspects of the pop-up from the main application file. One useful tool for developers is the ability to allow the application to respond to events dispatched in the pop-up.

Responding to pop-up events

The main application can control all aspects of the custom component that appears in the pop-up window. I've mentioned that the application can set properties of the base component, such as the title. We also saw that it can set the value of public properties in the custom component. The application hosting the pop-up can even respond to events dispatched from the pop-up. In this example, we'll control all aspects of the pop-up window from the main application file and respond to an event.

Create a new custom component in the components folder based on the TitleWindow. Set a width of 300 and a height of 150 for the component, and call it LoginForm4. The custom component will contain only controls without any ActionScript. Create the following interface, shown in bold, inside the custom component:

```
<?xml version="1.0" encoding="utf-8"?>
<mx:TitleWindow xmlns:mx="http://www.adobe.com/2006/mxml"
  layout="absolute" width="300" height="150">
  <mx:VBox x="10" y="10">
    <mx:HBox>
    <mx:Label text="Username" width="100"/>
    <mx:TextInput id="txtUsername"/>
  </mx:HBox>
  <mx:HBox>
    <mx:Label text="Password" width="100"/>
    <mx:TextInput/>
  </mx:HBox>
  <mx:HBox>
```

```
        <mx:Button label="Click me!" id="clickButton"/>
      </mx:HBox>
    </mx:VBox>
  </mx:TitleWindow>
```

We used the same structure as in the previous examples and added an id attribute for the button so we can respond to the click event in the main application.

Our application file is very simple as well. Create a new MXML application called PopUpManagerExample4.mxml and modify it to show the following structure:

```
<?xml version="1.0" encoding="utf-8"?>
<mx:Application xmlns:mx="http://www.adobe.com/2006/mxml"
  layout="absolute">
  <mx:VBox x="10" y="10">
    <mx:Button label="Click me"/>
    <mx:Text id="txtMessage"/>
  </mx:VBox>
</mx:Application>
```

The first task is to add a script block. We'll start by adding import statements and a variable declaration for the LoginForm4 component:

```
<mx:Script>
  <![CDATA[
    import flash.events.MouseEvent;
    import mx.managers.PopUpManager;
    import components.*;
    private var myLoginForm:LoginForm4;
  ]]>
</mx:Script>
```

We need to import the MouseEvent class so we can capture button click event objects. The PopUpManager class allows us to work with pop-ups, and we also need to import the custom component from the components package. We added a private variable that will refer to the LoginForm4 custom component.

We need to add a function that will display the pop-up and control its appearance. Add the following function to the script block:

```
private function showPopUp(e:MouseEvent):void {
  myLoginForm = LoginForm4(PopUpManager.createPopUp(this, LoginForm4,➥
    true));
  PopUpManager.centerPopUp(myLoginForm);
  myLoginForm.title = "Login";
  myLoginForm.showCloseButton=true;
}
```

Because we'll call the function by clicking a button, we need to pass in a MouseEvent event object as an argument. The second line of the function creates the pop-up and casts it to the data type LoginForm4—the name of the custom component. It creates the pop-up as a modal window.

We center the pop-up by using the static centerPopUp method, passing the name of the pop-up returned by the createPopUp method. The function also sets the title and showCloseButton properties of the pop-up.

Call this function when the user clicks the Click me button by modifying the <mx:Button> element, as shown in bold here:

```
<mx:Button label="Click me" click="showPopUp(event)"/>
```

We can modify the showPopUp function to add event listeners for the click event of the Login button and the close event of the pop-up window. Add the following lines at the end of the showPopUp function:

```
myLoginForm.addEventListener(Event.CLOSE, closeHandler);
myLoginForm.clickButton.addEventListener(MouseEvent.CLICK,➥
    loginClickHandler);
```

The lines add handlers for two events: the close event of the pop-up and the click event of the clickButton button. The closeHandler function will run when the pop-up closes while the loginClickHandler function will respond when the user clicks the Login button. Notice that we can refer to the controls in the custom component using dot notation, for example:

```
myLoginForm.clickButton
```

You can also use this:

```
myLoginForm["clickButton"]
```

The last task is to add these two handler functions in the script block:

```
private function loginClickHandler(e:Event):void {
    txtMessage.text = "Welcome back " + myLoginForm.txtUsername.text;
    PopUpManager.removePopUp(myLoginForm);
}
private function closeHandler(e:Event):void {
    PopUpManager.removePopUp(myLoginForm);
}
```

The loginClickHandler function sets the text in the txtMessage control, taking the value from the txtUsername control in the pop-up. The closeHandler function removes the pop-up using the static removePopUp method. That's all there is to it! The application controls all aspects of the pop-up.

Run the application and click the Click me button. Enter a username and log in. You should see the message Welcome back and your entered username displayed in the application. You can find this example in the resource files LoginForm4.mxml and PopUpManagerExample4.mxml.

I want to move the focus of the chapter away from things that pop up in applications and look at the Flex forms.

Working with forms

In XHTML, forms provide a way to group user interface controls in a collection. You include all controls inside a <form> tag. In Flex, forms work a little differently. They exist purely for layout purposes and make it easier to lay out individual form controls in an application.

Flex includes the familiar range of user interface controls for collecting and displaying data to users. Developers will be familiar with the functionality of controls such as TextInput, TextArea, RadioButton, and CheckBox. In addition, Flex includes more advanced controls that aren't available in XHTML, such as the DataGrid, Sliders, the NumericStepper, and the TileList.

So far in this book, you've seen how to work with some of the most common user interface controls. In this section, I'll introduce you to the Form layout container and show you how to use it with user interface controls. I'll also show you how to use built-in validators to check user input and how to apply built in-formatters to change the way data displays.

We'll start with a closer look at the Form container.

Understanding the Form container

You can use the Form container to control the layout of your form elements. It also includes functionality that allows you to specify which fields are required or optional and to add styling. One advantage of using the Form container is that you can bind the form to a data model to assist with management of your data. I'll show you more about that topic a little later in this chapter.

You create a Form container with the <mx:Form> element. When you create the form in Design view, each field within the form exists within an <mx:FormItem> element. This element is optional if you type the elements yourself in Source view. You can use the <mx:FormHeading> element to set the form's heading.

The following example shows a simple form inside a Panel container. The form collects the first name and last name of a user and displays the heading Enter your details. In this example, I added each control inside a <mx:FormItem> element:

```
<mx:Panel title="Form demonstration">
  <mx:Form id="userDetails">
    <mx:FormHeading label="Enter your details"/>
    <mx:FormItem label="First name">
      <mx:TextInput id="txtFirstName"/>
    </mx:FormItem>
    <mx:FormItem label="Last name">
      <mx:TextInput id="txtLastName"/>
    </mx:FormItem>
  </mx:Form>
</mx:Panel>
```

Figure 4-9 shows how this form appears when viewed in a web browser.

The form heading appears centered and in bold at the top of the form. The label of each <mx:FormItem> appears to the left of the control contained inside.

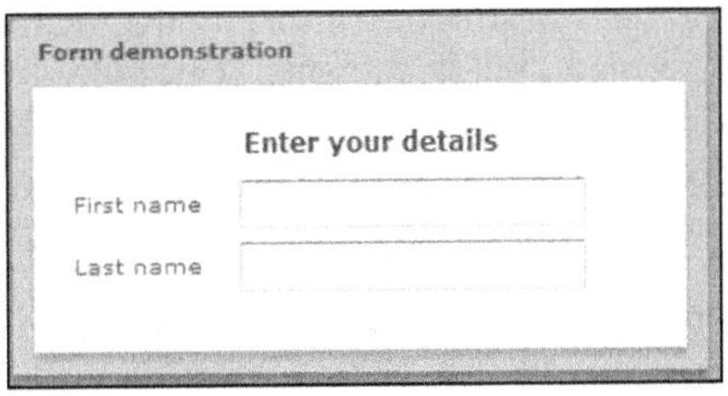

Figure 4-9. A simple Flex form

Forms often contain a set of related information for working with an external data source. For this reason, it's useful to bind form elements to a data model.

Working with a data model

A data model provides a way to store data in an organized manner within Flex. You might use a data model to organize data sent from a server-side page or to create a structure for data that you'll send to the server to update a database. Although data models are very useful for integrating server data into Flex applications, you can also use them on their own as a way of structuring client-side data. That's the approach we'll take in this section to simplify the examples.

You can use the <mx:Model> element to define a simple data model for your application. This approach embeds the data within the file, so you need to compile the application each time the data changes. You can also define a more complex data model using ActionScript, either within the application or using a class file. You can use these options to load data dynamically at run time. We'll cover those approaches later in the book.

Using the <mx:Model> tag

The <mx:Model> tag is normally used for creating very simple data structures within an application; it doesn't allow you to specify a data type. This tag uses XML tags to create the hierarchy and relationships as shown here:

```
<mx:Model id="books">
  <Library>
    <book>
      <title>Foundation Data-Driven Flex 3 Applications</title>
      <author>Sas Jacobs</author>
      <pubYear>2007</pubYear>
    </book>
    <book>
      <title>The Essential Guide to Flex 2 with ActionScript 3.0</title>
      <author>Charles E. Brown</author>
      <pubYear>2007</pubYear>
    </book>
  </Library>
</mx:Model>
```

The preceding data model provides information about two books within a library.

Because we use XML to describe the data structure in the model, we must make sure that the content conforms to the rules for well-formed XML documents. (One rule is that the model must contain a single root node.) In the previous example, it is the <Library> node. This node must contain all other nodes. You can see that the root node contains two <book> nodes that in turn contain nodes providing information about each book.

Other requirements for well-formed XML documents include these:

- Each node must close correctly.
- The case of both opening and closing tags must match.
- All attribute values must appear within quotation marks, either single or double.

You can also load the structure from an external file by using the source property, but we won't do that until later in the book:

```
<mx:Model source = "books.xml"/>
```

The data model can also be populated with content from an application by including data binding expressions inside each node or attribute. You might do this to bind the contents from form fields directly to your data model before updating an external data source. For example, we could bind the preceding model to user interface controls by specifying their id and a bound property inside curly braces as shown here:

```
<mx:Model id="books">
  <Library>
    <book>
      <title>{txtBookTitle.text}</title>
      <author>{txtAuthor.text}</author>
      <pubYear>{txtPubYear.text}</pubYear>
    </book>
  </Library>
</mx:Model>
```

In this example, the model populates from the text entered into the txtBookTitle, txtAuthor, and txtPubYear controls.

You can also use ActionScript expressions within the bindings:

```
<author>{"Author: " + txtAuthor.text}</author>
```

Let's work through a simple form example so that you can see how to use a form with a data model. Start by creating a new application file in your project and call it Forms1.mxml. Add the following MXML tags to the file:

```
<?xml version="1.0" encoding="utf-8"?>
<mx:Application xmlns:mx="http://www.adobe.com/2006/mxml"
  layout="absolute">
  <mx:Panel title="Form demonstration" width="500">
    <mx:Form id="userDetails">
      <mx:FormHeading label="Enter your details"/>
      <mx:FormItem label="First name">
```

```
            <mx:TextInput id="txtFirstName"/>
        </mx:FormItem>
        <mx:FormItem label="Last name">
            <mx:TextInput id="txtLastName"/>
        </mx:FormItem>
        <mx:FormItem label="Date of birth">
            <mx:TextInput id="txtDOB"/>
        </mx:FormItem>
        <mx:FormItem label="Email">
            <mx:TextInput id="txtEmail"/>
        </mx:FormItem>
        <mx:FormItem label="Gender">
            <mx:RadioButtonGroup id="rdoGender"/>
            <mx:RadioButton label="Female" groupName="rdoGender"/>
            <mx:RadioButton label="Male"  groupName="rdoGender"/>
            <mx:RadioButton label="Not telling" groupName="rdoGender"/>
        </mx:FormItem>
        <mx:FormItem label="Country">
            <mx:ComboBox id="cboCountry">
                <mx:dataProvider>
                    <mx:String>Choose...</mx:String>
                    <mx:String>Australia</mx:String>
                    <mx:String>United Kingdom</mx:String>
                    <mx:String>United States</mx:String>
                </mx:dataProvider>
            </mx:ComboBox>
        </mx:FormItem>
        <mx:ControlBar horizontalAlign="center" width="250">
            <mx:Button label="Update"/>
        </mx:ControlBar>
    </mx:Form>
  </mx:Panel>
</mx:Application>
```

Run the application and you should see a form that looks like the one displayed in Figure 4-10.

We'll use this form in the rest of the examples in the chapter. We'll extend it a little later to add validation and formatting.

Add the following data model to the top of the file below the <mx:Application> tag:

```
<mx:Model id="userData">
  <User>
    <firstName>{txtFirstName.text}</firstName>
    <lastName>{txtLastName.text}</lastName>
    <dateOfBirth>{txtDOB.text}</dateOfBirth>
    <email>{txtEmail}</email>
    <gender>{rdoGender.selectedValue}</gender>
    <country>{cboCountry.selectedItem}</country>
  </User>
</mx:Model>
```

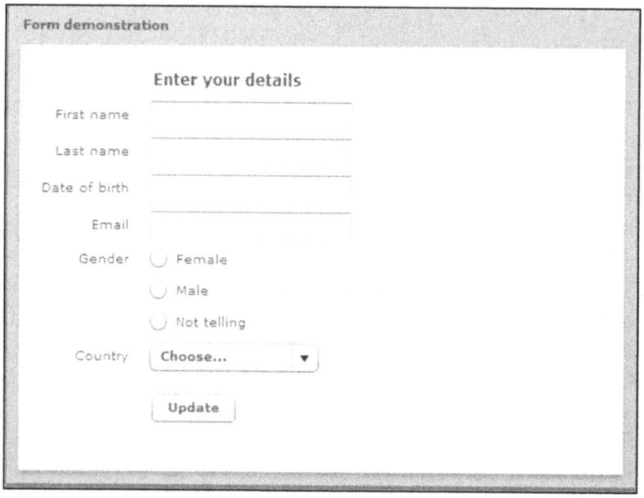

Figure 4-10. The form interface

The model creates a root node called <User> that contains other nodes corresponding to each field in the form. The model binds the child nodes to the relevant user controls with curly braces notation. Notice that we can't specify the data types of these values as if we were using an ActionScript class.

The <gender> and <country> nodes use an ActionScript expression in their bindings. To find gender, we choose the selectedValue property of the RadioButtonGroup element rdoGender. We can use the expression cboCountry.selectedItem to find what has been selected in the ComboBox because its dataProvider only specifies a string property rather than both a label and data.

There's no point in running the example at this point because we won't be able to tell whether the binding has been successful. There are no visual changes to indicate that the model updates.

Let's add functionality to the Update button to display some of the bound form details from the data model in a Text control.

Add the following Text control below the closing </mx:Form> element:

```
<mx:Text id="txtResponses" width="300"/>
```

Add a click handler to the Update button, as shown in bold:

```
<mx:Button label="Update" click="showEntries(event)"/>
```

Add a script block above the <mx:Model> element containing the following ActionScript code:

```
<mx:Script>
  <![CDATA[
    import flash.events.MouseEvent;
    private function showEntries(e:MouseEvent):void{
      txtResponses.text = "Thanks " + userData.firstName + " " +➥
        userData.lastName + " from " + userData.country;
    }
```

```
]]>
</mx:Script>
```

This block of code starts by importing the MouseEvent class, which is the type of event object dispatched when the user clicks the Update button. It then creates the showEntries function, which displays a message in the Text control txtResponses. The message accesses the values inside the data model using the id of the data model and the name of the relevant node. For example, to access the user's first name, we use userData.firstName.

Figure 4-11 shows what happens when you run the application, fill in the form, and click the Update button.

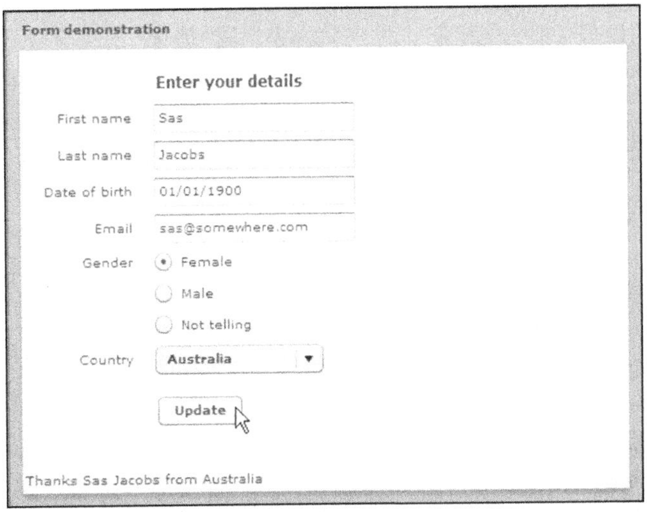

Figure 4-11. The completed example

The Text control updates with the bound values from the data model. This simple example shows how to bind a form to a data model and to retrieve the bound values from the model.

You can find the example saved as Forms1.mxml with the other resources. However, the example doesn't distinguish between required and optional form elements, and doesn't provide any type of validation to ensure that users have entered the correct types of values. Let's look at those topics now.

Determining required values

It's common for some values in a form to be required before the form is processed. For example, it isn't much use collecting user details that contain blank first and last names. If these fields are required in the database, you'll get an error when you try to add the record. For this reason, we try to validate required fields before sending their content for processing.

Flex provides a two-step process to deal with required fields. First, you can indicate that a field is required by displaying an asterisk in the label; to enforce the requirement, you can use a validator to ensure that the field contains a value.

The required property in the <mx:FormItem> element is a Boolean property that determines whether or not to display a red asterisk; it doesn't check that the user has entered a value. You can use the property as follows:

```
<mx:FormItem label="First name" required="true">
  <mx:TextInput id="txtFirstName"/>
</mx:FormItem>
```

Any <mx:FormItem> elements marked as required automatically display a red asterisk, as shown in Figure 4-12.

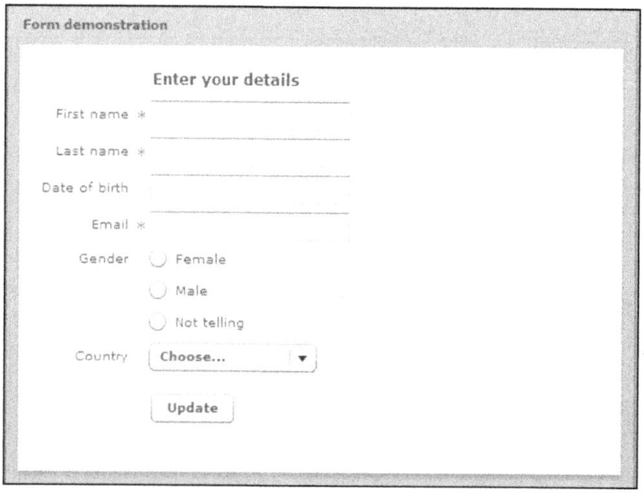

Figure 4-12. Required fields are marked with a red asterisk.

The required property displays an asterisk, but doesn't ensure that content has actually been entered into the field. You'll need to couple the declaration with an appropriate validator to ensure that data has been entered and that it is of the correct type.

Validating user input

Flex includes a number of built-in validators that you can use to make sure that users have entered the correct data in form fields. The Validator classes include CreditCardValidator, CurrencyValidator, DateValidator, EmailValidator, NumberValidator, PhoneNumberValidator, RegExpValidator, SocialSecurityValidator, StringValidator, and ZipCodeValidator. You must add these validators as children of the <mx:Application> tag.

All validators use the Validator base class, which provides attributes that are common to all. Table 4-1 shows these properties.

Table 4-1. Properties common to all validators

Property	Explanation
enabled	A Boolean value indicating whether the validator is enabled
listener	Specifies a listener for the validation
property	The name of the property to be validated in the source control
required	A Boolean value indicating whether entry in the source control is required
requiredFieldError	The error message to display if there is no entry in a required field
source	The id of the control containing the property to be validated
trigger	The id of the component that triggers validation
triggerEvent	The event triggering the validation

To set any field as required, you can set the required property to true. Unless you specify a trigger and triggerEvent, validation will occur when the user tabs out of the field. This provides immediate feedback to the user that they have entered incorrect or invalid data.

As an alternative, instead of validating each field one at a time, you might want to set validation for all fields to the click event of a single button control using the following attributes inside the validator:

```
trigger="{btnClick}" triggerEvent="click"
```

Whichever method you choose, an invalid entry will appear with a red border, as shown in Figure 4-13.

Figure 4-13. An invalid entry in a control displays a red border.

You can display the associated error message by moving your mouse over the control, as shown in Figure 4-14. Each validator has some standard error messages, and you can also set your own.

Figure 4-14. Displaying the error message associated with the invalid entry

It's worth knowing that you can assign a single validator to multiple fields and more than one validator to the same field.

You can also use ActionScript to work with validators (you'll see an example later in the chapter). To start with, we'll work through each validator in turn, starting with the CreditCardValidator.

Working with the CreditCardValidator

You can use the CreditCardValidator to check that a credit card meets all the criteria for the relevant card type, including the length, correct prefix, and Luhn mod10 algorithm. Even if the number is validated as meeting these criteria, the validator doesn't indicate that the credit card itself is valid.

You can specify the following card types: American Express, Diners Club, Discover, MasterCard, or Visa. The following example shows that you need to set two source objects and their properties to specify the credit card details. It specifies that the user can enter a space and hyphen in the formatting of credit card numbers:

```
<mx:CreditCardValidator
   allowedFormatChars=" -" required="true"
   cardTypeSource="{txtCreditCardType}" cardTypeProperty="text"
   cardNumberSource="{txtCreditCardNo}" cardNumberProperty="text"/>
```

You can specify the following errors associated with invalid data: invalidCharError, invalidNumberError, noNumError, noTypeError, wrongLengthError, and wrongTypeError. Assign a string to each type of error to display it as a message when the user enters invalid data:

```
invalidCharError ="You've entered an invalid character"
```

Working with the CurrencyValidator

The CurrencyValidator checks that the entry is a valid expression indicating a currency value. This validator can specify a range of values, whether negatives are allowed, and the number of decimal places. You can specify the currency symbol, where it is aligned, and the characters used for both the thousands and decimal places separators.

This example specifies that a currency value is required and must be between 1 and 10,000. It must use a $ sign on the left, with a dot for a decimal separator and a comma to separate thousands:

```
<mx:CurrencyValidator
source="{txtAmount}" property="text" required="true"
   currencySymbol="$" alignSymbol="left" allowNegative="false"
   decimalSeparator="." thousandsSeparator=","
   maxValue="10000" minValue="2" precision="1" />
```

The errors associated with this validator are currencySymbolError, decimalPointCountError, exceedsMaxError, invalidCharError, invalidFormatCharsError, lowerThanMinError, negativeError, precisionError, and separationError.

Working with the DateValidator

The DateValidator checks that a string matches a specific date format. You can either validate a single string containing the whole date or individual date parts for the day, month, and year in separate controls. You can specify the separator character as well as an input format using MM to indicate month, DD to indicate the day, and YYYY to indicate the year. If you don't specify a format, the

DateValidator validates that dates use the *MM/DD/YYYY* format used in the United States.

The code that follows shows an example of the DateValidator. It uses a European date format that allows for slashes, hyphens, dots, and spaces between the date parts. The validator validates the entry as a string because of the validateAsString property:

```
<mx:DateValidator source="{txtDate}" property="text"
    allowedFormatChars="/-. " inputFormat="DD/MM/YYYY"
    validateAsString="true" />
```

You can respond to the following types of errors in the DateValidator: formatError, invalidCharError, wrongDayError, wrongLengthError, wrongMonthError, and wrongYearError.

Working with the EmailValidator

The EmailValidator checks that an e-mail entry has a single @ sign and at least one dot; and that the top-level domain has two, three, four, or six characters. It can also check for valid IP addresses in the address, provided that you enclose them in square brackets.

The following tag shows one way to use this validator to determine that the user has entered a valid e-mail address:

```
<mx:EmailValidator source="{txtEmail}" property="text"
    required="true"/>
```

You can display the following types of error messages: invalidCharError, invalidDomainError, invalidIPDomainError, invalidPeriodsInDomainError, missingAtSignError, missingPeriodInDomainError, missingUsernameError, and tooManyAtSignsError.

Working with the NumberValidator

A NumberValidator checks for a valid number and can determine whether the number falls within a range or is an integer. You can also specify whether negative values are valid and how many decimal places the number can contain. As with the CurrencyValidator, you can specify the thousands and decimal places separator.

This example shows a required integer entry between –500 and 500:

```
<mx:NumberValidator
    source="{txtNumber}" property="text" required="true"
    allowNegative="true" precision="0"
    maxValue="500" minValue="-500" />
```

You can specify the following errors: decimalPointCountError, exceedsMaxError, integerError, invalidCharError, invalidFormatCharsError, lowerThanMinError, negativeError, precisionError, and separationError.

Working with the PhoneNumberValidator

The PhoneNumberValidator checks for a valid phone number. This is a number that contains at least 10 digits as well as formatting characters:

```
<mx:PhoneNumberValidator source="{txtPhone}" property="text"
allowedFormatChars="()- .+" />
```

The preceding example specifies that the phone number can include bracket, hyphen, space, dot, and plus characters. You can respond to the following errors: invalidCharError and wrongLengthError.

Working with the RegExpValidator

The RegExpValidator allows you to check that a string matches a specified regular expression. The validator allows you to specify an expression as well as any flags for the expression. The topic of regular expressions can be complex and is beyond the scope of this chapter, so you might want to find out more in the help topics.

The following example matches any expression starting with the letters AA with two digits to follow:

```
<mx:RegExpValidator source="{txtInput}" property="text"
  expression="/AA\d\d/"/>
```

You can specify two errors associated with the RegExpValidator: noExpressionError and noMatchError.

Working with the SocialSecurityValidator

You can use the SocialSecurityValidator to determine whether an entry is a valid U.S. Social Security number:

```
<mx:SocialSecurityValidator source="{txtSSN}" property="text"
  allowedFormatChars=".-"/>
```

The preceding example validates the text property of the txtSSN control, and allows for dot and hyphen characters. You can respond to the following errors: invalidCharError, wrongFormatError, and zeroStartError.

Working with the StringValidator

You use the StringValidator on string content to indicate that input is required and to set a minimum and maximum length for the entry. Like all validators, you can indicate whether the content is required, set the source control for the validator, and specify the property being validated.

The following example shows a StringValidator that checks the text property of the txtFirstName control. Entry is required and should be between 2 and 12 characters. The three possible error messages are shown in the following code block:

```
<mx:StringValidator required="true" source="{txtFirstName}"
  property="text" minLength="2" maxLength="12"
```

```
requiredFieldError="You must enter a value in this field"
tooShortError="Enter at least 2 characters"
tooLongError="You can't enter more than 12 characters"/>
```

Working with the ZipCodeValidator

The final built-in validator is the ZipCodeValidator, which checks for four- and five-digit U.S. or Canadian postal codes. The following example shows validation of U.S. Zip codes containing dot or hyphen characters:

```
<mx:ZipCodeValidator source="{txtZipCode}" property="text"
    allowedFormatChars=".-" domain="US Only"/>
```

You can respond to the following errors: invalidCharError, invalidDomainError, wrongCAFormatError, wrongLengthError, and wrongUSFormatError.

We'll work through an example in which we add validation to the previous user details form example.

Adding validation to a form

To see how some of the more common validators work, we'll extend the previous form example to include validation. We'll check that the required First name, Last name, and E-mail fields have been entered. We'll also check for a valid date of birth and e-mail address. Instead of validating each control individually, we'll carry out validation when the user clicks the Update button in the form.

Start by adding the id btnUpdate to the Update button, as shown here:

```
<mx:Button label="Update" id="btnUpdate" click="showEntries(event)"/>
```

We'll specify that this control triggers the validation and that the triggerEvent is click in each of our validators.

Because we'll use the U.S. date format for our DateValidator, it is a good idea to indicate the date format in the Date of birth FormLabel. Modify it as shown in bold:

```
<mx:FormItem label="Date of birth (MM/DD/YYYY)">
```

Note that for usability in a real-world application, I'd probably add three separate inputs—one each for the day, month, and year of the date of birth. I'd use a ComboBox for the month control and allow the user to select it by name so that they weren't tied to a single date format. However, I haven't done that here so that I can demonstrate how to use a DateValidator with a full date string.

Let's add the validators now. Enter the following tags in the application file. It doesn't matter where you put them as long as they're children of the <mx:Application> object. I have added mine below the <mx:Model> tag because I like to use a strict order in my files:

```
<mx:StringValidator id="fNameValidator" required="true"
    source="{txtFirstName}" property="text"
    trigger="{btnUpdate}" triggerEvent="click"
    requiredFieldError="You must enter your first name"/>
<mx:StringValidator id="lNameValidator" required="true"
```

```
      source="{txtLastName}" property="text"
      trigger="{btnUpdate}" triggerEvent="click"
      requiredFieldError="You must enter your last name"/>
   <mx:DateValidator id="DOBValidator" allowedFormatChars="/-. "
      source="{txtDOB}" property="text" required="false"
      trigger="{btnUpdate}" triggerEvent="click"
      invalidCharError="Check the characters in the date field"/>
   <mx:EmailValidator id="emailValidator" required="true"
      source="{txtEmail}" property="text"
      trigger="{btnUpdate}" triggerEvent="click"
      requiredFieldError="You must enter your email address"
      missingAtSignError="You're missing an @ sign in your email address"
      missingUsernameError="You've left out the email address username"/>
```

These tags create the validators that I described earlier. You can see that the source attribute contains the id of a control in curly brackets, and the property attribute indicates the bound property of that control. I've added some custom error messages as well. I could have added more error messages in the <mx:EmailValidator>, but I think you get the general idea!

You might notice that I specified a value for the required property. Even if I don't include this attribute, entry into the source will still be required because the property has a default value of true. Just adding a validator assumes that entry is required unless you explicitly set the required property to false to indicate otherwise.

Run the application and click the Update button without making any entries. Figure 4-15 shows how the form appears when we don't enter values in the required fields.

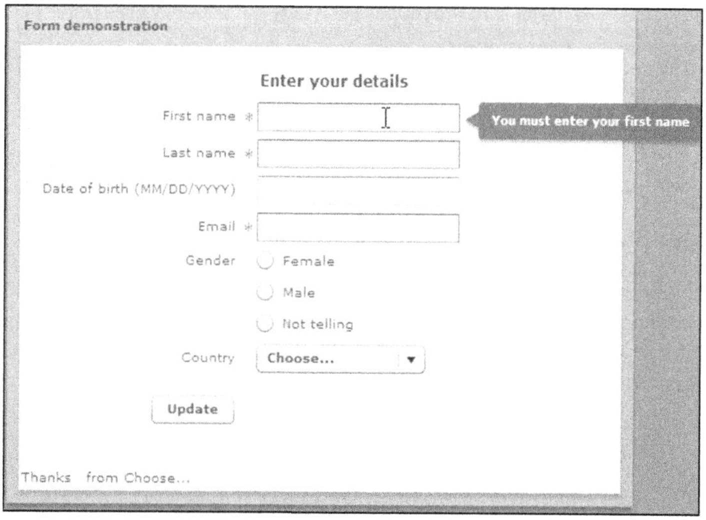

Figure 4-15. Validating the required fields

All the required fields are highlighted with a red border. You can move your mouse over each field to see the relevant error message.

Fill in the required fields and add a European formatted date (*DD-MM-YYYY*) as well as an incorrect e-mail address. Figure 4-16 shows the error message resulting from the incorrect e-mail address.

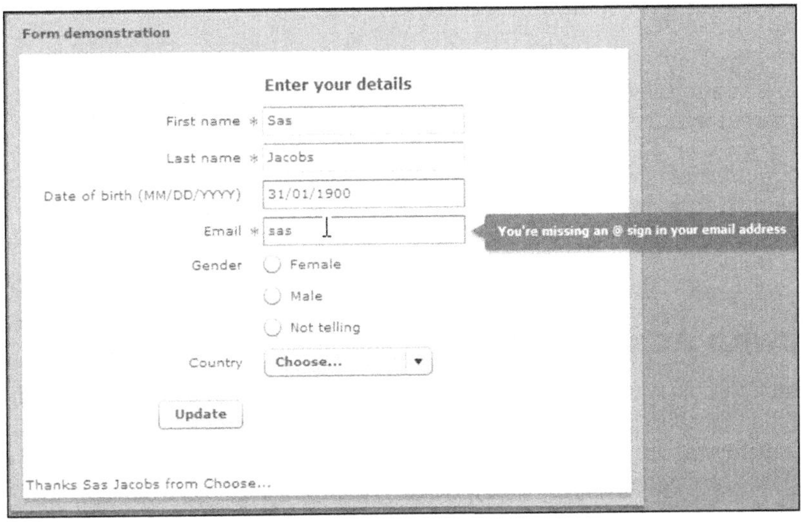

Figure 4-16. The e-mail validation message

You can see how easy it is to add validation to form elements in Flex. You can find this example saved as Forms2.mxml with your resources.

It's also possible to respond explicitly to validation within each component by detecting the valid and invalid events. We'll look at this topic now.

Validating with validator events

You can respond to the valid and invalid events associated with each validator if you want to write a custom function to handle validation. By assigning event handlers, you can listen for the events on each component and respond appropriately with ActionScript. This will allow you to do more than display a simple validation message in response to a valid or invalid entry. For example, you could change the application interface or state when the user makes a valid entry.

The following tag shows how to assign these event handlers:

```
<mx:StringValidator id="fNameValidator"
  source="{txtFirstName}" property="text"
  valid="handleValid(event)"
  invalid="handleInvalid(event)"/>
```

You can then include the appropriate handler functions to process the relevant outcomes:

```
private function handleValid(e:Event):void{
  //do something with valid result
}
private function handleInvalid(e:Event):void{
  //do something with invalid result
}
```

This approach is straightforward, so I won't work through an example. Instead, I want to fix up some issues that occurred with the previous example.

In our previous validation example, the user can select Choose... in the ComboBox control. We might want to prevent this from happening. We also might want to display all the validation error messages at the same time, so users don't have to move their mouse over each control highlighted in red to see the message.

Validating with ActionScript

We can be more flexible with our validation if we use ActionScript to detect invalid entries. We can assign a validation function to the click event of the button that checks the result of all validations. The validate method of each validation control will indicate whether the entry validated successfully. This method takes two arguments and returns a ValidationResultEvent:

```
validatorID.validate(value, suppressEvents);
```

You can pass in an entry to validate using the value argument. If this argument is blank or set to null, the validator uses the source and property attributes assigned in the MXML tag to determine which entry to validate. You can set the supressEvents argument to false if you want to notify the validation listener of the results of the validation. This is the default value if you omit the argument. In fact, it's common to call this method without either argument.

We can detect an invalid entry using something similar to the following code:

```
theValidationResult = validatorID.validate();
if (theValidationResult.type==ValidationResultEvent.INVALID) {
  //entry was invalid
}
```

Notice that we could find the outcome of the validation by using the type property of the ValidationResultEvent returned from the validate method. We can access an array of all ValidationResult objects using the results property or we can view all error messages as a single string using the message property.

By working through each validator, it's possible to respond programmatically to invalid entries; for example, displaying all validation errors in a single Text control.

We'll change the previous example so you can see how this approach might work. Start by changing the click handler function in the <mx:Button> control, as shown here:

```
<mx:Button label="Update" id="btnUpdate"
  click="doValidation(event)"/>
```

Change the name of the private function showEntries to doValidation and add the following import statement to the top of the script block:

```
import mx.events.ValidationResultEvent;
```

The validate method returns a ValidationResultEvent object, so we needed to import the class.

Add the following variable declarations below the import statements:

```
private var theValidationResult:ValidationResultEvent;
private var theResponse:String;
```

We'll use the theValidationResult variable for the results of each validation and we'll store error messages in the theResponse variable so we can display it in the Text control.

Change the doValidation function as follows:

```
private function doValidation(e:MouseEvent):void{
  theResponse = "<b>Error messages:</b>\n";
  theValidationResult = fNameValidator.validate();
  if (theValidationResult.type == ValidationResultEvent.INVALID) {
    theResponse += "<li>" + theValidationResult.message + "</li>\n";
  }
  theValidationResult = lNameValidator.validate();
  if (theValidationResult.type == ValidationResultEvent.INVALID) {
    theResponse += "<li>" + theValidationResult.message + "</li>\n";
  }
  theValidationResult = DOBValidator.validate();
  if (theValidationResult.type == ValidationResultEvent.INVALID) {
    theResponse += "<li>" + theValidationResult.message + "</li>\n";
  }
  theValidationResult = emailValidator.validate();
  if (theValidationResult.type == ValidationResultEvent.INVALID) {
    theResponse += "<li>" + theValidationResult.message + "</li>\n";
  }
  txtResponses.htmlText = theResponse;
}
```

The function starts by adding an HTML formatted string to the theResponse variable. It then goes through each validator, checking the outcome of the validate method. If the entry is invalid, the relevant message is added to the theResponse variable. We find the error message using the message property of the theValidationResult object. Finally, the results display in the txtResponses Text control, using the htmlText property.

Run the application and click the Update button without entering anything in the form. Figure 4-17 shows the result.

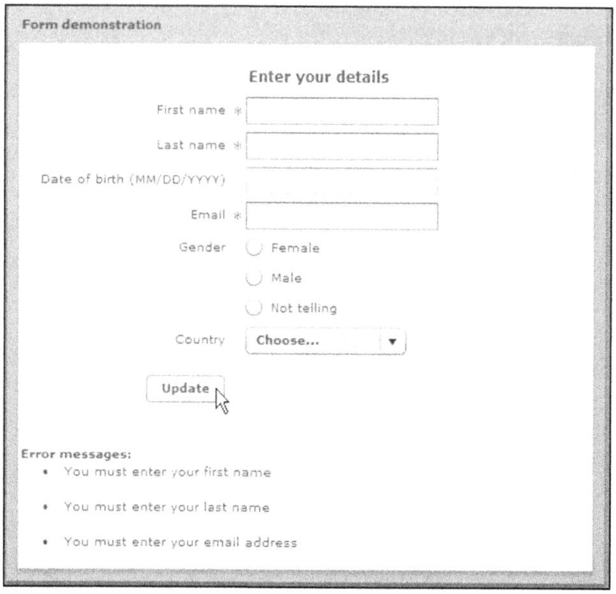

Figure 4-17. Validating the form with ActionScript

All validation error messages appear in the Text control underneath the form. Try entering incorrect values in the Date of birth (MM/DD/YY) and Email fields to see the other error messages.

The final step is to add manual validation to make sure that the user hasn't selected the Choose... option in the ComboBox control. Change the Country FormLabel so that it displays as a required field:

```
<mx:FormItem label="Country" required="true">
```

Modify the end of the doValidation function, as shown here in bold:

```
if (theValidationResult.type == ValidationResultEvent.INVALID) {
  theResponse += "<li>" + theValidationResult.message + "</li>\n";
}
if (cboCountry.selectedIndex == 0) {
  theResponse += "<li>You must choose a country</li>\n";
}
txtResponses.htmlText = theResponse;
```

If you run the application again, you'll see that clicking the Update button without making entries in the form will include the error message. You must choose a country in the Text control. You can find the finished file for this example saved as Forms3.mxml with the other resource files.

It's worth knowing that you can also declare validators using ActionScript. The following line declares a new StringValidator:

```
private var fNameValidator: StringValidator = new StringValidator();
```

You can then set the properties as follows:

```
fNameValidator.source = txtFirstName;
fNameValidator.property = "text";
```

You might want to explore that aspect of validation a little further. You can also declare custom validators by extending the mx.validators.Validator class. Again, I'll leave you to play with that topic yourself.

The final topic for this chapter is formatters, which change the appearance of bound data.

Formatting user input

Formatters modify the way that bound data displays in a component, and Flex includes several built-in formatters, all derived from the mx.formatters.Formatter base class. Formatters change the format after the bound data is sent from the source component, but before it is received in the target component. In our previous examples, we could apply formatters to change the data entered in the form controls before it is stored in the data model.

Flex includes the following built-in formatters: CurrencyFormatter, DateFormatter, NumberFormatter, PhoneFormatter, and ZipCodeFormatter. You can also create your own custom formatters. Let's work through each of these formatter types so you can see how they work; then we'll modify our form example to apply a formatter to one of the form fields.

Using the CurrencyFormatter

The CurrencyFormatter allows you to change to a currency-formatted number. You can specify the currency symbol, the thousands and decimal point separator, the number of digits of precision, and what to use for the negative symbol.

The following example shows a number formatted to display a left-aligned $ symbol with two decimal places. It uses a dot to separate decimal places and a comma to separate thousands:

```
<mx:CurrencyFormatter id="dollarFormat" precision="2"
    currencySymbol="$" alignSymbol="left"
    decimalSeparatorFrom="." decimalSeparatorTo="."
    thousandsSeparatorFrom="," thousandsSeparatorTo=","
    useNegativeSign="true" useThousandsSeparator="true"/>
```

You'll notice there are two values specified for the decimal and thousands separators: from and to. The from value indicates the unformatted value in the source control; the to value indicates the value to use in the formatted output.

Using the DateFormatter

The DateFormatter applies a date format to a date or string using any combination of the letters Y, M, D, A, E, H, J, K, L, N, and S. Table 4-2 shows the meaning of the letters that you can use.

Table 4-2. Explanation of letters used by the `DateFormatter`

Abbreviation	Meaning	Options
Y	Year	YY = 07, YYYY = 2007
M	Month	M = 9, MM = 09, MMM = Sep, MMMM = September
D	Day	D = 5, DD = 05
A	AM/PM indicator	
E	Day of the week	E = 1, EE = 01, EEE = Mon, EEEE = Monday
H	Hour in day	Values of 1 to 24
J	Hour in day	Values of 0 to 23
L	Hour in half day, am or pm	Values of 1 to 12
K	Hour in half day, am or pm	Values of 0 to 11
N	Minute	N = 5, NN = 05
S	Second	S = 5, SS = 05

The following code converts a U.S. date to a European-style date in *DD-MM-YYYY* format:

```
<mx:DateFormatter id="europeanDateFormat"
  formatString="DD-MM-YYYY"/>
```

Using the NumberFormatter

The `NumberFormatter` is similar to the `CurrencyFormatter`. It allows you to specify the number of decimal places, set the thousands and decimal separator, and determine how to display a negative sign.

This example formats a number to three decimal places, with a negative sign, and uses a comma as the thousands separator:

```
<mx:NumberFormatter id="myNumberFormat"
  decimalSeparatorFrom="." decimalSeparatorTo="."
  thousandsSeparatorFrom="," thousandsSeparatorTo=","
  precision="3" useThousandsSeparator="true"
  useNegativeSign="true"/>
```

Using the PhoneFormatter

The `PhoneFormatter` formats an entry into one of a number of different phone formats. You can specify the format of both the area code and number using the `areaCodeFormat` and `formatString` attributes. You can also specify which characters are valid using the `validPatternChars` attribute:

```
<mx:PhoneFormatter
    areaCode="-1"
    areaCodeFormat="(###)"
    formatString="(###) ###-####"
    validPatternChars="+()#-. "/>
```

In the next code example, the PhoneFormatter formats a 10-digit number into the Australian international phone format displayed as +61 (##) #### ####:

```
<mx:PhoneFormatter id="AusPhoneFormat"
   areaCode="-1"
   areaCodeFormat="(##)"
   formatString="+61 (##) #### ####"
   validPatternChars="+61 ()#"/>
```

Using the ZipCodeFormatter

The ZipCodeFormatter allows you to apply one of the following Zip code formats:

- #####-####
- ##### ####
- #####
- ### ###

You can format an entry to a five-, six- or nine-digit Zip code that you specify with the formatString attribute.

This example formats an entry into two blocks of five and four numbers, respectively, separated by a hyphen:

```
<mx:ZipCodeFormatter id="myZipFormatter"
   formatString="#####-####"/>
```

Now that you know how to construct formatter tags, it's time to see how they can be applied in a data binding example.

Applying the formatter

You can apply a formatter using the format method; for example, in the text property of a bound control. The following code shows how to apply a ZipCodeFormatter to the bound text property of a Text control:

```
<mx:ZipCodeFormatter id="myZipFormatter"
   formatString="#####-####"/>
<mx:TextInput id="sourceControl">
<mx:Text id="destinationControl
   text="{myZipFormatter.format(sourceControl.text)}" />
```

You apply the formatter by referring to its id and calling the format method, passing the id and bound property of the source control.

Let's see how we can add a formatter to the Date of birth field from our previous form example so we can store the date in the data model in European format. Remember that we're originally entering it in U.S. format.

Adding formatters to a form

I'll work through a simple example in which we store the user entry from the Date of birth field in the data model differently from the way it was originally entered. Basically, we're formatting a U.S.-style date to appear as a European-style date.

Start by adding a new Text control underneath the txtResponses control:

```
<mx:Text id="txtModelData" width="300"/>
```

We'll add the following formatter below the validators:

```
<mx:DateFormatter id="DOBFormatter" formatString="DD-MM-YYYY"/>
```

This formatter applies a European date format to a string, separated by hyphens.

We'll apply the formatter at the time the date of birth is bound to the data model. Change the <dateOfBirth> node in the data model, as shown here in bold:

```
<dateOfBirth>{DOBFormatter.format(txtDOB.text)}</dateOfBirth>
```

We apply the format from the DOBFormatter as the data is bound to the data model. The data model will receive the date of birth formatted as a European date.

To make sure that it is working correctly, we can display the formatted content in the new Text control by adding the following binding:

```
<mx:Text id="txtModelData" width="300"
    text="{'European date is ' + userData.dateOfBirth}"/>
```

Run the application and enter a date of birth in U.S. format. When you start to enter the year, you'll notice that the European date format starts to appear. After you enter the full date, you should see something similar to Figure 4-18.

Notice that the formatted date that appears in the Text control at the bottom of the screen uses European format with a full four-digit year, even though we entered only two digits in the TextInput. You can find this example saved as Forms4.mxml.

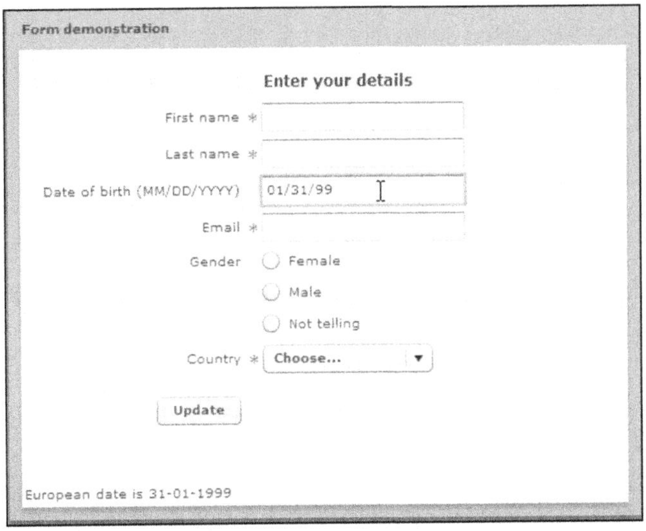

Figure 4-18. Applying a European date format during data binding

Summary

This chapter covered the most common ways applications can interact with their users. We started by looking at how to display simple alerts in an application. You learned that you can choose from four different buttons and display an icon within the alert. You can also change the appearance of some aspects of an alert.

Where you need a more complicated type of alert, it's possible to display a custom component in a pop-up window. The TitleWindow is a useful base class for this type of component, and I showed you how to create the component and how to pass values between the pop-up and the main application. We also explored how you could dispatch events from the pop-up and respond to them in the main application.

The chapter finished with a look at the Form component, which allowed us to lay out user interface controls in an application. We saw how to bind the form fields to a data model. We also learned how to validate and format data using built-in controls.

In the next chapter, I want to show you how you can allow Flex applications to interact with a web browser.

Chapter 5

INTERACTING WITH THE WEB BROWSER

Sometimes developers require their Flex applications to communicate with a web browser. Perhaps the SWF file needs to integrate with an existing JavaScript or Ajax-based application. Maybe the developer has strong JavaScript skills, but needs to use some of the components or multimedia capabilities available in the Flex framework. Whatever the requirement, it's possible for SWF movies to communicate with their Flash Player container, usually a web browser, and that's the topic for this chapter.

Communication between a Flex application and web browser may be as simple as sending a variable into a SWF file. It may involve more complicated communication in which the browser or the SWF file exchange values and wait to receive a response.

In this chapter, I want to look at the following topics:

- Loading a web page from a Flex application
- Sending variables from an HTML page into a SWF file
- Enabling communication between JavaScript and ActionScript with the External API
- Using the Flex-Ajax Bridge
- Understanding Flash Player security

ActionScript 3.0 also supports the fscommand method, which is a reworked version of the earlier method of the same name. The fscommand method is not very flexible, and Adobe recommends that you replace this functionality with the External API. For that reason, I didn't cover the flash.system.fscommand class in this chapter.

You can download the resources for this chapter from the friends of ED web site at www.friendsofed.com. We'll start by looking at how to load a web page from within a Flex application.

Loading a web page from Flex

Opening a web page is a common task within Flex applications. In earlier versions of ActionScript, developers used the getURL action to load a web page. That action has been replaced in ActionScript 3.0. Developers now have to use the new navigateToURL method to load a web page from a Flex application.

Just like the getURL action, the navigateToURL method loads a document from a specified URL. You can use it to load the document in the same or a new browser window, and you can optionally pass variables with the URL. As with getURL, you can also use the method to call a JavaScript function on the web page hosting the SWF file.

The navigateToURL method is subject to the same SWF security restrictions that apply to the External API. I'll take you through these restrictions later in the chapter. You can use the navigateToURL method in the following way:

```
navigateToURL(request, window);
```

The first argument, request, is a URLRequest object that specifies which web page to load. The window argument determines how the page loads, and it can be one of the following string values: _self, _blank, _parent, or _top. These values have the same meaning as in HTML. For example, a value of _blank loads the page into a new browser window. If you don't specify a value, the web page will replace the page hosting the Flex application.

To open the friends of ED web site in a new web browser window from a Flex application, you could use the following lines of ActionScript:

```
var site:URLRequest = new URLRequest("http://www.friendsofed.com");
navigateToURL(site, "_blank");
```

The navigateToURL method throws a SecurityError object if it encounters a security issue, so it's a good idea to wrap the method in a try-catch statement so you can specifically handle the error. For example, the following code block traces any error messages:

```
try {
  navigateToURL(request, "_blank");
}
catch (err:Error) {
  trace(err.Message);
}
```

You can optionally send variables from the Flex application with URLRequest.

Sending variables when calling a web page

Some Flex applications need to send variables to the web page that hosts the SWF file. You might need to do this so the web page can use the variable in a call to a database, perhaps in updating a record from the Flex interface. Another use is for a variable that notifies the web page of the Flex interface state so it can return in the case of a page refresh.

Whatever your need, one approach is to use the navigateToURL method to pass the values. There are two ways to do this:

1. Append variables to the URL, as in a GET operation.

2. Use a URLVariables object with POST.

You can add querystring variables from Flex by referring to the variable name at the end of the URL, as shown here:

```
var isbn:String = "1590597338";
var request:URLRequest ➡
    new URLRequest("http://www.friendsofed.com/book.html?isbn=" + isbn);
```

This has the same effect as using HTTP GET to send form variables.

You can also create a new URLVariables object and pass the variables from Flex that way. The following example shows how to POST username and password variables with a URLRequest:

```
var site:URLRequest = new URLRequest("http://www.friendsofed.com");
var urlVars:URLVariables = new URLVariables();
site.method = "POST";
urlVars.username = "sas";
urlVars.password= "1234";
site.data = urlVars;
navigateToURL(site);
```

Don't forget that you'll need to import the relevant classes, including the following:

```
import flash.net.navigateToURL;
import flash.net.URLRequest;
import flash.net.URLVariables;
```

You can also use the URLVariables class to send values to a server-side script (you'll see more about that later in the book).

As I mentioned, you can also call a JavaScript function using navigateToURL.

Calling JavaScript with navigateToURL

Instead of loading a web page, you can call a JavaScript function with the navigateToURL method. To do this, don't specify a URL. Use navigateToURL to reference a javascript command or function on the page containing the SWF file:

```
var jsRequest:URLRequest = new URLRequest("javascript: doWork();");
```

The preceding line calls the doWork JavaScript function in the web page that hosts the SWF file. Be aware that this approach might not work in all browsers, and security settings might prevent the JavaScript code from executing.

A more robust approach is to use the External API, which is preferable to the previous example because it allows for synchronous communication. You'll see how this works later in the chapter.

Let's work through a quick example showing how you can use the navigateToURL method to create a ComboBox that jumps to a specific URL.

Working through a simple example

Create a new Flex project and give it any name and location of your choosing. Add an interface for the application file, as follows:

```xml
<?xml version="1.0" encoding="utf-8"?>
<mx:Application xmlns:mx="http://www.adobe.com/2006/mxml"
  layout="absolute">
  <mx:HBox x="10" y="10">
    <mx:Label text="Visit site"/>
    <mx:ComboBox id="cboSites"/>
  </mx:HBox>
</mx:Application>
```

The interface contains a Label control and a ComboBox that we'll populate when the application is created. Add the following code to an <mx:Script> block at the top of the file to populate the ComboBox:

```
<mx:Script>
  <![CDATA[
    import mx.events.FlexEvent;
    private var dp:Array = new Array();

    private function populateCombo(e:FlexEvent):void {
      dp.push({label: "Choose site...", data: ""});
      dp.push({label: "Adobe Flex site",➥
        data: "http://www.adobe.com/products/flex/"});
      dp.push({label: "flex.org", data: "http://www.flex.org/"});
      dp.push({label: "Flexcoders",➥
        data: "http://groups.yahoo.com/group/flexcoders/"});
      cboSites.dataProvider = dp;
    }
  ]]>
</mx:Script>
```

The code block starts by importing the FlexEvent class. We need this class because we'll be passing a FlexEvent event object to the populateCombo function when it is called. We then create a new array variable called dp.

The populateCombo function populates the ComboBox component using the push method to add objects to the end of the array. Each object contains a label property, indicating the value to display and a data property, the data or URL associated with each item. By using the standard names label and data, we can access the URL of the selected item using selectedItem.data. The last line of the function assigns the dp array to the dataProvider property of the ComboBox.

We'll call the populateCombo function in the creationComplete event of the <mx:Application> tag. Change the tag as shown here in bold:

```
<mx:Application xmlns:mx="http://www.adobe.com/2006/mxml"
    layout="absolute" creationComplete="populateCombo(event)">
```

Notice that we pass an event object with the function. Figure 5-1 shows how the interface appears when you run the application.

Figure 5-1. The interface showing the loaded ComboBox control

When we select a site from the ComboBox control, we want to load it in a new web browser window. We'll make this happen with the following loadSite function that will run in response to a change in value in the ComboBox:

```
private function loadSite(e:Event):void {
  var site:String = e.target.selectedItem.data;
  if (site.length > 0) {
    var siteRequest:URLRequest = new URLRequest(site);
    navigateToURL(siteRequest, "_blank");
  }
}
```

The loadSite function receives an Event argument, passed from the ComboBox. It starts by identifying the data property of the selectedItem, identifying the ComboBox with e.target. The first option says Choose site... and has a zero-length string assigned to the data property. Because we don't want this option to open a new URL, we will proceed only if the site variable has a length greater than 0.

If we have a valid site to load, we create a new URLRequest object referencing that site. Then we use the navigateToURL method to load the URL in a new window by specifying _blank as the second argument.

The last step is to assign the loadSite function as the change handler for the ComboBox. Modify the <mx:ComboBox> tag as shown in bold:

```
<mx:ComboBox id="cboSites" change="loadSite(event)"/>
```

Run the application and check that making a new selection in the ComboBox opens the relevant URL in a new window, as shown in Figure 5-2.

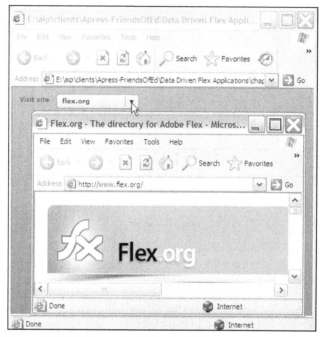

Figure 5-2. Selecting a value in the ComboBox opens the URL in a new window.

You can find the application file used in this example saved as jumpMenu.mxml in folder 5-1 with your resources. If you want to test my example, you have to import the file into a project first.

Now that you've seen how to open a new web page from Flex, we'll switch our focus to sending variables from a web page into a SWF application. You can do this in several ways, including working with the External API (you'll see this later). In the next section, you'll see how to use querystring parameters and flashVars to send variables into a SWF file.

Sending variables into a SWF file

In some cases, the hosting web page needs to send values into a Flex application. You might do this if you used server-side code to log in and you want to indicate to the Flex application that the user has logged-in privileges. You could also use values from the web page to load a specific Flex application state.

Other than working with the External API, there are two main approaches to sending variables into a SWF file so they can be used in your application:

- Using querystring parameters when loading the SWF file
- Using flashVars

Let's start by seeing how to use querystring parameters at the end of the SWF file name.

Using querystring parameters

Querystring parameters are name-value variable pairs that are added at the end of a URL or file name; for example:

```
mySWF.swf?userID=1234&admin=true
```

Once you add these parameters to the end of the SWF file name, they are accessible as variables in your Flex application. Note that you can't pass variables in this way to a SWF file that runs inside a standalone application.

It's easy to add the querystring variables when you're embedding the SWF file directly using <object> and <embed> tags within an HTML page. However, Flex generates a wrapper that hides these tags within JavaScript. If you're working with this default wrapper, you need to make modifications in the html-template folder first.

Modifying the Flex wrapper files

The standard Flex SWF wrapper is created from the AC_OETags.js and index.template.html files in the html-template folder of your project. You need to modify these template files as they're used to generate the hosting HTML page for your SWF file. Make sure you don't modify the files in the bin folder as those files can be overwritten each time you compile the SWF file. I'll show you how to add the parameters listed previously to the standard wrapper files and then we'll work through an example.

To add the querystring variables, open the AC_OETags.js file in the html-template folder of your project and locate the AC_FL_RunContent function. Modify the line that starts with the opening brackets, adding the querystring variables as shown in bold:

```
function AC_FL_RunContent(){
  var ret =
    AC_GetArgs
    ( arguments, ".swf?userID=1234&admin=true", "movie",➥
      "clsid:d27cdb6e-ae6d-11cf-96b8-444553540000"➥
      , "application/x-shockwave-flash"
    );
  AC_Generateobj(ret.objAttrs, ret.params, ret.embedAttrs);
}
```

You also open the index.template.html file for your project and locate the <noscript> block at the end of the page. Modify the following <param> attribute as shown, adding the parameters:

```
<param name="movie" value="${swf}.swf?userID=1234&admin=true" />
```

You also need to modify the start of the `<embed>` attribute:

```
<embed src="${swf}.swf?userID=1234&admin=true"
```

Accessing querystring variables in Flex

Once you've added the querystring parameters, you have to modify your Flex application file so it can receive them. To start, you need to declare a variable for each parameter you want to access in the `<mx:Script>` block of the MXML file:

```
private var myVar:String;
```

You can then assign the parameter value to the variable using the following:

```
myVar = Application.application.parameters.myVar;
```

You can do this in a single line of code if you want:

```
private var myVar:String = Application.application.parameters.myVar;
```

You might use the loaded variable in a function or bind it to the property of a component.

Let's work through a simple example so you can see how to use both approaches.

Working through an example

We'll work through an example using the project we created in the first exercise. Modify the `AC_OETags.js` and `index.template.html` files in the html-template folder of your project, as shown in the previous section, adding ?userID=1234&admin=true to the end of the SWF file references.

Create a new MXML application called `qsVars.mxml`. We don't normally have multiple application files in a project, but we'll do so here for simplicity.

Modify the interface so it looks like the following code block:

```
<?xml version="1.0" encoding="utf-8"?>
<mx:Application xmlns:mx="http://www.adobe.com/2006/mxml"
  layout="absolute">
  <mx:HBox x="10" y="10">
    <mx:Label text="UserID"/>
    <mx:Text id="txtUserID" width="100"/>
    <mx:CheckBox label="Admin" id="chkAdmin"/>
  </mx:HBox>
</mx:Application>
```

We'll display the userID parameter in the Text control, and bind the value of the admin parameter to the selected property of the chkAdmin CheckBox.

Add the following `<mx:Script>` block to the application file:

```
<mx:Script>
  <![CDATA[
```

```
      import mx.events.FlexEvent;
      private var userID:int = 0;
      [Bindable]
      private var isAdmin:Boolean = false;
      private function setVars(e:FlexEvent):void{
        userID = Application.application.parameters.userID;
        isAdmin = Boolean(Application.application.parameters.admin);
        txtUserID.text = String(userID);
      }
    ]]>
  </mx:Script>
```

Start by importing the FlexEvent class, as we'll use the creationComplete event to trigger the population of the variables. We then create a variable called userID to which we assign a default value of 0. We also create a Bindable Boolean variable called isAdmin with a default value of false. By assigning default values, we can easily check that we've changed the values with the querystring variables. Notice that we needed to set the data type of the variables appropriately using Boolean and String.

The setVars function assigns the values from the querystring to the new variables. Notice that it receives a FlexEvent event object as an argument. That's because we'll call the function in the creationComplete event of the <mx:Application> tag. As well as assigning variable values, the setVars function displays the userID in the txtUserID Text control.

We'll bind the isAdmin variable to the selected property of the CheckBox. Modify the <mx:CheckBox> tag as shown here in bold:

```
<mx:CheckBox label="Admin" id="chkAdmin" selected="{isAdmin}"/>
```

The final step is to call the setVars function in the creationComplete attribute of the <mx:Application> tag. This function passes a FlexEvent event, so modify the tag as shown in bold:

```
<mx:Application xmlns:mx="http://www.adobe.com/2006/mxml"
  layout="absolute" creationComplete="setVars(event)">
```

The complete code for the application follows:

```
<?xml version="1.0" encoding="utf-8"?>
<mx:Application xmlns:mx="http://www.adobe.com/2006/mxml"
  layout="absolute" creationComplete="setVars(event)">
  <mx:Script>
    <![CDATA[
      import mx.events.FlexEvent;
      private var userID:int = 0;
      [Bindable]
      private var isAdmin:Boolean = false;
      private function setVars(e:FlexEvent):void{
        userID = Application.application.parameters.userID;
        isAdmin = Boolean(Application.application.parameters.admin);
        txtUserID.text = String(userID);
      }
    ]]>
```

```
      </mx:Script>
      <mx:HBox x="10" y="10">
        <mx:Label text="UserID"/>
        <mx:Text id="txtUserID" width="100"/>
        <mx:CheckBox label="Admin" id="chkAdmin"
          selected="{isAdmin}"/>
      </mx:HBox>
    </mx:Application>
```

When you run the application, Figure 5-3 shows how the interface will appear, populated with variables sent from the wrapper.

Figure 5-3. Populating an application
interface using querystring parameters

You can see that it's easy to send in querystring parameters and use them in your Flex application. If you're using the default wrapper, the main challenge is modifying the AC_OETags.js and index. template.html tags in your html-template folder. The completed files for this example are available inside folder 5-2 with the other chapter resources.

An alternative approach is to use flashVars to pass variables to your Flex application.

Using flashVars

You can pass variables to a SWF file by setting the flashVars property in both the <object> and <embed> tags for the file:

```
<param name='flashVars' value='userID=1234&admin=true'>
<embed flashVars=' userID=1234&admin=true'...
```

As in the previous section, you need to modify the wrapper files if you're using the default Flex wrapper. This time you only need to change the index.template.html file. Add the relevant parameters as shown here in bold:

```
AC_FL_RunContent(
  "src", "playerProductInstall",
  "FlashVars", "userID=1234&admin=true&MMredirectURL="+MMredirectURL+ ➥
    '&MMplayerType='+MMPlayerType+'&MMdoctitle='+MMdoctitle+"",
```

You also need to add the parameters in the next else if block in the file:

```
else if (hasRequestedVersion) {
  // if we've detected an acceptable version
  // embed the Flash Content SWF when all tests are passed
  AC_FL_RunContent(
    "src", "${swf}",
    "width", "${width}",
    "height", "${height}",
    "align", "middle",
    "id", "${application}",
    "quality", "high",
    "bgcolor", "${bgcolor}",
    "name", "${application}",
    "flashvars",'userID=1234&admin=true&historyUrl=history.htm ➥
      %3F&lconid=' + lc_id + '',
```

Finally, you need to add them in the <noscript> block as well, as shown in bold:

```
<noscript>
  <object classid="clsid:D27CDB6E-AE6D-11cf-96B8-444553540000"
    id="${application}" width="${width}" height="${height}"
    codebase="http://fpdownload.macromedia.com/get/flashplayer/➥
      current/swflash.cab">
    <param name="movie" value="${swf}.swf" />
    <param name="quality" value="high" />
    <param name="bgcolor" value="${bgcolor}" />
    <param name="flashVars" value="userID=1234&admin=true" />
    <param name="allowScriptAccess" value="sameDomain" />
    <embed src="${swf}.swf" quality="high" bgcolor="${bgcolor}"
      width="${width}" height="${height}" name="${application}"
      align="middle" flashVars='userID=1234&admin=true'
```

You can access the parameters inside the flashVars value in the same way as previously discussed by using the following:

```
private var myVar:String = Application.application.parameters.myVar;
```

The qsVars.mxml application that we completed in the last example will work exactly the same way if you modify the index.template.html file as shown previously. You can find a completed example using flashVars in the 5-3 folder with the chapter resources.

You've seen two approaches to setting variables inside a Flex application from an external source. You've also learned how to pass variables from Flex to a web page. Both of these approaches are fairly basic and occur asynchronously—the Flex application or web page can't respond to the variables when they're sent. If you need synchronous communication between ActionScript and JavaScript, you can use the External API.

Understanding the External API

External API is the name given to the `ExternalInterface` class. This class resides within the `flash.external.ExternalInterface` package and allows ActionScript in a SWF movie to communicate with the hosting application. Usually this refers to communication with JavaScript on a web page, although the communication can occur with C#, VB.NET, Python, or any other language used to embed a Flash Player. In this section, I want to focus on communication between ActionScript and JavaScript in a web browser.

You can use the External API to call a JavaScript function from your Flex application or to call a function within a Flex application from a web page. Whichever type of communication you choose, the application that initiates the call can wait for a response from the other language and incorporate the response in its own code. In other words, the calls between the languages are synchronous.

You can use the External API only with a web browser that supports either ActiveX or the NPRuntime API. This includes the following major browsers:

- Internet Explorer 5.0 and above for Windows
- Firefox 1.0 and above for both Windows and Macintosh
- Mozilla 1.7.5 and above for both Windows and Macintosh
- Netscape 8 and above for both Windows and Macintosh
- Safari 1.3 and above for Macintosh

You can find out more about the NPRuntime API at www.mozilla.org/projects/plugins/npruntime.html. You can't use the External API inside Opera web pages because Opera doesn't support the NPRuntime API or ActiveX controls.

Scripting the ExternalInterface class

You can find out whether the External API is available by using the available property of the class:

```
ExternalInterface.available;
```

This property returns a Boolean value indicating whether the `EternalInterface` class is available. You can also find the id of the <object> tag or the name attribute of the <embed> tag using the `objectID` property of this class:

```
ExternalInterface.objectID;
```

The property returns null if you use it with containers other than web browsers.

The External API has two methods: `call` and `addCallback`. The `call` method allows ActionScript to call a JavaScript function in the hosting web page. You use `addCallback` to register an ActionScript function as a callback that can be accessed using JavaScript. You'll see examples of how to use both methods in the following sections.

The `ExternalInterface` class in ActionScript 3.0 is a little different from the previous version in AS2.0. You can target only Flash Player 9 with this class. If you need to target an earlier Flash Player, you have to use a different method of communication.

Let's see how to call a JavaScript function using ActionScript.

Calling a JavaScript function using ActionScript

You can use the call method to call a JavaScript function from ActionScript. You can also pass parameters with the function call, although this is optional:

```
ExternalInterface.call(functionName:String,➡
    [parameter1:Object, parameter2:Object]);
```

When working with JavaScript, the call method looks for a function of the name functionName within a <script> tag in the hosting web page. The method returns either the value returned by the JavaScript function or null if the function isn't available. The value can be any variable type.

The method can throw errors if the web browser or other container doesn't support outgoing calls, or if security restrictions stop the call from being successful. The first error is of type Error, while the second is of type SecurityError. For this reason, you may want to enclose your call method in a try-catch block:

```
try{
    response = call("functionName");
}
catch (error:SecurityError){
    trace("Security error: " + error.message);
}
catch (error:Error) {
    trace("Error: " + error.message );
}
```

By default, JavaScript on a web page can communicate only with Flex applications that are in the same domain. This means that the allowScriptAccess parameter in the web page is important for determining whether the call method is successful. You can find out more about this topic later in the chapter when we look at security.

Let's work through a simple example, in which we use a Flex application to call a JavaScript function that requests information about the web browser.

Create a new MXML application and call it callingJSFunction.mxml. Modify the interface so it looks like the following:

```
<?xml version="1.0" encoding="utf-8"?>
<mx:Application xmlns:mx="http://www.adobe.com/2006/mxml"
  layout="absolute">
  <mx:VBox x="10" y="10" height="100%">
    <mx:CheckBox id="chkEIAvail" label="External API available"/>
    <mx:Button label="Find browser details"/>
    <mx:Text id="txtResponses"/>
  </mx:VBox>
</mx:Application>
```

The interface contains a CheckBox that will display whether the External API is available. It also contains a Button control that will trigger the call to the JavaScript function, as well as a Text control for displaying messages. We'll start by determining whether the External API is available.

Create an <mx:Script> block at the top of the page and add the following import statements:

```
import mx.events.FlexEvent;
import flash.events.MouseEvent;
import flash.external.ExternalInterface;
```

Add the following variable declarations:

```
private var isAvail:Boolean = false;
private var jsResponse:String;
```

We'll use the first variable to determine whether the External API is available, and the second variable will receive a string response from the call to the JavaScript function.

Add the following function to check the availability of the External API and update the CheckBox accordingly:

```
private function checkEIAvailable(e:FlexEvent):void{
  isAvail = ExternalInterface.available;
  chkEIAvail.selected = isAvail;
}
```

This function receives a FlexEvent as we'll call it in the creationComplete event of the application. It sets the value of the isAvail variable to the value returned by the ExternalInterface.available property. The function finishes by assigning this Boolean variable to the selected property of the CheckBox. In other words, if the External API is available, you'll see that the CheckBox is checked.

Call the function by modifying the <mx:Application> tag as shown here:

```
<mx:Application xmlns:mx="http://www.adobe.com/2006/mxml"
  layout="absolute" creationComplete="checkEIAvailable(event)">
```

Run the application and, provided the External API is available, you should see the same interface as that shown in Figure 5-4.

Figure 5-4. The application interface shows that the External API is available.

We'll now add the click event handler for the Button. When we click the button, we'll use the ActionScript function getBrowserDetails to call the JavaScript function getBrowserInfo. The JavaScript function will return details about the web browser.

Add the following ActionScript function to the <mx:Script> block:

```
private function getBrowserDetails(e:MouseEvent):void {
  if (isAvail) {
    try{
      txtResponses.text = "Calling JavaScript function\n";
      jsResponse = ExternalInterface.call("getBrowserInfo");
      txtResponses.text += jsResponse + "\n";
    }
    catch (error:SecurityError){
      txtResponses.text = "Security error: " + error.message + "\n";
    }
    catch (error:Error) {
      txtResponses.text += "Error: " + error.message + "\n";
    }
  }
}
```

The getBrowserDetails function receives a MouseEvent event object as it is the handler for a button click. The function starts by checking that the External API is available using the variable isAvail. If so, it uses a try-catch block and displays the text Calling JavaScript function. It then calls the JavaScript function getBrowserInfo, receiving the response in the jsResponse string variable.

The function adds the response to the Text control. If there is either a SecurityError or other Error, the appropriate message displays in the Text control. We'll need to call the function when we click the Button, so modify the tag as shown in bold here:

```
<mx:Button label="Find browser details"
  click="getBrowserDetails(event)"/>
```

Run the application now. Figure 5-5 shows the result.

Figure 5-5. The application interface shows a call to a nonexistent JavaScript function.

You can see that the Text control displays null underneath the first message. This occurs because we haven't yet added the JavaScript function—the function name can't be located in a <script> block in the constrainer web page, so the call method returns null.

The JavaScript function getBrowserInfo will use a simple browser detection script to determine the browser name and its version. Copy the file detection.js from the 5-4 folder in the resource files to the html-template folder in your Flex project. Without going into details, the file contains a function that returns a BrowserDetect object that the HTML page will use to find the name and version of the current browser.

We'll add the new JavaScript function to the index.template.html file in the html-template folder. Open this file and add a reference to the detection.js file in the <head> section:

```
<script src="detection.js" language="javascript"></script>
```

Below it, add a <script> block, as shown here:

```
<script language="javascript">
  function getBrowserInfo() {
    var theBrowser = getBrowser();
    var theBrowserName = theBrowser.browser;
    var theBrowserVersion = theBrowser.version;
    var browserString = "You are using " + theBrowserName + " " ➥
    + theBrowserVersion;
    return browserString;
  }
</script>
```

This JavaScript function calls the getBrowser method in the detection.js file and uses the returned object to find out the name and version of the current web browser. The function returns the browserString string variable showing these details.

Switch back to the MXML file and run the application. Click the Find browser details button and you should see the details of your web browser (see Figure 5-6).

Figure 5-6. Clicking the button displays the browser type and version.

This example demonstrates how to call a JavaScript function from within a Flex application. You might need to do this to access functionality from JavaScript that isn't available in Flex. In this case, the JavaScript function returned details about the current web browser, and we displayed these details in the Flex interface. You can find the completed files from the example saved in the 5-4 folder with the other chapter resources.

Now it's time to explore the other side of the equation: calling an ActionScript function from JavaScript.

Calling an ActionScript function with JavaScript

For security reasons, you can call only ActionScript functions that you have made explicitly available to JavaScript. All other ActionScript functions remain unavailable to the container web page. You can make the ActionScript function available by using the addCallback method. Provided that the External API is available, the ActionScript function can then be called using JavaScript in the web page that hosts the SWF application.

The addCallback method takes the following arguments and returns nothing:

```
ExternalInterface.addCallback(functionName:String,closure:Function);
```

The functionName argument is the name that JavaScript will use to refer to the ActionScript function. The closure is the ActionScript name of the same function. It's usually best to keep these names the same, although this isn't a strict requirement.

Once you've registered the Flex callback, you can call it using JavaScript. In JavaScript, you need to call the function as if it is a method of the SWF object, which you can identify using its id or name from the <object> or <embed> tag:

```
flashObjectNameOrID.functionName(args);
```

For example:

```
function callAS() {
    flashMovieID.myFunction("Hi from JavaScript");
}
```

Be aware that you cannot call an ActionScript function from a web page if that page is not in the same domain because of Flash Player security settings. You can override this using the allowDomain method (and I'll cover that topic in more detail a little later when we look at Flash Player security).

Again, we'll work through a simple example in which we'll use JavaScript to call an ActionScript function that determines whether a microphone and camera are available to the current computer. This functionality isn't available using JavaScript alone.

Start by creating a new MXML application called callingASFunction.mxml. Modify the interface as shown here:

```
<?xml version="1.0" encoding="utf-8"?>
<mx:Application xmlns:mx="http://www.adobe.com/2006/mxml"
  layout="absolute">
  <mx:VBox x="10" y="10" height="100%">
    <mx:CheckBox id="chkEIAvail" label="External API available"/>
    <mx:CheckBox id="chkMicAvail" label="Microphone available"/>
    <mx:CheckBox id="chkCameraAvail" label="Camera available"/>
  </mx:VBox>
</mx:Application>
```

The application shows three CheckBox controls that we'll use to display if the External API, a microphone, and a camera are available to the current user. Add the following variable declarations and function in an <mx:Script> block so we can set the selected property of each control correctly:

```
<mx:Script>
  <![CDATA[
    private var mic:Microphone;
    private var cam:Camera;
    private var isAvail:Boolean
    private var isMicAvail:Boolean;
    private var isCamAvail:Boolean;
    private function checkAvailable(e:FlexEvent):void{
      isAvail = ExternalInterface.available;
      if (isAvail) {
        ExternalInterface.addCallback("returnStatus",returnStatus);
        chkEIAvail.selected = isAvail;
      }
      mic = Microphone.getMicrophone();
      cam = Camera.getCamera();
      if (mic !=null) {
        isMicAvail = true;
      }
      else {
        isMicAvail = false;
      }
      if (cam !=null) {
        isCamAvail = true;
      }
      else {
        isCamAvail = false;
      }
      chkMicAvail.selected = isMicAvail;
      chkCameraAvail.selected = isCamAvail;
    }
  ]]>
</mx:Script>
```

We declare variables for the Microphone and Camera objects, as well as three Boolean variables that will reflect their availability and the availability of the External API. We'll set the values of these variables in the checkAvailable function.

The checkAvailable function receives a FlexEvent because we'll call it in the creationComplete event of the <mx:Application> tag. It first checks for the availability of the External API. If it is available, the function checks the CheckBox and creates a callback to the ActionScript function returnStatus. We'll add this function shortly. The function also checks whether a microphone and camera are available, and, if so, sets the values of the isMicAvail and isCamAvail variables. These values are then used to check the appropriate CheckBox controls.

We also need to make sure that the correct import statements appear at the top of the <mx:Script> block. They should include the following:

```
import mx.events.FlexEvent;
import flash.external.ExternalInterface;
import flash.media.Microphone;
import flash.media.Camera;
```

Modify the <mx:Application> tag as shown in bold to call the checkAvailable function:

```
<mx:Application xmlns:mx="http://www.adobe.com/2006/mxml"
    layout="absolute" creationComplete="checkAvailable(event)">
```

Run the application. Figure 5-7 shows how the interface might appear, depending on what accessories are available.

Figure 5-7. Testing the interface

It's useful to display the microphone and camera check boxes so we know what values to expect when we display the results in the JavaScript function.

The JavaScript function will call an ActionScript function named returnStatus. I used the same name for both the JavaScript and ActionScript names in the addCallback method. Although it isn't a necessity, it is good practice and will make coding easier. Add the ActionScript function to the <mx:Script> block:

```
private function returnStatus():String {
  return isMicAvail + "," + isCamAvail;
}
```

This function returns a string made up of the two Boolean variables isMicAvail and isCamAvail. As the values are separated by a comma, we'll be able to use the JavaScript split method to separate the values into an array.

We need to modify the HTML template to include a form and <div> element for displaying the ActionScript response. Open the index.template.html file from the html-template folder and add the following immediately below the opening <body> element:

```
<form id="frmAvailable">
  <input type="button" value="Check accessories"
    onclick="checkAccess();"/>
</form>
<div id="accessInfo"></div>
```

Clicking the button will call the JavaScript checkAccess function. We need to add this function inside a <script> block in the <head> section of the web page:

```
function checkAccess() {
  var response = callingASFunction.returnStatus();
  var tempArray = response.split(",");
  document.getElementById("accessInfo").innerHTML = "Microphone: " + ➡
    tempArray[0] + "<br/>Camera: " + tempArray[1];
}
```

The checkAccess function calls the ActionScript function returnStatus using the following:

```
callingASFunction.returnStatus();
```

Notice that I had to call the function using the id or name of the SWF file, callingASFunction, which is taken from the name of the Flex application file.

We capture the returned value from the ActionScript function in a variable called response and use the split method to separate the values into an array. Then we display the results in the interface using the innerHTML property of the accessInfo <div> element.

Switch back to the MXML application and run the file. Figure 5-8 shows the interface after clicking the Check accessories button in the web page.

The example isn't pretty, but it demonstrates how easy it is to call an ActionScript function using JavaScript and use the returned value in a web page. You can find the completed files in the 5-5 folder with the other resources.

So far in this chapter, you've seen two examples of one-way communication. Let's work through a more complicated example showing how to achieve two-way communication using ActionScript and JavaScript.

Figure 5-8. Calling an ActionScript function using JavaScript

Working through a two-way communication example

In this example, I want to show how to send and receive simple information between a web page and Flex application. Start by creating a new application file called twoWayCommunication.mxml and modify the interface as shown here:

```
<?xml version="1.0" encoding="utf-8"?>
<mx:Application xmlns:mx="http://www.adobe.com/2006/mxml"
  layout="absolute">
  <mx:VBox x="10" y="10">
    <mx:HBox>
      <mx:Label text="Flex says" id="txtFlex" fontWeight="bold"/>
      <mx:TextInput id="txtAS" width="334"/>
    </mx:HBox>
    <mx:Button label="Communicate"/>
    <mx:Label text="The conversation so far" fontWeight="bold"/>
    <mx:TextArea width="400" height="204" id="txtMessages"
      editable="false"/>
  </mx:VBox>
</mx:Application>
```

We also need to modify the interface in the index.template.html file. Remove the previous reference to the detection.js file as well as the functions you added earlier. Modify the form element underneath the <body> tag as shown and change the id of the <div> element:

```
<form id="frmAvailable">
  <strong>JavaScript says </strong> 
  <input type="text" id="txtJS"/><br/>
  <input type="button" value="Communicate" onclick="sendToFlex();"/>
</form>
<div id="flexResponse"></div>
```

Clicking the HTML Communicate button will call the sendToFlex function. We'll add that a little later.

Switch back to the MXML application and click the Run button. Figure 5-9 shows how the interface should appear.

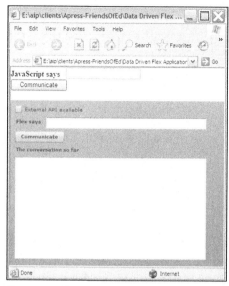

Figure 5-9. The completed interface

We'll start by determining whether the External API is available and update the interface accordingly. Add an <mx:Script> block containing the following code:

```
<mx:Script>
  <![CDATA[
    import mx.events.FlexEvent;
    import flash.external.ExternalInterface;
    private var isAvail:Boolean;
    private var jsResponse:String;
    private function checkAvailable(e:FlexEvent):void{
      isAvail = ExternalInterface.available;
      chkEIAvail.selected = isAvail;
      if (isAvail) {
        ExternalInterface.addCallback("communicate",communicate);
      }
    }
  ]]>
</mx:Script>
```

The code imports the relevant classes and creates the variables we'll need. It also creates the checkAvailable function, which determines whether the External API is available. If it is, we add a callback to make the ActionScript function called communicate available to JavaScript using the name communicate. We'll add these functions a little later.

If you run the application again, you'll see that the CheckBox is ticked. When we click the Flex Communicate button, we want to send whatever has been entered in the TextBox control to the web page. We'll do this by adding a call to a JavaScript function called receiveFromFlex. Add the following sendToJS function to the <mx:Script> block:

```
private function sendToJS(e:MouseEvent):void {
  if (txtAS.text.length > 0) {
    jsResponse = ExternalInterface.call("receiveFromFlex",[txtAS.text]);
    txtMessages.text += "\n" + jsResponse;
  }
}
```

The function checks for an entry in the txtAS TextInput and uses the call method to call the JavaScript receiveFromFlex function, passing the value from the control. It captures the JavaScript response in the string jsResponse variable and adds it to the txtMessages TextArea control.

We need to add the JavaScript function that we just called, receiveFromFlex, to an <mx:Script> block in the index.template.html page:

```
function receiveFromFlex(flexComment){
  document.getElementById("flexResponse").innerHTML = "Flex said: " ➡
    + flexComment;
  return "AS said: " + flexComment;
}
```

This JavaScript function receives a parameter from Flex that we called flexComment. It displays this value in the flexResponse <div> element and returns it to the ActionScript function after the text AS said. Figure 5-10 shows what happens when you run the application, enter some Flex text, and click the Flex Communicate button.

Figure 5-10. Calling a JavaScript function from Flex and receiving a response

You can see that the text entered in the TextInput appears in the <div> element in the web page, preceded by the text Flex said:. The text AS said: with the original text is passed back to Flex from the JavaScript function and displays in the TextArea control in Flex.

Now we need to enable the JavaScript side of the communication. The HTML Communicate button calls the sendToFlex function, so you need to add it now to the <mx:Script> block in the index.template.html file:

```
function sendToFlex() {
    var comment = document.getElementById("txtJS").value;
    var response = twoWayCommunication.communicate(comment);
    document.getElementById("flexResponse").innerHTML = "Flex replied: " + ➥
        response;
}
```

The sendToFlex function gets the value entered in the HTML input control with the id of txtJS and calls the ActionScript communicate function, passing this value. The function captures the value returned from the ActionScript function in a variable called response and displays it in the <div> element preceded by the text Flex replied:.

Before we can test the function, we need to add the following communicate function to the Flex application:

```
private function communicate(comment:String):String{
    txtMessages.text += "\nJS said: " + comment;
    return "Thanks for the comment"
}
```

This function receives a string value from the JavaScript call and adds it to the TextArea control, with the words JS said: beforehand. It returns the string Thanks for the comment.

Run the application and you should be able to send text back and forth between the Flex application and the web page. Figure 5-11 shows some sample communications.

In this example, we set up two-way communication between ActionScript and JavaScript and displayed it in both HTML and Flex elements. You can find the completed files in the 5-6 resource folder.

While it's easier to use the External API compared with earlier methods of JavaScript communication, this approach still suffers from some limitations.

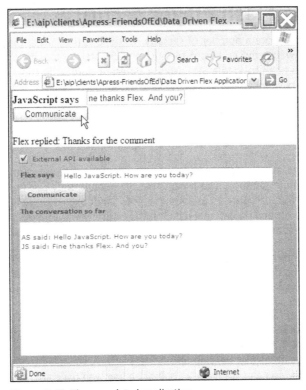

Figure 5-11. The completed application

Limitations of the External API

The External API provides more functionality than the use of the navigateToURL method with URLVariables, querystring variables, or flashVars. Unlike these other options, the External API allows for synchronous communication so the ActionScript or JavaScript functions can wait and receive a response. However, the External API does have some limitations.

You can use the External API to pass only certain data types between ActionScript and JavaScript. You're limited to primitive data types and arrays. Even though it's common to create ActionScript classes to describe complex data types, you can't send these data types as part of ExternalInterface communication.

Developers who want to use the External API in a web browser need to have a reasonably good understanding of both ActionScript and JavaScript. If this is likely to be an issue, the Flex-Ajax Bridge (FABridge) allows developers to create two-way communication from a web page using JavaScript alone. If you want to find out more, the FABridge is available as part of the Adobe LiveCycle Data Services 2.5 Beta at http://labs.adobe.com/downloads/livecycle_dataservices2_5.html.

The final topic in this chapter is the Flash Player security model.

Understanding Flash Player security

As mentioned earlier, there are a number of security restrictions that affect the way Flex applications communicate with the web browser. I want to finish the chapter by looking at security a little more closely. Developers who need to load a SWF from a different domain in their web page will need to consider security settings when working with the External API.

Flash Player security is based on the concept of security sandboxes. Flash Player allocates SWF files to different sandboxes for security purposes, depending on their location when they were loaded. Basically, files in the same sandbox can interact fully with each other.

SWF files on the Internet are placed into separate remote sandboxes where they can access content only from the same remote sandbox. This means that, by default, they can only access content from the same domain. SWF files can only access other remote sandboxes if there is a cross-domain policy file in place, in the case of loading external data, or if they use the allowDomain method. SWF files in a remote sandbox cannot access local files.

The sandbox security system has implications for the External API. By default, the SWF movie and web page must be in the same domain before they can communicate with each other. The default settings can be changed using the allowScriptAccess property and the allowDomain method.

Within the ExternalInterface class, the value of the allowScriptAccess property in the <object> and <embed> elements determines whether the call method will be successful. If the value is set to never, the call method will fail. If it is set to sameDomain, the default value, the method will succeed only if the application is in the same domain as the web page. Finally, if the value is set to always, the call method will always succeed as the domains of the Flex application and web page are not relevant.

The allowDomain method allows an ActionScript function to be called using JavaScript in a web page located in a different domain. You would use it in the same function that adds the callback to specify allowed domains:

    Security.allowDomain(myDomain);

The method can list the following types of domains:

- Text-based domains such as mysite.com
- IP addresses such as 192.168.1.1
- An asterisk (*) to signify all domains

If you specify an IP address, access isn't granted to a domain that maps to that IP address.

There's a little more to security when you're loading external data, and we'll cover that in the next chapter.

Summary

This chapter looked at the most common ways that a Flex application can communicate with a web browser. You saw that the navigateToURL method can load a web page, optionally passing variables. You also saw how to pass variables from a web browser into a Flex application. Even though these approaches offer some basic forms of communication, the External API offers the most flexible method.

The External API allows developers to communicate with the Flash Player container. Most commonly, this is done to allow ActionScript and JavaScript to communicate, although it's possible for ActionScript to communicate with other languages. In this chapter, we concentrated on JavaScript communications and worked through several examples showing one- and two-way communication.

We finished the chapter by looking at the implications of the Flash Player security model for the External API. By default, both the Flash Player and web browser have to be within the same domain, although this can be overridden.

In the next chapter, I want to introduce the topic of working with data in Flex applications. You'll see the different ways to load external content in Flex and look at some of the tools that specifically help out with data-driven applications.

Chapter 6

WORKING WITH DATA IN FLEX APPLICATIONS

So far in this book, you've seen many examples of Flex applications that work with client-side data; that is, data stored inside the application. While it's useful to be able to work with this type of data, it's not a very flexible approach. Every time you need to update the data, you have to modify the Flex application and recompile the SWF file.

A better approach is to store the data in an external data source such as a static file or within a database. You can then change the external data source as you need, and the Flex application updates without the need for it to be recompiled. As a developer, this means that you can allow clients to update the content themselves.

Because Flex is designed specifically for data-driven applications, it includes a number of different options to help, including the following:

- The ability to interact with a range of external data sources
- An <mx:Model> tag for storing simplistic data models client-side
- ActionScript classes for storing complex data structures
- Data-binding capabilities to make component updating easier
- Formatters for changing the appearance of bound data
- Validators for ensuring that users enter valid data

In this chapter, we'll look at all of these areas. I covered some of these areas earlier in the book, but I'll touch on them briefly here and extend the examples. You can download the resource files for this chapter from the friends of ED web site at www.friendsofed.com.

We'll start by looking at the different external sources of data that you can include in a Flex application.

Sources of external data

Flex can connect with a variety of different external data sources, including the following:

- Text files
- Binary files
- Requests from server-side pages
- XML documents
- Web services

In this chapter, I want to look at the topics of text files and requests from server-side pages. The next two chapters will look at working with XML content and web services.

There is a range of choices for accessing the content in external data sources, including these:

- Using the <mx:HTTPService> tag
- Scripting the HTTPService class
- Scripting the URLLoader class
- Working with Adobe LiveCycle Data Services ES
- Using socket connections for real-time communication

In this chapter, I'll cover the first three options. We'll look at Adobe LiveCycle Data Services ES later in the book.

In earlier versions of ActionScript, developers used the LoadVars and XML classes to load external data. The LoadVars action has been removed, and the XML class has changed significantly in ActionScript 3.0. The LoadVars class has been replaced by the URLLoader and URLRequest classes. The ActionScript 2.0 XML class has been renamed to the XMLDocument class and replaced with a new ActionScript 3.0 XML class. We'll see more about this in Chapter 8.

Let's start by seeing how to work with the HTTPService class.

Working with the HTTPService class

The HTTPService class allows you to make a request from a URL and to receive a response, optionally sending parameters with the request. You can use work with the <mx:HTTPService> tag or use ActionScript to create and work with the class.

Creating an HTTPService request

To create an HTTPService request using an MXML tag, you need to specify an id attribute and a url for the component, as shown here:

```
<mx:HTTPService id="txtLoader" url="text.txt" />
```

You can also use the following ActionScript:

```
var txtLoader:HTTPService = new HTTPService();
txtLoader.url = "text.txt";
```

The two approaches are equivalent.

Making the request

You will request the URL using the send method. If you need to load the data so it is available with the application, it's common to call this method in the initialize or creationComplete attribute of the <mx:Application> tag:

```
<mx:Application xmlns:mx="http://www.adobe.com/2006/mxml"
  layout="absolute" creationComplete="txtLoader.send()">
```

You could also call it in response to a button click or some other event.

Receiving a response

When the HTTPService makes a response, it dispatches a result event. If the request fails, a fault event is dispatched.

You can specify handlers for each of these events in the component:

```
<mx:HTTPService id="txtLoader" url="text.txt"
  result="resultHandler(event)"
  fault="faultHandler(event)"/>
```

You can also use the ActionScript addEventListener method:

```
txtLoader.addEventListener(ResultEvent.RESULT, resultHandler);
txtLoader.addEventListener(FaultEvent.FAULT, faultHandler);
```

In the preceding examples, the resultHandler function is called when the result event is dispatched, and the faultHandler function is called when the fault event is dispatched.

Another approach is to bind the returned data directly to other components. You'll see examples of this shortly.

Specifying a return type

You can specify how the results are to be returned by using the resultFormat property. By default, you'll receive the content as a tree of ActionScript objects, but there are a number of other choices. Table 6-1 shows the type of value that is returned and the relevant formats.

Table 6-1. Summary of values for the resultFormat property

Format	Returned value	Explanation
object (default)	XML	Parsed as a tree of ActionScript objects.
array	XML	Parsed as a tree of ActionScript objects. If the top-level object is not an Array, a new Array is created, and the result set is the first item.
xml	XML	Content provided as an ActionScript 2.0 XMLNode object.
flashvars	Name-value pairs	Parsed into an ActionScript object.
text	Text	Value remains as raw text.
e4x	XML	Content provided as an ActionScript 3.0 XML object. Can be accessed using E4X expressions.

You set the property as follows:

```
<mx:HTTPService id="txtLoader" url="text.txt"
  result="resultHandler(event)" resultFormat="e4x"/>
```

The equivalent ActionScript follows:

```
txtLoader.resultFormat = "e4x";
```

Accessing loaded content

Once the request has been successfully processed, you can access the response in the lastResult property of the HTTPService object. You can deal with this in ActionScript using the function handling the result event:

```
function resultHandler(e:ResultEvent):void {
  //do something with e.target.lastResult
}
```

You can also bind a property within the result directly to a target component property:

```
<mx:Text text="{txtLoader.lastResult.textResponse}"/>
```

In this case, we bound the textResponse property from the response to the text within a Text control using curly braces notation. As you can see, you can use dot notation to access the relevant properties within the lastResult property.

Sending variables with the request

You might want to send parameters with the request. For example, if you're requesting a server-side file, you might send one or more parameters to filter the results returned in the response.

There are several ways to send parameters with the request. First, you can send variables at the same time that you call the send method. If you choose this approach, you need to specify an object containing the variable pairs inside the call, as shown here:

```
countryLoader.send({continent: 'Europe'};
```

You can also use the <mx:request> tag to list the parameters. Here, the tag sends an XML-formatted parameter called continent that has a value of Europe:

```
<mx:HTTPService id="countryLoader"
  url="http://localhost/FlexApp/getCountries.apx">
  <mx:request>
    <continent>Europe</continent>
  </mx:request>
</mx:HTTPService>
```

Notice that the <mx:request> property of the <mx:HTTPService> element contains the parameter. It's interesting to note that properties can act as containers in MXML syntax.

Another approach is to add the parameters with ActionScript by creating an object, adding parameters to it, and assigning the object to the request property of the HTTPService:

```
var params:Object = new Object();
params.continent = "Europe";
countryLoader.request = params;
```

Specifying a request method and format

Parameters are always sent using HTTP GET unless you specify something else with the method property. You can also specify POST, HEAD, OPTIONS, PUT, TRACE, or DELETE.

The format for the parameters is set with the contentType property. The default value of this property is application/x-www-form-urlencoded, which equates to name-value variable pairs. You can also use the setting application/xml if your URL expects to receive raw XML data.

Before we move on to an example, let's see a summary of the properties, methods, and events of the HTTPService class. There are a few additional options here that I haven't covered yet.

Properties of the HTTPService class

Table 6-2 summarizes the properties of the HTTPService class.

Table 6-2. Properties of the HTTPService class

Property	Data type	Explanation
channelSet	ChannelSet	Provides access to the ChannelSet used by the service. These are the channels used to send messages to the destination.
contentType	String	Specifies the type of content being sent. Choose from application/x-www-form-urlencoded (default) or application/xml.
concurrency	String	Indicates how to handle multiple calls to the same service. Choose from multiple (default), single, or last.
destination	String	Indicates the HTTPService destination name specified in the services-config.xml file.
headers	Object	Custom HTTP headers to send with the request.
lastResult	Object	The result from the last service request.
makeObjectsBindable	Boolean	Determines whether returned anonymous objects are forced to bindable objects.
method	String	HTTP method for making the request. Choose from GET (default), POST, HEAD, OPTIONS, PUT, TRACE, and DELETE.
request	Object	Object containing name-value pairs to be sent to the URL. For a contentType of application/xml, this should be an XML document.
requestTimeout	int	Sets the timeout for the request in seconds.
resultFormat	String	Determines how data should be returned from the service. Choose from object (default), array, xml, flashvars, text, and e4x.
showBusyCursor	Boolean	Determines whether to display a busy cursor while the call is in progress. Default value is false. Note that this is available only when using the MXML tag.
rootURL	String	The URL to use as the basis for calculating relative URLs. Used only when useProxy is set to true.
url	String	The location of the service.
useProxy	Boolean	Determines whether to use the Flex proxy service. Default value is false.
xmlDecode	Function	Sets the function to use to decode XML returned with the resultFormat of object.
xmlEncode	Function	Sets the function to use to encode a service request as XML.

The HTTPService class also has three methods.

Methods of the HTTPService class

Table 6-3 summarizes the methods of the HTTPService class.

Table 6-3. Methods of the HTTPService class

Method	Parameters	Explanation	Returns
cancel		Overrides the most recent request	Nothing
initialized	document: Object, id: String	Used for validation with ActionScript	Nothing
send	parameters: Object	Sends an HTTPService request with optional parameters	AsyncToken

The HTTPService class dispatches three events.

Events of the HTTPService class

Table 6-4 summarizes the events dispatched by the HTTPService class.

Table 6-4. Events of the HTTPService class

Event	Type	Explanation
fault	FaultEvent	Dispatched when the service call fails
invoke	InvokeEvent	Fired when the service call is invoked and an error is not thrown
result	ResultEvent	Dispatched when the service call successfully returns

We've covered the HTTPService class in some detail. Let's move on to looking at the URLLoader class. After that, we'll work through some examples so you can see the different approaches to requesting external content. When we've finished, we'll compare the two classes.

Understanding the URLLoader class

The URLLoader class makes server requests and handles responses. It is not a Flex component, so you need to work with it in ActionScript.

Creating a URLLoader request

You can create a URLLoader object using the following ActionScript:

```
var loader:URLLoader = new URLLoader();
```

Making the request

To send the request, you use the load method and specify a URLRequest object. The URLRequest object specifies the URL to load as well as the loading method: GET or POST. It can also specify header information and MIME type.

The following code shows an example of how to request a simple text file from the server:

```
var request:URLRequest = new URLRequest("myText.txt");
var loader:URLLoader = new URLLoader();
loader.load(request);
```

Receiving a response

When a successful response is received from the server, the complete event is dispatched by the URLLoader. You can add an event handler to respond to this event, as shown here:

```
loader.addEventListener(Event.COMPLETE, completeHandler);
```

You can capture the returned data in the data property of the URLLoader:

```
loader.data
```

By default, the response from the URLLoader is treated as a string. For other types of data, such as XML, you will need to cast the response appropriately. The following line casts the response as an XML object:

```
var returnedXML:XML = XML(loader.data);
```

Specifying a return type

You can also specify the dataFormat property to handle different types of responses. Table 6-5 summarizes the different dataFormat types that are available.

Table 6-5. The values for the dataFormat property of the URLLoader class

dataFormat	Explanation
URLLoaderDataFormat.BINARY	The URLLoader.data property contains binary data stored in a ByteArray object.
URLLoaderDataFormat.TEXT (default)	The URLLoader.data property contains text in a String object.
URLLoaderDataFormat.VARIABLES	The URLLoader.data property contains URL-encoded name-value variable pairs in a URLVariables object.

Sending variables with the request

You can also send parameters with the URLLoader object using the data property of the URLRequest object:

```
var serverPage:String = "http://localhost/FlexApp/getCountries.apx";
var request:URLRequest = new URLRequest(serverPage);
var params:URLVariables = new URLVariables();
params.continent = "Europe";
request.data = params;
```

In this code snippet, the URLRequest object sends the variable continent with a value of Europe.

Specifying a request method

If you don't specify the loading method, Flex uses GET by default. You can override this by specifying POST as the value of the method property:

```
var serverPage:String = "http://localhost/FlexApp/getCountries.apx";
var request:URLRequest = new URLRequest(serverPage);
request.method = URLRequestMethod.POST;
```

Let's look at the properties, methods, and events of the URLLoader class.

Properties of the URLLoader class

Table 6-6 shows the properties of the URLLoader class.

Table 6-6. Properties of the URLLoader class

Property	Data type	Explanation
bytesLoaded	uint	The number of bytes loaded so far.
bytesTotal	uint	The total number of bytes to be downloaded, populated when the operation is complete.
data		The data received from the load method.
dataFormat	String	Format for received data. Choose from URLLoaderDataFormat.TEXT, URLLoaderDataFormat.BINARY, or URLLoaderDataFormat.VARIABLES.

Methods of the URLLoader class

Table 6-7 summarizes the two methods of the URLLoader class.

Table 6-7. Methods of the URLLoader class

Method	Parameters	Explanation	Returns
close		Closes the current load operation	Nothing
load	request: URLRequest	Sends and loads data to the specified URLRequest	Nothing

Events of the URLLoader class

Table 6-8 summarizes the events dispatched by the URLLoader class.

Table 6-8. The events dispatched by the URLLoader class

Event	Type	Explanation
complete	Event	Dispatched after all received data is decoded and placed in the data property.
httpStatus	HTTPStatusEvent	Dispatched if the load method attempts to access data over HTTP and the Flash Player can detect and return the status code for the request.
ioError	IOErrorEvent	Dispatched if the load method results in a fatal error that terminates the download.
open	Event	Dispatched when downloading commences after a call to the load method.
progress	ProgressEvent	Dispatched when downloaded data is received.
securityError	SecurityErrorEvent	Dispatched if the load method attempts to load data from outside of the security sandbox.

You can see that the URLLoader class dispatches a number of different events, which makes it easy to respond to the errors and to determine the progress of the request.

I've covered the code that you need to make requests with both the HTTPService and the URLLoader classes, but you might be asking yourself what the difference is between them.

Comparing the HTTPService and URLLoader

The HTTPService and URLLoader classes can both be used to make requests and receive responses, optionally passing parameters. You can work with the HTTPService class by using either MXML or ActionScript, whereas you must use ActionScript with the URLLoader class. If you don't want to write ActionScript or if you're working with simple content that you want to bind to other controls, the logical choice is the <mx:HTTPService> tag.

While both the HTTPService and URLLoader classes can return content, the HTTPService allows you to work with more data types than the URLLoader. For example, you can use the HTTPService with XML content and specify that you want to use E4X expressions to locate data. This isn't possible with the URLLoader, although you can cast the returned response as an XML object.

The URLLoader class allows you to monitor the progress of the download by providing access to the bytesLoaded and bytesTotal properties. It provides access to a wider range of events, including httpStatus, ioError, open, progress, and securityError. If you need more complicated error handling, this makes the URLLoader class a better choice.

Now that you understand the difference between these two classes, let's see some simple examples of loading information from text files.

Loading information from text files

In this section of the chapter, we'll see three different ways to load content from an external text file. We'll see how to load information using the following:

- The <mx:HTTPService> tag
- ActionScript with the HTTPService class
- The URLLoader class

We'll start by using the <mx:HTTPService> tag.

Using the <mx:HTTPService> tag

In this example, we'll request a text file using the <mx:HTTPService> tag. This example won't use any ActionScript, and we'll bind the loaded content so it displays in a Text component.

Start by creating a new MXML Project without specifying the main source folder. Give it the name and location of your choosing and add a new folder called assets. We'll use this folder for all the external files that we're going to load. Copy the file textOnly.txt from the resources to the assets folder.

Modify the application file to show the following interface:

```
<?xml version="1.0" encoding="utf-8"?>
<mx:Application xmlns:mx="http://www.adobe.com/2006/mxml"
  layout="absolute">
  <mx:VBox x="10" y="10">
    <mx:Text id="txtLoadedContent"/>
  </mx:VBox>
</mx:Application>
```

We now need to add an <mx:HTTPService> tag above the VBox container, as shown here:

```
<mx:HTTPService id="textService" url="assets/textOnly.txt"
  resultFormat="text"/>
```

This tag loads the textOnly.txt file from the assets folder and specifies a resultFormat of text. To load the document, we need to call the send method, as shown in the <mx:Application> tag:

```
<mx:Application xmlns:mx="http://www.adobe.com/2006/mxml"
  layout="absolute" creationComplete="textService.send()">
```

When the application has been created, the creationComplete event is dispatched and calls the send method of the HTTPService.

The final step is to bind the returned text from the textService control to the text property of the Text component:

```
<mx:Text id="txtLoadedContent" text="{textService.lastResult}"/>
```

Notice that we specified the lastResult property of the textService HTTPService. Because we specified that the results would be returned as text, we can bind the lastResult directly using curly braces notation.

The complete code for this example follows:

```
<?xml version="1.0" encoding="utf-8"?>
<mx:Application xmlns:mx="http://www.adobe.com/2006/mxml"
  layout="absolute" creationComplete="textService.send()">
  <mx:HTTPService id="textService" url="assets/textOnly.txt"
    resultFormat="text"/>
  <mx:VBox x="10" y="10">
    <mx:Text id="txtLoadedContent" text="{textService.lastResult}"/>
  </mx:VBox>
</mx:Application>
```

You can see that this is a very simple way to bind the contents from a text file to display directly in a component. Figure 6-1 shows what happens when you run the application.

Figure 6-1. Simple binding using content loaded from a text file

The text from the file appears within the Text control. You can find the file LoadSimpleTextHttpService. mxml saved with your resources if you want to see my finished example. You'll need to import the file into a Flex project first before you can run it.

Using the HTTPService class with ActionScript

The ActionScript equivalent for the preceding example is saved as LoadSimpleTextHttpServiceAS.mxml and looks like the following block of code:

```
<?xml version="1.0" encoding="utf-8"?>
<mx:Application xmlns:mx="http://www.adobe.com/2006/mxml"
  layout="absolute" creationComplete="loadText(event)">
  <mx:Script>
    <![CDATA[
      import mx.rpc.events.ResultEvent;
      import mx.rpc.http.HTTPService;
      import mx.events.FlexEvent;
      private var textService:HTTPService = new HTTPService();
      private function loadText(e:FlexEvent):void{
        textService.url = "assets/textOnly.txt"
        textService.resultFormat = "text";
        textService.addEventListener(ResultEvent.RESULT, resultHandler);
        textService.send();
      }
      private function resultHandler(e:ResultEvent):void {
        txtLoadedContent.text = e.target.lastResult;
      }
    ]]>
  </mx:Script>
  <mx:VBox x="10" y="10">
    <mx:Text id="txtLoadedContent"/>
  </mx:VBox>
</mx:Application>
```

You can see that there's a lot more work involved in re-creating this example using ActionScript. The code starts with the relevant import statements, referencing the ResultEvent, HTPPService, and FlexEvent classes. It then declares a variable called textService, which is a new HTTPService object.

The code includes the loadText function, which is called to handle the creationComplete event of the application. This function sets the relevant properties of the textService object and finishes by calling the send method.

The second function, resultHandler, handles the ResultEvent dispatched when a response is received from the server. This function displays the loaded content in the Text control.

Running the application shows the same result shown in Figure 6-1. You can see that the first approach took a lot fewer lines to load this text file. However, there are times when you need to use ActionScript instead of MXML. For example, you might create a reusable class file to handle the loading of external data.

Using the URLLoader class

Another approach is to use the URLLoader class to load the text file. The following code re-creates the previous example using this class:

```
<?xml version="1.0" encoding="utf-8"?>
<mx:Application xmlns:mx="http://www.adobe.com/2006/mxml"
  layout="absolute" creationComplete="loadText(event)">
  <mx:Script>
    <![CDATA[
      import flash.net.URLLoader;
      import flash.net.URLRequest;
      import mx.events.FlexEvent;
      private var loader:URLLoader = new URLLoader();
      private function loadText(e:FlexEvent):void {
        loader.addEventListener(Event.COMPLETE, completeHandler);
        loader.load(new URLRequest("assets/textOnly.txt"));
      }
      private function completeHandler(e:Event):void{
        txtLoadedContent.text = e.target.data;
      }
    ]]>
  </mx:Script>
  <mx:VBox x="10" y="10">
    <mx:Text id="txtLoadedContent"/>
  </mx:VBox>
</mx:Application>
```

The code starts by importing the relevant classes and creating a new URLLoader object. When the application is created, the creationComplete event calls the loadText function.

The loadText function loads the text, assigning an event listener and calling the load event, passing a URLRequest object. When the loading completes, the completeHandler function displays the loaded content in the txtLoadedContent control, using the data property of the URLLoader.

Running the application will create the same outcome as is displayed in Figure 6-1. You can find the completed code saved in the resource file LoadSimpleTextURLLoader.mxml.

The examples covered in this section show three different approaches to loading text content from an external file. While you can use any approach, you can see that using the <mx:HTTPService> tag with data binding offered the simplest solution in terms of the amount of code required.

Let's move on to look at loading content stored in a text file using variable pairs.

Loading information stored in variable pairs

In previous versions of Flash, the LoadVars class required that external content was formatted into name-value variable pairs before it was loaded. It was common to see text files with content similar to the following:

```
label=Country&countries=Australia|England|United States
```

The file contains two variable names: label and countries. The value of the label variable is Country, while the countries variable contains a pipe-delimited set of three values: Australia, England, and United States. Structuring the countries variable this way allows us to pass in the equivalent of an array variable in the text file.

In earlier versions of ActionScript, we had to use the split method to separate out these values and assign them to an ActionScript array. If we had many variables to process, we could end up with a large number of arrays or even an array of arrays! Many developers will remember how much work was required to load external data into an application.

You can still use variable pairs to load external content into Flex applications, but Flex makes processing a lot easier.

Using variable pairs with the HTTPService class

If you want to load name-value pairs using the HTTPService class, you can still use the same external file structures. However, you'll need to specify the flashvars resultFormat for the external data when loading the content:

```
resultFormat="flashvars"
```

You can then access the variables as properties of the lastResult of the HTTPService. If we use the following external data:

```
label=Country
```

we could access the value Country as follows:

```
service.lastResult.label
```

The value of the label variable is found with the following:

```
service.lastResult.countries
```

We can then use split to separate the countries into an array of country names that might be suitable to be bound as a data provider:

```
var arrCountry:Array = textVars.countries.split("|");
```

We'll work through an example shortly.

Using variable pairs with the URLLoader class

If you're working with the URLLoader class, you can use the URLVariables class to access the variable pairs, by passing in the data property of the URLLoader:

```
var textVars:URLVariables = new URLVariables(loader.data);
```

You can then access the variables using the following:

```
textVars.label
textVars.countries
```

As before, you could use split to separate out the individual country names:

```
var arrCountry:Array = textVars.countries.split("|");
```

If you're working with numeric data, you may need to cast the data types before using them as they'll be treated as strings by the loading process.

Let's see some examples of accessing variable pairs with both the HTTPService and URLLoader classes. In the following examples, I'm working with the contents of the resource file variablePairs.txt, which you will need to add to your assets folder. It contains the following content:

```
label=Country&countries=Australia|England|United States
```

Let's start by using the <mx:HTTPService> tag to load this content.

Using the <mx:HTTPService> tag

In this example, we'll load a text file containing variable pairs and use it to populate a Label and ComboBox control. Create a new application with the following interface:

```
<?xml version="1.0" encoding="utf-8"?>
<mx:Application xmlns:mx="http://www.adobe.com/2006/mxml"
  layout="absolute">
  <mx:HBox x="10" y="10">
    <mx:Label id="txtLabel"/>
    <mx:ComboBox id="cboCountries"/>
  </mx:HBox>
</mx:Application>
```

This application contains a Label and ComboBox control that we'll populate from the loaded text file. We'll bind the loaded content directly to the text and dataProvider properties, respectively.

Add the following <mx:HTTPService> tag:

```
<mx:HTTPService id="varPairsSvc" url="assets/variablePairs.txt"
  resultFormat="flashvars"/>
```

This tag requests the variablePairs.txt file using the resultFormat flashvars as the file contains name-value variable pairs.

You'll need to call the send method of the HTTPService class in the <mx:Application> tag, as shown here, so it loads when the application interface is created:

```
<mx:Application xmlns:mx="http://www.adobe.com/2006/mxml"
  layout="absolute" creationComplete="varPairsSvc.send()">
```

The final step is to bind the returned values from the HTTPService to the Label and ComboBox controls. Modify the tags as shown here in bold:

```
<mx:Label id="txtLabel" text="{varPairsSvc.lastResult.label}"/>
<mx:ComboBox id="cboCountries"
    dataProvider="{varPairsSvc.lastResult.countries.split('|')}"/>
```

We've bound the text property of the label using the expression varPairsSvc.lastResult.label. Using the split method inside the second binding allows us to bind the value of the dataProvider property directly to the varPairsSvc.lastResult.countries property of the HTTPService object.

The complete code for this example follows:

```
<?xml version="1.0" encoding="utf-8"?>
<mx:Application xmlns:mx="http://www.adobe.com/2006/mxml"
  layout="absolute" creationComplete="varPairsSvc.send()">
  <mx:HTTPService id="varPairsSvc" url="assets/variablePairs.txt"
    resultFormat="flashvars"/>
  <mx:HBox x="10" y="10">
    <mx:Label id="txtLabel" text="{varPairsSvc.lastResult.label}"/>
    <mx:ComboBox id="cboCountries"
        dataProvider="{varPairsSvc.lastResult.countries.split('|')}"/>
  </mx:HBox>
</mx:Application>
```

Figure 6-2 shows what happens when you run the application.

Figure 6-2. The ComboBox and Label controls populate from an external text file using variable pairs.

The Label control displays the text Country, and the ComboBox is populated with the loaded countries array.

I've saved this file as LoadVarPairsHttpService.mxml with the other resources if you want to test my version of the file.

Using the HTTPService class with ActionScript

The ActionScript equivalent of the previous file follows:

```
<?xml version="1.0" encoding="utf-8"?>
<mx:Application xmlns:mx="http://www.adobe.com/2006/mxml"
  layout="absolute" creationComplete="loadVarPairs(event)">
  <mx:Script>
    <![CDATA[
      import mx.rpc.events.ResultEvent;
      import mx.rpc.http.HTTPService;
      import mx.events.FlexEvent;
      private var varPairsSvc:HTTPService = new HTTPService();
      private function loadVarPairs(e:FlexEvent):void {
        varPairsSvc.url = "assets/variablePairs.txt"
        varPairsSvc.resultFormat = "flashvars";
        varPairsSvc.addEventListener(ResultEvent.RESULT,  ➡
          resultHandler);
        varPairsSvc.send();
      }
      private function resultHandler(e:ResultEvent):void {
        txtLabel.text = e.target.lastResult.label;
        cboCountries.dataProvider = e.target.lastResult.countries ➡
          .split("|");
      }
    ]]>
  </mx:Script>
  <mx:HBox x="10" y="10">
    <mx:Label id="txtLabel"/>
    <mx:ComboBox id="cboCountries"/>
  </mx:HBox>
</mx:Application>
```

In this example, we create the HTTPService object using ActionScript after importing the relevant classes. The creationComplete event of the application calls the loadVarPairs function, which sets the properties of the object, including the url, the resultFormat, and the event listener. It finished by making the request using the send method.

When the response is received, the resultHandler function assigns the relevant values to the text property of the txtLabel control and the dataProvider of the cboCountries control.

Running the application shows the same result as that shown in Figure 6-2. You can find this example saved as LoadVarPairsHttpServiceAS.mxml with the other resources.

Using the URLLoader class

Compare the previous example with this one using the URLLoader class:

```
<?xml version="1.0" encoding="utf-8"?>
<mx:Application xmlns:mx="http://www.adobe.com/2006/mxml"
  layout="absolute" creationComplete=" loadVarPairs(event)">
  <mx:Script>
    <![CDATA[
      import flash.net.URLLoader;
      import flash.net.URLRequest;
      import mx.events.FlexEvent;
      private var loader:URLLoader = new URLLoader();
      private function loadVarPairs(e:FlexEvent):void {
        loader.addEventListener(Event.COMPLETE, completeHandler);
        loader.load(new URLRequest("assets/variablePairs.txt"));
      }
      private function completeHandler(e:Event):void{
        var txtVars:URLVariables = new URLVariables(e.target.data);
        txtLabel.text = txtVars.label;
        cboCountries.dataProvider = txtVars.countries.split("|");
      }
    ]]>
  </mx:Script>
  <mx:HBox x="10" y="10">
    <mx:Label id="txtLabel"/>
    <mx:ComboBox id="cboCountries"/>
  </mx:HBox>
</mx:Application>
```

After importing the relevant classes, the code creates a new URLLoader object. The loadVarPairs function sets the event listener and loads the variablePairs.txt file. When the file completes loading, the completeHandler function assigns the data property to a URLVariables object. It then uses these variables to set the text and dataProvider properties of the relevant controls. Notice that we specified the path from the URLVariables object; for example, txtVars.label.

I've saved this example as LoadVarPairsURLLoader.mxml with the other resource files. Running it produces the same outcome as shown in Figure 6-2.

> We could use any of the previous approaches to load results returned by a call to a server-side file. In that case, we'd need to make sure that the file was running through a web server so that it was parsed correctly. To do that, we'd be using a URL similar to http://localhost/FlexApp/getCountries.apx.

So far in the chapter, we've worked with text files that store external content. We might want to be able to update these text files or a database by sending data to the server with the request.

Sending data to the server

Flex applications can use exactly the same techniques that we've seen so far to send values to server-side scripts. You might do this if you want to save content to a text file or update a database. For security reasons, you can't use Flex to create, modify, or delete external files so you'll need to use a server-side file to carry out the work.

You can use either the HTTPService class or URLLoader class to send values to a server-side script for processing.

Sending variables with the HTTPService class

If you are using the HTTPService class, you can send variables to the server-side page for processing using several different methods.

First, you can include parameters in the send method using the following approach:

```
countryLoader.send({continent: 'Europe'});
```

If you need to send XML content, you can use the <mx:request> tag within an <mx:HTTPService> tag:

```
<mx:HTTPService id="countryLoader"
  url="http://localhost/FlexApp/getCountries.apx">
  <mx:request>
    <continent>Europe</continent>
  </mx:request>
</mx:HTTPService>
```

The advantage of this approach is that you can bind the value to be sent with the service request:

```
<mx:request>
  <continent>{txtContinent.text}</continent>
</mx:request>
```

You can also add the variables in ActionScript using the following:

```
var params:Object = new Object();
params.continent = "Europe";
xmlLoader.request = params;
```

Sending variables with the URLLoader

If you're working with the URLLoader class, you can use a URLVariables object to send parameters to a server-side page:

```
var serverPage:String = "http://localhost/FlexApp/getCountries.apx";
var request:URLRequest = new URLRequest(serverPage);
var params:URLVariables = new URLVariables();
params.continent = "Europe";
request.data = params;
```

If you're using this method, make sure that you use %26 to encode any & characters in the parameters because this character is used as a delimiter for variable pairs. If you don't do this, you may get an error message.

Other considerations

When you specify the URL for the HTTPService or URLLoader, make sure that you include the full server path so that the server-side file can be correctly processed by the web server:

```
http://localhost/FlexApp/getCountries.apx
```

Parameters are sent using HTTP GET unless you specify something else with the method property. For the HTTPService class, you can also specify POST, HEAD, OPTIONS, PUT, TRACE, or DELETE. You can only specify POST as an alternative for the URLLoader class.

You may also need to specify the format of the parameters using the contentType property. As previously mentioned, the default value is application/x-www-form-urlencoded, which equates to name-value variable pairs. You can also use application/xml if you need to send raw XML data to the server-side page for processing.

This explanation will make more sense if we work through an example.

Working through an example

Let's work through a simple example in which we load a news item from a text file using an <mx:HTTPService> tag. We'll use Flex to save a new text file with the same name using a server-side file. The editable text from the file will display in a TextArea, so we can update it prior to sending it server-side for processing.

You'll need to run the server-side scripts in this example through a web server to make it work. I'll be using the server-side language ASP.NET. You can use any server-side language that you like as an alternative, provided you have the correct web server installed. I've also included a PHP version of the file with the resources and I'll run through it briefly as well.

We'll start by using the <mx:HTTPService> tag in an example.

Updating content with the HTTPService class

The first step in the example is to create the Flex application. Create a new MXML application file and modify the interface as follows:

```
<?xml version="1.0" encoding="utf-8"?>
<mx:Application xmlns:mx="http://www.adobe.com/2006/mxml"
  layout="absolute">
  <mx:VBox x="10" y="10">
    <mx:Label id="txtTitle" fontWeight="bold"/>
    <mx:TextArea id="txtNews" width="400" height="100/>
    <mx:Button x="20" y="142" label="Update news"/>
    <mx:Label id="txtMessages"/>
  </mx:VBox>
</mx:Application>
```

The interface consists of a Label to show the title of the news item, a TextArea for the news item content, a Button to update the content, and another Label to display messages.

We'll start by loading the text file into the interface. You'll need to copy the resource file news.txt to your assets folder. The file contains the following content:

```
title=Developer builds Flex application&content=A developer built
    the first Flex application to read content from a text file and
    then use a server-side file to update the content.
```

Notice that the file contains two variables: title and content. We'll load the title into the Label control and the content into the TextArea.

Add the following <mx:HTTPService> tag:

```
<mx:HTTPService id="loadTextService" url="assets/news.txt"
    resultFormat="flashvars"/>
```

This <mx:HTTPService> tag loads the relevant file, specifying the content as flashvars because we're loading name-value variable pairs.

We'll need to call the send method of this service in the creationComplete event of the <mx:Application> tag, so modify it as shown:

```
<mx:Application xmlns:mx="http://www.adobe.com/2006/mxml"
    layout="absolute" creationComplete="loadTextService.send()">
```

We'll bind the results from this HTTPService directly to the two controls. Modify them as shown in bold here:

```
<mx:Label id="txtTitle" fontWeight="bold"
    text="{loadTextService.lastResult.title}" />
<mx:TextArea id="txtNews" width="400" height="100"
    text="{loadTextService.lastResult.content}"/>
```

The binding expressions start with loadTextService.lastResult and then specify the relevant variable name.

Run the application. Figure 6-3 shows how the interface appears when loaded with the content from the text file.

Although we can enter any text we like in the TextArea, it won't update until we enable the Update news button. Modify this button to call the updateText function when clicked:

```
<mx:Button x="20" y="142" label="Update news"
    click="updateText(event)"/>
```

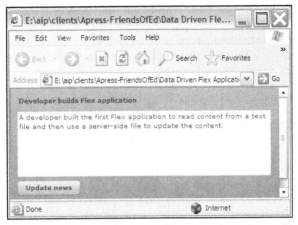

Figure 6-3. The interface loaded with content from the text file

Before we add that function, we'll need to add a second HTTPService element to send the updated details to the server-side page:

```
<mx:HTTPService id="updateTextService" method="POST"
    url="http://localhost/DataDrivenFlex/updateTextFile.aspx"
    showBusyCursor="true"
    result="resultHandler(event)" fault="faultHandler(event)"/>
```

This HTTPService tag uses the POST method to send details to the server-side page. Notice that it specifies the full path to the updateTextFile.aspx file. At this point, the server-side file is running through the web server, but the Flex application isn't. This will work while we're testing locally, but we'll need to locate everything on the web server if we move the application to a network location.

I've set the showBusyCursor attribute to true to provide feedback to the user. I've also set a result and fault handler. We'll add those shortly.

Add a script block containing the updateText function below the opening <mx:Application> tag. Remember that this is the function called when we click the Update news button:

```
<mx:Script>
  <![CDATA[
    import flash.events.MouseEvent;
    private function updateText(e:MouseEvent):void {
      updateTextService.send({title: txtTitle.text, content: ➥
        txtNews.text});
      txtMessages.text = "Contacting server-side page"
    }
  ]]>
</mx:Script>
```

This code block imports the relevant class, MouseEvent, and creates the updateText function. The function receives the MouseEvent as an argument and calls the send method of the updateTextService. The send method passes two variables to the server-side page, using the values displaying in the controls. The function also displays a message in the txtMessages control saying Contacting server-side page.

Add the following event handlers to the script block to handle the server response:

```
private function resultHandler(e:ResultEvent):void {
  txtMessages.text = "The text file has been updated"
}
private function faultHandler(e:FaultEvent):void {
  txtMessages.text = e.message.toString();
}
```

These functions respond to the result and fault events, respectively. The first function displays the message The text file has been updated when a response is received from the service. The second function displays the fault message if a FaultEvent is dispatched by the service.

That's it for the Flex file. Now it's time to turn our attention to the ASP.NET file. As I said previously, you can use a different server-side language, but don't forget to update the url of the second service in the Flex file if that's the case.

I've included the ASP.NET file with your resources, and the full declarative code appears here. You'd probably create it in Visual Studio and compile it instead of using the code on the page in this way. However, for simplicity, this approach will serve our purposes:

```
<%@ Page Language="VB" %>
<script runat="server">
  Dim strTitle As String = ""
  Dim strContent As String = ""
  Dim strFilePath As String = ""
  Protected Sub Page_Load(ByVal sender As Object, ByVal e As  ➥
    System.EventArgs)
    strFilePath = "E:\aip\clients\Apress-FriendsOfEd\Data Driven  ➥
      Flex Applications\chapter 06\Flex project\assets\news.txt"
    strTitle = Request.Form("title")
    strContent = Request.Form("content")
    If Len(strContent) > 0 Then
      Dim StreamWriter1 As System.IO.StreamWriter =  ➥
        New System.IO.StreamWriter(strFilePath)
      StreamWriter1.WriteLine("title=" & strTitle & "&content="  ➥
        & strContent)
      StreamWriter1.Close()
    End If
  End Sub
</script>
```

Make sure you change the value of the variable strFilePath to point to the correct path for the assets folder in your Flex project. I'd normally use Server.Mappath to find out this value, but that's not possible given that the server-side file is located in a different location from the text file.

The code starts by declaring variables and creates a subroutine that runs when the page loads. The sub assigns the strFilePath variable and uses Request.form to access the title and content variables passed from Flex. I need to use this method because I used POST in the Flex service.

If we have content from the text file, the sub declares a StreamWriter and uses it to create the news.txt file. It then writes both the title and content from Flex to this file and closes the StreamWriter.

Remember that you need to locate this server-side file on your web server. I referred to the path http://localhost/DataDrivenFlex/updateTextFile.aspx in my Flex application file, which equates to the C:\Inetpub\wwwroot\DataDrivenFlex\ folder on my computer.

If you prefer to work with PHP, your resources include the relevant code in the file updateTextFile.php. You need to change the url property within the second HTTPService element as shown here:

```
<mx:HTTPService id="updateTextService" method="POST"
  url="http://localhost/DataDrivenFlex/updateTextFile.php"
  showBusyCursor="true"
  result="resultHandler(event)" fault="faultHandler(event)"/>
```

The updateTextFile.php code follows:

```
<?php
$strFilePath = 'E:\aip\clients\Apress-FriendsOfEd\Data Driven Flex ➥
  Applications\chapter 06\Flex project\assets\news.txt';
$strTitle = $_POST['title'];
$strContent = $_POST['content'];
if ($strTitle != "") {
  $output = 'title=' . $strTitle . '&content=' . $strContent;
  $fileOpener = fopen($strFilePath, 'w');
  fwrite($fileOpener, $output);
  fclose($fileOpener);
}
?>
```

This code block starts by declaring a variable for the path and file name to update. As with the ASP.NET example, you'll need to change the value of the $strFilePath variable to the correct path on your own computer. The code then requests the title and content values from the Flex application. The PHP page expects that the application will use the POST method.

If we have a title from Flex, we create another variable, $output, containing the string to write to the text file. We then open the text file using fopen. The second parameter, w, indicates that we want to open the file for writing. Next we use fwrite to write the string to the file we indicated in the $output variable. Finally, we close the file using fclose.

Whichever version of the code you used, run the application, update the content, and click the Update news button. Figure 6-4 shows the interface after updating the content.

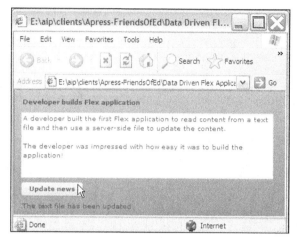

Figure 6-4. The completed application

This example shows how to pass a value to a server-side page from Flex for updating. In this case, we saved a text file, but we could just as easily have updated a database or XML document.

The finished application file is saved with your resources as ServerInteractionHttpService.mxml. The .NET 2.0 file is saved as updateTextFile.aspx, while the PHP version is saved as updateTextFile.php. Remember that these files must be located on the web server if you want to try the example for yourself.

Updating content with the URLLoader class

The following code shows how to re-create the example using the URLLoader class:

```
<?xml version="1.0" encoding="utf-8"?>
<mx:Application xmlns:mx="http://www.adobe.com/2006/mxml"
  layout="absolute" creationComplete="loadText(event)">
  <mx:Script>
    <![CDATA[
      import flash.net.URLLoader;
      import flash.net.URLRequest;
      import mx.events.FlexEvent;
      import flash.events.MouseEvent;
      private var loader:URLLoader = new URLLoader();
      private var sender:URLLoader = new URLLoader();
      private var serverPage:String = "http://localhost/ ➥
        DataDrivenFlex/updateTextFileURLLoader.aspx";
      private function loadText(e:FlexEvent):void {
        loader.addEventListener(Event.COMPLETE, completeHandler);
        loader.load(new URLRequest("assets/news.txt"));
      }
```

```
        private function completeHandler(e:Event):void{
          var txtVars:URLVariables = new URLVariables(e.target.data);
          txtTitle.text = txtVars.title;
          txtNews.text = txtVars.content;
        }
        private function updateText(e:MouseEvent):void {
          sender.dataFormat = URLLoaderDataFormat.VARIABLES;
          sender.addEventListener(Event.COMPLETE, sendCompleteHandler);
          var request:URLRequest = new URLRequest(serverPage);
          var params:URLVariables = new URLVariables();
          params.title = txtTitle.text;
          params.content = txtNews.text;
          request.data = params;
          request.method = URLRequestMethod.POST;
          try {
            sender.load(request);
            txtMessages.text = "Contacting server-side page"
          }
          catch (e:Error) {
              txtMessages.text = e.message.toString();
          }
        }
        private function sendCompleteHandler(e:Event):void {
          var txtVars:URLVariables = new URLVariables(e.target.data);
          txtMessages.text = txtVars.response;
        }
      ]]>
    </mx:Script>
    <mx:VBox x="10" y="10">
      <mx:Label id="txtTitle" fontWeight="bold"/>
      <mx:TextArea id="txtNews" width="400" height="100"/>
      <mx:Button x="20" y="142" label="Update news"
        click="updateText(event)"/>
      <mx:Label id="txtMessages"/>
    </mx:VBox>
  </mx:Application>
```

In this example, we import the relevant classes and create two URLLoader objects: one to load the external text file, called loader, and the second, called sender, to call a server-side file to update text content. We've also declared a variable for the server-side page and you'll notice that I'm using a slightly different page from the last time: updateTextFileURLLoader.aspx. The difference is that this page provides a response that we'll load into the Flex interface.

The creationComplete event of the application calls the loadText function. This function adds an event handler to deal with the loaded text, completeHandler, and loads the document news.txt from the assets folder. The completeHandler function displays the title and content variables from the text file in the interface.

When you click the Update news button, the updateText function sets the dataFormat for the URLLoader to send variables. It also adds an event listener to process the response from the server-side file: sendCompleteHandler. The function adds the variables to the request and sets the method property to POST the values.

The load method is called inside a try-catch block. If successful, we display the message Contacting server-side page; otherwise we display an error message. When the server-side page finishes and sends a response, it is processed by the sendCompleteHandler function. The function captures the response in a URLVariables object and displays it in the txtMessages control.

Running the application shows the same outcome as seen in Figure 6-4. You can find the files referred to in this example saved as ServerInteractionURLLoader.mxml and updateTextFileURLLoader.aspx.

We've seen several examples of loading and updating content using Flex applications. When you request data, you're subject to Flash Player security restrictions, so it's important to understanding them before we move on to our next data-related topic.

Understanding Flash Player 9 security

When accessing external data, Flash Player 9 security is based on the relative locations of SWF files loading the data and the data source. Note that earlier versions of the Flash Player have different approaches to security, which aren't discussed here.

The basic rule is that a SWF file can access any data from the same domain as its own location. By default, it's not possible for the SWF file to load content from a different domain or subdomain. This restriction also prevents SWF files on the network from accessing local data.

Understanding security sandboxes

Flash Player 9 allocates SWF files to their own security sandbox, which equates to their exact domain. For example, SWF files located in the following domains are considered to be in separate sandboxes:

- http://www.friendsofed.com
- http://friendsofed.com
- http://65.19.150.101

Even though the IP address 65.19.150.101 may resolve to the first domain, it is still considered to be in a separate security sandbox.

If you need to load data from another domain into your Flex application, you can choose from the following two alternatives:

- Specifically allow access by using a cross-domain policy file on the server hosting the data source
- Use a server-side proxy file to access the remote data and locate it within the local domain

Creating a cross-domain policy file

A cross-domain policy file is an XML file called crossdomain.xml that resides in the root of the web server hosting the external data. The file grants permission to allow specific domains to access the data stored there.

The file needs to have the following structure:

```
<?xml version="1.0"?>
<cross-domain-policy>
  <allow-access-from domain="www.friendsofed.com" />
  <allow-access-from domain="*.friendsofed.com" />
  <allow-access-from domain="65.19.150.101" />
</cross-domain-policy>
```

This policy file allows access to the data to www.friendsofed.com, any subdomain of friendsofed.com, and the IP address 65.19.150.101. If the SWF requesting the data appears in any of the preceding domains, it will be granted access by Flash Player 9. If not, the SWF won't be granted permission to load the data.

You can also use a wildcard to grant access to all domains:

```
<?xml version="1.0"?>
<cross-domain-policy>
  <allow-access-from domain="*" />
</cross-domain-policy>
```

It's possible to include the secure attribute within an <allow-access-from> tag. This attribute has a default value of true that restricts data on a secure HTTPS server from being accessed by anything other than another HTTPS server. You can set this value to false if you want a secure server to be able to be accessed by both secure and insecure servers.

If the crossdomain.xml file does not reside in the root directory of the server, the SWF file can request it from a different location using the Security.loadPolicyFile method. The policy file will apply only to the directory from which it is loaded and any child directories. For example, you might use this method to restrict access to data in the _data folder and any child folders.

Proxying data locally

If you can't add a cross-domain policy file to a remote server, you can use a server-side file to request the data and provide it to your Flex application. As long as the server-side file is in the same domain as the Flex application, you can load the proxied content.

You can write the server-side file in the language of your choice and find out more about the topic at www.macromedia.com/cfusion/knowledgebase/index.cfm?id=tn_16520. At the time of writing, the article had examples of proxy files written in ColdFusion, PHP, and ASP, and using a Java Servlet.

The next section of the chapter looks at how to separate data from the interface in Flex applications.

Separating data from presentation

One of the underlying principles in modern web development is the separation of presentation from structure and content. A common way to structure web applications is to use the Model-View-Controller (MVC) architecture. This type of application architecture divides the application into three areas: the Model, the View, and the Controller. Figure 6-5 shows a representation of this architecture. The way this architecture applies to the Flex framework appears in italics, and I'll explain it shortly.

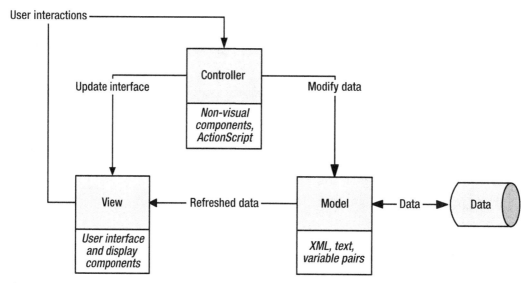

Figure 6-5. MVC architecture and Flex

The Model stores the data for the application and informs the View when the data changes. In Flex applications, the Model consists of XML, text, or other content that will appear in the interface. Flex applications can include the `<mx:Model>` tag to represent the data layer within an application, even though it is stored externally.

The View represents the user interface or visual elements of the application. It displays data from the Model and refreshes itself when informed by the Model that the data has been refreshed. User interactions in the View call the appropriate functionality in the Controller. Flex provides a range of user interface and display components to create the View.

The Controller provides the logic behind the user interactions in the application. It contains the methods that are called by the View. In Flex, this layer is represented by ActionScript logic that responds to user interactions. It also includes nonvisual components such as bindings, validators, and formatters.

MVC architecture is very common in web applications because it abstracts the data layer and keeps it separate from the presentation layer.

In the next section, I'd like to look more closely at the `<mx:Model>` tag to see how Flex represents data within an application.

Working with the <mx:Model> tag

Developers can use the <mx:Model> tag to create an XML representation of data structures within an application. You can't use the <mx:Model> tag to specify a data type, so this method isn't suitable for anything but very simplistic approaches.

Chapter 4 provides an introduction to the <mx:Model> tag. Basically, this tag is useful because it allows simple data binding between user interface elements and model elements. The following example is taken from Chapter 4 and shows a model with the id books:

```
<mx:Model id="books">
  <Library>
    <book>
      <title>{txtBookTitle.text}</title>
      <author>{txtAuthor.text}</author>
      <pubYear>{txtPubYear.text}</pubYear>
    </book>
  </Library>
</mx:Model>
```

You can see that the data in each of the <title>, <author>, and <pubYear> nodes is bound to the text property of a relevant control.

Instead of specifying the content for the model within the application, you can load it from an external file using the source attribute, as shown in the following code:

```
<mx:Model id="books" source="myFile.xml"/>
```

The data is loaded from the file when the application is compiled. This means that you don't need to provide the source for the model file inside the SWF file. It does mean, however, that if you change the external file, you'll need to recompile the application.

Even though you might load an XML document into the model, it is treated as an Object, an ObjectProxy to be precise, by Flex. This means that, as with other types of data, you can access the content within the model using dot notation, starting from the root node. The root node of the XML file can be accessed using the model id.

In the preceding example, you can access the title of the book using the following:

```
books.book.title
```

The path starts with the id of the model, books, and moves to the <book> node and then the child node <title>.

You can assign values to nodes within the model in the same way:

```
books.book.title = "Flex 3 with ActionScript 3.0"
```

Where you have multiple objects of the same name, for example, multiple <book> nodes, you can access a specific node using array notation:

```
books.book[0].title
```

177

The preceding example accesses the title details within the first book element.

You can also use ActionScript to loop through each element in the collection:

```
for (var i:int=0; i<books.book.length;i++) {
  //do something with books.book[i]
}
```

The simple example that follows shows how to load a model from an external XML document and use it to populate a ComboBox control. The external XML document follows:

```
<?xml version="1.0" encoding="UTF-8"?>
<countries>
  <country>
    <countryName>Australia</countryName>
    <countryHemisphere>Southern</countryHemisphere>
  </country>
  <country>
    <countryName>England</countryName>
    <countryHemisphere>Northern</countryHemisphere>
  </country>
  <country>
    <countryName>United States</countryName>
    <countryHemisphere>Northern</countryHemisphere>
  </country>
</countries>
```

This document is saved as countryList.xml with the other chapter resources if you want to have a closer look.

We'll use the following application to load and reference the content:

```
<?xml version="1.0" encoding="utf-8"?>
<mx:Application xmlns:mx="http://www.adobe.com/2006/mxml"
  layout="absolute" creationComplete="loadCountries(event)">
  <mx:Script>
    <![CDATA[
      import mx.events.FlexEvent;
      private var arrCountryNames:Array = new Array();
      private function loadCountries(e:FlexEvent):void{
        for (var i:int=0; i< countryData.country.length;i++) {
          arrCountryNames.push({label: countryData.country[i] ➥
            .countryName})
        }
        cboCountry.dataProvider = arrCountryNames;
      }
    ]]>
  </mx:Script>
  <mx:Model id="countryData" source="assets/countryList.xml"/>
  <mx:HBox x="10" y="10">
```

```
        <mx:Label text="Country"/>
        <mx:ComboBox id="cboCountry"/>
      </mx:HBox>
    </mx:Application>
```

The `<mx:Model>` tag countryData uses as its source the file countryList.xml within the assets folder. It uses the loaded content to populate the ComboBox in the loadCountries function. This function loops through each `<country>` element and pushes the `<countryName>` node to the arrCountryNames array. We then assign this array to the dataProvider property of the cboCountry control.

You can find this simple example saved as LoadModel.mxml. When you run the application, it populates the ComboBox control with the country names. If you want to test the content, make sure you move the countryList.xml file to the assets folder first.

It's worth noting that another tag, `<mx:XML>`, allows you to work with literal XML data. You can find out more about that topic in Chapter 8.

If you need to work with more complex data structures or assign data types to your loaded content, you can use ActionScript classes.

Using ActionScript to work with complex data structures

You can create ActionScript classes to work with more complex data structures. The advantage of this approach is that you can specify data types for each piece of data. You can create getter and setter methods to retrieve and set the values of your data and include error handling and validation. You can also create methods for manipulating the stored data.

An ActionScript data model needs to use getter and setter methods for each piece of data. These pieces of data equate to private properties of the class. You can then create an instance of the model in your application, using either an MXML tag or ActionScript.

If you want to be able to bind the data in the custom class, you'll need to add the [Bindable] metatag above the class definition. This metatag sets all public properties and all getter and setter methods as available for data binding. You'll also need to add the [Bindable] metatag to instances of the class created in ActionScript.

It can be hard to picture this approach, so let's work through an example to see how it might work. In Chapter 4, we saw how to create a user form to collect data. The user form used an `<mx:Model>` tag to store the data. We'll revisit the example and see how to use an ActionScript class instead. We'll populate the form from the ActionScript class, and initial values will come from a text file. We'll bind the form controls to the ActionScript class so we can update it easily.

Start by creating a new application and modify it to display the following interface:

```
<?xml version="1.0" encoding="utf-8"?>
<mx:Application xmlns:mx="http://www.adobe.com/2006/mxml"
  layout="absolute">
  <mx:VBox x="10" y="10">
    <mx:Form id="userFormData">
      <mx:FormHeading label="Enter your details"/>
      <mx:FormItem label="First name">
```

179

```
                <mx:TextInput id="txtFirstName"/>
            </mx:FormItem>
            <mx:FormItem label="Last name">
                <mx:TextInput id="txtLastName"/>
            </mx:FormItem>
            <mx:FormItem label="Date of birth">
                <mx:TextInput id="txtDOB"/>
            </mx:FormItem>
            <mx:FormItem label="Email">
                <mx:TextInput id="txtEmail"/>
            </mx:FormItem>
            <mx:FormItem label="Gender">
                <mx:RadioButtonGroup id="rdoGender"/>
                <mx:RadioButton label="Female" groupName="rdoGender"/>
                <mx:RadioButton label="Male"   groupName="rdoGender"/>
                <mx:RadioButton label="Not telling" groupName="rdoGender"/>
            </mx:FormItem>
        </mx:Form>
        <mx:HBox>
            <mx:Label text="Full name from class:" fontWeight="bold"/>
            <mx:Text id="txtFullName" width="300"/>
        </mx:HBox>
    </mx:VBox>
</mx:Application>
```

Figure 6-6 shows how the interface appears when you run the application.

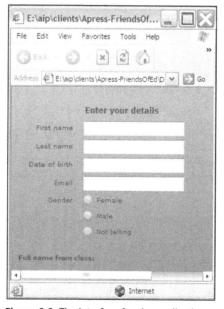

Figure 6-6. The interface for the application

Add the file user.txt to your assets folder. It contains the following variable pairs that we'll initially use to populate the form:

```
firstName=sas&lastName=jacobs&dob=01/01/1900&email=sas@somewhere.com
  &gender=Female
```

We need to create a class that will store the data for this form. The class will need to define getter and setter methods for each of the form fields. It will also need to have a setter method that allows us to set all values at the same time from an external file. Finally, we'll need to make sure that the class uses the [Bindable] metatag so we can bind the individual values from the ActionScript class to each of the form fields.

Create a new class called UserDetails in the package com.aip. We don't need to base this class on any super class because we'll use it only for working with data. Add the following import statements after the package declaration:

```
import flash.net.URLLoader;
import flash.net.URLRequest;
import flash.net.URLVariables;
```

We'll need to make the class bindable, so add the [Bindable] metatag before the class declaration, as shown here:

```
[Bindable]
public class UserDetails
```

This tag makes all public properties bindable—as well as all the getter and setter methods in the class file.

We'll need to create a series of private variables, one for each of the form values, as well as a variable for the URLLoader that we'll use to load the text file that will populate the form. Add the following private variables underneath the class definition:

```
private var userFirstName:String;
private var userLastName:String;
private var userDateOfBirth:String;
private var userEmail:String;
private var userGender:String;
private var loader:URLLoader = new URLLoader();
```

Because it's good practice, we'll add a constructor method, even though it will remain empty. Add the following lines below the variable declarations:

```
public function UserDetails() {
}
```

Now we'll add setter methods for each of the variables that we will need for the form. Add the following code underneath the constructor method:

```
public function set firstName(fName:String):void {
  userFirstName = fName;
```

```
    }
    public function set lastName(lName:String):void {
        userLastName = lName;
    }
    public function set dateOfBirth(DOB:String):void {
        userDateOfBirth = DOB;
    }
    public function set email(theEmail:String):void {
        userEmail = theEmail;
    }
    public function set gender(theGender:String):void {
        userGender = theGender;
    }
```

Each setter method takes a single argument and uses it to set the value of the relevant private variable. The methods don't return anything.

We'll also need to add the following getter methods so that we can retrieve the values of the private variables:

```
    public function get firstName():String {
        return userFirstName;
    }
    public function get lastName():String {
        return userLastName;
    }
    public function get dateOfBirth():String {
        return userDateOfBirth;
    }
    public function get email():String {
        return userEmail;
    }
    public function get gender():String {
        return userGender;
    }
```

Each of these getter methods returns the value of the relevant private variable.

To be able to set the initial values from a text file, I'll create another setter method called dataSource that sets the values of all private properties at once. Because I'll want to bind the initial values to the form fields, I'll need to set the values within this method using the individual setter methods that I just created. This will allow the values to be bound to the form fields automatically.

Add the following setter method:

```
    public function set dataSource(fileName:String):void {
        loader.addEventListener(Event.COMPLETE, completeHandler);
        loader.load(new URLRequest(fileName));
    }
```

This method receives a fileName argument, adds an event listener, and uses the load method to request the external document. The results will be handled when the complete event is dispatched using the completeHandler private function. Add that function now:

```
private function completeHandler(e:Event):void {
  var txtVars:URLVariables = new URLVariables(e.target.data);
  this.firstName = txtVars.firstName;
  this.lastName = txtVars.lastName;
  this.dateOfBirth = txtVars.dob;
  this.email = txtVars.email;
  this.gender = txtVars.gender;
}
```

This function creates a new URLVariables variable called txtVars that we'll use to extract the individual values from the variable pairs. We initially assign the value to the data property of the event object. We then call each of the setter functions, assigning the relevant value from the txtVars variable.

That's it for the class file. The complete code follows:

```
package com.aip {
  import flash.net.URLLoader;
  import flash.net.URLRequest;
  import flash.net.URLVariables;
  [Bindable]
  public class UserDetails {
    private var userFirstName:String;
    private var userLastName:String;
    private var userDateOfBirth:String;
    private var userEmail:String;
    private var userGender:String;
    private var loader:URLLoader = new URLLoader();
    public function UserDetails() {
    }
    public function set firstName(fName:String):void {
      userFirstName = fName;
    }
    public function set lastName(lName:String):void {
      userLastName = lName;
    }
    public function set dateOfBirth(DOB:String):void {
      userDateOfBirth = DOB;
    }
    public function set email(email:String):void {
      userEmail = email;
    }
    public function set gender(gender:String):void {
      userGender = gender;
    }
    public function set dataSource(fileName:String):void {
      loader.addEventListener(Event.COMPLETE, completeHandler);
```

```
        loader.load(new URLRequest(fileName));
      }
      public function get firstName():String {
        return userFirstName;
      }
      public function get lastName():String {
        return userLastName;
      }
      public function get dateOfBirth():String {
        return userDateOfBirth;
      }
      public function get email():String {
        return userEmail;
      }
      public function get gender():String {
        return userGender;
      }
      private function completeHandler(e:Event):void {
        var txtVars:URLVariables = new URLVariables(e.target.data);
        this.firstName = txtVars.firstName;
        this.lastName = txtVars.lastName;
        this.dateOfBirth = txtVars.dob;
        this.email = txtVars.email;
        this.gender = txtVars.gender;
      }
    }
  }
```

Switch to the application file and add a namespace declaration to the <mx:Application> tag as shown:

```
<mx:Application xmlns:mx="http://www.adobe.com/2006/mxml"
  xmlns:aip="com.aip.*" layout="absolute">
```

The xmlns attribute associates the text aip with the package com.aip. We'll use the aip prefix when we add the UserDetails class as a component. Do so with the following line underneath the <mx:Application> tag:

```
<aip:UserDetails id="userData"/>
```

This tag creates an instance of the UserDetails class and assigns it the id of userData.

We want to populate this instance with the details from the loaded text file, so we need to set the dataSource attribute of this tag. We'll do so in the creationComplete event of the application as shown in bold here:

```
<mx:Application xmlns:mx="http://www.adobe.com/2006/mxml"
  xmlns:aip="com.aip.*"
  creationComplete="userData.dataSource='assets/user.txt'"
  layout="absolute">
```

Before we can see the loaded values in the form, we'll need to bind each of the form controls to the relevant property of the userData instance. Modify each of the form controls as shown here to add a binding expression using curly braces:

```
<mx:Form id="userFormData">
  <mx:FormHeading label="Enter your details"/>
  <mx:FormItem label="First name">
    <mx:TextInput id="txtFirstName" text="{userData.firstName}"/>
  </mx:FormItem>
  <mx:FormItem label="Last name">
    <mx:TextInput id="txtLastName" text="{userData.lastName}"/>
  </mx:FormItem>
  <mx:FormItem label="Date of birth">
    <mx:TextInput id="txtDOB" text="{userData.dateOfBirth}"/>
  </mx:FormItem>
  <mx:FormItem label="Email">
    <mx:TextInput id="txtEmail" text="{userData.email}"/>
  </mx:FormItem>
  <mx:FormItem label="Gender">
    <mx:RadioButtonGroup id="rdoGender"
      selectedValue="{userData.gender}"/>
    <mx:RadioButton label="Female" groupName="rdoGender"/>
    <mx:RadioButton label="Male"   groupName="rdoGender"/>
    <mx:RadioButton label="Not telling" groupName="rdoGender"/>
  </mx:FormItem>
</mx:Form>
<mx:HBox>
<mx:Label text="Full name from class:" fontWeight="bold"/>
<mx:Text id="txtFullName" width="300"
  text="{userData.firstName+ ' ' + userData.lastName}"/>
</mx:HBox>
```

Figure 6-7 shows what happens when you run the application.

Each of the form controls is bound to the relevant property in the userData instance, which in turn is loaded from the file user.txt. Notice that the txtFullName control displays the relevant values from the class file.

The final step is to bind the setter methods to the form controls by modifying the UserDetails tag, as shown here:

```
<aip:UserDetails id="userData"
  firstName="{txtFirstName.text}"
  lastName = "{txtLastName.text}"
  dateOfBirth = "{txtDOB.text}"
  email = "{txtEmail.text}"
  gender = "{rdoGender.selectedValue}"/>
```

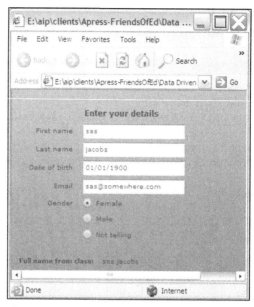

Figure 6-7. The form controls bound to the loaded text content

When we modify a value in the form, the stored data will update in the UserDetails class. Figure 6-8 shows what happens when we type a new value in the first and last name fields. You should see the Text control at the bottom update at the same time.

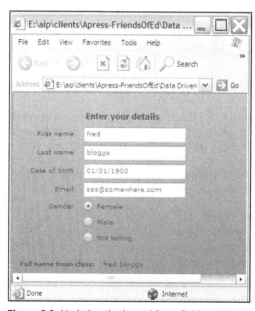

Figure 6-8. Updating the bound form fields updates the data stored in the userData instance.

This example shows how you can store data in an ActionScript class and use an MXML class with data binding. We could extend the example by adding validation to the setter methods. For example, we could add a regular expression to check for a valid e-mail address. I haven't done this to keep the example simple, but feel free to explore these areas yourself. You can find the finished files saved as UserForm.mxml, user.txt, and UserDetails.as.

You could also have created the userData instance using ActionScript by importing the relevant class:

```
import com.aip.UserDetails;
```

You could then declare a variable of the relevant type and use it to create a new instance and assign property values; for example:

```
private var userData:UserDetails = new UserDetails;
userData.firstName= "sas";
```

I'll leave you to try that example on your own.

In the previous example, you saw how important data binding was in displaying the content in each of the controls in the interface. So far in the book you've seen only very simple examples of data binding using curly braces notation. In the next section, I want to look at other ways to bind data.

Understanding data binding

Data binding allows you to bind one property of a component to a property of a second component. For example, you can bind the text property of a Text control to a value loaded from a text file. A property in the source component—in this case, data within the lastResult property from the HTTPService that loads the text file—provides a value to the text property of the target component.

The previous scenario describes a one-way binding, but it's also possible for two components to update each other in a two-way binding. That might occur when a TextInput is bound to a property within a data model. When the data model first loads, it populates the TextInput. The user can also update the TextInput, which in turn updates the data model. The two components remain synchronized, regardless of which one initiates the change.

Bindings are triggered by an event that dictates when the property should be updated in the target component. This may happen when the contents of an XML document finish loading or when the user makes a change to a user interface component.

There are many different ways to set up a binding between two components. You can use the following:

- Curly braces syntax
- The <mx:Binding> tag
- ActionScript

We'll look at each of these approaches in turn.

Binding with curly braces syntax

The easiest way to add a binding is to use curly braces, and you've seen many examples of this approach already in this chapter. The following example shows a simple binding between two controls:

```
<mx:TextInput id="txtSource" />
<mx:Text id="txtDestination" text="{txtSource.text}"/>
```

In this case, the text property in the txtSource TextInput is bound to the text property of the txtDestination control. When you update the txtSource control, the Text control updates as well.

Because the examples shown so far have been simplistic, let's look at how we can extend the use of curly braces by including ActionScript expressions within the curly braces.

You can use ActionScript expressions and functions to transform the bound property in some way before it appears in the destination component. You might want to do this to include calculations, concatenate values, add conditional expressions, or even apply a more complex transformation using a function.

Including a calculation

If you expect a numeric value from the source of the binding, you can include calculations within the binding expression:

```
<mx:TextInput id="txtSource" />
<mx:Text id="txtDestination" text="{Number(txtSource.text)*100}"/>
```

The example here multiplies a number provided in a TextInput control by 100. Notice that I had to cast the text property as a number first before performing the calculation.

Where the source value is provided by a user, you might want to add a validator first to make sure you actually get a numeric value. You'll see how to validate content a little later in the chapter.

Concatenating values

You can include text within the curly braces if you need to concatenate content with the bound source property. The following example adds text as well as the text property from the txtSource control:

```
<mx:TextInput id="txtSource" />
<mx:Text id="txtDestination"
   text="The source component contained the text {txtSource.text}"/>
```

Adding conditions

You can also add bindings that contain conditions that affect the displayed value:

```
<mx:CheckBox id="chkSource" label="Over 65?"/>
<mx:Textt id="txtDestination"
   text="(chkSource.selected) ? 'Can retire' : 'Keep working' "/>
```

In this example, if the user checks the Over 65? Checkbox, the txtDestination control will display the text Can retire; otherwise it will display Keep working.

Using an ActionScript function

You can specify a more complicated transformation during the binding by using an ActionScript function:

```
<mx:ComboBox id="cboCountry">
  <mx:dataProvider>
    <mx:String>England</mx:String>
    <mx:String>France</mx:String>
    <mx:String>United States</mx:String>
  </mx:dataProvider>
</mx:ComboBox>
<mx:Text id="txtCurrencyName"
  text = "{showCurrency(String(cboCountry.selectedItem))}"/>
```

In this example, the Text control displays text returned by the showCurrency function. The binding passes the selectedItem from the ComboBox to the function. The showCurrency function follows:

```
private function showCurrency(country:String):String{
  var strReturn:String;
  if (country == "England") {
    strReturn = "Pounds sterling";
  }
  else if (country == "France") {
    strReturn = "Euros";
  }
  else if (country == "United States") {
    strReturn = "US dollars";
  }
  return strReturn;
}
```

This function returns a string which displays in the txtCurrencyName control. When the user picks a country from the ComboBox, the relevant currency will display in the txtCurrencyName control. The text that appears is set by the showCurrency function. This is a simplistic example but you can see how the binding is routed through this function before the final value appears in the target component.

An alternative to using curly braces is to include the <mx:Binding> tag.

Binding with the <mx:Binding> tag

Developers can also use the <mx:Binding> tag to create bindings that are distinct from the user interface components. Like the curly braces syntax, this tag can also include ActionScript expressions and functions.

The <mx:Binding> tag requires a source and destination:

```
<mx:Binding source="src.property" destination="dest.property"/>
```

For example:

```
<mx:Binding source="sourceTI.text"
  destination="destinationText.text" />
<mx:TextInput id="sourceTI" />
<mx:TextInput id="destinationTI"/>
```

You can include multiple <mx:Binding> tags in an application.

As you saw in the previous examples, it's also possible to include a calculation, concatenation, condition, and ActionScript function in the source property of the binding.

Including a calculation

The following example shows how to use a calculation in the source attribute for a numeric component source property:

```
<mx:Binding source="Number(txtSource.text) * 100"
  destination="txtDestination.text" />
<mx:TextInput id="txtSource" />
<mx:TextInput id="txtDestination"/>
```

This example includes a simple multiplication within the source attribute of the binding.

Concatenating values

You can also concatenate values within the binding:

```
<mx:Binding
  source="'The source component contained the text '+ txtSource.text"
  destination="txtDestination.text" />
<mx:TextInput id="txtSource" />
<mx:TextInput id="txtDestination"/>
```

Again, this example includes the concatenation within the source attribute.

Adding conditions

As with the curly braces syntax, you can add conditional bindings in the source attribute:

```
<mx:Binding source="(chkSource.selected) ? 'Can retire' : 'Keep working'"
  destination="txtDestination.text" />
<mx:CheckBox id="chkSource" label="Over 65?"/>
<mx:TextInput id="txtDestination"/>
```

Using an ActionScript function

You can specify a more complicated transformation during the binding by using an ActionScript function:

```
<mx:Binding source="showCurrency(String(cboCountry.selectedItem))"
  destination="destinationText.text" />
```

```
<mx:ComboBox id="cboCountry">
  <mx:dataProvider>
    <mx:String>England</mx:String>
    <mx:String>France</mx:String>
    <mx:String>United States</mx:String>
    </mx:dataProvider>
  </mx:ComboBox>
<mx:Text id="txtCurrencyName"}"/>
```

As with the previous example, the Text control displays text returned by the showCurrency function.

Working through an example

Before we start creating ActionScript bindings, let's work through a more detailed data binding example. We'll load an external XML document containing country details and bind the list of countries to a ComboBox component. When we choose a country, the interface will show facts about the selected country. We'll also show the entire XML document in a TextArea control, so you check what's been loaded.

We'll use the document countryDetails.xml, so copy it from your resources and add it to the assets folder in your project. The file contains three countries and each has the following structure:

```
<?xml version="1.0" encoding="UTF-8"?>
<countries>
  <country>
    <countryName>Australia</countryName>
    <hemisphere>Southern</hemisphere>
    <population>20,000,000 approx</population>
    <capital>Canberra</capital>
    <areaSqKM>7,692,024</areaSqKM>
    <areaSqMiles>2,969,906</areaSqMiles>
  </country>
</countries>
```

Create a new Flex application and modify the interface to appear as follows:

```
<?xml version="1.0" encoding="utf-8"?>
<mx:Application xmlns:mx="http://www.adobe.com/2006/mxml"
  layout="absolute">
  <mx:VBox x="10" y="10">
    <mx:HBox>
      <mx:Label text="Country" fontWeight="bold" width="100"/>
      <mx:ComboBox id="cboCountry"/>
    </mx:HBox>
    <mx:HBox>
      <mx:Label text="Hemisphere" fontWeight="bold" width="100"/>
      <mx:Text id="txtHemisphere"/>
    </mx:HBox>
    <mx:HBox>
      <mx:Label text="Population" fontWeight="bold" width="100"/>
      <mx:Text id="txtPopulation"/>
```

```
          </mx:HBox>
          <mx:HBox>
            <mx:Label text="Capital" fontWeight="bold" width="100"/>
            <mx:Text id="txtCapital"/>
          </mx:HBox>
          <mx:HBox>
            <mx:Label text="Area" fontWeight="bold" width="100"/>
            <mx:Text id="txtArea"/>
          </mx:HBox>
        </mx:VBox>
      </mx:Application>
```

We'll display a list of countries in the ComboBox. When we choose a country, we'll show further details in the Text controls. Figure 6-9 shows how the interface appears at this point.

Figure 6-9. The application interface

We need to load the external XML document into the application, so add an <mx:HTTPService> tag above the VBox container as shown:

```
<mx:HTTPService id="countriesService" url="assets/countryDetails.xml"
    result="showCountries(event)" resultFormat="e4x"/>
```

Notice that I specified that we'll use the e4x format so we can use E4X expressions to target the loaded XML data. You'll find out more about these expressions in Chapter 8, but for now, you'll see that they're fairly self-explanatory. When we receive a result, we'll call the showCountries function to populate the interface.

We'll call the send method to make the request in the creationComplete event of the application. Modify the opening <mx:Application> tag as shown in bold here:

```
<mx:Application xmlns:mx="http://www.adobe.com/2006/mxml"
    layout="absolute" creationComplete="countriesService.send()">
```

After the interface is created, the application will request the XML document using the countriesService HTTPService component.

We need a variable to store the loaded content from the XML document. Add a script block below the opening <mx:Application> tag containing the following code:

```
<mx:Script>
  <![CDATA[
    import mx.rpc.events.ResultEvent;
    [Bindable]
    private var countryXML:XML;
  ]]>
</mx:Script>
```

The code imports the ResultEvent class and creates a bindable variable called countryXML of the type XML. We'll populate this variable using the result handler.

We now need to add the result handler function showCountries to this script block. Before we do so, add a TextArea above the closing </VBox> element:

```
<mx:TextArea id="txtLoadedXML" width="400" height="200"/>
```

We'll use this to display the loaded content. This technique can be useful to double-check what loads into the application.

Add the showCountries function that follows to the script block:

```
private function showCountries(e:ResultEvent):void {
  countryXML = e.target.lastResult;
  txtLoadedXML.text = countryXML.toXMLString();
}
```

The function receives a ResultEvent object, passed with the function call. We'll assign the lastResult property of the target of this event, the HTTPService, to the countryXML variable. Then we use the toXMLString method to display the loaded content in the txtLoadedXML control.

Run the application now and you should see the TextArea populated with the details from the external file, as shown in Figure 6-10.

Now we need to populate the ComboBox component from the <countryName> node in the XML variable. We'll use an E4X expression and bind it to the dataProvider property as shown here:

```
<mx:ComboBox id="cboCountry"
  dataProvider="{countryXML.country}" labelField="countryName"/>
```

The expression countryXML.country starts by targeting the root node of the loaded XML document, which is equivalent to the variable countryXML. It then finds the country nodes that are children of the root node. There are three of these in the XML document. If you run the application again, you should see that the ComboBox is populated with the three country names.

The dataProvider contains all the data from the <country> node downward and includes all child elements. If we bind the selectedItem property from the ComboBox, we can display the selected country details in the other controls by using E4X expressions.

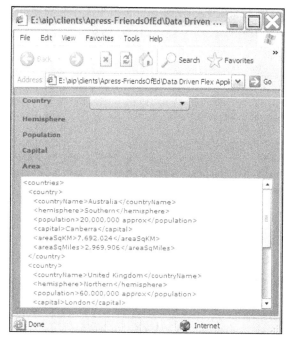

Figure 6-10. The TextArea displays content from the loaded XML document.

Modify the Text controls as shown in bold. Note that they don't appear next to each other in the application file:

```
<mx:HBox>
  <mx:Label text="Hemisphere" fontWeight="bold" width="100"/>
  <mx:Text id="txtHemisphere"
    text="{cboCountry.selectedItem.hemisphere}"/>
</mx:HBox>
<mx:HBox>
  <mx:Label text="Population" fontWeight="bold" width="100"/>
  <mx:Text id="txtPopulation"
    text="{cboCountry.selectedItem.population}"/>
</mx:HBox>
<mx:HBox>
  <mx:Label text="Capital" fontWeight="bold" width="100"/>
  <mx:Text id="txtCapital"
    text="{cboCountry.selectedItem.capital}"/>
</mx:HBox>
<mx:HBox>
  <mx:Label text="Area" fontWeight="bold" width="100"/>
  <mx:Text id="txtArea"
    text="{cboCountry.selectedItem.areaSqKM + ' square kms (' + ➥
    cboCountry.selectedItem.areaSqMiles + ' square miles)'}"/>
</mx:HBox>
```

In each case, we located the path to the relevant node using dot notation, starting from cboCountry.selectedItem. For example, to find the <hemisphere> element, we use cboCountry.selectedItem.hemisphere.

If you run the application, you should see that the interface appears, as shown in Figure 6-11. You should be able to choose different countries from the ComboBox and see the details update.

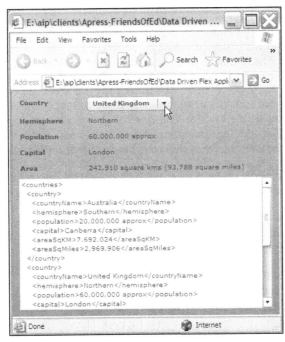

Figure 6-11. The completed application

This example shows how you can bind a loaded XML document to different controls using curly braces notation. I saved the file as Binding1.mxml with your other resources.

Let's see how we can add bindings with ActionScript.

Binding with ActionScript

Developers can create bindings entirely in ActionScript by using the mx.binding.utils.bindingUtils ActionScript 3.0 class. The static bindProperty method allows you to create a binding to a property. You can also use the static bindSetter method to bind to a property value set with a method.

Using bindProperty

The bindProperty method binds one property to another using ActionScript to create a direct binding. This method has the following structure:

```
bindProperty(site:Object, prop:String, host:Object, chain:Object, ➡
  commitOnly:Boolean - default is false):ChangeWatcher
```

The site argument specifies the id of the destination control while the prop argument identifies the bound property. The host represents the source control, while the chain provides details of the property to be bound. You would normally use the method this way:

```
BindingUtils.bindProperty(destControlID, "text", srcControlID, "text");
```

In addition, you can use the chain property to specify an object:

```
{name: propertyName, getter:function(host) {return host[name]}}
```

You can also specify an Array of chained bindable properties from the source, as an array of String properties. For example, the property src.a.b.c would be defined as ["a", "b", "c"]. This approach can be useful for drilling down into a hierarchy of properties.

The commitOnly, which is not commonly required, allows you to specify which events cause the event handler to be called. If you set the value to true, the handler is called on committing change events. Otherwise, both committing and noncommitting change events will call the handler. Noncommitting change events are specified with the [NonCommittingChangeEvent(<event-name>)] metatags.

When you use the bindProperty method, it returns a ChangeWatcher object that allows you to define an event handler to detect and respond when the binding occurs. Again, it's not common to use the returned object.

You can see an example in the following code block, in which we use ActionScript to create a binding between a TextInput and Text control (we won't work through this example here):

```
<?xml version="1.0"?>
<mx:Application xmlns:mx="http://www.adobe.com/2006/mxml"
  layout="absolute" creationComplete="createBinding(event);">
  <mx:Script>
    <![CDATA[
      import mx.events.FlexEvent;
      import mx.binding.utils.BindingUtils;
      private function createBinding(e:FlexEvent):void {
        BindingUtils.bindProperty(destinationText, "text", sourceTI, ➥
          "text");
      }
    ]]>
  </mx:Script>
  <mx:HBox x="10" y="10">
    <mx:VBox>
      <mx:Label text="Source control" fontWeight="bold"/>
      <mx:Label text="Destination control" fontWeight="bold"/>
    </mx:VBox>
    <mx:VBox>
      <mx:TextInput id="sourceTI"/>
      <mx:Text id="destinationText"/>
    </mx:VBox>
  </mx:HBox>
</mx:Application>
```

The binding is created in the creationComplete event of the application with the createBinding function. This function uses bindProperty to create the binding from the text property of the sourceTI control to the text property of the destinationText.

If you enter text into the TextInput control, it will appear within the Text control because of the binding. You can find the example saved as Binding2.mxml with your resources if you want to run it and see the result yourself.

Using bindSetter

As an alternative, you can use bindSetter to specify a method that sets the value of the destination property. You can use this method as follows:

```
bindSetter(setter:Function, host:Object, chain:Object, ➠
  commitOnly:Boolean - default is false):ChangeWatcher
```

You'd normally use it in the following way:

```
BindingUtils.bindSetter(setterFunction, srcControlID, "text");
```

The chain and commitOnly parameters work in the same way as with the bindProperty method. The bindSetter method also returns a ChangeWatcher object.

The code that follows shows how to use bindSetter to re-create the previous scripted binding:

```
<?xml version="1.0"?>
<mx:Application xmlns:mx="http://www.adobe.com/2006/mxml"
  layout="absolute" creationComplete="createBinding(event);">
  <mx:Script>
    <![CDATA[
      import mx.events.FlexEvent;
      import mx.binding.utils.*;
      private function setTextValue(textValue:String):void {
        destinationText.text = textValue;
      }
      private function createBinding(e:FlexEvent):void {
        var watcherSetter:ChangeWatcher = BindingUtils.bindSetter ➠
          (setTextValue, sourceTI, "text");
      }
    ]]>
  </mx:Script>
  <mx:HBox x="10" y="10">
    <mx:VBox>
      <mx:Label text="Source control" fontWeight="bold"/>
      <mx:Label text="Destination control" fontWeight="bold"/>
    </mx:VBox>
    <mx:VBox>
      <mx:TextInput id="sourceTI"/>
      <mx:Text id="destinationText"/>
    </mx:VBox>
  </mx:HBox>
</mx:Application>
```

197

In this example, I imported the entire mx.binding.utils.* package because it also contains the ChangeWatcher class. The createBinding function uses bindSetter to specify the source for the binding, the text property of the sourceTI control. The bindSetter method calls the setTextValue function to set the value of the bound property in the destinationText control. You can find this example saved as Binding3.mxml.

The previous two examples are simplistic, so let's re-create our earlier example of displaying country details using scripted bindings.

Working through a scripted binding example

In this example, I'll use ActionScript to create bindings from data in a loaded document to other user interface controls. You'll be able to see how to use both the bindProperty and bindSetter methods. If you didn't previously add the countryDetails.xml file to your assets folder, do so now.

Create a new Flex application with the following interface:

```
<?xml version="1.0" encoding="utf-8"?>
<mx:Application xmlns:mx="http://www.adobe.com/2006/mxml"
  layout="absolute">
  <mx:VBox x="10" y="10">
    <mx:HBox>
      <mx:Label text="Country" fontWeight="bold" width="100"/>
      <mx:ComboBox id="cboCountry"/>
    </mx:HBox>
    <mx:HBox>
      <mx:Label text="Hemisphere" fontWeight="bold" width="100"/>
      <mx:Text id="txtHemisphere"/>
    </mx:HBox>
    <mx:HBox>
      <mx:Label text="Population" fontWeight="bold" width="100"/>
      <mx:Text id="txtPopulation"/>
    </mx:HBox>
    <mx:HBox>
      <mx:Label text="Capital" fontWeight="bold" width="100"/>
      <mx:Text id="txtCapital"/>
    </mx:HBox>
    <mx:HBox>
      <mx:Label text="Area" fontWeight="bold" width="100"/>
      <mx:Text id="txtArea"/>
    </mx:HBox>
    <mx:TextArea id="txtLoadedXML" width="400" height="200"/>
  </mx:VBox>
</mx:Application>
```

The interface is identical to the one we used in the earlier example.

Add the following <mx:HTTPService> tag above the VBox container:

```
<mx:HTTPService id="countriesService" url="assets/countryDetails.xml"
   result="showCountries(event)" resultFormat="e4x"/>
```

The service loads the file countryDetails.xml using the e4x format. When the service receives a result, it calls the showCountries function. We'll add that function shortly.

Call the send method of the service in the creationComplete event of the application, as shown here in bold:

```
<mx:Application xmlns:mx="http://www.adobe.com/2006/mxml"
   layout="absolute" creationComplete="countriesService.send()">
```

Add a script block and import the relevant classes:

```
<mx:Script>
  <![CDATA[
    import mx.rpc.events.ResultEvent;
    import mx.binding.utils.BindingUtils;
  ]]>
</mx:Script>
```

We'll also create a private variable to store the content from the loaded document. We must make it bindable, so add the following to the code block:

```
[Bindable]
private var countryXML:XML;
```

When we load the document, the response will be processed with the showCountries function. Add it now:

```
private function showCountries(e:ResultEvent):void {
  countryXML = e.target.lastResult;
  txtLoadedXML.text = countryXML.toXMLString();
  createBindings();
}
```

The function finds the lastResult property of the service and assigns it to the countryXML variable. We then display a string representation in the TextArea control using the toXMLString method. We finish by calling the createBindings function.

The createBindings function binds the loaded content to the dataProvider property of the ComboBox control. It specifies the countryName nodes in the countryXML.country path. Add the function to the script block now:

```
private function createBindings():void {
  BindingUtils.bindProperty(cboCountry, "dataProvider", countryXML, ➥
    "country");
  cboCountry.labelField = "countryName";
}
```

If you run the application now, the TextArea component will display the loaded content, and the ComboBox control will display a list of country names.

We can finish by creating bindings that display the details of the selected country in the other controls. Add the following line at the end of the createBindings function before the closing brace:

```
BindingUtils.bindProperty(txtHemisphere, "text", cboCountry, ➡
    ["selectedItem", "hemisphere"]);
```

Notice that we needed to specify a chain of bound properties from the ComboBox using array notation. We specify the selectedItem property followed by the hemisphere node.

Add the following additional bindings to the createBindings function for the population and capital details:

```
BindingUtils.bindProperty(txtPopulation, "text", cboCountry, ➡
    ["selectedItem", "population"]);
BindingUtils.bindProperty(txtCapital, "text", cboCountry, ➡
    ["selectedItem", "capital"]);
```

We'll bind the area property a little differently. Using the bindSetter method, we can apply our own transformation to the bound square kilometers area value. Add the following line to the createBindings function:

```
BindingUtils.bindSetter(displayArea, cboCountry, ➡
    ["selectedItem", "areaSqKM"]);
```

This method assigns the displayArea function to handle the binding of the areaSqKM property. Add the function now:

```
private function displayArea(areaSqKM:String):void {
  txtArea.text = areaSqKM + " square kms"
}
```

The function accepts the passed property as an argument and assigns it to the text property of the txtArea control, followed by the text square kms.

If you run the application, you should see the same outcome as in the previous example, but with one small difference: the area will display only in square kilometers.

This example showed how to add bindings using ActionScript. The completed file is saved as Binding4.mxml with the other chapter resources.

Once we have bound data in an application, we may need to change the way it displays with a formatter or check for valid entry with a validator.

Adding validators and formatters

Both formatters and validators are useful Flex tools for working with data-driven applications. Validators allow developers to ensure that anything entered by users matches predetermined requirements such as the correct data type or format. Formatters allow you to change the way bound data displays in the destination control. They are applied during the binding process.

Chapter 4 provides an introduction to the built-in validators and formatters. In this chapter, I want to look at how developers can create their own validators and formatters. We'll start by looking at validators.

Understanding validators

Validators check that anything entered by users is valid. This might involve making sure that an e-mail address is constructed in the correct way or that a number in a specific range has been entered where one is required.

When building data-driven applications, best practice is to check that user entry is valid before making a call to the server. This approach can reduce the amount of data sent to the server and increase application response time for the user.

Flex includes a number of built-in validators and developers can also create their own. The built-in validators include CreditCardValidator, CurrencyValidator, DateValidator, EmailValidator, NumberValidator, PhoneNumberValidator, RegExpValidator, SocialSecurityValidator, StringValidator, and ZipCodeValidator. You can use these validators either as MXML tags or within ActionScript.

Basically, all validators extend the Validator base class so they share several common features: whether the input is required, specifying a source for the input, and a trigger for the validation process. In addition, each of the built-in validators has its own properties, including the capability to set custom error messages. Turn to Chapter 4 for a more detailed exploration of the built-in validators. I'd like to focus on custom validation here.

Creating a custom validator

Developers can create custom validators that are useful when they need to carry out the same type of validation more than once. All custom validators extend the Validator class and override the doValidation method. They return an array of ValidationResult objects that contain details about each validation error.

We'll create a custom validator that checks a text entry to ensure that it is a valid state or territory in Australia. I would have chosen the U.S. as an example, but in Australia we have a lot fewer states and territories!

Start with a new ActionScript class in the com.aip package called AusStateValidator.as. This class will extend the Validator class, as do all custom validators.

Add the following import statements above the class declaration:

```
package com.aip
{
  import mx.validators.Validator;
  import mx.validators.ValidationResult;
  public class AusStateValidator extends Validator {
  }
}
```

Declare the states, results, and booValid variables, as shown in the class:

```
private var states:Array = ["ACT","NSW","NT","QLD","SA","TAS", ➥
  "VIC","WA"];
private var results:Array;
private var booValid:Boolean;
```

The states array holds a list of valid state and territory abbreviations in Australia. We'll use the results array to store our ValidationResult objects and the booValid variable will act as a flag, tracking whether an entry is valid.

We need to call the super method in the constructor function to call the base class constructor, so add the following code inside the class declaration:

```
public function AusStateValidator() {
  super();
}
```

Now we need to override the doValidation method from the base class. In addition to calling the doValidation method from that class, the new method must return an array of ValidationResult objects that will provide the details about each custom validation error. Add the following to your class file:

```
override protected function doValidation(value:Object):Array {
  results  = [];
  results = super.doValidation(value);
  if (value != null) {
    for (var i:int=0; i<states.length;i++) {
      if (states[i] == value.toString()) {
        booValid = true;
        break;
      }
    }
  }
  if (!booValid) {
    results.push(new ValidationResult(true, null, "notState", "This is ➥
      not a valid Australian state or territory"));
  }
  return results;
}
```

The doValidation function receives a value that is the user input value being validated. It starts by clearing the results array and calling the doValidation method on the base class. This allows any default validations to be added to the array.

The function then checks that a value has been passed in, and if so, loops through the array of states and territories, checking if the value matches one of the array entries. If the code finds a match, it sets the booValid flag to true and breaks out of the loop. If it finds an error (that is, booValid is false), we add a new ValidationResult object to the results array.

When creating the ValidationResult object, we need to specify that the result is an error (the first argument is true), any subfield if multiple fields are required in the validation (null), the error code (notState), and an error message (This is not a valid Australian state or territory):

```
new ValidationResult(true, null, "notState", ➡
    "This is not a valid Australian state or territory")
```

That's it for the custom validator class. Now we'll create an application that uses this validator.

Create a new application file with the following interface:

```
<?xml version="1.0" encoding="utf-8"?>
<mx:Application xmlns:mx="http://www.adobe.com/2006/mxml"
  layout="absolute">
  <mx:VBox x="10" y="10">
    <mx:HBox>
      <mx:Label text="Enter state or territory" fontWeight="bold"/>
      <mx:TextInput id="txtState"/>
    </mx:HBox>
    <mx:Button label="Validate" id="btnValidate"/>
  </mx:VBox>
</mx:Application>
```

The interface includes a simple Label and TextInput. We'll add the custom validator to the text property of the txtState control and carry out the validation when we click the Validate button.

We need to add a namespace to the <mx:Application> tag so we can include our custom validator class as a tag in the application. Modify the <mx:Application> tag as shown in bold here:

```
<mx:Application xmlns:mx="http://www.adobe.com/2006/mxml"
    xmlns:aip="com.aip.*" layout="absolute">
```

The new namespace specifies that we'll use the aip prefix to refer to any classes in the com.aip package.

Add the following custom validator tag below the <mx:Application> tag:

```
<aip:AusStateValidator id="stateValidator"
    source="{txtState}" property="text"
    trigger="{btnValidate}" triggerEvent="click"
    required="true"/>
```

The tag creates an instance of our custom validator. We use the aip prefix as well as the name of the class file AusStateValidator to create the tag. We use the source and property attributes inherited from the base class to reference the entry in the TextInput control. The tag specifies that validation will occur when the btnValidate button is clicked and that entry in the field is required.

This time, we'll use standard validation instead of a custom validation function. When we click Validate, any invalid entries will cause the control to have a red border, and we'll need to move the mouse over the control to see the error message.

Run the application and enter an invalid entry. When you click Validate, the TextInput should show a red border indicating a validation error. When you move your mouse over the TextInput, you should see something similar to Figure 6-12.

Figure 6-12. The TextInput uses a custom validator.

In this example, we created a custom validator and used it to validate a TextInput. Because the custom validator uses the Validator as the base class, it inherits the methods and properties of that class. We used override to redefine the doValidation method and add our own custom validation routine.

You can find this file saved as StateValidation.mxml with your resources. I've also included the AusStateValidator.as custom validator class.

Let's move on to the topic of formatters.

Understanding formatters

Formatters change the appearance of bound raw data when it appears in the destination control. Flex includes a range of built-in formatters based on the Formatter class, including CurrencyFormatter, DateFormatter, NumberFormatter, PhoneFormatter, and ZipCodeFormatter. Chapter 4 provides a more detailed overview of the built-in formatters included in Flex. It is also possible to create custom formatters, and that's the topic for the next section.

Creating a custom formatter

If you need a custom formatter, you have to create an ActionScript 3.0 class that extends the mx.formatters.Formatter base class or one of the other built-in formatters. The class must contain a public format method that takes an argument (the input) and returns a string (the formatted output).

Let's work through an example in which we take an abbreviation and use a formatter to display the expanded version of that text. We'll do this with the Australian states and territories abbreviations that we used in the custom validator example.

Create a new ActionScript class called AusStateFormatter.as in the com.aip package, extending the Formatters class. Declare the following two private variables in the class definition:

```
package com.aip {
  import mx.formatters.Formatter;
  public class AusStateFormatter extends Formatter {
    private var stateDetails:Object = new Object();
    private var stateName:String;
  }
}
```

We'll use the first variable to create an associative array of state and territory abbreviations, and their full names. The second variable will hold the state name.

Add the following constructor method:

```
public function AusStateFormatter(){
  stateDetails["ACT"] = "Australian Capital Territory";
  stateDetails["NSW"] = "New South Wales";
  stateDetails["NT"] = "Northern Territory";
  stateDetails["QLD"] = "Queensland";
  stateDetails["SA"] = "South Australia";
  stateDetails["TAS"] = "Tasmania";
  stateDetails["VIC"] = "Victoria";
  stateDetails["WA"] = "Western Australia";
  super();
}
```

This constructor function assigns the name-value pairs to the associative array and calls the constructor of the base class using the super method.

The next step is to override the format method. Add the following method to the class file:

```
override public function format(value:Object):String {
  if(value.length == 0) {
    error="No abbreviation was provided";
    return "";
  }
  else {
    stateName = stateDetails[value];
  }
  if (stateName.length > 0) {
    return stateName;
  }
  else {
    return ""
  }
}
```

This method starts by checking for a zero length formatted value. If this is the case, an error message is set and the method returns a zero length string because we don't want to display a formatted value in this case.

If a value is provided, we look it up in the stateDetails associative array, assigning the returned name to the stateName variable. We then check that this variable has a value and return it; otherwise, we return a zero length string.

We'll use this custom formatter in a simple example. Create a new application with the following interface:

```
<?xml version="1.0" encoding="utf-8"?>
<mx:Application xmlns:mx="http://www.adobe.com/2006/mxml"
  layout="absolute">
  <mx:VBox x="10" y="10">
    <mx:HBox>
      <mx:Label text="Enter state or territory abbreviation"
        fontWeight="bold" width="220"/>
      <mx:TextInput id="txtState"/>
    </mx:HBox>
    <mx:HBox>
      <mx:Label text="Full name"
        fontWeight="bold" width="220"/>
      <mx:Text id="txtFullStateName"/>
    </mx:HBox>
  </mx:VBox>
</mx:Application>
```

The application provides a TextInput for a user to enter a state or territory abbreviation. A formatter will be used during binding to display the formatted results in the txtFullStateName control.

Add the following namespace to the <mx:Application> tag:

```
<mx:Application xmlns:mx="http://www.adobe.com/2006/mxml"
  xmlns:aip="com.aip.*" layout="absolute">
```

This will allow us to use the components in the com.aip package by referencing the aip namespace. Add the custom formatter tag:

```
<aip:AusStateFormatter id="stateFormatter"/>
```

We'll need to apply the formatter during binding, so add the following text property to the txtFullStateName control:

```
<mx:Text id="txtFullStateName"
  text="{stateFormatter.format(txtState.text)}"/>
```

This binding calls the format method of the stateFormatter control. We've finished creating the application!

Run the application and test it by entering an Australian state abbreviation. Figure 6-13 shows the formatted output when I enter the state WA. If you enter a value that isn't in the associative array, no formatted value will display.

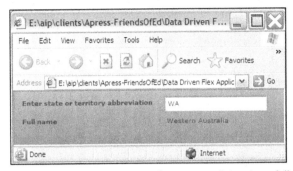

Figure 6-13. Applying a custom formatter to determine a full state name

In this example, we created and applied a simple custom formatter. You can find the saved application file StateFormatting.mxml and ActionScript class AusStateFormatter.as saved with the chapter resources.

That ends our look at the Flex tools available for working with data.

Summary

In this chapter, you've seen several ways to load and update external content from text files. We worked through examples that used both the HTTPService and URLLoader classes. During these examples you saw some simple data binding approaches using curly braces syntax. The chapter also explained the security model within Flash Player 9 so that you'd be aware of restrictions that apply where data exists in a different domain from the compiled Flex application.

We saw how to store external data on the client using the <mx:Model> tag and ActionScript classes. We finished with a detailed look at data binding and touched on the topic of validators and formatters. The topic of built validators and formatters was covered in more detail in Chapter 4. In this chapter, you saw how to create a custom validator and a custom formatter.

Throughout the book, you've seen that XML plays an important role in Flex applications. In the next chapter, I want to explore the topic of XML in more detail. Then, in Chapter 8, I'll show you how you can work with XML in your Flex applications.

Chapter 7

INTRODUCTION TO XML

If you've worked through the chapters in order up until now, you'll see that I have referred to the term **Extensible Markup Language (XML)** throughout each one. In fact, you've been working with XML all along because **Multimedia Extensible Markup Language (MXML)**, the language of Flex applications, is an XML vocabulary.

XML is one of the most important technologies underpinning modern web development. Every developer needs to have a sound understanding of the topic and how it affects the building of web applications. As a Flex developer, this is important because XML underpins the way you construct your applications as well as providing a source for external data.

In this chapter, I'll explore the topic of XML in more detail. I want to answer the following questions:

- What is XML and why is it useful?
- What can you do with XML?
- What is an XML document and what does it contain?
- What are the rules for creating XML documents?

If you know the answers to all these questions, please feel free to skip forward to the next chapter, where we'll look at using XML as an external data source. Otherwise, read on!

Understanding XML

Let's start by looking at what the term XML means. The term is a little misleading because it stands for Extensible Markup Language. In fact, XML is not a language on its own; instead it is a metalanguage that specifies how to create other languages, called vocabularies, using markup. MXML is a vocabulary of XML because it is created according to the rules of XML.

XML creates text-based languages that work with structured content. You might use XML to describe database or document content. In the case of Flex, MXML describes an application interface. The markup can provide descriptive tags for the data and describe how one piece of content relates to another.

The MXML tag `<mx:ComboBox>` describes a ComboBox control. It has a visual appearance associated with the tag as well as a set list of properties and methods that are attributes of the tag, for example, the `id` attribute. The related tag `<mx:dataProvider>` describes how to populate the ComboBox.

You can use the XML construction rules to invent tags that describe a particular set of data and the data structures. There are also many standardized XML vocabularies for use in specific industries and situations. Web developers will be most familiar with XHTML, an XML vocabulary used to describe the structure and content in a web page. Other examples include Scalable Vector Graphics (SVG), Structured Graph Format (SGF), and Synchronized Multimedia Integration Language (SMIL).

What is an XML document?

Any file containing content marked up by tags following XML rules is called an XML document. This type of file can be a physical document or it can be a stream of digital data, perhaps created from a call to a database or from another software package. A web service or RSS feed is one example of XML data that is provided in a digital stream.

At its simplest, an XML document is a way to store data in a text file. At its most complex, XML allows you to describe and structure content so that an XML processor, software that reads an XML document can render it in a specific way. A web browser is an example of an XML parser as it can read and render XHTML content. Similarly, Flex Builder contains an XML processor that renders the MXML tags visually in Design view.

There are many rules that surround the construction of an XML document, and we'll get into those a little later in the chapter. You've seen examples of XML documents each time you've created a Flex application in Flex Builder.

Understanding the XML framework

XML exists within a framework of other recommendations so there are XML-based languages to do the following (to name but a few):

- Document the rules for an XML language (XML schemas)
- Specify how to transform an XML document for other purposes (Extensible Stylesheets Language)
- Identify parts of an XML document (XPath)
- Consume and provide web services (Simple Object Access Protocol [SOAP] and Web Services Description Language [WSDL])

You can find out more about these languages at the W3C web site.

Let's see how XML started.

A brief history

The World Wide Web Consortium (W3C) released the XML recommendation in 1998. XML is based on **Standard Generalized Markup Language (SGML)**, which was in turn was created out of General Markup Language (GML) in the 1960s. XML is actually a simplified version of SGML.

SGML describes how to write languages, specifically those that work with text in electronic documents. SGML is also an international standard: ISO 8879. Interestingly enough, SGML was one of the considerations for HTML when it was first developed so both HTML and XML share a common ancestor. As I'm sure you're aware, HTML has since been reformulated into XHTML using the rules of XML construction.

Since its introduction, XML has been used in many situations and for a variety of purposes. Both human beings and software packages can work with XML documents. Most databases can provide their information in XML format, and Office 2007 uses XML languages as the basis for all Office documents. XML provides one means for software packages to exchange information.

The W3C provides the following definition for XML in its glossary at www.w3.org/TR/DOM-Level-2-Core/glossary.html.

> *XML is an extremely simple dialect of SGML. The goal is to enable generic SGML to be served, received, and processed on the Web in the way that is now possible with HTML. XML has been designed for ease of implementation and for interoperability with both SGML and HTML.*

You can read more about XML at the W3C's Web site at http://www.w3c.org/XML/. At the time of writing, the current specification was for XML 1.1, second edition. You can view this specification at http://www.w3.org/TR/xml11/.

When it created XML, the W3C published the following goals at www.w3.org/TR/REC-xml/#sec-origin-goals:

1. XML shall be straightforwardly usable over the Internet.

2. XML shall support a wide variety of applications.

3. XML shall be compatible with SGML.

4. It shall be easy to write programs which process XML documents.

5. The number of optional features in XML is to be kept to the absolute minimum, ideally zero.

6. XML documents should be human-legible and reasonably clear.

7. The XML design should be prepared quickly.

8. The design of XML shall be formal and concise.

9. XML documents shall be easy to create.

10. Terseness in XML markup is of minimal importance.

In other words, XML should be easy to use over the Internet and in a variety of other settings, by both people and software applications. The rules for XML documents should be clear so they are easy to create. XML documents should be easy to work with for both software and human beings and their conciseness isn't important. The last point is interesting as one of the key criticisms of XML documents is that they can be verbose.

Understanding why you should use XML

At this point, you might be asking yourself why XML is so important and what benefits it provides to developers. Some of the benefits are that XML is

- Simple to construct
- Flexible for a variety of purposes
- Both machine and human readable
- Accessible
- Platform and vendor independent

I want to look at each of these benefits a little more closely.

Simplicity

XML documents are relatively simple. It's easy for both humans and software packages to create XML documents as they are basically text files that follow the XML constructions rules. At a minimum, humans creating XML documents only need a basic text editor. They can also be automatically generated by a variety of different software packages.

Reading an XML document is also simple. Tag names are generally descriptive so that humans can easily work out what type of data each element contains. Because you can write the tags in a hierarchy, it's easy to determine the relationships between each piece of information.

Flexibility

One key aspect of XML is its flexibility. Unless you're working with an existing XML-based language such as XHTML or MXML, you are not restricted to a standard list of tags. As long as you follow some simple rules, you can structure an XML document in any way you like. The choice of tag names, attributes, and structures is completely flexible, so you can tailor it to suit your data.

As a metalanguage, XML has created other languages for a variety of purposes. It is so flexible that it can describe topics as diverse as vector graphics to mathematical formulae. Of particular interest to developers is the use of XML to construct languages such as XHTML, MXML, and server-side approaches like ASP.NET.

The way XML information can be used is also flexible. You can display any XML document in a web browser to see the structure of elements. You can also use other technologies or software packages to change the display quite dramatically. For example, you can do the following:

- Create printed representations of data within an XML document
- Create a web page from an XML document
- Read out XML content using a screen reader

Readability

XML documents are often called **self-describing** because the tag names that surround content are usually descriptive. This makes it easy for humans to interpret the contents in an XML document by looking at the tag names.

Because XML documents are standardized in their construction rules, it's also unambiguous for software packages to read the content. In the case of standard vocabularies, provided that a software package knows the rules or "grammar" for that language (the schema), it can easily interpret the contents of an XML document.

The hierarchy in elements means that XML documents show relationships between information in a similar way to a database. It's easy to create one-to-one and one-to-many relationships by using a hierarchical structure.

Accessibility

XML documents are stores of data or content separate from the presentation of that data. The presentation is usually governed by an XML processor or a stylesheet. By separating the data or content from its presentation, developers can repurpose their information for a number of different target audiences.

XML documents use Unicode and specify an encoding for their standard character sets, so you can write XML documents in any number of different languages. This allows developers to provide the same content for people or software packages located in different countries

Platform and vendor independence

XML is a central standard in a whole family of related standards. These recommendations work together to create an independent framework for managing markup languages.

XML is platform-, device-, and vendor-independent. It doesn't matter if you view an XML document on a PC, Macintosh, handheld computer, or mobile phone. The content is still the same and can be exchanged seamlessly. This independence allows data to be shared among software packages that otherwise couldn't communicate with each other.

People don't need to rely on a specific software package to work with XML documents. XML content can be created in a basic text editor and can be viewed in a web browser or any other XML processor. In the case of Web Services, XML is an intermediary between a user and a remote database.

The XML specification isn't owned by any company or commercial enterprise. so it's free to use. In fact, most major software packages either support XML or are moving so that they will support it in the future.

Using XML information

Software packages that process XML documents are called **XML processors**. Many different software packages, including Flex Builder, fall into this category. An XML processor can view, extract, display, and validate XML content.

XML parsers are one category of XML processors. Parsers can read through the content of an XML document and extract individual elements, attributes, and text. Parsers need to be able to separate the different parts of an XML document. For example, Flex Builder includes an XML parser that allows applications to work through the structure of an XML document to extract different parts for inclusion in the user interface.

XML parsers first check to see whether a document is well-formed, and you'll learn more about what this term means a little later in the chapter. XML parsers can't work with documents that aren't well-formed and will usually throw an error.

XML parsers fall into two categories: nonvalidating and validating. All parsers check to see whether a document is well-formed. In addition, validating parsers also compare the structure of the document with a DTD or schema to check that it is constructed correctly. A document that meets the rules listed within a DTD or schema is considered **valid** by the validating parser. Flex Builder cannot validate loaded XML content.

We've covered much of the background so you have an understanding of XML and its place in the world. Now it's time to start looking at the specifics of working with XML documents.

Understanding the structure of an XML document

XML documents are structured in a specific way, made up of a document prolog and a tree. The prolog contains information about the XML document as a whole, while the tree contains the actual data or content within the document.

Before we get started, I want to cover two basics. First, it's important to realize that the content in the document is case sensitive. Second, you can add comments to your XML document in the same way as you would with an XHTML document. Comments begin with the characters <!-- and end with -->:

```
<!-- here is a commented line -->
```

Let's start by looking at the document prolog.

The document prolog

The document prolog sits at the top of an XML document and must appear before any of the data in the document. It usually includes an XML declaration, any processing instructions, and links to other files. It can also include comments, although comments can appear anywhere in the document.

The XML declaration

The prolog usually starts with an XML declaration, although this is optional. You'll notice that MXML files always start with the following declaration:

```
<?xml version="1.0" encoding="utf-8"?>
```

If you do include a declaration, it must be on the first line of your XML document, with nothing before it, not even a space. The XML declaration tells software applications and humans that the document contains XML:

```
<?xml version="1.0"?>
```

You can optionally include an XML version in the declaration. The preceding line shows a version of 1.0. Even though the latest recommendation is for XML 1.1, you should continue to use the version="1.0" attribute value for backward compatibility with XML processors, including Flex Builder.

The XML declaration can also include an encoding attribute. Encoding determines the character set for the XML document. You can use Unicode character sets UFT-8 and UTF-16; or ISO character sets such as ISO 8859-1, Latin-1 Western Europe. These character sets are all part of the Unicode standard, which is maintained by the Unicode Consortium. You can find out more about this topic at www.unicode.org.

If no encoding attribute is included, it is assumed that the document uses UTF-8 encoding. Languages such as Japanese and Chinese need UTF-16 encoding. Western European languages often use ISO 8859-1 to cope with the accents that aren't part of the English language.

If you include the encoding attribute, it must appear after the version attribute:

```
<?xml version="1.0" encoding="UTF-8"?>
<?xml version="1.0" encoding="UTF-16"?>
<?xml version="1.0" encoding="ISO-8859-1">
```

The standalone attribute indicates whether the XML document uses external information such as a Document Type Definition (DTD) to specify the rules for how to construct the document. The attribute takes a value of either yes or no. This attribute is optional but, if used, must appear as the last attribute in the declaration:

```
<?xml version="1.0" encoding="UTF-8" standalone="yes"?>
```

The preceding line shows a complete XML declaration with all attributes in the correct order.

Processing instructions

The prolog of an XML document can also include processing instructions. Processing instructions (PIs) pass information about the XML document to other applications.

PIs start with the characters <? and finish with ?>. The first item in a PI is a name, called the **PI target**. PI names that start with xml are reserved.

A common processing instruction is the inclusion of an external XSLT stylesheet. **Stylesheets** transform the XML document into other types of documents. If included, this PI must appear before the document root. The following line shows how a stylesheet PI might appear:

```
<?xml-stylesheet type="text/xsl" href="listStyle.xsl"?>
```

Some processing instructions can also appear at the end of the XML document.

Document Type Definitions (DTDs)

DTDs or DOCTYPE declarations, which appear in the prolog of an XML document, are rules about the elements and attributes within the XML document and provide information about what is valid within the document. The prolog can include a set of declarations about the XML document, a reference to an external DTD, or both. The lines that follow show an external DTD reference:

```
<?xml version="1.0"?>
<!DOCTYPE phoneBook SYSTEM "phoneBook.dtd">
```

The document tree

All other content within an XML document that isn't in the prolog is contained within the document tree. The tree equates to the data or content within the XML document, described in elements and attributes. The tree starts with the document root, which contains all of the other content.

The content in the document tree contains information and markup. You can divide markup into the following:

- Elements
- Attributes
- Text
- CDATA

The document root

The document root contains all data within the XML document. An XML document can only ever have a single root element.

In MXML application files, the document root is often the `<mx:Application>` element:

```
<mx:Application xmlns:mx="http://www.adobe.com/2006/mxml"
    layout="absolute">
```

This element contains all the other MXML tags. It's also possible for the root of an MXML document to be another element; for example, in the case of a custom component.

Elements

Each XML document contains one or more **elements** that are also called **nodes**. An example of an MXML element is this:

```
<mx:VBox></mx:VBox>
```

All MXML elements that start with the prefix `mx:` are predetermined by the Flex SDK. You'll find out more about what the prefix means a little later in the chapter. It's possible to create your own elements by writing custom ActionScript classes.

Elements serve many functions in an XML document, including the following:

- Mark up content
- Use descriptive tag names to describe the content they mark up
- Provide information about the order of data in an XML document
- Indicate the relative importance of pieces of data
- Show relationships between blocks of information

Elements usually have a starting and ending tag, as well as some text or other elements:

```
<mx:String>England</mx:String>
```

XML tags start and end with less than and greater than signs, and the name of the tag appears between these signs:

```
<mx:String>
```

Elements may also include other elements:

```
<mx:dataProvider>
  <mx:String>England</mx:String>
</mx:dataProvider>
```

In the preceding example, the `<mx:String>` element is a child element within the `<mx:dataProvider>` element.

Some elements are empty; that is, they contain no text or other elements. These can be written in either of the two following ways:

```
<mx:Label text="Country"></mx:Label>
<mx:Label text="Country"/>
```

Each element has a name that usually describes the content. In the previous lines it's easy to see that tag describes a label. The mx: portion of the tag is not actually the name; it's the prefix before the name.

Each name must follow a standard naming convention. The names start with either a letter or an underscore and can't start with a number. Element names can contain any letter or number, but no spaces. Names don't usually contain colons because, as you have seen, these are usually used for prefixes.

If you're creating your own XML vocabulary, it's best to give elements a meaningful name that describes the content inside the tags; for example:

```
<fullName>Sas Jacobs</fullName>
```

Elements inside other elements are called **child elements** or **child nodes**. Not surprisingly, the element that contains the children is called the **parent**. The parent of the parent is called the **grandparent**. Elements that share the same parent are **siblings**.

You can mix the content of elements so that they contain text as well as child elements:

```
<tagname>
  Text being <childTagName>marked up</childTagName>
</tagname>
```

This approach doesn't normally happen with built-in MXML tags.

Attributes

Attributes provide more about an element to clarify or modify the information already provided. For example, it's common to store an id as an attribute of an element:

```
<mx:ComboBox id="cboCountry">
```

Attributes appear in the start tag of an element after the element name. They are pairs of names and related values, and each attribute must include both the name and the value:

```
<mx:RadioButton label="Female" groupName="rdoGender"/>
```

In the preceding example, the RadioButton has two attributes: label and groupName. In MXML, the relevant attributes for each tag are determined by the methods, properties, and events of the ActionScript class corresponding to the element.

Attribute values must appear within quotation marks after the attribute name, with an equals sign in between:

```
label="Female"
```

You can use either single or double quotes around the attribute value:

```
label="Female"
label='Female'
```

You're not limited in the number of attributes you can include within an element, but each attribute in a single element has to have a unique name. You couldn't repeat the label attribute twice in an element.

The rules for naming attribute are the same as for elements. You can't start the name with a number and you can't include spaces in the name.

If you're creating your own XML content, you can rewrite attributes as nested elements:

```
<contact id="1"/>
  <name>Sas Jacobs</name>
</contact>
```

They can also be written as follows:

```
<contact>
  <id>1</id>
  <name>Sas Jacobs</name>
</contact>
```

There is no single correct way to structure elements and attributes. The method you choose depends on your data and the way you're going to process the XML document

Text

Text refers to any information contained between opening and closing element tags. In the following line, the text England is stored between the `<mx:String>` and `</mx:String>` tags:

```
<mx:String>England</mx:String>
```

Unless you specify otherwise, the text between the opening and closing tags in an element will always be processed as if it were XML. Suppose that you want to include special characters such as < and >, as follows:

```
<mx:String><b>England</b></mx:String>
```

You'll have to replace them with the entities < and >:

```
<mx:String>&lt;b&gt;England&lt;/b&gt;</mx:String>
```

Entities

Character entities are symbols that represent a single character. In XHTML, character entities are used for symbols such as an ampersand & and a nonbreaking space . In XML, you use entities so that reserved text inside elements isn't processed as XML. For example, the following line would cause an error in an XML parser:

```
<expression>3 < 5</expression>
```

If you want to include a less than sign in text, you must use the entity <:

```
<expression>3 &lt; 5</expression>
```

You can also use the equivalent Unicode number.

Table 7-1 lists the common entities that you'll need to use in XML documents.

Table 7-1. Entities commonly used in XML documents

Character	Entity
<	<
>	>
'	'
"	"
&	&

An alternative is to use a CDATA block.

CDATA

The term CDATA stands for character data. You use this declaration to mark blocks of text so that they aren't processed as XML. You could use CDATA to enclose information containing characters such as < and > instead of using entitles.

CDATA sections start with <![CDATA and finish with]>. The character data is contained within square brackets [ ] inside the section:

```
<mx:String><![CDATA[<b>England</b>]]></mx:String>
```

You'll notice that when you use Flex Builder to add a script block to an MXML file, a CDATA declaration is automatically added:

```
<mx:Script>
  <![CDATA[
    import mx.events.FlexEvent;
  ]]>
</mx:Script>
```

Using a CDATA block ensures that any ActionScript that you add inside the <mx:Script> block isn't interpreted as an MXML tag.

There are a couple of other areas to consider when interpreting an XML document: the topics of white space and namespaces.

White space

XML documents contain white space in the form of spaces, returns, and tabs. The purpose of white space is to make the XML document easier for humans to read by laying out the hierarchy of elements. For example, it's common to indent child elements within their parent. The only place you can't have white space is at the top of the file before the XML declaration.

White space can be interpreted by the XML processor, although it usually isn't. You'll notice that you can have as many returns, tabs, or spaces as you like within an MXML file, without it affecting the way the application displays or runs when compiled.

Namespaces

Namespaces allow tags within an XML document to be identified as coming from a particular source. Flex applications always reference the following namespace:

```
xmlns:mx="http://www.adobe.com/2006/mxml"
```

This namespace declaration says that anything beginning with the prefix mx: is associated with the preceding URI. It isn't necessary to use the mx: prefix; you can replace that text with anything of your choosing. However, convention and best practice indicate that you probably shouldn't do so.

In Chapter 3, you saw that you can reference custom ActionScript classes with a namespace so that we can add them as tags to an application file. The following line declares a namespace aip: that corresponds to the package com.aip:

```
xmlns:aip="com.aip.*"
```

Any time we want to refer to a class within the com.aip package, we can use the aip prefix:

```
<aip:UserDetails id="userData"/>
```

This tag corresponds to the custom ActionScript class UserDetails.as within the com/aip folder.

A simple MXML document

In this book, we're particularly concerned with MXML XML vocabulary. To this point, you've worked with many MXML files, so let's take one apart so you can apply the concepts covered in this chapter:

```
<?xml version="1.0" encoding="utf-8"?>
<mx:Application xmlns:mx="http://www.adobe.com/2006/mxml"
  xmlns:aip="com.aip.*" layout="absolute">
  <!-- add UserDetails control -->
<aip:UserDetails id="userData"/>
  <mx:HBox x="10" y="10">
    <mx:VBox>
      <mx:Label text="First name" fontWeight="bold"/>
      <mx:Label text="Last name" fontWeight="bold"/>
    </mx:VBox>
    <mx:VBox>
      <mx:TextInput id="txtFName"/>
      <mx:Text id="txtLName"/>
    </mx:VBox>
  </mx:HBox>
</mx:Application>
```

The file starts with an xml declaration that specifies version 1.0 and utf-8 encoding. This is the only item that appears in the document prolog.

The root element of this document is the <mx:Application> element. All the other tags appear between the <mx:Application> and </mx:Application> tags. The <mx:Application> element contains the standard MXML namespace declaration as well as another namespace declaration for the prefix aip:. The element also contains a layout attribute that has a value of absolute.

A comment appears underneath the <mx:Application> tag. This comment won't affect the display of the interface when the application is compiled.

The first child of the <mx:Application> element is an <aip:UserDetails> element with an id attribute that has the value userData. This element is within the aip: namespace and can be found in the package com.aip.

The second child of the <mx:Application> element is an <mx:HBox> element that contains two child <mx:VBox> elements. These <mx:VBox> elements are grandchildren of the <mx:Application> element.

The <mx:VBox> elements contain other child elements such as <mx:Label>, <mx:TextInput>, and <mx:Text>. Each of these elements has attribute values assigned such as id, text, and fontWeight.

This document is simple, but it illustrates most of the main concepts that you'll need to consider when working with XML content.

I've referred to the term well-formed several times in the chapter, so now it's time to see what this means when creating an XML document.

Understanding the term "well-formed"

The construction rules for an XML document are a set of rules that ensure that the XML document is **well-formed**. Documents that aren't well-formed can't be processed by an XML parser and will generate an error. All MXML documents need to be well-formed before they can be compiled.

Well-formed documents meet the following criteria:

- The document contains one or more elements.
- The document contains a single root element that may contain other nested elements.
- Each element closes properly.
- Elements nest correctly.
- Attribute values are contained in quotes.

Let's examine each of these rules in a little more detail.

Element structure

An XML document must have at least one element: the document root. It doesn't have to have any other content, although in most cases it probably will.

The following MXML document is well-formed because it contains a single empty element <mx:Application>:

```
<?xml version="1.0" encoding="utf-8"?>
<mx:Application xmlns:mx="http://www.adobe.com/2006/mxml"
  layout="absolute"/>
```

Just how useful this document will be remains to be seen as it doesn't contain any information!

You're much more likely to create an MXML document that contains a hierarchy of elements like this one:

```
<?xml version="1.0" encoding="utf-8"?>
<mx:Application xmlns:mx="http://www.adobe.com/2006/mxml"
  layout="absolute">
```

```
            <mx:HBox>
                <mx:Label text="Country"/>
                <mx:ComboBox id="cboCountry">
                    <mx:dataProvider>
                        <mx:String>England</mx:String>
                        <mx:String>France</mx:String>
                        <mx:String>United States</mx:String>
                    </mx:dataProvider>
                </mx:ComboBox>
            </mx:HBox>
        </mx:Application>
```

As long as all the elements are contained inside a single root element, the document is well-formed.

Elements must be closed

Within an XML document, you must close all elements correctly. You can include a closing tag, as follows:

```
        <mx:Label></mx:Label>
```

Or, in the case of empty elements, you can add a forward slash to the opening tag:

```
        <mx:Label/>
```

As XML is case sensitive, start and end tag names must match exactly. You can't use the opening tag <mx:Label> with the closing element <mx:label> or even <mx:LABEL>. Most MXML elements start with an uppercase letter, corresponding to the name of the relevant ActionScript class.

Elements must nest correctly

You must also close elements in the correct order. In other words, each child element must close before its parent element.

You can't write this:

```
        <mx:ComboBox id="cboCountry">
            <mx:dataProvider>
                <mx:String>England</mx:String>
            </mx:ComboBox>
        </mx:dataProvider>
```

Instead, you must use this:

```
        <mx:ComboBox id="cboCountry">
            <mx:dataProvider>
                <mx:String>England</mx:String>
            </mx:dataProvider>
        </mx:ComboBox>
```

Use quotes for attributes

All attribute values must be contained in quotes, either double or single. The following two lines are equivalent:

```
<mx:Label text="Country"/>
<mx:Label text='Country'/>
```

If your attribute value contains a single quote, you'll have to use double quotes, and vice versa:

```
<mx:Label text="O'Malley"/>
```

Or use the following:

```
<mx:Label text='John "Bo bo" Smith'/>
```

You can also replace the quote characters inside an attribute value with character entities:

```
<mx:Label text="O&apos;Malley"/>
<mx:Label text='John &quot;Bo bo&quot; Smith'/>
```

And that's it for our look at XML.

Summary

In this chapter, I introduced you to the key concepts that you'll need for understanding XML and, in particular, MXML. I defined XML and gave you a brief history. Remember, XML is a metalanguage instead of a language in its own right.

We explored the structure of XML documents and looked at the different types of content. We worked through a simple MXML document to put the theory into practice and finished with a look at the definition of the term **well-formed**.

Flex Builder is both an XML processor (as it can process the tags in the MXML language) and an XML parser. It's capable of parsing other XML content, such as that loaded from external files. We'll look at that concept in the next chapter.

Chapter 8

USING XML IN FLEX BUILDER

In Chapter 6, we saw some different ways to work with external data stored in text files. I showed how to load raw text or text formatted into variable pairs, and you saw several different approaches using the HTTPService and URLLoader classes. You can also use these classes to load content from external XML documents and even web services.

In the previous chapter, I introduced you to XML and covered the types of content you can include in XML documents. I also introduced the rules for creating well formed documents. In this chapter, you'll learn about how to use XML as a data source for your Flex applications.

Within Flex, you can work with XML documents in many different ways. ActionScript 3.0 has completely reworked the XML class as well as introducing a new class: XMLList. You can also declare and explicitly assign content to XML objects, in much the same way that you would with strings and numeric types.

In this chapter, I want to cover the following topics:

- Working with ECMAScript for XML expressions
- Using the XML and XMLList classes
- Manipulating XML content
- Using the <mx:XML> tag
- Loading external XML documents
- Consuming web services

We'll start by learning more about ECMAScript for XML. You can download the resources for this chapter from www.friendsofed.com.

Working with XML

If you've worked with earlier versions of ActionScript, you'll be familiar with the ActionScript 2.0 XML class. Unfortunately, you'll need to forget what you've previously learned because ActionScript 3.0 changes things quite significantly.

ActionScript 3.0 includes a completely new XML class based on the ECMAScript for XML (E4X) specification: ECMA-357. It also introduces a new XMLList class, which works with one or more XML elements. It refers to a collection of nodes or attributes, often returned by applying an E4X expression to an XML document.

The old ActionScript 2.0 XML class has been renamed to the XMLDocument class for support of legacy applications, but it's suggested that you no longer use this class for new Flex applications.

E4X is an extension to ECMAScript (JavaScript) specifically targeted at working with XML documents. It is a standard managed by an international body called the European Computer Manufacturers Association (ECMA), which allows an XML document to be defined as a JavaScript object (or an ActionScript object, in our case). E4X is implemented in a number of different areas, including within Flex. Unfortunately, there is only limited support for E4X within the current web browsers.

The advantages of introducing E4X to ActionScript 3.0 are the following:

- Flex now uses a standardized approach compared with the ActionScript 2.0 XML class.
- E4X usually produces less code than the equivalent functionality in ActionScript 2.0.
- E4X expressions are simple and are generally easier to understand than the equivalent ActionScript 2.0 expressions.
- E4X is easy to learn, especially for developers with experience in XPath.

You can find out more about E4X by reading the specification at www.ecma-international.org/publications/standards/Ecma-357.htm. If you want to know more about the XPath specification, you can find it at www.w3.org/TR/xpath.

Let's look at E4X a little more closely.

Understanding E4X expressions

E4X expressions allow you to navigate through an XML document using node names in paths separated by dots. Instead of complicated and not very descriptive ActionScript 2.0 paths, such as the following:

```
theXML.childNodes[0].childNodes[0].firstChild.nodeValue;
```

E4X expressions describe a path to the data using the names of nodes and attributes to create expressions. If we wanted to find the title of the first book of an author, we could use an expression similar to this one:

```
theXML.author.book[0].title;
```

In this example, theXML equates to the root node of the XML document. Within that root node, we target a node called <author>. The <author> node has multiple <book> nodes, and the path above selects the first one. The final part of the expression indicates that we're targeting the <title> node of the first book. I'll explain E4X expressions in more detail shortly.

Besides specifying nodes by their name, you can also use an at sign (@) to target an attribute within a node. The following expression targets the id attribute within the <author> node of the XML object:

```
theXML.author.@id
```

You can even filter nodes and attributes using an expression like this one:

```
theXML.author.(@id=="2")
```

This expression finds the author with the id of 2.

If you've worked with XPath, this approach will be familiar to you. If you're not familiar with the term **XPath**, it is a World Wide Web Consortium (W3C) recommendation that explains how to address different parts of an XML document. You can read more about this recommendation at www.w3.org/TR/xpath.

To explore E4X expressions a little more closely, we'll use the following XML object and see how to extract different pieces of information from it:

```
var countryXML:XML = <countries>
  <country abbreviation="AU">
    <countryName>Australia</countryName>
    <countryHemisphere>Southern</countryHemisphere>
    <countryCurrency symbol="$">AUD</countryCurrency>
  </country>
  <country abbreviation="US">
    <countryName>United States</countryName>
    <countryHemisphere>Northern</countryHemisphere>
    <countryCurrency symbol="$">USD</countryCurrency>
  </country>
</countries>
```

As I mentioned in the introduction, in ActionScript 3.0 it's possible to create an XML object in exactly the same way that you'd create any other type of variable: by assigning the literal XML content directly to the object. An alternative approach is to assign an XML string to the variable, as shown here:

```
var strXML:String = "<countryName>Australia</countryName>";
var theXML:XML = new XML(strXML);
```

In either approach, you need to make sure the XML content is well formed or else you'll get a run time error.

Let's get back to the countryXML object shown previously. In terms of E4X expressions, the variable countryXML is equivalent to the root node of the XML content: <countries>. All paths start from the root node, so whenever you're writing an E4X expression, it must start from the countryXML object.

The expressions can then go on to target child nodes and attributes within the XML object using their names and position. A simple example appears in the following expression:

```
countryXML.country[0]
```

This line targets the first <country> element beneath the root node. Notice that the first element appears at position 0. You can then target child nodes of this country; for example, the <countryName> node using the following:

```
countryXML.country[0].countryName
```

When we have a collection of child nodes, specifying a path to the node name will create a list of all nodes of that name. Consider the following expression:

```
countryXML.country
```

This expression retrieves all <country> elements within the root node and returns an XMLList object. You'll find out more about this class a little later in the chapter. In our example, the list will consist of two elements, each with its own child nodes.

You can then use ActionScript to loop through each element in the XMLList. One approach is to use a for loop, as shown here:

```
var allCountries:XMLList = countryXML.country;
for (var i:int=0; i<allCountries.length();i++) {
  //do something with each country using allCountries[i]
}
```

You can also use a for each loop:

```
for each (var nodeValue:String in countryXML.country) {
  //do something with the country node using nodeValue
}
```

The descendant operator .. allows you to retrieve all nodes that exist within the XML content. It doesn't specify an exact path to the node or attribute. The following expression locates all <countryName> elements within the root node, regardless of their position:

```
countryXML..countryName
```

The expression would return an XMLList that you could then loop through using a for or for each expression.

You can use the wildcard * operator if you want to find all children or descendants of a node:

```
countryXML.country[0].*
```

To target an attribute, we can use the @ operator. So, to get the abbreviation of the first country, we'd use the following expression:

```
countryXML.country[0].@abbreviation
```

To find the currency symbol for the second country, we could use the following:

```
countryXML.country[1].countryCurrency.@symbol
```

The wildcard operator * also works with attributes, and the following expression finds all attributes within the first <country> node:

```
countryXML.country[0].@*
```

You can also use E4X expressions to apply filters by writing a predicate or condition inside parentheses. In the following example, we can find the <countryName> element that has the abbreviation attribute equal to US:

```
countryXML.country.(@abbreviation=="US").countryName
```

Notice that the equality operator is == (as with other ActionScript expressions).

> It's important to note that Flex treats all node and attribute values as strings, so you may need to cast values of a different data type; for example, if you want to use a number in a calculation. Otherwise, when you use the + operator, you'll be concatenating instead of performing an addition.

In the preceding example, we saw an ActionScript 3.0 XML object and a collection of nodes, or an XMLList. It's important to understand these new ActionScript 3.0 classes and see how we can use them to create and manipulate XML content.

Understanding the XML and XMLList classes

The ActionScript 3.0 XML class allows you to work with XML content, and you've seen that it implements the E4X standard for working with XML documents. In the previous section, you saw that it was possible to declare an XML variable and assign a value using ActionScript. You can also populate an XML object from content in an external XML document.

You can create an XMLList through various E4X expressions. When you apply an E4X expression to an XML document, you'll often return an XMLList, maybe a collection of child nodes or of attributes. The E4X expression acts like a filter for the XML content.

The XMLList class represents an ordered collection of properties. Many of the XML class methods that you'll see shortly return an XMLList. One useful feature of an XMLList is that you can assign it as a dataProvider for Flex components.

The difference between XMLList and XML objects is that the XML object is a single object containing any number of child nodes, whereas an XMLList is a collection of one or more objects. In any case, the distinction blurs somewhat because an XMLList object containing a single item is treated in the same way as an XML object.

It's worth exploring the properties and methods of the XML class a little further.

Properties of the XML class

The XML class has five static properties that determine how the XML content is treated, shown in Table 8-1.

Table 8-1. Static properties of the XML class

Property	Type	Explanation	Default value
ignoreComments	Boolean	Determines whether to ignore comments in the XML document	true
ignoreProcessingInstructions	Boolean	Determines whether to ignore processing instructions in the XML document	true
ignoreWhitespace	Boolean	Determines whether to ignore white space in the XML document	true
prettyIndent	int	Determines the amount of indenting in spaces when prettyPrinting is set to true	2
prettyPrinting	Boolean	Determines whether white space is preserved when the XML document displays with the toString or toXMLString methods	true

These properties are used to determine the global settings for XML objects in ActionScript 3.0.

You can see this in an example using the following XML object created in ActionScript:

```
private var snippet:XML = <login>
  <!-- login details -->
    <username>
      sas
    </username>
    <password>
      9876
    </password>
  </login>
```

Figure 8-1 shows how the values of the static properties can affect the appearance of XML content displayed with the toXMLString method.

Figure 8-1. Setting static properties of the XML class

The application that appears on the left side uses the following settings:

```
XML.ignoreComments = true;
XML.prettyPrinting = false;
```

Comments are ignored, and the content renders without pretty printing.

The application appearing on the right uses different settings:

```
XML.ignoreComments = false;
XML.prettyIndent = 4;
XML.prettyPrinting = true;
```

It displays the comment because of the ignoreComments = false setting. The application also lays out the content neatly with four characters of spacing between indented lines because of the prettyIndent and prettyPrinting property settings.

In addition to the static properties, the XML class also has a number of methods.

Methods of the XML class

The XML class has several methods that return an XMLList. There are several methods that developers can use to create and modify XML content.

Table 8-2 shows the common methods that allow you to work with content in an XML document. These methods also apply to the XMLList class. You'll notice that some methods refer to **simple** and **complex** content. Simple content contains only text, whereas complex content contains child nodes.

Table 8-2. Methods of the XML class that assist in identifying XML content

Method	Explanation
attribute	Returns the value of a specified attribute as an XMLList.
attributes	Returns a list of attribute values for a specified node as an XMLList.
child	Lists all children of a specified node as an XMLList.
childIndex	Identifies the position of the child within its parent node, starting from zero.
children	Returns all children of the specified node as an XMLList.
comments	Returns all comments within an XML object.
descendants	Returns all descendants of an XML object as an XMLList.
elements	Lists the elements of an XML object as an XMLList.
hasComplexContent	Determines whether an XML object contains complex content.
hasSimpleContent	Determines whether an XML object contains simple content.
nodeKind	Returns the node kind: text, attribute, comment, processing-instruction, or element.
parent	Returns the parent of the specified XML object as an XMLList.
processingInstructions	Returns all processing instructions.
text	Returns all text nodes.
toString	For complex content, returns XML content as a string containing all tags. Returns text only for simple content.
toXMLString	Returns all XML content as a string including all tags, regardless of whether the content is simple or complex.
XML	Constructor method. Creates a new XML object.

You can use these methods to locate specific parts of an XML document. For example, the following E4X expression:

```
countryXML.child("country");
```

returns the same XMLList as the following E4X expression:

```
countryXML.country;
```

You might use the first option when you need to use a string variable to refer to the node name. For example, you may need to generate the expression dynamically by passing the node name to a function.

You can use an index with the child method to return a specific child node:

```
countryXML.child("country")[0]
```

The attribute method works in the same way as the @ operator. The advantage of using the @ symbol is that it makes the E4X expressions shorter:

```
countryXML.country[0].attribute("abbreviation")
```

The toString and toXMLString methods deserve some special attention. You can use both methods to return a string representation of an XML object. However, there is a slight difference. Consider the following XML object:

```
private var simpleXML:XML = <username>sas</username>
```

The expression simpleXML.toString returns the text sas, whereas simpleXML.toXMLString returns <username>sas</username>.

In this case, the XML object contains only simple content; that is, a single node containing text. It means that the toString method will only return the text content inside the <username> element. The toXMLString method returns the full element, including the opening and closing tags.

If the XML object contained child elements or complex content, both the toString and toXMLString methods would return the same content. It would include all elements and text. If you use the trace method to display an XML or XMLList object *without* using either toString or toXMLString, the data will display using the toString method.

You can find whether an element contains complex content using the hasComplexContent and hasSimpleContent methods. Both return a Boolean value. Remember that simple content contains only text, whereas complex content contains child nodes.

In addition to the methods mentioned previously, several methods allow you to manipulate the content in an XML and XMLList object. Table 8-3 summarizes these methods.

Table 8-3. Methods of the XML class for modifying XML content

Method	Explanation
appendChild	Inserts a child node at the end of the child nodes collection of the specified node
copy	Creates a copy of a node
insertChildAfter	Inserts a child node after a specified child node
insertChildBefore	Inserts a child node before a specified child node
prependChild	Inserts a child node at the beginning of the child nodes of the specified node
replace	Replaces a specified property with a value
setChildren	Replaces children of an XML object with specified content

Let's see some of these methods in action.

Manipulating XML content

When manipulating XML content, common tasks include the following:

- Changing the values of nodes and attributes
- Adding new nodes
- Copying nodes
- Deleting nodes

We'll look at each task using the XML object from our earlier example:

```
var countryXML:XML = <countries>
  <country abbreviation="AU">
    <countryName>Australia</countryName>
    <countryHemisphere>Southern</countryHemisphere>
    <countryCurrency symbol="$">AUD</countryCurrency>
  </country>
  <country abbreviation="US">
    <countryName>United States</countryName>
    <countryHemisphere>Northern</countryHemisphere>
    <countryCurrency symbol="$">USD</countryCurrency>
  </country>
</countries>
```

Changing node and attribute values

You can update values by identifying the node or attributes to change with a valid path and then assigning a value using an equals = sign. For example, we can modify the following XML object:

```
var newCountry:XML = <country></country>;
```

by using the following ActionScript:

```
newCountry.@abbreviation = "NZ";
newCountry.countryName = "New Zealand";
newCountry.countryHemisphere = "Southern";
newCountry.countryCurrency = "NZD";
newCountry.countryCurrency.@id = "$";
```

We have added attributes with the @ operator and new nodes using dot notation. This approach is the same one that we'd use to add properties to any other type of object.

The preceding example gives the following XML output:

```
<country abbreviation="NZ">
  <countryName>New Zealand</countryName>
  <countryHemisphere>Southern</countryHemisphere>
  <countryCurrency id="$">NZD</countryCurrency>
</country>
```

Adding new nodes

You can add a new node after existing child nodes by using the appendChild method with an XML object:

```
var newCountry:XML = <country abbreviation="NZ">
    <countryName>New Zealand</countryName>
    <countryHemisphere>Southern</countryHemisphere>
    <countryCurrency symbol="$">NZD</countryCurrency>
  </country>
countryXML.appendChild(newCountry);
```

In this example, the <newCountry> child node will appear after all other <country> nodes within the countryXML object. We could add the new country after the first child using the following line:

```
countryXML.insertChildAfter(countryXML.country[0], newCountry);
```

We could also have used the insertChildBefore method to achieve the same result:

```
countryXML.insertChildBefore(countryXML.country[1], newCountry);
```

To add the child node to the beginning of the list, use the prependChild method:

```
countryXML.prependChild(newCountry);
```

Copying nodes

The copy method allows you to create a copy of an XML object. Doing so copies all the child nodes underneath the specified nodes. However, the copied XML object doesn't have any parent or location in an existing XML tree. You'll need to use appendChild, prependChild, insertChildAfter, or insertChildBefore to locate the copied object within another XML object:

```
var copyXML:XML = countryXML.country[0].copy();
countryXML.appendChild(copyXML);
```

The preceding example copies the first <country> node and uses appendChild to add it after the other <country> nodes.

Deleting nodes

You can use the delete operator to remove nodes from an XML object. In the following example, the second <country> node is removed from the countryXML object:

```
delete countryXML.country[1];
```

In the examples that we've worked through so far, we assigned XML content directly to an XML object. It's also possible to use the <mx:XML> tag to work with XML content.

Working with the <mx:XML> tag

The <mx:XML> tag allows you to work with literal XML content in an XML data model. It's similar to the <mx:Model> tag covered in Chapter 6. However, unlike the <mx:Model> tag, which creates a tree of ActionScript objects, the <mx:XML> tag compiles the data into an XML object. You can then work through this object using E4X expressions.

You can either add the content directly to the <mx:XML> tag or specify an external document source. The following shows how to declare the content of an <mx:XML> element explicitly:

```
<mx:XML id="books">
  <Library>
    <book>
      <title>{txtBookTitle.text}</title>
      <author>{txtAuthor.text}</author>
      <pubYear>{txtPubYear.text}</pubYear>
    </book>
  </Library>
</mx:XML>
```

In this example, we described a book, and the contents of each node are bound to components using curly braces notation. The <mx:XML> tag has the id of books, and we could use that within other binding expressions.

The content inside an <mx:XML> tag must be well formed XML. This means that it must have a single root element, use consistent case, nest correctly, and enclose attributes in quotes. You can find a summary of the term **well formed** in Chapter 7.

Another approach is to specify an external document source for the <mx:XML> tag using the source attribute, as shown here:

```
<mx:XML id="countryData" source="assets/countryList.xml"/>
```

As with the <mx:Model> tag, the <mx:XML> tag compiles the data into the SWF file instead of loading it at run time. This means that you can't modify the XML document and expect the application to update the content automatically.

You can traverse the contents of the <mx:XML> tag using E4X expressions. If you need to override this setting, you can use the ActionScript 2.0 XMLNode object instead by setting the format attribute of the tag to xml:

```
<mx:XML id="countryData" format="xml"/>
```

As you saw earlier, you can also use data binding expressions with content inside an XML data model.

The simple example that follows shows how to load a model from an XML document called countryXML.xml and use it to populate a ComboBox control. The external XML document follows:

```
<?xml version="1.0" encoding="UTF-8"?>
<countries>
  <country abbreviation="AU">
```

```
        <countryName>Australia</countryName>
        <countryHemisphere>Southern</countryHemisphere>
        <countryCurrency symbol="$">AUD</countryCurrency>
      </country>
      <country abbreviation="US">
        <countryName>United States</countryName>
        <countryHemisphere>Northern</countryHemisphere>
        <countryCurrency symbol="$">USD</countryCurrency>
      </country>
    </countries>
```

I've saved the document as countryXML.xml with the other chapter resources if you want to have a closer look at its structure. Add it to an assets folder within a new Flex project first if you are going to work through the following example.

The following application loads the external XML document using the <mx:XML> tag. It uses E4X expressions to reference the content:

```
<?xml version="1.0" encoding="utf-8"?>
<mx:Application xmlns:mx="http://www.adobe.com/2006/mxml"
  layout="absolute" creationComplete="loadCountries(event)">
  <mx:Script>
    <![CDATA[
      import mx.events.FlexEvent;
      private function loadCountries(e:FlexEvent):void{
        var countryNames:XMLList = countryData.country.countryName;
        cboCountry.dataProvider = countryNames;
      }
    ]]>
  </mx:Script>
  <mx:XML id="countryData" source="assets/countryXML.xml"/>
  <mx:HBox x="10" y="10">
    <mx:Label text="Country"/>
    <mx:ComboBox id="cboCountry"/>
  </mx:HBox>
</mx:Application>
```

The <mx:XML> tag countryData uses as its source the file countryXML.xml within the assets folder. The contents from this tag populate the cboCountry ComboBox when the application is complete using the loadCountries function.

The loadCountries function creates an XMLList called countryNames using the E4X expression countryData.country.countryName. It then assigns the XMLList directly to the dataProvider of the ComboBox control.

You can find this simple example saved as LoadXMLObject.mxml with the resource files. When you run the application, it populates the ComboBox control with the country names from the XML document. Note that because we're working with XML content, all element and attribute values are treated as strings.

So far in this chapter, most of our work has been with XML content stored within the application; in other words, client-side XML content. Even when we loaded XML content from an external source using the `<mx:XML>` tag, we couldn't dynamically update the XML content. These approaches aren't very flexible, so now we'll turn our attention to loading content from an external XML source using the same approaches as we saw with text content in Chapter 6.

Loading an external XML document

While you can create XML variables with ActionScript, it's much more flexible to load XML content from an external data source—either by accessing a static XML document or by requesting data from a server-side page. To do this, you can use the following classes:

- HTTPService class
- URLLoader class
- XMLSocket class

In this section, I want to focus on the first two approaches: the HTTPService and URLLoader classes. It's important to note that these classes use a request-response approach. The classes request the content, and the server responds by providing the relevant XML. If the XML content changes externally, the application would need to make a further request.

The XMLSocket class allows you to create a real-time connection to XML content so that any changes are pushed to the application automatically. This is in contrast with the HTTPService and URLLoader classes that must request information. When the external document changes, these classes must request the updated information again, although it is available automatically to the XMLSocket class. The XMLSocket class requires that the application runs on a socket server, so we won't explore that topic here.

You can use the HTTPService and URLLoader classes to load external XML content. You'd use the same approaches that we've seen in Chapter 6. The difference is that if we want to traverse the loaded content with E4X expressions, the HTTPService class needs to use the e4x resultFormat. If you're working with the URLLoader class, you need to cast the data property into XML format to be able to work with the loaded content using E4X expressions.

Let's work through examples of each of these approaches using the XML content that we saw earlier. The XML document that we'll use is called countryXML.xml, so you should add this file from your resources to the assets folder.

Using the <mx:HTTPService> tag

Let's work through an example in which we use the content from an XML document to populate a ComboBox control. If you haven't already created a new Flex application, do so now. In it, create an application with the following interface:

```
<?xml version="1.0" encoding="utf-8"?>
<mx:Application xmlns:mx="http://www.adobe.com/2006/mxml"
  layout="absolute">
  <mx:HBox x="10" y="10">
    <mx:Label id="txtLabel" text="Country"/>
```

```
        <mx:ComboBox id="cboCountries" />
    </mx:HBox>
</mx:Application>
```

This is a very simple application that will display a Label and ComboBox control inside an HBox container.

Add an <mx:HTTPService> tag, as shown above the <mx:HBox> element:

```
<mx:HTTPService id="xmlService" url="assets/countryXML.xml"
    resultFormat="e4x"/>
```

Notice that I've specified the resultFormat of e4x so I can use E4X expressions to target the content in the XML file.

We'll load the external document by calling the send method. We'll do this in the creationComplete event of the application by modifying the <mx:Application> tag, as shown here in bold:

```
<mx:Application xmlns:mx="http://www.adobe.com/2006/mxml"
    layout="absolute" creationComplete="xmlService.send()">
```

After the application is created, the send method will request the countryXML.xml document. The contents will be returned as an XML object, capable of being accessed with E4X expressions.

The final step is to bind the results returned from the xmlService to the dataProvider of the ComboBox control. Modify that control so the tag appears as shown here:

```
<mx:ComboBox id="cboCountries"
    dataProvider="{xmlService.lastResult.country.countryName}"/>
```

In this case, the dataProvider property of the ComboBox control is bound directly to the loaded content from the <mx:HTTPService> tag using an E4X expression. The expression xmlService.lastResult. country.countryName returns an XMLList object made up of the two country names Australia and United States. Notice that we didn't have to specify the root node <countries> because that is equivalent to the lastResult property of the <mx:HTTPService> tag.

Run the application and you should see a screen identical to the one shown in Figure 8-2.

Figure 8-2. The ComboBox populated from an XML document

You can find my finished file saved as LoadXMLHttpService.mxml with the other resources for the chapter. This simple example shows how easy it is to bind loaded external content directly to user interface components.

An alternative approach is to script the HTTPService class.

Using the HTTPService class with ActionScript

The following code block shows how you would script the same example. You might use this approach if you're working with ActionScript custom classes:

```
<?xml version="1.0" encoding="utf-8"?>
<mx:Application xmlns:mx="http://www.adobe.com/2006/mxml"
  layout="absolute" creationComplete="loadXML(event)">
  <mx:Script>
    <![CDATA[
      import mx.rpc.events.ResultEvent;
      import mx.rpc.http.HTTPService;
      import mx.events.FlexEvent;
      private var xmlService:HTTPService = new HTTPService();
      private function loadXML(e:FlexEvent):void {
        xmlService.url = "assets/countryXML.xml"
        xmlService.resultFormat = "e4x";
        xmlService.addEventListener(ResultEvent.RESULT, resultHandler);
        xmlService.send();
      }
      private function resultHandler(e:ResultEvent):void {
        cboCountries.dataProvider = e.target.lastResult.country.countryName;
      }
    ]]>
  </mx:Script>
  <mx:HBox x="10" y="10">
    <mx:Label id="txtLabel" text="Country"/>
    <mx:ComboBox id="cboCountries"/>
  </mx:HBox>
</mx:Application>
```

The script block starts by importing the relevant classes and declaring an HTTPService object called xmlService. The creationComplete event calls the loadXML function, which sets the url and resultFormat of the object. It also adds an event listener so that the function resultHandler is called when the response is received from the server. The function finishes by calling the send method to make the request for the XML document.

When the service receives a result in e4x format, it assigns the <countryName> nodes to the dataProvider of the ComboBox component. It does this by locating the lastResult property and appending the E4X expression country.countryName. Again, we didn't need to specify the <countries> node because it's equivalent to e.target.lastResult.

Running this application shows the same result as the one that appears in Figure 8-2. You can find the completed application saved in the file LoadXMLHttpServiceAS.mxml if you want to look at it more closely.

Using the URLLoader class

You can also load an external XML document using the URLLoader class. The loaded content is treated as a string, so you'll need to cast it as an XML object before you can traverse it with E4X expressions.

The following code shows how to load the same XML document into a ComboBox component using the URLLoader class:

```
<?xml version="1.0" encoding="utf-8"?>
<mx:Application xmlns:mx="http://www.adobe.com/2006/mxml"
  layout="absolute" creationComplete="loadXML(event)">
  <mx:Script>
    <![CDATA[
      import flash.net.URLLoader;
      import flash.net.URLRequest;
      import mx.events.FlexEvent;
      private var xmlLoader:URLLoader = new URLLoader();
      private var countryXML:XML;
      private function loadXML(e:FlexEvent):void {
        xmlLoader.addEventListener(Event.COMPLETE, completeHandler);
        xmlLoader.load(new URLRequest("assets/countryXML.xml"));
      }
      private function completeHandler(e:Event):void{
        countryXML = XML(e.target.data);
        cboCountries.dataProvider = countryXML.country.countryName;
      }
    ]]>
  </mx:Script>
  <mx:HBox x="10" y="10">
    <mx:Label id="txtLabel" text="Country"/>
    <mx:ComboBox id="cboCountries"/>
  </mx:HBox>
</mx:Application>
```

This application starts by loading the relevant classes, including URLLoader and URLRequest. It declares two variables, one for the URLLoader object, called xmlLoader, and one for the loaded XML variable, called countryXML.

The loading of the external XML file is handled with the loadXML function, which is called in response to the creationComplete event of the application. The function adds an event listener to the URLLoader object that calls the completeHandler function when the response is received and the complete event is dispatched. The function finishes by calling the load method to request the XML document.

When the external content finishes loading, the completeHandler function targets the loaded content using e.target.data. It casts this content as an XML object and assigns it to the countryXML object. We can then use the E4X expression countryXML.country.countryName to create an XMLList of the country names and set that object as the dataProvider for the ComboBox control.

I've saved this example under the name LoadXMLURLLoader.mxml with the other resources. Running the application shows the same result as that depicted in Figure 8-2.

Problem solving

If you are having difficulties writing the correct E4X expressions to target specific parts of the loaded XML document, you can always trace the loaded content using the toXMLString method. A good approach is to add the following to the result handler function for the HTTPService and click the debug button instead of running the application:

```
trace (e.target.lastResult.toXMLString());
```

In debug mode, the content will display in the Console view in Flex Builder, as shown in Figure 8-3.

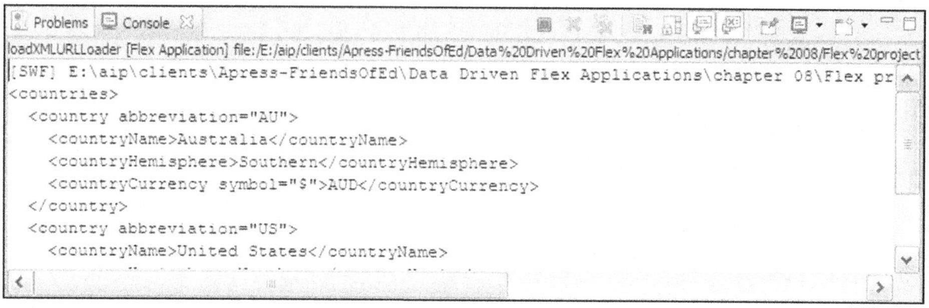

Figure 8-3. The toXMLString method provides a string representation of an XML object.

You can use the following with the URLLoader class:

```
trace (XML(e.target.data).toXMLString());
```

You can also write trace statements that use E4X expressions to check that you've constructed the expression correctly.

In our first example, we used a curly braces binding expression to assign the loaded content from the <mx:HTTPService> tag to the dataProvider of a ComboBox control. You can also use data binding when working with ActionScript.

Binding XML content with E4X expressions

Curly braces binding expressions allow you to bind a property of a control directly to a value or property from a loaded XML document. You can use an E4X expression to identify which part of the document should be bound to the property of the target component.

If you assign the loaded XML content to an ActionScript XML object, you can still use curly braces binding with properties of other controls. Before you do this, though, you need to make sure that the XML object is a bindable variable by adding the [Bindable] metatag above its declaration:

```
[Bindable]
private var loadedXML:XML;
```

Once you populate this variable with XML content, you can then add E4X expressions within curly braces as shown here:

```
<mx:ComboBox id="cboCountries"
  dataProvider="{loadedXML.lastResult.country.countryName}"/>
```

The previous example would bind the <countryName> XMLList within the <country> nodes to the dataProvider property of the cboCountries component.

Another approach is to use the <mx:Binding> tag to create the binding using an E4X expression. Again, make sure that the XML document is loaded into a bindable variable by adding the [Bindable] metatag above its declaration.

If you're not familiar with the <mx:Binding> tag, it has source and destination properties that create a binding just as you would do using curly braces. You can include E4X expressions in the source property, as shown here:

```
<mx:Binding source="{loadedXML.lastResult.country.countryName}"
  destination="cboCountries.dataProvider" />
```

This example achieves the same outcome as in the previous example.

Before we move on to look at web services, let's see a more complex example in which we load an RSS feed into a Flex application. As before, we'll use both the HTTPService and URLLoader classes in the next sections.

Working through an example

RSS feeds are a very common way for web site owners to provide up-to-date information to site visitors. Because of their popularity, it's common for developers to build applications that consume these feeds. RSS feeds provide their information using a standard XML vocabulary. In fact, there are several different standards that feeds can use and they can target different parts of the feed using E4X expressions, provided that the developer knows which vocabulary is in use.

In this example, we'll load content from the Adobe Flex Top issues feed at http://rss. adobe.com/www/support/top/top_flex.xml. You'll see how to do this using the <mx:HTTPService> tag with data binding.

Start by creating a new Flex application with the following interface:

```
<?xml version="1.0" encoding="utf-8"?>
<mx:Application xmlns:mx="http://www.adobe.com/2006/mxml"
  layout="absolute">
  <mx:VBox x="10" y="10">
    <mx:Label text=" Flex: Top Issues" fontWeight="bold"/>
    <mx:TextArea id="txtMessages" width="400" height="100"/>
    <mx:List id="lstHeadlines" width="400" height="100"/>
    <mx:HBox>
      <mx:Label text="Summary" fontWeight="bold" width="80"/>
      <mx:Text id="txtSummary" width="300"/>
```

```
          </mx:HBox>
          <mx:HBox>
          <mx:Label text="Date" fontWeight="bold" width="80"/>
            <mx:Text id="txtDate"/>
          </mx:HBox>
          <mx:Button label="Read more"/>
        </mx:VBox>
    </mx:Application>
```

Figure 8-4 shows how the interface appears when you run the application.

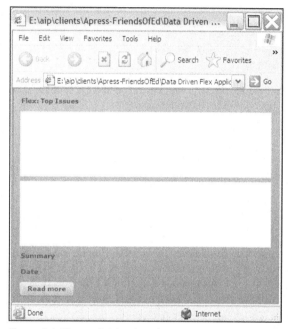

Figure 8-4. The application interface

We'll add an <mx:HTTPService> tag that requests the news feed. Add the following below the opening <mx:Application> tag:

```
    <mx:HTTPService id="rssService" resultFormat="e4x"
      url="http://rss.adobe.com/www/support/top/top_flex.xml"
      showBusyCursor="true"/>
```

This tag requests the feed at the specified url, returning the results in e4x format. This will allow us to use E4X expressions to target specific parts of the feed. Notice that the tag also specifies that it will display a busy cursor while the request is under way.

We'll send the request by modifying the <mx:Application> tag, as shown here:

```
    <mx:Application xmlns:mx="http://www.adobe.com/2006/mxml"
      layout="absolute" creationComplete="rssService.send()">
```

To check what is loaded, we'll bind the results of the request directly to the TextArea control. Modify the control as shown here:

```
<mx:TextArea id="txtMessages" width="400" height="100"
    text="{rssService.lastResult.toXMLString()}"/>
```

The binding expression uses the toXMLString method to display the response from the rssService request, retrieved with the lastResult property. We need to do this so we can display a string representation of the XML object in the TextArea.

When you test the application, you should see that the XML returned from the RSS feed displays in the TextArea control. You may need to wait for a second or two while the content loads. Figure 8-5 shows how this appears.

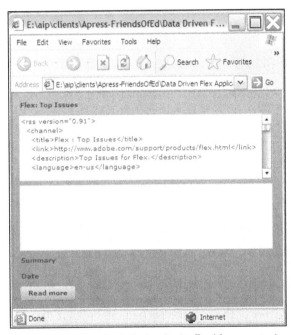

Figure 8-5. The RSS feed displays in the TextArea control.

Provided that we've successfully requested the feed, we can now bind the news items from the loaded results directly to the dataProvider property of the List control. Each news item appears as an <item> element inside the <channel> element of the feed. You can check this by loading the feed into a web browser to see the structure or simply by scrolling through the TextArea.

We'll bind the entire <item> element to the dataProvider property, even though we only want the title to display. By doing this, we can then bind other controls to the selectedItem from the List control and specify exactly which child node we want to appear.

Modify the List control as shown here:

```
<mx:List id="lstHeadlines" width="400" height="100"
    dataProvider="{rssService.lastResult.channel.item}"
    labelField="title"/>
```

We've used the E4X expression `channel.item` as a path from the `rssService.lastResult` property to return an XMLList containing all items within the news feed. To display the title, we need to set the `labelField` property.

Before testing the application, remove the TextArea element completely to make the interface a little less crowded. Figure 8-6 shows what happens when you do this and test the application.

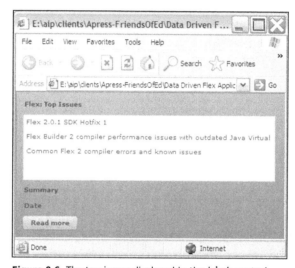

Figure 8-6. The top issues displayed in the List control

The last steps are to display the summary and date for the selected news item, and to enable the Read more button so that we can click it to see the news item at the external site. In each case, we can use a binding to the `selectedItem` of the List control because the List `dataProvider` includes all child elements.

Modify the txtSummary control as shown here:

```
<mx:Text id="txtSummary" width="300"
    text="{lstHeadlines.selectedItem.description}"/>
```

The Text control will display the `description` associated with the item selected from the List. You can use the same approach with the txtDate control:

```
<mx:Text id="txtDate" text="{lstHeadlines.selectedItem.edited}"/>
```

Finally, we'll modify the button so that we can view more details about the selected news item:

```
<mx:Button label="Read more"
  click="{navigateToURL(new URLRequest(lstHeadlines.selectedItem. ➥
  link), '_blank')}"/>
```

We've added a click handler that calls the navigateToURL method, passing the selected link as a URLRequest and specifying that we want to open the URL in a new browser window.

Figure 8-7 shows the effect of running the application and choosing an item from the List control. When you click the Read more button, the page containing further details of the feed item should open in a new browser window.

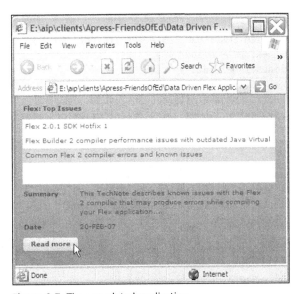

Figure 8-7. The completed application

In this example, we used an <mx:HTTPService> tag with data binding expressions to load and display information from an RSS feed. I saved the finished example file as RssFeedHttpService.mxml with the other resources in case you want to have a closer look.

The following code block shows how to achieve the same outcome by scripting the HTTPService class. You can see that it's a lot more complicated than using the <mx:HTTPService> tag. However, there may be times when you need to create this functionality using ActionScript; for example, in a custom class:

```
<?xml version="1.0" encoding="utf-8"?>
<mx:Application xmlns:mx="http://www.adobe.com/2006/mxml"
  layout="absolute" creationComplete="requestRSS(event)">
  <mx:Script>
    <![CDATA[
```

```
        import mx.rpc.http.HTTPService;
        import mx.events.FlexEvent;
        import flash.events.Event;
        import mx.rpc.events.ResultEvent;
        import flash.events.MouseEvent;
        private var rssService:HTTPService = new HTTPService();
        private function requestRSS(e:FlexEvent):void {
          rssService.url = "http://rss.adobe.com/www/support/top/➥
            top_flex.xml"
          rssService.resultFormat = "e4x";
          rssService.addEventListener(ResultEvent.RESULT, ➥
            resultHandler);
          rssService.send();
        }
        private function resultHandler(e:ResultEvent):void {
          lstHeadlines.dataProvider = e.target.lastResult.channel.item;
          lstHeadlines.labelField = "title";
        }
        private function showDetails(e:Event):void{
          txtSummary.text = lstHeadlines.selectedItem.description;
          txtDate.text = lstHeadlines.selectedItem.edited;
          btnReadMore.addEventListener(MouseEvent.CLICK, showURL);
        }
        private function showURL(e:MouseEvent):void {
          var link:String = lstHeadlines.selectedItem.link;
          var request:URLRequest = new URLRequest(link);
          navigateToURL(request, "_blank");
        }
      ]]>
    </mx:Script>
    <mx:VBox x="10" y="10">
      <mx:Label text="Flex: Top Issues" fontWeight="bold"/>
      <mx:List id="lstHeadlines" width="400" height="100"
        change="showDetails(event)"/>
      <mx:HBox>
        <mx:Label text="Summary" fontWeight="bold" width="80"/>
        <mx:Text id="txtSummary" width="300"/>
      </mx:HBox>
      <mx:HBox>
        <mx:Label text="Date" fontWeight="bold" width="80"/>
        <mx:Text id="txtDate"/>
      </mx:HBox>
      <mx:Button id="btnReadMore" label="Read more"/>
    </mx:VBox>
</mx:Application>
```

In this application, all the RSS processing is handled with ActionScript. The script block imports the relevant classes and creates an HTTPService object called rssService. The requestRSS function configures the object in response to the creationComplete event of the application. The function finishes by calling the send method to make the request.

When the HTTPService responds, the resultHandler function processes the content, setting the dataProvider for the List control. We use the same E4X expression e.target.lastResult. channel.item to target the <item> nodes. The resultHandler function also sets the labelField so that the title displays within the List control.

The List control has a change handler attribute that calls the showDetails function when a new item is selected. When the user selects an item in the control, the function sets the text properties of the txtSummary and txtDate controls using the selectedItem from the List control. It also sets the click handler for the Button control.

When a user clicks the Read more button, the showURL function requests the relevant URL, specifying that is should load into a blank browser window.

Running the application will create the same outcome as with the previous example. Neither approach is better than the other, although using ActionScript creates more lines of code. The approach you choose depends on whether you prefer to script the HTTPService class or work with the corresponding tag.

This application is saved as RssFeedHttpServiceAS.mxml with your resources.

As a final example, the following code block uses a URLLoader object to request the RSS feed:

```
<?xml version="1.0" encoding="utf-8"?>
<mx:Application xmlns:mx="http://www.adobe.com/2006/mxml"
  layout="absolute" creationComplete="requestRSS(event)">
  <mx:Script>
    <![CDATA[
      import flash.net.URLLoader;
      import flash.net.URLRequest;
      import mx.rpc.events.ResultEvent;
      import mx.events.FlexEvent;
      import flash.events.MouseEvent;
      private var rssLoader:URLLoader = new URLLoader();
      private var rssXML:XML;
      private function requestRSS(e:FlexEvent):void {
        lstHeadlines.addEventListener(Event.CHANGE, showDetails);
        rssLoader.addEventListener(Event.COMPLETE, completeHandler);
        var strURL:String = "http://rss.adobe.com/www/support/top/➥
          top_flex.xml";
        rssLoader.load(new URLRequest(strURL));
      }
```

```
            private function completeHandler(e:Event):void{
              rssXML = XML(e.target.data);
              lstHeadlines.dataProvider = rssXML.channel.item;
              lstHeadlines.labelField = "title";
            }
            private function showDetails(e:Event):void{
                txtSummary.text = lstHeadlines.selectedItem.description;
                txtDate.text = lstHeadlines.selectedItem.edited;
                btnReadMore.addEventListener(MouseEvent.CLICK, showURL);
            }
            private function showURL(e:MouseEvent):void {
              var link:String = lstHeadlines.selectedItem.link;
              var request:URLRequest = new URLRequest(link);
              navigateToURL(request, "_blank");
            }
        ]]>
      </mx:Script>
      <mx:VBox x="10" y="10">
        <mx:Label text="Flex: Top Issues" fontWeight="bold"/>
        <mx:List id="lstHeadlines" width="400" height="100"/>
          <mx:HBox>
          <mx:Label text="Summary" fontWeight="bold" width="80"/>
          <mx:Text id="txtSummary" width="300"/>
        </mx:HBox>
        <mx:HBox>
          <mx:Label text="Date" fontWeight="bold" width="80"/>
          <mx:Text id="txtDate"/>
        </mx:HBox>
        <mx:Button id="btnReadMore" label="Read more"/>
      </mx:VBox>
    </mx:Application>
```

In this application, the RSS feed is requested with a URLLoader object. As much of the code is the same as in the previous example, I'll focus on the main differences here.

The requestRSS function sets up the URLLoader object and adds a change handler for the List control. The relevant event that we need to capture to detect the successful loading of the RSS feed is the complete event instead of the result event used by the HTTPService class. We will respond with the completeHandler function when this event is dispatched.

The requestRSS function calls the load method to access the RSS feed instead of the send method used with the HTTPService class.

The completeHandler function accesses the loaded content using the data property of the URLLoader. The code must cast this as an XML object so we can use E4X expressions to find our way through the content. As before, this function sets the dataProvider and labelField for the List control.

The rest of the code is the same as in the previous example. You can find the file saved as RssFeedURLLoader.mxml with the other chapter resources. You should see the same outcome when you run the example.

Let's move on to look at the topic of web services. In its broadest sense, an RSS feed is a web service; however, we'll focus on a different type of web service, those using the SOAP protocol in the next section.

Consuming web services

A web service is a remote procedure that provides results in XML format. You might use it to look up a currency exchange rate, to access local weather information, or even as a way to connect to a local server. The key point is that the services are usually provided on remote computers; that is, those computers running at a different location from the current application.

Web services exist to provide access to important enterprise-level systems to users in a way that can be regulated. They are an intermediate layer that defines what the users can and cannot do when they interact with the system.

Each web service has an associated Web Services Description Language (WSDL) file that describes the different functions that are available and how to access them. The functions available at the web service are operations within the WSDL file. This file describes what parameters are required, their data types, as well as what the operation returns to the user. WSDL is a vocabulary of XML, so you can view the URL of the WSDL file in a web browser if you want to see what details it contains.

There are many different protocols for working with web services, and Flex includes support for SOAP-based services. SOAP messages are requests and responses from a web service that use a particular XML structure. You don't need to know this structure because Flex will create the SOAP messages automatically, provided that you can specify a WSDL file. Flex will also interpret the returned SOAP message containing the response from the server.

If you're interested in finding out more, you can read about SOAP 1.2 at the W3C web site in the following pages:

- www.w3.org/TR/2003/REC-soap12-part0-20030624/ (SOAP primer)
- www.w3.org/TR/2003/REC-soap12-part1-20030624/ (Messaging framework)
- www.w3.org/TR/2003/REC-soap12-part2-20030624/ (Adjuncts)

Flex includes a class dedicated to working with SOAP web services: the WebService class.

Working with the WebService class

You can use the WebService class to make requests of a SOAP web service. You can either use the <mx:WebService> tag or write corresponding ActionScript. You'll need to know the WSDL of the web service, the name of any operations that you want to call, the parameters required by those operations, and the data and type returned.

You can find all of these details within the WSDL file for the web service. Because it's just an XML document, you can view it in a web browser by loading the URL. Figure 8-8 shows a sample WSDL with the relevant elements displayed.

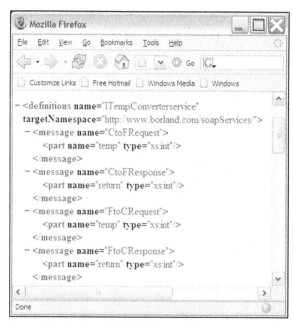

Figure 8-8. Viewing a WSDL file in a web browser

As far as developers are concerned, the most important parts within the WSDL file are the <message> elements. These elements contain details about the operation request and response, including the name of the operation. Remove the text Request and Response from the <message> name attribute to find the name of the operation. In Figure 8-8 you can see the CtoF and FtoC operations.

Each message indicates the parameters that are either required or returned, and they are identified by the <part> element. The <part> element also identifies the data type of the parameter. These can either be one of the built-in data types or a custom data type also defined in the WSDL file.

In Figure 8-8, the CtoF operation requires that a single parameter temp is sent with the request. It is an xs:int data type that corresponds to the ActionScript type int. The operation returns a single parameter, return, which is also of the same data type.

Let's learn more about the WebService class by looking at its properties and methods.

Properties of the WebService class

The WebService class has many properties, and Table 8-4 shows the most commonly used.

Table 8-4. Properties of the WebService class

Property	Type	Explanation	Default value
description	String	Provides the description of the service	
destination	String	Determines the destination for the service and matches an entry in the services-config.xml file	

Property	Type	Explanation	Default value
endpointURI	String	Sets the location of the web service if overriding the WSDL location	
headers	Array	Returns the SOAP headers registered for the web service	
port	String	Specifies the port to use with the web service	
ready	Boolean	Indicates whether the web service is ready for requests	
service	String	Specifies which remote operation the web service should use	
useProxy	Boolean	Specifies whether to use the Flex proxy service	false
wsdl	String	Specifies the location for the WSDL for the web service	

The WebService class also has a number of methods.

Methods of the WebService class

Table 8-5 shows the methods of the WebService class.

Table 8-5. Methods of the WebService class

Method	Explanation
canLoadWSDL	Returns a Boolean value indicating whether the web service has a valid WSDL or destination specified.
getOperation	Returns the operation specified from the web service.
loadWSDL	Loads the WSDL for the web service. Requires a value for the destination or wsdl property.
WebService	Constructor that creates a new web service.

In the next section, we'll see how to consume a SOAP web service using the <mx:WebService> tag.

Creating the web service request

You can create a web service request using the following tag:

```
<mx:WebService id="wsRequest"
    wsdl="urlToTheWSDL">
```

255

In the preceding tag, I've included an id attribute as well as the wsdl attribute, which specifies the URL for the WSDL file describing the operations of the web service. In ActionScript, you'd do it like this:

```
var wsRequest:WebService = new WebService();
wsRequest.loadWSDL("urlToTheWSDL");
```

In ActionScript, you can also set the wsdl property and call the loadWSDL method without passing in any parameters:

```
wsRequest.wsdl = "urlToTheWSDL";
wsRequest.loadWSDL();
```

If you want to bind the results from a web service request made with ActionScript, you'll need to use the [Bindable] tag when you declare the web service object:

```
[Bindable]
var wsRequest:WebService = new WebService();
```

This will allow you to use curly brace expressions in the bound properties of your other components.

You may also want to display a busy cursor while the request is taking place using the following showBusyCursor attribute:

```
<mx:WebService id="wsRequest"
  wsdl=" urlToTheWSDL"
  showBusyCursor="true">
```

There is no corresponding ActionScript property of the WebService class.

Once you've set up the <mx:WebService> tag, you need to specify which operations you'll call.

Specifying the operation

Each type of remote procedure available in the web service is called an operation, and you need to specify the operation that you want to call, optionally sending the relevant arguments to the web service. The values for these arguments frequently come from entries made to user interface components in the application, so it's common to see binding expressions in this area.

As you saw earlier, any required arguments and their data type are available by looking at the WSDL file. You need to add them using an <mx:operation> tag between the opening and closing <mx:WebService> elements. Every argument that you want to send appears inside the <mx:request> element:

```
<mx:operation name="operationName">
  <mx:request>
    <param1>Value 1</param1>
    <param2>Value 2</param2>
  </mx:request>
</mx:operation>
```

You may want to bind these arguments to other components in the application. The following code shows how you might use bindings when specifying parameters:

```
<mx:operation name="operationName">
  <mx:request>
    <param1>{controlID.boundProperty}</param1>
    <param2>{controlID.boundProperty}</param2>
  </mx:request>
</mx:operation>
```

It's a little more complicated to specify the operation in ActionScript. You can do so in the following way by creating an AbstractOperation object:

```
var wsOperation:AbstractOperation;
wsOperation = wsRequest["operationName"];
```

You need to declare the operation as the type AbstractOperation and associate it with the web services request, passing a string for the name of the operation.

Each of the arguments for the operation must be created as properties of an object. You can then set that object as the arguments property of the web service request, as shown here:

```
var args = new Object();
args.param1 = "value 1";
args.param2 = "value 2";
wsRequest.arguments = args;
```

Once you've set up the WebService object, you need to make the request.

Making the request

You can consume the web service by referring to the id of the WebService component, the operation name, and calling the send method, as shown here:

```
wsRequest.operationName.send();
```

In ActionScript, it's even simpler. You just use the name of the web service and call the send method:

```
wsRequest.send();
```

You can also call the operation directly:

```
wsRequest.wsOperation();
```

This approach allows you to pass parameters with the call to the operation using either approach contained within the following two lines of code:

```
wsRequest.wsOperation("value 1", "value 2");
wsRequest.wsOperation.send("value 1", "value 2");
```

Requesting the web service will result in a response that either contains the results of the request or an error message.

Receiving a response

The web service will respond, sending either the response arguments specified in the WSDL file or by notifying that a fault occurred. You can specify handlers for both the result and fault events dispatched by the web service in the <mx:WebService> tag:

```
<mx:WebService id="wsRequest"
  wsdl=" urlToTheWSDL"
  showBusyCursor="true"
  result="resultHandler(event)"
  fault="faultHandler(event)"/>
```

In ActionScript, you can use the addEventListener method to assign event handlers that respond when either event is dispatched:

```
wsRequest.addEventListener(ResultEvent.RESULT, resultHandler);
wsRequest.addEventListener(FaultEvent.FAULT, faultHandler);
```

The result event handler receives a ResultEvent as an argument while the fault handler receives a FaultEvent.

Accessing the web service response

Like the HTTPService class, you can identify the returned results from the web service by accessing the lastResult property of the operation. You need to use the name of the returned parameter to identify which value to display:

```
wsRequest.operationName.lastResult.returnedParam;
```

If the request returns a single parameter, it's also possible to access the response using the toString method:

```
wsRequest.operationName.lastResult.toString();
```

You use the same approach regardless of whether you're using the <mx:WebService> tag or ActionScript. If the web service is declared as Bindable, you can use either expression above inside curly braces within a bound component property.

Understanding data types

One advantage of using the WebService class is that many of the built-in data types specified in the WSDL are converted to ActionScript 3.0 data types. For example, if the WSDL specifies a return value that uses the data type xs:int, Flex recognizes this as an int data type once the content is loaded. This doesn't occur when you load an external XML document, in which all element and attributes values are treated as strings. Bear in mind that custom data types won't have an equivalent value in ActionScript.

Table 8-6 shows how the data types listed in the WSDL document convert to ActionScript 3.0 data types.

Table 8-6. Actionscript conversions of SOAP data types

SOAP data type	ActionScript data type
xs:string	String
xs:int	int
xs:float	Number
xs:boolean	Boolean
xs:date	Date

We'll work through an example so you can see the different ways to consume a web service.

Consuming a web service with the <mx:WebService> tag

In this example, we'll consume a web service that provides temperature conversion services. We can convert from Celsius to Fahrenheit or the reverse. We need to specify the starting temperature as an integer, as well as the direction of the conversion.

The WSDL for the web service is located at http://developerdays.com/cgi-bin/tempconverter.exe/ wsdl/ITempConverter. Figure 8-8 shows this WSDL file viewed in a web browser. You can see that it shows CtoF and FtoC operations that take an integer called temp as a parameter.

These operations both return a parameter that is an integer called return. Because return is a reserved word in Flex, using this variable name is likely to cause a compiler error, so we'll need to deal with that minor issue when we access the response.

Start by creating a new application file with the following interface:

```
<?xml version="1.0" encoding="utf-8"?>
<mx:Application xmlns:mx="http://www.adobe.com/2006/mxml"
  layout="absolute">
  <mx:VBox x="10" y="10">
    <mx:Label text="Temperature converter" fontWeight="bold"/>
    <mx:HBox>
      <mx:Label text="Enter temperature" width="120"/>
      <mx:TextInput id="txtTemp" width="50"/>
    </mx:HBox>
    <mx:HBox>
      <mx:Label text="Choose type" width="120"/>
      <mx:ComboBox id="cboTempType">
        <mx:dataProvider>
          <mx:Object label="Celsius to Fahrenheit" data="CtoF"/>
          <mx:Object label="Fahrenheit to Celsius" data="FtoC"/>
        </mx:dataProvider>
      </mx:ComboBox>
```

```
        </mx:HBox>
        <mx:Button id="btnConvert" label="Convert" />
        <mx:Text id="txtConvertedTemp"/>
      </mx:VBox>
    </mx:Application>
```

Figure 8-9 shows how the interface appears when you run the application.

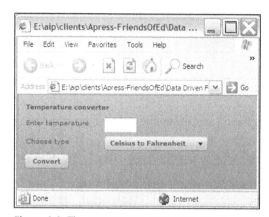

Figure 8-9. The temperature conversion interface

You can enter a temperature in a `TextInput` control and choose a conversion type from a `ComboBox`. When you want to carry out the conversion, click the Convert button.

If you look at the WSDL for the web service that we'll be using, you can see that it takes an integer as the parameter for the temperature conversion. We'll add a validator to detect that the user has made a correct entry before requesting the web service. We don't want to create an error by sending a blank value or a string.

Add the following element below the opening `<mx:Application>` tag:

```
<mx:NumberValidator id="tempValidator"
  source="{txtTemp}" property="text"
  trigger="{btnConvert}" triggerEvent="click"
  precision="0" required="true"
  invalid="txtConvertedTemp.text='Please enter a whole number'"/>
```

The validator validates that the entry in the `txtTemp` `TextInput` is a whole number by using a precision value of 0. The `required` property indicates that we must also have an entry before the content is considered to be valid. Validation occurs when we click the `Button` control because we specified the `click` event of the bound `btnConvert` control as the trigger. If the entry is invalid, we display the message Please enter a whole number in the `txtConvertedTemp` control.

We'll make the web service request using a `WebService` tag. Add the following tag above the opening `<mx:VBox>` element:

```
<mx:WebService id="tempService"
  wsdl="http://developerdays.com/cgi-bin/tempconverter.exe/wsdl/➥
```

```
        ITempConverter" showBusyCursor="true"
        result="resultHandler(event)" fault="faultHandler(event)">
        <mx:operation name="CtoF">
          <mx:request>
            <temp>{int(txtTemp.text)}</temp>
          </mx:request>
        </mx:operation>
        <mx:operation name="FtoC">
          <mx:request>
            <temp>{int(txtTemp.text)}</temp>
          </mx:request>
        </mx:operation>
      </mx:WebService>
```

The tag creates a WebService with the id of tempService that uses the WSDL that I listed earlier. It will show a busy cursor while the request is in progress. The web service sets two handlers: one for the result event and one for the fault event.

The web service identifies two operations, CtoF and FtoC, corresponding with the direction of the conversion. In each operation, we send a single parameter temp, which is bound to the value in the txtTemp control. Notice that we have used int to cast the string contents as an integer:

```
        <temp>{int(txtTemp.text)}</temp>
```

We'll make the web service request after determining that the entry in the txtTemp control is valid. We do this in response to the valid event, so modify the validator as shown in bold here:

```
        <mx:NumberValidator id="tempValidator"
          source="{txtTemp}" property="text"
          trigger="{btnConvert}" triggerEvent="click"
          precision="0" required="true"
          invalid="txtConvertedTemp.text='Please enter a whole number'"
          valid="callWS(event)"/>
```

Clicking the btnConvert button invokes the validator. If the entry is valid, the tag calls the callWS function passing a ValidationResultEvent object. We need to add that function now inside an ActionScript block below the opening <mx:Application> tag:

```
        <mx:Script>
          <![CDATA[
            import mx.events.ValidationResultEvent;
            private function callWS(e:ValidationResultEvent):void {
              if (cboTempType.selectedItem.data == "CtoF") {
                tempService.CtoF.send();
              }
              else {
                tempService.FtoC.send();
              }
            }
          ]]>
        </mx:Script>
```

Flex Builder should automatically add the import statement when you enter the ValidationResultEvent type. The callWS function tests the data associated with the selectedItem of the ComboBox control. It calls the send method, specifying the appropriate operation name.

We also need to write the handler functions for the result and fault events. Add the following functions to the script block:

```
private function resultHandler(e:ResultEvent):void {
  if (cboTempType.selectedItem.data == "CtoF") {
    txtConvertedTemp.text = txtTemp.text + " Celsius converts to " + ➡
      e.target.CtoF.lastResult.toString() + " Fahrenheit";
  }
  else {
    txtConvertedTemp.text = txtTemp.text + " Fahrenheit converts to "➡
      + e.target.FtoC.lastResult.toString() + " Celsius";
  }
}
private function faultHandler(e:FaultEvent):void {
  txtConvertedTemp.text = e.fault.faultString;
}
```

The resultHandler function responds when we receive a response from the web service. It accesses the result using e.target.CtoF.lastResult.toString(). The function checks for the type of conversion and displays an appropriate message, including this response.

Unfortunately for us, the operation returns a single value called return. As I mentioned earlier, this will cause some errors when we try to compile the SWF file because return is a reserved word in ActionScript. As we're only receiving a single value from the web service, we can cheat a little and access it through the lastResult property. This property will only contain the integer corresponding to the converted value. We can then display the value in the interface as a string by calling the toString method.

The faultHandler function responds when a fault message is returned from the web service. It displays the returned faultString value in the txtConvertedTemp control.

Before you run the application, check that the script block includes the following import statements. If they haven't been added automatically, you need to enter them yourself:

```
import mx.rpc.events.FaultEvent;
import mx.rpc.events.ResultEvent;
import mx.events.ValidationResultEvent;
```

Run the application and enter a temperature value to convert. Choose the type of conversion and click the Convert button. Figure 8-10 shows the resulting output when we convert 40 degrees Celsius to Fahrenheit.

You can find the completed file saved as WebServiceTempConvert.mxml with your chapter resources.

You can also set up the web service using ActionScript.

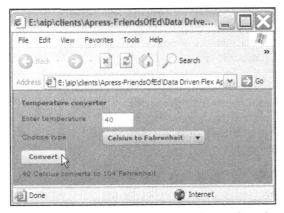

Figure 8-10. Converting a temperature using a web service

Consuming a web service with ActionScript

The complete code for the ActionScript version of the application follows:

```
<?xml version="1.0" encoding="utf-8"?>
<mx:Application xmlns:mx="http://www.adobe.com/2006/mxml"
  layout="absolute" creationComplete="initWS(event)">
  <mx:Script>
    <![CDATA[
      import mx.events.ValidationResultEvent;
      import mx.rpc.events.FaultEvent;
      import mx.rpc.events.ResultEvent;
      import mx.events.FlexEvent;
      import mx.rpc.soap.WebService;
      import mx.rpc.AbstractOperation;
      private var tempService:WebService = new WebService();
      private var wsOperation:AbstractOperation;
      private var operationArguments:Object = new Object();
      private function initWS(e:FlexEvent):void {
        var wsdlURL:String = "http://developerdays.com/cgi-bin/➥
        tempconverter.exe/wsdl/ITempConverter";
        tempService.loadWSDL(wsdlURL);
        tempService.addEventListener(ResultEvent.RESULT, ➥
          resultHandler);
        tempService.addEventListener(FaultEvent.FAULT, faultHandler);
      }
      private function callWS(e:ValidationResultEvent):void {
        if (cboTempType.selectedItem.data == "CtoF") {
          wsOperation = tempService["CtoF"];
        }
        else {
          wsOperation = tempService["FtoC"];
        }
```

```
            txtConvertedTemp.text = "Calling web service";
            operationArguments.temp = int(txtTemp.text);
            wsOperation.arguments = operationArguments;
            wsOperation.send();
          }
          private function resultHandler(e:ResultEvent):void{
            if (cboTempType.selectedItem.data == "CtoF") {
              txtConvertedTemp.text = txtTemp.text + " Celsius converts➡
                to " + e.target.CtoF.lastResult.toString() + ➡
                " Fahrenheit";
            }
            else {
              txtConvertedTemp.text = txtTemp.text + " Fahrenheit➡
              converts to " + e.target.FtoC.lastResult.toString()➡
              + " Celsius";
            }
          }
          private function faultHandler(e:FaultEvent):void {
            txtConvertedTemp.text = e.fault.faultString;
          }
      ]]>
    </mx:Script>
    <mx:NumberValidator id="tempValidator"
      source="{txtTemp}" property="text"
      trigger="{btnConvert}" triggerEvent="click"
      precision="0" required="true"
      invalid="txtConvertedTemp.text='Please enter a whole number'"
      valid="callWS(event)"/>
    <mx:VBox x="10" y="10">
      <mx:Label text="Temperature converter" fontWeight="bold"/>
      <mx:HBox>
        <mx:Label text="Enter temperature" width="120"/>
        <mx:TextInput id="txtTemp" width="50"/>
      </mx:HBox>
      <mx:HBox>
        <mx:Label text="Choose type" width="120"/>
        <mx:ComboBox id="cboTempType">
          <mx:dataProvider>
            <mx:Object label="Celsius to Fahrenheit" data="CtoF"/>
            <mx:Object label="Fahrenheit to Celsius" data="FtoC"/>
          </mx:dataProvider>
        </mx:ComboBox>
      </mx:HBox>
      <mx:Button id="btnConvert" label="Convert"/>
      <mx:Text id="txtConvertedTemp"/>
    </mx:VBox>
</mx:Application>
```

The code block starts by importing the relevant classes and declaring variables for the WebService, the operation, and the operation arguments object, operationArguments. The first function, initWS, is called in the creationComplete event of the application. This function loads the WSDL for the web service using the loadWSDL method. It also adds event listeners for the result and fault events of the web service.

We don't call the send method of the web service until we've validated the contents of the txtTemp control. When we know we have an integer value, we determine which operation to use from the data property of the selectedItem in the ComboBox.

The function then displays the text Calling web service. It adds the temp argument to the operation and sends the web service request using the send method.

The resultHandler function handles the response from the web service and operates in the same way as you saw in the previous example. The faultHandler function does the same.

Running the application will display the same screenshot that appears in Figure 8-10. You can find the completed example with the other resources saved as WebServiceTempConvertAS.mxml.

Summary

In this chapter, we saw how to include XML content within a Flex application. We started by understanding the changes to the XML class introduced with ActionScript 3.0. We looked at how to construct E4X expressions to traverse an XML document. We also explored the methods and properties of both the XML and XMLList classes and used them to manipulate XML content.

I briefly covered the <mx:XML> tag, which operates in much the same way as the <mx:Model> tag. You then saw the different ways to load an external XML document using the HTTPService and URLLoader classes. We finished the chapter with a look at web services and saw how to consume a web service using the WebService class.

In the next chapter, we'll look more closely at some of the components specifically designed to work with data. In particular, we'll look at the Repeater, DataGrid, TileList, and Tree components.

Chapter 9

FLEX DATA-DRIVEN CONTROLS

The Flex framework includes a rich class library that gives developers access to many different types of controls. So far in the book, you've seen how to use the standard user interface controls and layout containers, as well as some of the nonvisual controls.

Included in the Flex framework are a number of controls specifically designed for working with data. These controls are populated using a dataProvider property, and you've already used the ComboBox control in several examples. In the case of dynamic data-driven applications, the dataProvider property is typically populated from an external data source such as an XML document or a call to a database, although you've also seen that it's possible to use content stored within the application.

The range of data-driven controls includes the following:

- ComboBox
- List
- HorizontalList
- TileList
- Repeater
- DataGrid
- Tree

In this chapter, I want to focus on the Repeater, the TileList, and the DataGrid controls. We'll see how you can populate each control by setting its dataProvider property and look at the other properties that you need to set. For each control, we'll work through an example where we load content from an external data source.

You can download the resources for the chapter from the friends of ED web site at www.friendsofed.com. Before we start looking at controls, we'll take a closer look at working with the dataProvider property.

Working with a dataProvider

Data-driven controls have one thing in common: they all have a dataProvider property that references the source of data for that control. The controls can then display and manipulate data from this data source.

One of the advantages of working with dataProvider property is that you can use data binding expressions within Flex controls. Data binding allows you to bind the property of one component to the property of another, so updates happen automatically. Using this approach simplifies the process of creating applications greatly and can speed up development time.

The dataProvider property will usually reference an Array object or perhaps an XMLList object. You can embed these objects as static content within the application. In this case, if you want to take advantage of data binding, you'll need to declare this content as bindable using the [Bindable] metatag:

```
[Bindable]
private var myArray:Array = new Array("value1", "value2", "value3");
```

In the case of dynamic data-driven applications, you'll associate the dataProvider property with an external data source. You might load content from the following:

- A request to a server-side page that contacts a database
- A web service
- A static text or XML file

You've already seen how to use the HTTPService, URLLoader, and WebService classes to request these types of information.

The Flex controls actually use collection classes for a wrapper for data when working with data providers because these classes provide more functionality when compared with raw Arrays and Objects. Collections contain a group of objects and provide methods specifically for reading and writing content, sorting, and filtering the items in the collection.

If you set the dataProvider for a control to an object such as an Array or XMLList, Flex will automatically wrap the object in a collection wrapper. For example, if you set the dataProvider for a control to an Array, Flex will convert it to an ArrayCollection object, while an XMLList will be converted to an XMLListCollection.

Now that you understand a little more about dataProvider property, let's look more closely at the Repeater control.

Using the Repeater control

You use the Repeater control when you need to repeat a small number of simple components within an application. They might be user interface controls, containers, or a combination of both. Repeater controls are useful if you don't know how many groups of components need to appear in the final application. For example, if you're loading dynamic content from an external file, you might not know how many records you'll be accessing, but you do know that you need one for each set of components for each record in the source.

A good example is a multiple-choice questionnaire in which the questions load from a database. You might vary the number of questions in each questionnaire. You can use a Repeater to add a Label for each question as well as a set of radio buttons containing the standard answers. In fact, we'll look at this example a little later in the chapter.

You create a Repeater using the <mx:Repeater> tag. Any tags that have to repeat must appear within the opening and closing <mx:Repeater> tags. You can place just about any tag you like inside a Repeater and use it anywhere you'd use other controls. Obviously, you can't include an <mx:Application> tag inside a Repeater because you can have only one of these tags in any application. You can have multiple Repeater controls in your application and you can nest one inside the other.

A Repeater isn't a container in the same sense as VBox and HBox controls because they don't include any automatic layout functionality. If you need to use automatic layouts, you can add containers inside the Repeater or place the Repeater inside a container.

The content being repeated comes from the dataProvider.

Setting the dataProvider

The <mx:Repeater> tag has a dataProvider property that you can bind to an Array, Object, XML object, or XMLList object. Once you've set the dataProvider, you can bind the relevant item within the source data to a control using the currentItem property. Make sure you declare any variables or objects as bindable.

Let's see a simple example of how this might work. In this case, I will create radio buttons from an array created in ActionScript. The following ActionScript block shows the array we'll use:

```
<mx:Script>
 <![CDATA[
    [Bindable]
    private var arrGender:Array = ["Female", "Male", "Not telling"];
 ]]>
</mx:Script>
```

Notice that I've used the metatag [Bindable] so I can access it in a curly braces binding expression within the Repeater.

The next block of code demonstrates placing a RadioButton control inside a Repeater. It uses binding expressions for both the dataProvider of the Repeater and the label for each RadioButton:

```
<mx:VBox x="10" y="10">
  <mx:Label text="Choose your gender"/>
  <mx:Repeater id="responses" dataProvider="{arrGender}">
    <mx:RadioButton label="{responses.currentItem}"
      groupName="rdoGender"/>
  </mx:Repeater>
</mx:VBox>
```

The <mx:Repeater> tag has a dataProvider property that is bound to the arrGender variable using the expression {arrGender}. A RadioButton appears inside this tag and takes its label property from the currentItem property of the Repeater using the binding expression responses.currentItem.

Figure 9-1 shows the effect of running this application.

Figure 9-1. Creating radio buttons using a Repeater

Each item in the array creates a new RadioButton instance in the application. Because they share the same group name, only one RadioButton can be selected at a time.

An alternative data source would be XML-formatted data.

Using XML as a dataProvider

You can create the same effect using an XML or XMLList object. For example, the following ActionScript creates an XML object that provides the same options for the dataProvider:

```
<mx:Script>
  <![CDATA[
    [Bindable]
    private var questionXML:XML= <question>
      <option><gender>Female</gender></option>
      <option><gender>Male</gender></option>
      <option><gender>Not telling</gender></option>
      </question>;
  ]]>
</mx:Script>
```

In this case, the text that we'll need to access is stored inside the <gender> nodes within each <option>. We can use an E4X expression within curly braces to target these nodes for binding.

The Repeater portion of the application would need to change to the following:

```
<mx:Repeater id="responses" dataProvider="{questionXML.option}">
  <mx:RadioButton label="{responses.currentItem.gender}"
    groupName="rdoGender"/>
</mx:Repeater>
```

In this case, the dataProvider is bound using the E4X expression questionXML.option. Remember that questionXML is equivalent to the root node of the XML content: <question>. The E4X expression returns an XMLList of all <option> elements. We set the RadioButton label property using the gender property from the XMLList: responses.currentItem.gender.

We've seen how to create a simple control within a Repeater, but what if we want to be able to access content from the control?

Iterating through controls in a Repeater

You can iterate through each of the children of a Repeater component using ActionScript. Before you can do this, however, you need to set an id property for any component inside the Repeater that you want to be able to access in this way.

Using the same XML object as previously, the following code block shows how to work through each RadioButton control using ActionScript to retrieve the label property. The relevant code appears in the showRepeaterChildren function:

```
<?xml version="1.0" encoding="utf-8"?>
<mx:Application xmlns:mx="http://www.adobe.com/2006/mxml"
  layout="absolute">
  <mx:Script>
    <![CDATA[
      [Bindable]
      private var questionXML:XML= <question>
        <option><gender>Female</gender></option>
        <option><gender>Male</gender></option>
        <option><gender>Not telling</gender></option>
        </question>;
      private function showRepeaterChildren(e:MouseEvent):void {
        for (var i:int = 0; i < rdoGenderOption.length;i++) {
          txtOutput.text += "Radio " + i + " has value " + ➥
            rdoGenderOption[i].label +  "\n";
        }
      }
    ]]>
  </mx:Script>
  <mx:VBox x="10" y="10">
    <mx:Label text="Choose your gender"/>
    <mx:Repeater id="responses" dataProvider="{questionXML.option}">
```

```
        <mx:RadioButton id="rdoGenderOption" groupName="rdoGender"
          label="{responses.currentItem.gender}"/>
      </mx:Repeater>
      <mx:Button label="Click me" click="showRepeaterChildren(event)"/>
      <mx:TextArea id="txtOutput" width="200" height="50"/>
    </mx:VBox>
  </mx:Application>
```

The application includes a function, showRepeaterChildren, which iterates through each child in the Repeater. It does this by referencing the id from the RadioButton control: rdoGenderOption. To find the label for each control, you'll need to use the following:

```
    rdoGenderOption[i].label
```

The application demonstrates how to call this function when clicking the Click me button. The label from each RadioButton displays in the TextArea. Figure 9-2 shows how this appears when the application is run.

Figure 9-2. Iterating through the child of a Repeater component

Let's see a more complex example of the Repeater component. We'll populate a short questionnaire from an external XML document.

Working through a simple example

In this example, we'll create a simple application that loads content from an external XML document into two nested Repeater controls. The first Repeater will display a statement in a Label control, while the second will display a set of standard responses in RadioButton controls.

Start by creating a new Flex application. You can give it any name and location that you like. Create a new folder called assets and add the resource file questionnaire.xml. That file contains the data that we'll use to populate the Repeater controls, and I've reproduced it as follows:

```
<questionnaire>
  <question questionID="1" statement="The sky is purple"/>
  <question questionID="2" statement="Jupiter has six moons"/>
  <question questionID="3" statement="Neptune is larger than Earth"/>
  <response responseID="1">True</response>
  <response responseID="2">False</response>
  <response responseID="3">I haven't got a clue</response>
</questionnaire>
```

The XML file includes three statements and three standard responses to these statements.

Modify the interface of the application as shown here:

```
<?xml version="1.0" encoding="utf-8"?>
<mx:Application xmlns:mx="http://www.adobe.com/2006/mxml"
  layout="absolute">
  <mx:VBox x="10" y="10">
    <mx:Repeater id="questionList">
      <mx:Label id="txtQuestion" fontWeight="bold"/>
    </mx:Repeater>
  </mx:VBox>
</mx:Application>
```

The components are all contained within an outer VBox container. Inside it, the Repeater questionList will display each of the statements from the XML file in the txtQuestion Label. We'll add a second Repeater a little later. There's no point in running the application now as we need to populate it with data first.

Add the following <mx:HTTPService> tag below the opening <mx:Application> tag:

```
<mx:HTTPService id="questions" url="assets/questionnaire.xml"
  resultFormat="e4x"/>
```

This tag sets the url for the request to the external XML document and specifies the resultFormat e4x. We can request this file using the send method, which we'll call in the creationComplete event of the application. Modify the opening <mx:Application> tag as shown here:

```
<mx:Application xmlns:mx="http://www.adobe.com/2006/mxml"
  layout="absolute" creationComplete="questions.send()">
```

We'll use E4X expressions to bind the loaded XML content to the relevant controls, starting with the first Repeater. Set the dataProvider for this control as follows:

```
<mx:Repeater id="questionList"
  dataProvider="{questions.lastResult.question}">
```

The expression accesses the lastResult property of the HTTPService tag and targets the <question> element. The expression will return an XMLList made up of all these elements.

273

To display each statement, we'll need to add a text property to the Label. We'll bind this property to the statement attribute in the <question> element. Modify the Label control as shown in bold here:

```
<mx:Label id="txtQuestion" fontWeight="bold"
    text="{questionList.currentItem.@statement}"/>
```

The expression uses the @ symbol to target the attribute of the current item in the dataProvider.

Run the application now and you should see the list of statements displayed, as shown in Figure 9-3.

Figure 9-3. The statements from the external XML document displayed within a Repeater control

The next step is to add a second repeater inside the first and set its dataProvider property to access the list of responses from the XML file.

Add the following tags underneath the Label control:

```
<mx:Repeater id="responseList"
    dataProvider="{questions.lastResult.response}">
</mx:Repeater>
```

We'll populate the Repeater using the <response> elements in the XML document. Add the following elements inside the second Repeater:

```
<mx:HBox>
  <mx:Spacer width="20"/>
  <mx:RadioButton groupName="{'rdo'+questionList.currentIndex}"
     label="{responseList.currentItem}"/>
</mx:HBox>
```

The second Repeater will display RadioButton controls, one for each of the standard responses in the XML document. I've used a spacer and an HBox control to arrange them in the interface.

The RadioButton control uses data binding to set the groupName dynamically. We need to do this so that each group of radio buttons has a unique groupName. Doing this will allow us to keep the groups separate, but it restricts us to selecting a single value within each group. The expression uses the currentIndex property to create the group names rdo0, rdo1, and rdo2. The label for each radio button comes from the currently selected <response> element.

You should be able to run the application and see the result shown in Figure 9-4. You should be able to select only a single value from each of the groups of radio buttons.

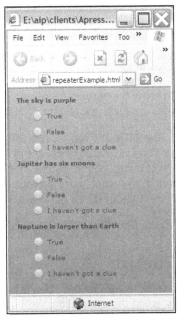

Figure 9-4. The completed application

In this example, we used nested Repeater controls to display data from an external XML document. We were able to create a simple questionnaire with a set of standard answers. You can find this application saved as repeaterExample.mxml with the chapter resources.

In the help files, Adobe states that the Repeater control isn't suitable for use with two-dimensional arrays that are programmatically generated. In the previous example, if you wanted to associate a different set of values with each statement, the Repeater control wouldn't be suitable. For more complicated data structures, a better approach is to use custom ActionScript classes to store the data and to create methods and properties to populate the nested content.

Adobe also states that when the application uses large amounts of data, the List, HorizontalList, and TileList controls provide better performance. The List control displays data in a single vertical column, while the HorizontalList displays data horizontally from left to right, in the same way as an HBox container. The TileList displays data in a tiled layout, and you can specify the direction. We'll look at this control in the next section.

Using the TileList

As the name suggests, the TileList control displays items in equal-sized tiles. It's common to use this control to display images in rows and columns. When there are more items than can be displayed in the visible area, you can specify either a horizontal or vertical scrollbar so that the user can access the additional items. You can also specify the size of the tiles or let Flex set them, based on the size of the first item.

You use the <mx:TileList> tag to create this control. It has width, height, rowHeight, and columnWidth properties that allow you to control the way content appears in the TileList. As usual, you specify the width and height in either pixels or a percentage value. The maximum size for a TileList is 5000 pixels in either direction.

The rowHeight and columnWidth properties allow you to specify an exact size for each of the tiles. You can also specify the maximum number of rows or columns to display using the maxRows and maxColumns properties. If you don't specify the number of rows or columns, the default is a 4 × 4 grid, with each tile 50 pixels high and wide. This gives a total area of 200 pixels high and wide.

Like the other data-driven controls, the TileList has a dataProvider property that you can use to bind the data that you'll display. The TileList determines how to display the data using an item renderer and it has a built-in renderer that allows you to display a label and optionally an icon. You can also specify a custom item renderer if you want more control over the layout of content in the TileList.

Let's see a simple example of how to use the TileList to display images.

Displaying images in a TileList

In this simple example, we'll show some images in the TileList. The images are all the same size, 150 × 100 pixels, and we'll embed them in the application. We'll use the built-in item renderer label and icon properties to display a caption and the image.

The code for the example follows, and I'll explain it afterward. It assumes that the images exist within a folder called assets in the project. If you're working through the example, make sure you create the folder and add the images from the resources download:

```
<?xml version="1.0" encoding="utf-8"?>
<mx:Application xmlns:mx="http://www.adobe.com/2006/mxml"
  layout="absolute">
  <mx:Script>
  <![CDATA[
    [Bindable]
    [Embed(source="assets/olgas.jpg")]
    public var photo1:Class;
    [Bindable]
    [Embed(source="assets/operahouse.jpg")]
    public var photo2:Class;
    [Bindable]
    [Embed(source="assets/porthedland.jpg")]
    public var photo3:Class;
```

```
    [Bindable]
    [Embed(source="assets/waterhole.jpg")]
    public var photo4:Class;
    [Bindable]
    private var photosArray:Array = new Array(➥
      {icon: photo1, label: "The Olgas"},➥
      {icon: photo2, label: "Sydney Opera House"},➥
      {icon: photo3, label: "Pretty Pool, Port Hedland"},➥
      {icon: photo4, label: "Waterhole"});
    ]]>
  </mx:Script>
    <mx:Panel title="Photo gallery" x="10" y="10">
      <mx:TileList id="photos" height="130" width="350"
        maxColumns="2" dataProvider="{photosArray}"/>
    </mx:Panel>
  </mx:Application>
```

The application consists of a TileList that displays up to two columns of images. The dataProvider for the TileList is set to an array of objects called photosArray, each containing both a label and icon property. The icon values refer to an embedded photo within the assets folder. Note that this TileList is specifically sized to work with the images provided. Using images of different sizes is likely to create some strange results!

The application uses the [Embed] metatag to include each image and to give it a reference class name. In the example, these images are called photo1, photo2, photo3, and photo4, and we use those names with the icon property for the objects stored in photosArray.

Figure 9-5 shows the effect of running the application.

Figure 9-5. Photos displayed in a TileList control

We can see two columns of images, each with a label. The vertical scrollbar allows us to access the remaining images in the TileList. Notice that you can click an image to select it in the TileList, although this doesn't do anything other than change the background color. You'll see more about this feature a little later.

We can also change the direction that the images display in the TileList.

Changing the direction

Notice that the default direction for the TileList is horizontal. That is, items are laid out horizontally in each row until we display the maximum number of columns specified with the maxColumns property. Because we display more than one row, a vertical scrollbar appears.

It's also possible to specify a vertical direction so that items are laid out vertically in each column by including the direction property. When you do this, the maxRows property specifies the number of rows to include. Modifying the TileList control, as shown in bold, creates the output shown in Figure 9-6:

```
<mx:TileList id="photos" height="350" width="350"
  maxRows="3" dataProvider="{photosArray}"
  direction="vertical" horizontalScrollPolicy="auto"/>
```

Figure 9-6. Setting the direction of the TileList to vertical

We have a horizontal scrollbar and we display the items in the TileList in rows of one item. Notice that I had to set the horizontalScrollPolicy attribute explicitly to make the horizontal scrollbar appear in the application.

Using a custom item renderer

In the previous example, we took advantage of the label and icon properties of the TileList default item renderer. The item renderer uses the TileListItemRenderer class and allows for the text display associated with each display item and an optional icon.

We can also create a custom item renderer that overrides the TileListItemRenderer. This approach allows you to determine how each item will display in the TileList. You can set a custom item renderer using the itemRenderer property in the tag. By the way, you can also use custom renderers with other data-aware controls (for example, List and DataGrid controls).

It's possible to create a custom item renderer in an MXML file or by using ActionScript. This means that you can base the custom renderer on any control you like. You need to bind the relevant properties in each control to display the data passed in from the dataProvider of the TileList. You access each property of the dataProvider through the data property. For example, you could access the caption property using data.caption.

The following example shows how to display photos in the TileList using a custom item renderer. The custom renderer loads the images as required instead of referring to embedded images. The custom renderer file photoRenderer.mxml follows. It is based on a VBox component:

```
<?xml version="1.0" encoding="utf-8"?>
<mx:VBox xmlns:mx="http://www.adobe.com/2006/mxml"
  width="180" height="130" paddingLeft="20">
  <mx:Label id="txtLabel" fontWeight="bold" width="150"
    text="{data.caption}"/>
  <mx:Image id="imgPhoto" width="150" height="100"
    source="{'assets/'+data.file}"/>
</mx:VBox>
```

The custom renderer uses a VBox control and specifies the width, height, and paddingLeft properties in the root element. It includes a Label and Image control. The text property of the Label is bound to the caption property of the TileList dataProvider. It is passed in with the data property and accessed with the expression data.caption. The source for the image is a binding expression made up of the folder name assets and the file property from the TileList dataProvider.

The main application file can use the custom renderer in the itemRenderer property, as shown here:

```
<?xml version="1.0" encoding="utf-8"?>
<mx:Application xmlns:mx="http://www.adobe.com/2006/mxml"
  layout="absolute">
  <mx:Script>
  <![CDATA[
    [Bindable]
    private var photosArray:Array = new Array(➡
      {file: "olgas.jpg", caption: "The Olgas"},➡
```

```
                {file: "operahouse.jpg", caption: "Sydney Opera House"},➡
                {file: "porthedland.jpg", caption: "Pretty Pool,Port Hedland"},➡
                {file: "waterhole.jpg", caption: "Waterhole"});
        ]]>
    </mx:Script>
      <mx:Panel title="Photo gallery" x="10" y="10">
        <mx:TileList id="photos" height="140" width="390"
          maxColumns="2" dataProvider="{photosArray}"
          itemRenderer="photoRenderer"/>
      </mx:Panel>
    </mx:Application>
```

In this case, the array now refers to the file names of the images that will display in the TileList. The application uses file and caption properties within each object in the photosArray. The name isn't significant.

The TileList has changed height and width properties compared with the previous example, and it assigns an itemRenderer property with the value of photoRenderer. This means that the itemRenderer will use the file photoRenderer.mxml for its layout of each item.

Running the application shows the result displayed in Figure 9-7.

Figure 9-7. The TileList using a custom item renderer

Unlike in the previous example, the caption appears in bold above each image.

The advantage of using a custom renderer approach is that we don't need to embed all photos in the application. Instead, we load them from external files, reducing the overall size of the application. We can also add any formatting that we want, including padding and bolding.

If you click an image in the TileList, you'll see that the display changes color to indicate that you've selected the image. It's possible to respond to a user's click, for example, to display further details about the image.

Responding to user interactions

Within a TileList, one of the most common user interactions that developers need to deal with is clicking an item. By default, clicking selects a single item, although it's possible to use a Ctrl-click or Shift-click key combination to select multiple items. You need to set the allowMultipleSelection property to true first.

You can also move the selection using the arrow keys on the keyboard. When you change the selection, the TileList broadcasts the change event that you can respond to with an event handler. This process works in the same way as for any other change handler.

Working through an example

In this example, we'll use an XML file to provide information about the images to display in a TileList. We'll load the images and display them using a custom item renderer. Clicking an image will show the user a description of the photo.

Before you start, make sure that all the JPEG files from the chapter resources have been copied to the assets folder. Copy the photos.xml resource file to your assets folder in the Flex project. The structure of the file follows, although I've shown only one element for brevity:

```
<gallery>
  <photo file="galah.jpg" location="Cervantes, Western Australia"
    caption="Pink and grey galah">Galahs are one of the most common
    cockatoos in Australia. They are found almost everywhere in the
    continent and are about 35cm long. They are very loud birds, showing little
    fear of man.</photo>
</gallery>
```

You can see the full details of the photos in the photos.xml file.

Start by creating a new MXML application in your project and give it the name of your choosing. Add the following interface elements:

```
<mx:VBox x="10" y="10">
  <mx:Panel title="Photo gallery">
    <mx:TileList id="photos" height="280" width="580"
      maxColumns="2" />
  </mx:Panel>
  <mx:Text id="txtDescription" width="100%" />
</mx:VBox>
```

The application includes a VBox containing a Panel with a TileList and a Text control. We'll populate the TileList from an external XML document using the <mx:HTTPService> tag. Add this tag below the opening <mx:Application> tag:

```
<mx:HTTPService id="photoService" url="assets/photos.xml"
  resultFormat="e4x"/>
```

We're requesting the photos.xml file from the assets folder using an e4x format. This format will allow us to retrieve the content from the XML file using E4X expressions. You can find out more about E4X expressions in Chapter 8 of this book.

To request the XML document, we need to call the send method of this service in the creationComplete event of the application as shown here. I'll also modify the background color of the application to display a plain white page because I think the photos will look better that way:

```
<mx:Application xmlns:mx="http://www.adobe.com/2006/mxml"
    layout="absolute" backgroundColor="#FFFFFF"
    backgroundGradientAlphas="[0,0]"
    creationComplete="photoService.send()">
```

The next step is to set the results from this request as the dataProvider for the TileList. Modify the <mx:TileList> tag as shown here in bold:

```
<mx:TileList id="photos" height="280" width="580"
    maxColumns="2" dataProvider="{photoService.lastResult.photo}"/>
```

We access the loaded content from the HTTPService object using the lastResult property. The TileList uses the <photo> elements from this property. The E4X expression photoService.lastResult.photo returns an XMLList of all these elements, so we can set it directly as the dataProvider for the TileList.

We won't be able to display the results until we create a custom item renderer for the TileList. I want to display the image, a caption, and a location for each <photo> element that appears in the XML document. I'll also display the description.

Create a new component called galleryRenderer based on the VBox container. Make the component 280 pixels wide and 160 high. Modify the root element to add padding to the left as shown in bold here:

```
<mx:VBox xmlns:mx="http://www.adobe.com/2006/mxml"
    width="280" height="160" paddingLeft="20">
```

Add the following interface elements between the opening and closing <mx:VBox> tags:

```
<mx:Image id="imgPhoto" width="150" height="100"/>
<mx:HBox>
  <mx:Label fontWeight="bold" width="60" text="Caption:"/>
  <mx:Label id="txtLabel"/>
</mx:HBox>
<mx:HBox>
  <mx:Label fontWeight="bold" width="60" text="Location:"/>
  <mx:Label id="txtLocation"/>
</mx:HBox>
```

We've added an Image and several Label controls inside two HBox elements. We'll need to bind the relevant properties of these controls to the data coming from the TileList.

Start by modifying the Image control:

```
<mx:Image id="imgPhoto" width="150" height="100"
    source="{'assets/'+data.@file}"/>
```

The preceding binding expression sets the source for the Image to the assets folder and takes the file name from the file attribute in the <photo> element. Remember that an XMLList of these elements makes up the dataProvider for the TileList. If you check the XML document, you'll see this attribute:

```
<photo file="galah.jpg"...
```

We also need to set the bindings for the two Label controls with id attributes. Modify them as shown here. Note that they're not located next to each other in the MXML file:

```
<mx:Label id="txtLabel" text="{data.@caption}"/>
<mx:Label id="txtLocation" text="{data.@location}"/>
```

The text properties of each control are set to the relevant attributes in the <photo> element, caption, and location.

Switch back to the main application file and add the galleryRenderer as the custom itemRenderer for the TileList:

```
<mx:TileList id="photos" height="280" width="580"
    maxColumns="2" dataProvider="{photoService.lastResult.photo}"
    itemRenderer="galleryRenderer"/>
```

The last step is to bind the text property of the Text control in this file so it displays the description. Modify the control as shown here in bold:

```
<mx:Text id="txtDescription" width="100%"
    text="{photos.selectedItem}"/>
```

We're binding the text property of the control to the selectedItem in the TileList. This allows us to display the text inside each of the <photo> elements.

Figure 9-8 shows the effect of running the application and selecting an image from the TileList.

In this example, we used an external XML document to provide content for a TileList control. By using a custom item renderer, we could choose how to display the external content in the TileList. We also added a binding from the item selected in the TileList to a Text control so that we could display a description.

You can find the completed files for this exercise saved as tileListExample.mxml and galleryRenderer.mxml with the other chapter resources. The download includes copies of all images referred to in the photos.xml file.

The next control that I want to cover is the DataGrid, which allows us to display complex data in a grid layout. Bear in mind that the topic of working with the DataGrid control is very large, so the next section aims to provide an overview of the most important points instead of being a complete reference.

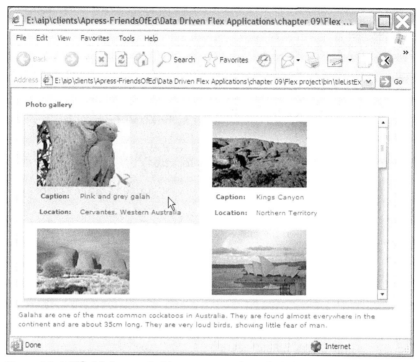

Figure 9-8. A TileList control with a custom renderer displaying content from an external XML document

Using the DataGrid

The DataGrid component is one of the most important controls available to data-driven applications. The control allows you to display a list of data rows showing more than one column for each record, like a table of data. Like the TileList, you can specify custom item renderers for the display of data in each cell. One important point about this component is that it allows for the editing of data within the DataGrid using item editors.

You can create a DataGrid using the <mx:DataGrid> control. Again, you need to specify the dataProvider for the control. The columns displayed in the DataGrid will take their names from the property names provided in the dataProvider unless you specify otherwise.

A very simplistic example of a DataGrid populated with an Array follows:

```
<?xml version="1.0" encoding="utf-8"?>
<mx:Application xmlns:mx="http://www.adobe.com/2006/mxml"
  layout="absolute">
  <mx:Script>
```

```
        <![CDATA[
          [Bindable]
          private var personArray:Array = new Array(➥
            {FirstName: "Santa", Surname: "Claus", Age: 1000},➥
            {FirstName: "Tooth", Surname: "Fairy", Age: 250},➥
            {FirstName: "Sas", Surname: "Jacobs", Age: 102});
        ]]>
      </mx:Script>
      <mx:DataGrid id="personsDG" dataProvider="{personArray}"/>
    </mx:Application>
```

Figure 9-9 shows the effect of running the application shown previously.

Figure 9-9. Populating a DataGrid from an Array

The column headings come from the properties defined in each Object within the Array: Age, FirstName, and Surname. Notice that the columns appear in alphabetical order and are sized with a standard width. If you click one of the column headings, the DataGrid will sort into that order. Clicking a second time applies a reverse sort order to the column.

If you want more control over the DataGrid, you may want to specify the order and width for columns.

Specifying column settings

You can specify a custom list of columns to include in the DataGrid using the <mx:columns> tag. Within this tag, you can then specify which columns to include using the <mx:DataGridColumn> tag. You need to set the field to display using the dataField property as shown here (you'll see this in an example shortly):

```
<mx:columns>
  <mx:DataGridColumn dataField="Surname"/>
  <mx:DataGridColumn dataField="Age"/>
</mx:columns>
```

The default width for each column containing content is 100 pixels. Empty columns have a default width of 300 pixels. You can add a width attribute to the <mx:DataGridColumn> tag to specify your own width settings. You can also change the text that displays in the header with the headerText property, as follows:

```
<mx:DataGridColumn dataField="Surname" width="80"
   headerText="Last name"/>
```

The following application re-creates the previous code sample. In this case, the content comes from an XML object, and the application specifies the order for the columns. It also sets the width and headerText properties for each column:

```
<?xml version="1.0" encoding="utf-8"?>
<mx:Application xmlns:mx="http://www.adobe.com/2006/mxml"
  layout="absolute">
  <mx:Script>
    <![CDATA[
      [Bindable]
      private var personXML:XML= <persons>
        <person><FirstName>Santa</FirstName>
        <Surname>Claus</Surname>
        <Age>1000</Age></person>
        <person><FirstName>Tooth</FirstName>
        <Surname>Fairy</Surname>
        <Age>250</Age></person>
        <person><FirstName>Sas</FirstName>
        <Surname>Jacobs</Surname>
        <Age>102</Age></person>
        </persons>;
    ]]>
  </mx:Script>
  <mx:DataGrid id="personsDG" dataProvider="{personXML.person}">
    <mx:columns>
      <mx:DataGridColumn dataField="FirstName" width="80"
        headerText="First name"/>
      <mx:DataGridColumn dataField="Surname" width="80"
        headerText="Last name"/>
      <mx:DataGridColumn dataField="Age" width="50" />
    </mx:columns>
  </mx:DataGrid>
</mx:Application>
```

Figure 9-10 shows the effect of running the application.

The columns display in a custom order, and each has a specific width. The DataGrid uses custom names for each column.

Figure 9-10. Customizing the order
and other column settings

If you don't want to display column headers, set the showHeaders attribute to false:

```
<mx:DataGrid id="personsDG" dataProvider="{personXML.person}"
    showHeaders="false">
```

Another common task for developers is changing the way data sorts within a DataGrid.

Sorting columns

By default, it's possible to sort every column in the DataGrid by clicking the column headers. Clicking the same column a second time sorts in reverse order. You can override the default sorting behavior to remove this functionality from an individual column or from the entire DataGrid.

To turn off sorting for the entire DataGrid, set the sortableColumns attribute of the DataGrid to false:

```
<mx:DataGrid id="personsDG" dataProvider="{personXML.person}"
    sortableColumns="false">
```

You can also use the sortable attribute with individual columns:

```
<mx:DataGridColumn dataField="Age" width="50" sortable="false"/>
```

If you want to specify the initial order of the DataGrid, the best approach is to make sure that the data source is sorted first.

Reordering columns

By default, a user can rearrange the columns in a DataGrid by dragging and dropping. You can turn off this feature by setting the value of the draggableColumns attribute to false:

```
<mx:DataGrid id="personsDG" dataProvider="{personXML.person}"
    draggableColumns="false">
```

Setting the display of data within a column

The labelFunction property of the DataGridColumn class allows you to specify how the data appears in each column. You might use this property to change the display of text in a column, perhaps to concatenate content from two data fields for display in a single column, as shown in this example:

```
<?xml version="1.0" encoding="utf-8"?>
<mx:Application xmlns:mx="http://www.adobe.com/2006/mxml"
  layout="absolute">
  <mx:Script>
    <![CDATA[
      [Bindable]
      private var personXML:XML= <persons>
        <person><FirstName>Santa</FirstName>
        <Surname>Claus</Surname>
        <Age>1000</Age></person>
        <person><FirstName>Tooth</FirstName>
        <Surname>Fairy</Surname>
        <Age>250</Age></person>
        <person><FirstName>Sas</FirstName>
        <Surname>Jacobs</Surname>
        <Age>102</Age></person>
        </persons>;
      private function showFullName(item:Object, ➥
        column:DataGridColumn):String {
        var fullName:String = item.FirstName + " " + item.Surname;
        return fullName;
      }
    ]]>
  </mx:Script>
  <mx:DataGrid id="personsDG" dataProvider="{personXML.person}">
    <mx:columns>
      <mx:DataGridColumn width="150" headerText="Full name"
        labelFunction="showFullName"/>
      <mx:DataGridColumn dataField="Age" width="50" />
    </mx:columns>
  </mx:DataGrid>
</mx:Application>
```

The labelFunction, in this case showFullName, has two arguments. The first, item, corresponds to the data item for that row. The second argument specifies the DataGrid column. The preceding showFullName function returns a string made up of the FirstName value, a space, and the Surname.

Figure 9-11 shows what happens when the application runs.

Figure 9-11. A labelFunction is used to concatenate two data fields for display in a single column.

The DataGrid displays two columns, the first of which uses a labelFunction attribute to display content from two fields.

Another common requirement for developers is to be able to wrap text within a column.

Wrapping text within a column

In order to wrap column text, you need to set the wrapText property of the relevant DataGrid column:

```
<mx:DataGridColumn dataField="FirstName" width="80"
    wordWrap="true"/>
```

This step isn't the only one, however. If the first item in the column doesn't wrap, it can cause problems for other values in later rows that do need to wrap. Word wrapping seems to be an all-or-nothing setting, based on the value from the first cell.

You can fix this issue by setting the variableRowHeight property of the DataGrid to true, as shown here:

```
<mx:DataGrid id="personsDG" dataProvider="{personXML.person}"
    variableRowHeight="true">
```

The DataGrid can then include some cells that wrap in the same column as cells that don't wrap.

Using renderers

As with the TileList component, the DataGrid also allows you to modify the way items display in each column of the DataGrid. In addition to the default renderer, which appears as text, you can use a drop-in renderer, use an inline renderer, or create a custom renderer.

Working with a drop-in renderer

You'd use a drop-in item renderer to display the content in another control. The control that you choose for the renderer must implement the IDropInListItemRenderer interface. Effectively, this means that it must be one of the following controls:

- Button (selected property)
- CheckBox (selected property)
- DateField (selectedDate property)
- Image (source property)
- Label (text property)
- NumericStepper (value property)
- Text (text property)
- TextArea (text property)
- TextInput (text property)

The list shows which property of the control uses the data from the dataProvider. The value that you specify in the dataProvider must be of an appropriate data type for this property. For example, the CheckBox selected property must reference a Boolean value.

The following example shows how to use a CheckBox and Image control as a drop-in item renderer within a DataGrid:

```
<?xml version="1.0" encoding="utf-8"?>
<mx:Application xmlns:mx="http://www.adobe.com/2006/mxml"
  layout="absolute">
  <mx:Script>
    <![CDATA[
      [Bindable]
      private var productsArray:Array = new Array({Product: "Shoes", ➥
        Sale: true, File: "assets/shoes.jpg"},{Product: "Jewelry", ➥
        Sale: false, File: "assets/jewelry.jpg"});
    ]]>
  </mx:Script>
  <mx:DataGrid id="productsDG" dataProvider="{productsArray}"
    variableRowHeight="true" width="400" height="250">
    <mx:columns>
      <mx:DataGridColumn dataField="Product" width="90" />
      <mx:DataGridColumn dataField="Sale" width="80"
        itemRenderer="mx.controls.CheckBox" />
      <mx:DataGridColumn dataField="File" headerText="Image"
        itemRenderer="mx.controls.Image"/>
    </mx:columns>
  </mx:DataGrid>
</mx:Application>
```

The application uses an array to provide content to the DataGrid. The DataGrid lists the columns to display and specifies a width. The Sale column uses the mx.controls.CheckBox class as a drop-in renderer. It uses the value of the Sale property in productsArray, which is set to either true or false.

The third column uses the mx.controls.Image class, specifying the file path and name. These values are used in the source property of the control. The application sets the variableRowHeight property of the DataGrid to true so that the image doesn't scale down to the default row height of 20 pixels. It could also have set the rowHeight property to an exact value to choose a constant height for each row.

Running the application shows the output shown in Figure 9-12.

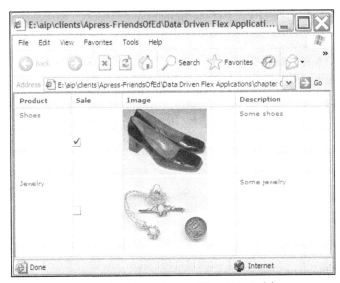

Figure 9-12. Using a drop-in renderer within a DataGrid

The second column displays a CheckBox that indicates whether or not the item is on sale. The third column displays an image of the item.

If you need to set other properties of the control rendering the content, you can use an inline renderer.

Working with an inline renderer

The second option is to use an inline renderer. This approach works in a similar way to the drop-in renderer, but you can specify additional properties for each control. You need to specify <mx:itemRenderer> and <mx:Component> tags containing the relevant control for each DataGrid column.

The following code block shows how to add an inline renderer that includes a CheckBox and sets the label property, as well as an Image control with a drop shadow filter. You'd modify the <mx:DataGrid> element from the previous example as shown in bold here:

```
<mx:DataGrid id="productsDG" dataProvider="{productsArray}"
    variableRowHeight="true" width="400" height="250">
    <mx:columns>
```

```
        <mx:DataGridColumn dataField="Product" width="90" />
        <mx:DataGridColumn dataField="Sale" width="80">
          <mx:itemRenderer>
            <mx:Component>
              <mx:CheckBox label="On sale"/>
            </mx:Component>
          </mx:itemRenderer>
        </mx:DataGridColumn>
        <mx:DataGridColumn dataField="File" headerText="Image">
          <mx:itemRenderer>
            <mx:Component>
              <mx:Image filters="{[new DropShadowFilter(5, 30,0x8C8C8C,
                0.8)]}"/>
            </mx:Component>
          </mx:itemRenderer>
        </mx:DataGridColumn>
      </mx:columns>
    </mx:DataGrid>
```

Replacing the DataGrid from the previous example with the preceding one would display the label On sale for each CheckBox, while the image would appear with a light gray drop shadow. You can see the result in Figure 9-13.

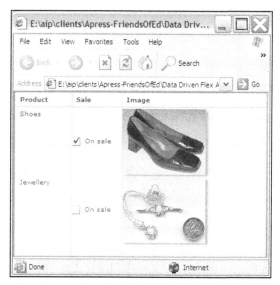

Figure 9-13. Using inline renderers

For even greater control over the display in each column, you can use a custom renderer.

Working with a custom renderer

The third alternative is to use a custom item renderer to display the content within each column. The advantage of this approach is that you have much greater control over the layout of each cell. You can set a custom renderer for the header using the headerRenderer property of the DataGrid column or for the displayed content using the itemRenderer property. As we covered a custom renderer example in the section on the TileList control, I won't go through it again here because it works in much the same way.

Choosing a renderer

How do you choose which type of renderer to use? Table 9-1 provides a summary of when to choose which type of renderer.

Table 9-1. Choosing an item renderer

Renderer type	Use when
Default item renderer	Displaying text only within the column
Drop-in renderer	Displaying data using a standard property of one of the supported controls
Inline renderer	Displaying data within one or more controls and accessing other properties of that control at the same time
Custom renderer	Displaying data within a customized control or set of controls, or creating a reusable renderer for multiple columns or DataGrid controls

DataGrid controls also allow for editing of content within each cell. You are faced with the same renderer choices when adding editing functionality to columns.

Editing content

You can edit the content in a DataGrid by using an item editor. The List control also supports an item editor, as does the Tree component. You need to make sure that the editable property of the DataGrid or column is set to true before you can edit content. You can prevent the editing of individual columns by setting their editable attribute to false.

There are several different types of item editors that you can use with the DataGrid, including the following:

- The default item editor
- A drop-in item editor
- An inline item editor
- Using a custom item editor

Using the default item editor

The default item editor works with a single text-based data item. When you click an item, it displays the content inside a TextInput control, so you can modify the text property of that control.

In the following code sample, we use the editable attribute to make all columns editable using the default TextInput editing control. I've returned to our earlier example because I want to demonstrate how editable text appears in a DataGrid:

```
<?xml version="1.0" encoding="utf-8"?>
<mx:Application xmlns:mx="http://www.adobe.com/2006/mxml"
  layout="absolute">
  <mx:Script>
    <![CDATA[
      [Bindable]
      private var personArray:Array = new Array({FirstName: "Santa",➦
        Surname: "Claus", Age: 1000}, {FirstName: "Tooth", Surname: ➦
        "Fairy", Age: 250}, {FirstName: "Sas", Surname: "Jacobs", ➦
        Age: 102});
    ]]>
  </mx:Script>
  <mx:DataGrid id="personsDG" dataProvider="{personArray}"
    editable="true"/>
</mx:Application>
```

Figure 9-14 shows how editing appears when an item is clicked.

Figure 9-14. Editing the DataGrid with the default item editor

When you finish editing, the dataProvider will update with the new value.

Using a drop-in item editor

As with item renderers, you can use a drop-in editor to display the cell contents in a single control. You do this by specifying the control inside the itemEditor attribute of the DataGrid column.

Switching back to the products list, the following example shows a DataGrid where only the Description column is editable. It uses a TextArea control as a drop-in item editor:

```
<?xml version="1.0" encoding="utf-8"?>
<mx:Application xmlns:mx="http://www.adobe.com/2006/mxml"
  layout="absolute">
  <mx:Script>
    <![CDATA[
      [Bindable]
      private var productsArray:Array = new Array({Product: "Shoes",➥
        Sale: true, File: "assets/shoes.jpg", Description: ➥
        "Some shoes"},{Product: "Jewelry", Sale: false, File: ➥
        "assets/jewelry.jpg", Description: "Some jewelry"});
    ]]>
  </mx:Script>
  <mx:DataGrid id="productsDG" dataProvider="{productsArray}"
    width="500" height="250" variableRowHeight="true"
    editable="true">
    <mx:columns>
      <mx:DataGridColumn dataField="Product" width="90"
        editable="false"/>
      <mx:DataGridColumn dataField="Sale" width="80"
        itemRenderer = "mx.controls.CheckBox" editable="false"/>
      <mx:DataGridColumn dataField="File" headerText="Image"
        itemRenderer="mx.controls.Image" editable="false"/>
      <mx:DataGridColumn dataField="Description" width="150"
        wordWrap="true" editable="true"
        itemEditor="mx.controls.TextArea"/>
    </mx:columns>
  </mx:DataGrid>
</mx:Application>
```

Running this application and editing the description shows the result that displays in Figure 9-15.

We can edit the description for each item in a TextArea control. Note that even though the CheckBox column has an editable attribute of false, it will still be possible to check and uncheck the control. However, the underlying dataProvider won't update each time you do this.

You can set extra properties in the renderer control by using an inline item editor.

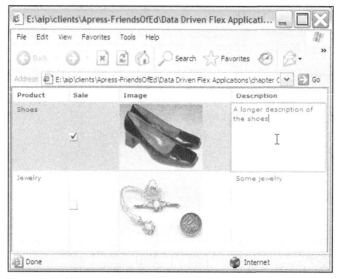

Figure 9-15. Using a TextArea as a drop-in item editor

Using an inline item editor

You can use an inline item editor in much the same way as an inline item renderer. The following DataGrid column demonstrates how to set both a drop-in itemRenderer and an inline itemEditor:

```
<mx:DataGridColumn dataField="Sale" width="80" editable="true"
  editorDataField="selected" itemRenderer="mx.controls.CheckBox">
  <mx:itemEditor>
    <mx:Component>
      <mx:CheckBox/>
    </mx:Component>
  </mx:itemEditor>
</mx:DataGridColumn>
```

In this case, we needed to specify that the property to update is the selected property within the editorDataField attribute. If we didn't do this, the default property is text, which is not available within the CheckBox control.

Another alternative to this approach is to specify that the column should use the same renderer as the editor, and I'll deal with that in the next section when we look at custom editors.

Using a custom item editor

You can specify a custom item editor by referring to an MXML component. This topic is dealt with in more detail in the section on the TileList control, so I won't cover it again here.

However, if you create a custom item renderer, you can also use it as the editor for the item by specifying a value of true for the rendererIsEditor attribute of the column. You'll need to do this where your renderer uses an editable control such as a CheckBox; otherwise, even though you can modify the control, it won't update the underlying dataProvider. You'll also need to specify the editorDataField property when you're updating a property other than text—in a CheckBox, for example.

Using the previous products example, the following code block shows a DataGrid in which the Sale column renders as a CheckBox:

```
<mx:DataGrid id="productsDG" dataProvider="{productsArray}"
  variableRowHeight="true" width="400" height="250" editable="true">
  <mx:columns>
    <mx:DataGridColumn dataField="Product" width="90"
      editable="false" />
    <mx:DataGridColumn dataField="Sale" width="80" editable="true"
      rendererIsEditor="true" itemRenderer="mx.controls.CheckBox"
      editorDataField="selected"/>
    <mx:DataGridColumn dataField="File" headerText="Image"
      editable="false"
      itemRenderer="mx.controls.Image"/>
  </mx:columns>
</mx:DataGrid>
```

Because the rendererIsEditor property is set to true, the dataProvider can also be updated by making changes to this control. Notice that I had to specify the selected property in the editorDataField attribute. In this case, checking and unchecking the CheckBox will also update the dataProvider.

Some other useful properties include the ability to resize and show and hide columns.

Other column properties

It's possible to determine whether or not the user can resize a column by setting its resizable property:

```
<mx:DataGridColumn dataField="Age" resizable="false"/>
```

If you need to show and hide columns, use the visible property:

```
<mx:DataGridColumn dataField="Age" visible="false"/>
```

Let's look at how we might affect the display of rows.

Working with rows

Each record of data in the dataProvider displays as a row in the DataGrid. You can customize how these rows appear by choosing how many to display at once or how tall each row should appear.

The DataGrid displays seven rows by default, and each row has a default height of 20 pixels. You can modify these settings using the rowCount and rowHeight attributes, as shown here:

```
<mx:DataGrid id="personsDG" dataProvider="{personXML.person}"
  rowCount="5" rowHeight="30">
```

As we saw earlier, you can also set variable row heights using the variableRowHeight property:

```
<mx:DataGrid id="personsDG" dataProvider="{personXML.person}"
  rowCount="5" variableRowHeight ="true">
```

Using common DataGrid events

A DataGrid control dispatches many different events. Some useful events for developers are the change and itemClick events.

Working with the change event

The change event is dispatched when the selectedItem or selectedIndex property changes because the user selects a new row in the DataGrid. You can access which row has been selected from the dataProvider using the event object passed to the change handler. Use the currentTarget property of the event object with the relevant property of the selectedItem, as shown in the following example:

```
private function changeHandler(e:Event):void {
  trace(e.currentTarget.selectedItem.Product);
}
```

The code block is taken from the following application, which shows how to display the text from the Product column of the DataGrid using a changeHandler:

```
<?xml version="1.0" encoding="utf-8"?>
<mx:Application xmlns:mx="http://www.adobe.com/2006/mxml"
  layout="absolute">
  <mx:Script>
    <![CDATA[
      [Bindable]
      private var productsArray:Array = new Array(➡
        {Product: "Shoes", Sale: true, File: "assets/shoes.jpg"},➡
        {Product: "Jewelry", Sale: false, ➡
        File: "assets/jewelry.jpg"});
      private function changeHandler(e:Event):void {
        txtMessage.text = "You selected the " + ➡
          e.currentTarget.selectedItem.Product;
      }
    ]]>
  </mx:Script>
  <mx:VBox>
    <mx:DataGrid id="personsDG" dataProvider="{productsArray}"
      variableRowHeight="true" width="400" height="250"
      change="changeHandler(event)">
      <mx:columns>
        <mx:DataGridColumn dataField="Product" width="90" />
        <mx:DataGridColumn dataField="Sale" width="80"
```

```
                 itemRenderer="mx.controls.CheckBox"/>
              <mx:DataGridColumn dataField="File" headerText="Image"
                itemRenderer="mx.controls.Image"/>
          </mx:columns>
        </mx:DataGrid>
        <mx:Text id="txtMessage" fontWeight="bold"/>
      </mx:VBox>
    </mx:Application>
```

Figure 9-16 shows the effect of running the application and selecting a row of data.

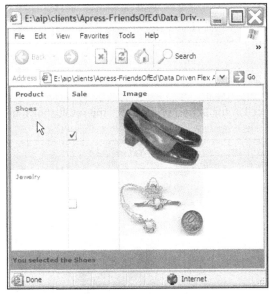

Figure 9-16. Determining a column value from a selected row using the change event

The value of the Product column displays in a Text control underneath the DataGrid. Note that the message updates whenever you click a row in the DataGrid, not when you click the check box.

Another useful event is itemClick.

Working with the itemClick event

You can use the itemClick event to respond when the user clicks content in a specific cell in the DataGrid. The event handler receives a ListEvent object, and you can use this object to determine exactly which column and row was clicked. Note that you need to click the contents, *not* an empty area of the cell.

The event object contains the columnIndex and rowIndex properties, which are zero-based numbers indicating the position of the item in the DataGrid.

You can see the effect if the <mx:DataGrid> tag is modified from the previous example to include an itemClick attribute, as shown here:

```
<mx:DataGrid id="personsDG" dataProvider="{productsArray}"
  variableRowHeight="true" width="400" height="250"
  itemClick="itemClickHandler(event)">
```

The corresponding event handler might look something like the following:

```
private function itemClickHandler(e:ListEvent):void {
  txtMessage.text = "You selected row " + e.rowIndex + ", ➥
    column " + e.columnIndex;
}
```

If you're working through this code yourself, make sure that you have the following import statement in your application:

```
import mx.events.ListEvent;
```

Clicking the contents of a cell in the DataGrid produces the result shown in Figure 9-17.

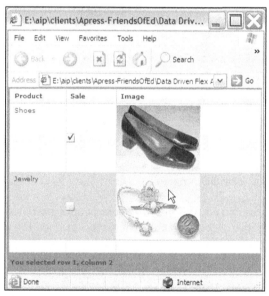

Figure 9-17. Using the itemClick event to detect the row and column clicked in a DataGrid

We can detect the clicked row and column through the itemClick event, and clicking the second image displays the selection of row 1, column 2.

Let's work through a more complicated example in which we display the contents from an RSS feed in a DataGrid.

Working through a DataGrid example

In this example, we'll load details from the Adobe MXNA RSS feed into a DataGrid. You can see the formatted version of the feed at http://weblogs.macromedia.com/mxna/. The DataGrid will display the title and date of each item, along with a Button control to view further details. Clicking a row in the DataGrid will display the item details in a TextArea control.

Start by creating a new Flex application, giving it any name and location that you like. Add the following interface elements:

```
<mx:VBox x="10" y="10">
  <mx:DataGrid id="MXNAData">
  </mx:DataGrid>
  <mx:TextArea id="txtDescription" width="500" height="100"/>
</mx:VBox>
```

We'll use a URLLoader control to load the raw RSS feed. You can see the XML structure of the feed at http://weblogs.macromedia.com/mxna/xml/rss.cfm?query=byMostRecent&languages=1. If you view the feed, you should see that the root element, RDF, contains several namespaces:

```
<rdf:RDF xmlns:rdf="http://www.w3.org/1999/02/22-rdf-syntax-ns#"
  xmlns="http://purl.org/rss/1.0/"
  xmlns:dc="http://purl.org/dc/elements/1.1/">
```

This will affect the way that we use E4X expressions to access the content from the feed. Instead of using simple expressions, we'll need to set Namespaces and QNames.

Start by adding the following code to your application:

```
<mx:Script>
  <![CDATA[
    import flash.net.URLLoader;
    import flash.net.URLRequest;
    import mx.events.FlexEvent;
    private var MXNALoader:URLLoader = new URLLoader();
    private function loadMXNA(e:FlexEvent):void {
      var strURL:String = "http://weblogs.macromedia.com/mxna/xml➥
        /rss.cfm?query=byMostRecent&languages=1"
      MXNALoader.addEventListener(Event.COMPLETE, completeHandler);
      MXNALoader.load(new URLRequest(strURL));
    }
    private function completeHandler(e:Event):void{
    }
  ]]>
</mx:Script>
```

The script block starts by importing the relevant classes and creates a variable called MXNALoader, which we'll use to load the RSS feed. The code block also includes the loadMXNA function, which receives a FlexEvent event object as an argument. We need to include this argument because we'll call the function in the creationComplete event of the application.

301

The loadMXNA function defines the variable strURL to represent the URL of the RSS feed. It adds an event listener called completeHandler to deal with the complete event, dispatched when the URL loads successfully. It also calls the load method to request the RSS feed. We've added an empty completeHandler function, which we'll come back to later.

Modify the opening <mx:Application> tag as shown here in bold:

```
<mx:Application xmlns:mx="http://www.adobe.com/2006/mxml"
  layout="absolute" creationComplete="loadMXNA(event)">
```

We'll call the loadMXNA function after the application is created, passing a FlexEvent.

Before we add to the completeHandler function, we need to deal with the namespaces listed in the root element of the RSS feed. We'll do this by defining the MXNA and dc namespaces because they contain the elements that we need to reference.

Add the following private variables to the script block:

```
private var mxna:Namespace = new Namespace("http://purl.org/rss/1.0/");
private var dc:Namespace = new Namespace("http://purl.org/dc/➥
    elements/1.1/");
```

The URI http://purl.org/rss/1.0/ is the default namespace for the RSS feed. All elements that aren't qualified with a namespace prefix will exist within this namespace. The dc prefix references namespaces at the URI http://purl.org/dc/elements/1.1.

We need to add a QName object for each of the details we'll need to access from the RSS feed. We need to use a QName because each of the nodes that we want to access is within a namespace. The majority are within the default namespace which we've defined as mxna, although the <date> element is within the dc namespace.

Add the following declarations to the script block:

```
private var rssItems:QName = new QName(mxna, "item");
private var rssTitle:QName = new QName(mxna, "title");
private var rssLink:QName = new QName(mxna, "link");
private var rssDescription:QName = new QName(mxna, "description");
private var rssDate:QName = new QName(dc, "date");
```

In each case, we create a QName object that refers to one of the RSS feed elements within the specified namespace. We'll be able to access these objects using the descendants method of the loaded XML content.

We'll also add two more variable declarations to deal with the XML content loaded from the RSS feed and so that we can reference an XMLList of all <item> elements from the feed. Each <item> contains the details that we want to display in the application. Add the following to the script block:

```
private var MXNAContent:XML;
[Bindable]
private var allItems:XMLList;
```

Notice that we need the allItems variable to be bindable because we'll bind it as the dataProvider for the DataGrid.

Modify the opening <mx:DataGrid> element to reference the dataProvider, as shown here:

```
<mx:DataGrid id="MXNAData" dataProvider="{allItems}">
```

We can't display any content in columns until we finish creating the completeHandler function. Change the function as shown in bold here:

```
private function completeHandler(e:Event):void{
    MXNAContent = XML(e.target.data);
    MXNAContent.addNamespace(mxna);
    allItems = MXNAContent.descendants(rssItems);
}
```

The function sets the value of the MXNAContent XML object, casting the RSS feed as the data type XML. It adds the mxna namespace that we defined earlier to this content. It finishes by creating an XMLList of all <item> elements using the expression MXNAContent.descendants(rssItems). We can reference this XMLList using the name allItems.

Now that we've populated the relevant data for the application, we can add some columns to the DataGrid. We'll display the title and date in columns, with a third column containing a button that we'll be able to click to see more details. Modify the <mx:DataGrid> tag as shown here:

```
<mx:DataGrid id="MXNAData" dataProvider="{allItems}">
    <mx:columns>
        <mx:DataGridColumn dataField="title" headerText="Title"/>
        <mx:DataGridColumn dataField="date" headerText="Date"/>
        <mx:DataGridColumn>
            <mx:itemRenderer>
                <mx:Component>
                    <mx:Button label="See more"/>
                </mx:Component>
            </mx:itemRenderer>
        </mx:DataGridColumn>
    </mx:columns>
</mx:DataGrid>
```

We've added three columns, one for the title, one for the date, and a third containing an inline item renderer that displays a button with the label See more. In order to display the title and date details correctly, we'll need to add a labelFunction attribute.

We'll start with the title column. Modify the tag as shown here:

```
<mx:DataGridColumn dataField="title" headerText="Title"
    labelFunction="showTitle"/>
```

We'll display the title using the showTitle function, which we'll add now in the script block:

```
private function showTitle(item:Object, column:DataGridColumn):String {
    return item.descendants(rssTitle).toString();
}
```

The function finds the <title> element using the rssTitle QName object as an argument to the descendants method of the XMLList dataProvider.

We'll also add a labelFunction attribute for the date column:

```
<mx:DataGridColumn dataField="date" headerText="Date"
    labelFunction="showDate"/>
```

Add this function to the script block:

```
private function showDate(item:Object, column:DataGridColumn):String {
    var dateString:String;
    var formatMXNADate:DateFormatter = new DateFormatter();
    formatMXNADate.formatString = "DD-MMM-YYYY";
    dateString = formatMXNADate.format(item.descendants(rssDate).➥
        toString());
    return dateString;
}
```

Check that Flex Builder has added the following import statement:

```
import mx.formatters.DateFormatter;
```

The function uses a DateFormatter object to display the date using a DD-MMM-YYYY format. We create the string to display by calling the format method of the DateFormatter and passing in a reference to the <date> element from the RSS feed.

Run the application to check that the RSS feed loads correctly, and that the title and date display in the DataGrid. Figure 9-18 shows how the application should look at this point.

So far, so good! We still need to set the column widths and deal with word wrapping in case we load a long title.

Change the <mx:DataGrid> tag as shown here in bold:

```
<mx:DataGrid id="MXNAData" dataProvider="{allItems}"
    variableRowHeight="true">
```

This attribute allows us to have rows of variable heights. Modify the first two columns as follows:

```
<mx:DataGridColumn dataField="title" headerText="Title"
    labelFunction="showTitle" width="250" wordWrap="true"/>
<mx:DataGridColumn dataField="date" headerText="Date"
    labelFunction="showDate" width="150"/>
```

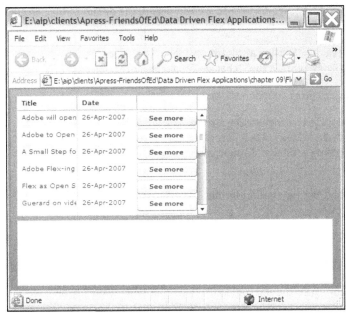

Figure 9-18. The DataGrid loaded from the MXNA RSS feed

Running the application now shows the DataGrid looking a little better, as seen in Figure 9-19.

Figure 9-19. Formatting the columns in the DataGrid

The next step is to add a change handler so we can display the details of the selected news item in the TextArea component. Add the change attribute to the opening <mx:DataGrid> element:

```
<mx:DataGrid id="MXNAData" dataProvider="{allItems}"
    variableRowHeight="true" change="changeHandler(event)">
```

Now add the changeHandler function to the script block:

```
private function changeHandler(e:Event):void {
    txtDescription.text = e.currentTarget.selectedItem.➥
        descendants(rssDescription).toString();
}
```

This function displays the description in the TextArea. It accesses the <description> element using the following expression:

```
e.currentTarget.selectedItem.descendants(rssDescription)
```

It also uses the toString method to render the content as text for display in the TextArea control.

We also need to configure the Button controls so that when we click one, we load the URL of the clicked item in a new web browser window. We'll do that in the itemClick event of the DataGrid rather than in the button click handler. If we click a nonheader item in the third column, we'll load the URL specified in the <link> element.

Add the itemClick attribute to the opening <mx:DataGrid> element:

```
<mx:DataGrid id="MXNAData" dataProvider="{allItems}"
    variableRowHeight="true"   change="changeHandler(event)"
    itemClick="itemClickHandler(event)">
```

You'll also need to add the itemClickHandler function to the code block:

```
private function itemClickHandler(e:ListEvent):void {
    if (e.columnIndex == 2 && e.rowIndex > 0) {
        var link:String = e.currentTarget.selectedItem.➥
            descendants(rssLink).toString();
        navigateToURL(new URLRequest(link), '_blank');
    }
}
```

This function receives a ListEvent object as an argument, so check that Flex Builder has added the following import statement:

```
import mx.events.ListEvent;
```

The event handler function checks to see that we've selected an item from the third column using the comparison e.columnIndex ==2. If that item isn't in a header row (that is, e.rowIndex > 0), we create the link variable by identifying the rssLink QName object. We then use the navigateToURL action to load the URL into a new web browser window.

Run the application. You should see the description populate when you select a row, as shown in Figure 9-20.

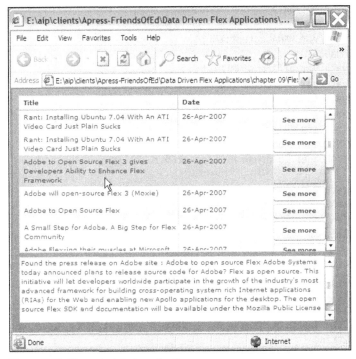

Figure 9-20. The completed application

You should also see the details of the selected news item load into a new browser window when you click the Button control for that news item.

The complete source for the application follows:

```
<?xml version="1.0" encoding="utf-8"?>
<mx:Application xmlns:mx="http://www.adobe.com/2006/mxml"
  layout="absolute" creationComplete="loadMXNA(event)">
  <mx:Script>
    <![CDATA[
      import mx.events.ListEvent;
      import flash.net.URLLoader;
      import flash.net.URLRequest;
      import mx.events.FlexEvent;
      import mx.formatters.DateFormatter;
      import mx.controls.dataGridClasses.DataGridColumn;
      private var mxna:Namespace = new Namespace("http://purl.org/➥
        rss/1.0/");
      private var dc:Namespace = new Namespace("http://purl.org/dc/➥
        elements/1.1/");
      private var rssItems:QName = new QName(mxna, "item");
```

```
                private var rssTitle:QName = new QName(mxna, "title");
                private var rssLink:QName = new QName(mxna, "link");
                private var rssDescription:QName = new QName(mxna, ➥
                  "description");
                private var rssDate:QName = new QName(dc, "date");
                private var MXNAContent:XML;
                [Bindable]
                private var allItems:XMLList;
                private var MXNALoader:URLLoader = new URLLoader();
                private function loadMXNA(e:FlexEvent):void {
                  var strURL:String = "http://weblogs.macromedia.com/mxna/xml/➥
                    rss.cfm?query=byMostRecent&languages=1"
                  MXNALoader.addEventListener(Event.COMPLETE, completeHandler);
                  MXNALoader.load(new URLRequest(strURL));
                }
                private function completeHandler(e:Event):void{
                  MXNAContent = XML(e.target.data);
                  MXNAContent.addNamespace(mxna);
                  allItems = MXNAContent.descendants(rssItems);
                }
                private function showTitle(item:Object, column:DataGridColumn)➥
                  :String {
                  return item.descendants(rssTitle).toString();
                }
                private function showDate(item:Object, column:DataGridColumn)➥
                  :String {
                  var dateString:String;
                  var formatMXNADate:DateFormatter = new DateFormatter();
                  formatMXNADate.formatString = "DD-MMM-YYYY";
                  dateString = formatMXNADate.format(item.descendants(rssDate)➥
                    .toString());
                  return dateString;
                }
                private function changeHandler(e:Event):void {
                  txtDescription.text = e.currentTarget.selectedItem.➥
                    descendants(rssDescription).toString();
                }
                private function itemClickHandler(e:ListEvent):void {
                  if (e.columnIndex == 2 && e.rowIndex > 0) {
                    var link:String = e.currentTarget.selectedItem.➥
                      descendants(rssLink).toString();
                    navigateToURL(new URLRequest(link), '_blank');
                  }
                }
              }
            ]]>
          </mx:Script>
          <mx:VBox x="10" y="10">
            <mx:DataGrid id="MXNAData" dataProvider="{allItems}"
              variableRowHeight="true" change="changeHandler(event)"
```

```
            itemClick="itemClickHandler(event)">
            <mx:columns>
              <mx:DataGridColumn dataField="title" headerText="Title"
                labelFunction="showTitle" width="250" wordWrap="true"/>
              <mx:DataGridColumn dataField="date" headerText="Date"
                labelFunction="showDate" width="150"/>
                <mx:DataGridColumn>
                  <mx:itemRenderer>
                      <mx:Component>
                        <mx:Button label="See more"/>
                      </mx:Component>
                  </mx:itemRenderer>
                </mx:DataGridColumn>
            </mx:columns>
          </mx:DataGrid>
          <mx:TextArea id="txtDescription" width="500" height="100"/>
        </mx:VBox>
      </mx:Application>
```

You can find this file saved as dataGridExample.mxml with the other chapter resources.

Summary

In this chapter, we looked at three of the data-driven controls available within the Flex framework: the Repeater, the TileList, and the DataGrid. These controls operate in a similar way, each having a dataProvider property that can be bound to external content. For each control, I worked through a simple example that demonstrated the most important features.

In the next chapter, I want to look at the debugging tools that are available to help out when things go wrong in a Flex application.

Chapter 10

DEBUGGING FLEX APPLICATIONS

As a developer, I've added my fair share of errors into applications by making typing mistakes, by writing incorrect code, and sometimes through plain old sloppy coding. It's impossible to get things right every time.

Flex Builder provides a range of approaches that can help to track down the errors that all developers make. From adding simple trace commands to more-sophisticated debugging tools, Flex Builder offers it all. You can display a range of warnings and error messages in the Console view, and Flex Builder automatically alerts you to potential issues in the Problems view.

If you've built applications with earlier versions of Flash, you'll find that Flex Builder includes the same range of debugging tools. I actually find them easier to use in Flex Builder. You can work with breakpoints; suspend, resume, and terminate an application; step into the code; watch variables; and evaluate expressions.

In order to debug a Flex application using Flex Builder, you need to click the Debug button on the Flex Builder toolbar instead of the Run button. This button allows you to compile the application and view it using the debug version of Flash Player 9.

You must make sure that you've installed this Flash Player version before you start the debugging process. Flex Builder will complain if you try to debug an application without having installed the debug Flash Player. You can download and install it from www.adobe.com/support/flashplayer/downloads.html.

In this chapter, I want to cover the following topics:

- Working with the trace method
- Working with the `<mx:TraceTarget>` tag
- The types of errors that occur in Flex applications
- Using ActionScript to trap errors
- Working with breakpoints
- Stepping into code
- Watching variables
- Evaluating expressions

You can download the resource files for this chapter from www.friendsofed.com. Let's start with a look at the changes to the trace method in ActionScript 3.0.

Working with the trace method

Most developers who have experience with Flash will have used the global trace method extensively. It's usually the first option that developers use to try and locate errors when things go wrong. In earlier versions of ActionScript, the trace action displayed content in the Output window when testing the Flash file.

In Flex Builder, you can only see the results of the global trace method when you debug an application using the Debug button. Any output from a trace statement appears in the Console view of Flex Builder, as shown in Figure 10-1. You usually have to switch from the web browser back to Flex Builder to view the results of trace statements.

Figure 10-1. Displaying the results of a trace statement

In this case, the output in the Console view comes from the following application, saved as SimpleTrace1.mxml with your resources:

```
<?xml version="1.0" encoding="utf-8"?>
<mx:Application xmlns:mx="http://www.adobe.com/2006/mxml"
  layout="absolute">
  <mx:Script>
    <![CDATA[
      private function traceHello(e:MouseEvent):void {
        trace ("Hello world");
      }
    ]]>
```

```
      </mx:Script>
      <mx:VBox x="10" y="10">
        <mx:Button label="Click me" click="traceHello(event)"/>
      </mx:VBox>
    </mx:Application>
```

Because we clicked the Debug button, Flex Builder takes us into a debugging session. You can tell that we're currently debugging the application because the red button is active in the toolbar at the top right of the Console view. Closing the browser window will end the debugging session. You can also click the red button on the toolbar to end the session and close the browser at the same time.

By default, calling the trace method displays the output in the Console view, but it's also possible to write the output to a text file.

Logging to a text file

You can log the output from your trace methods to a text file. This approach might be useful if you want to keep a record of your debugging efforts or if you want to be able to analyze the output more thoroughly. You'll need to set up logging by creating a file called mm.cfg.

The mm.cfg file must contain the appropriate settings as shown here:

```
ErrorReportingEnable=1
TraceOutputFileEnable=1
```

I've included a simple mm.cfg file with your chapter resources if you want to see how the file should look.

You can create the mm.cfg file using a text editor and you need to save it to the home directory, usually the folder C:\Documents and Settings*user_name*\ for Windows XP machines. (Don't forget to replace *user_name* with your own username.) On a Macintosh computer, you need to save the file to MacHD:Library:Application Support.

By default on a Windows computer, the log file is saved under the name flashlog.txt to C:\Documents and Settings*user_name*\Application Data\Macromedia\Flash Player\Logs\. The log file is saved with the same name to Macintosh users/*user_name*/library/preferences/macromedia/ flash player/logs/ on a Macintosh computer.

Note that you can add the setting TraceOutputFileName to change the location and file name of the log file. However, the Flash Player 9 update ignores this property.

Each time you debug the application, you'll overwrite the log file, so don't forget to save it under a different name if you need to keep a record of your successive debugging efforts.

An alternative to using the global trace method is the <mx:TraceTarget> tag. This tag is particularly useful for debugging the loading of external data.

Working with the <mx:TraceTarget> tag

One of the most common frustrations for developers is trying to debug the process of loading data from an external source. You run the application and nothing happens when you try to request the external document. It's hard to know where the error exists. You're not sure if there a problem with the URL you're using or whether there's a problem with the requested document itself. There could also be an error in the code you're using to access the content in Flex.

One solution to this problem is to use the <mx:TraceTarget> tag. When you add this tag to your application and click the Debug button, you'll see all relevant output in the Console view. You can see an example of this using the following simple application:

```
<?xml version="1.0" encoding="utf-8"?>
<mx:Application xmlns:mx="http://www.adobe.com/2006/mxml"
  layout="absolute" creationComplete="textService.send()">
  <mx:TraceTarget/>
  <mx:HTTPService id="textService" url="assets/textOnly.txt"
    resultFormat="text"/>
  <mx:VBox x="10" y="10">
    <mx:Text id="txtLoadedContent" text="{textService.lastResult}"/>
  </mx:VBox>
</mx:Application>
```

You can find this code saved as TraceTag1.mxml with your resources. When you debug it, you'll see something similar to the output displayed in Figure 10-2. Flex Builder may prompt you to switch to the Debugging Perspective to view this output.

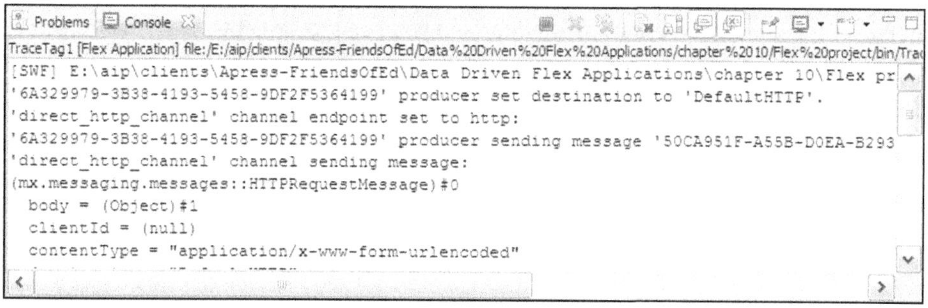

Figure 10-2. The output from the <mx:TraceTarget> tag

You can see that this tag displays a wealth of information about the request in the Console view. Most importantly, because we can see the details of the request without error messages, we can confirm that the request was successful.

The <mx:TraceTarget> tag is especially useful when working with web services because it provides information about each step of the request, including the returned SOAP envelope.

As a tip, don't forget to remove any <mx:TraceTarget> tags from your code before you move a Flex application to the production environment.

Now that we've covered the simplest of debugging approaches, let's look more closely at the type of errors that you're likely to receive.

Understanding Flex errors

In Flash 8 and earlier, you'd often see compiler errors where you had included incorrect or misspelled code in your applications. However, when you actually ran the application, Flash Player would fail silently if it hit some incorrect ActionScript. This behavior has changed with Flash Player 9.

As with Flash, Flex will still present you with error messages when you try to compile ActionScript that contains syntactical errors. These are called compiler errors. You may also see some compiler warnings, and I'll explain those shortly. Flash Player 9, however, will also display run-time errors in the web browser instead of failing silently when you run an application containing certain types of errors. This change in behavior can cause some nasty dialog boxes for unsuspecting users!

Compiler warnings and compile errors occur when you try to compile the code in the application, usually when you save the file.

Compiler warning messages

Compiler warning messages appear in the Problems view within Flex Builder and are there to alert developers to potential issues with their coding. These messages don't prevent the application from running successfully and they won't appear in the finished application.

Warning messages may relate to the developer's coding style, for example, leaving out a variable type or scope declaration. These messages may also occur when trying to migrate ActionScript 2.0 code to ActionScript 3.0. A third class of warnings relates to valid statements that may behave differently from what the developer expects.

Figure 10-3 shows an example of warnings displayed within the Problems view.

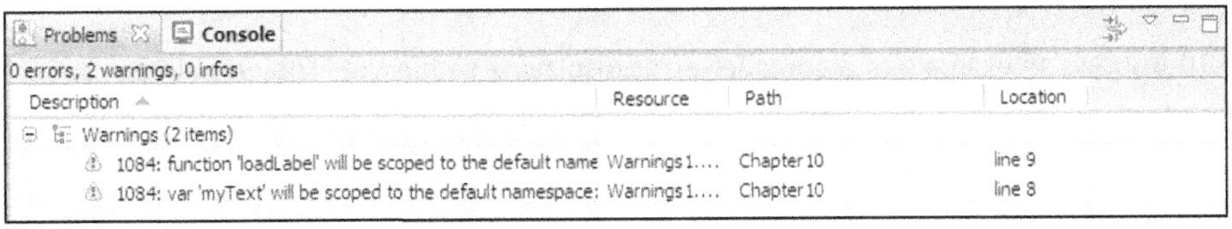

Figure 10-3. Warning displayed in the Problems panel

The warnings come from the following application, saved as Warnings1.mxml with your resources:

```
<?xml version="1.0" encoding="utf-8"?>
<mx:Application xmlns:mx="http://www.adobe.com/2006/mxml"
  layout="absolute" creationComplete="loadLabel(event)">
  <mx:Script>
    <![CDATA[
      import mx.events.FlexEvent;
      var myText = "Hello world";
      function loadLabel(e:FlexEvent):void {
        lblMessage.text = myText;
      }
    ]]>
  </mx:Script>
  <mx:VBox x="10" y="10">
```

```
    <mx:Label id="lblMessage"/>
  </mx:VBox>
</mx:Application>
```

In this case, the warnings occur because the developer hasn't added a scope for the variable and function declared in the script block.

The message indicates that the default scope, internal, will apply to both the variable and function. Regardless of this warning, the application will still compile and run successfully.

There are too many compiler warning messages to cover here. At the time of writing, you can find a list of compiler messages that you're likely to encounter at the Adobe web site at http://livedocs.adobe.com/flex/201/langref/compilerWarnings.html.

The display of warnings is turned on by default. You can check this in the settings for the Flex Builder compiler. Choose Project ➤ Properties and select the Flex Compiler category on the left. Make sure that the Enable warnings option is selected.

Let's move on to the topic of compiler errors, which are errors detected when the SWF file is compiled. These errors are likely to stop an application from working correctly.

Compiler errors

Compiler errors occur when Flex tries to compile code that you've written. They happen when the compiler encounters a code error during the process of creating a SWF file. These code errors are often due to spelling mistakes or incorrect use of property, method, and event references.

The error messages associated with compiler errors will display in the Problems panel. Some of these errors are easy to track down from their descriptions, while others can seem very cryptic.

Figure 10-4 shows an example of a compiler error displaying within the Problems view.

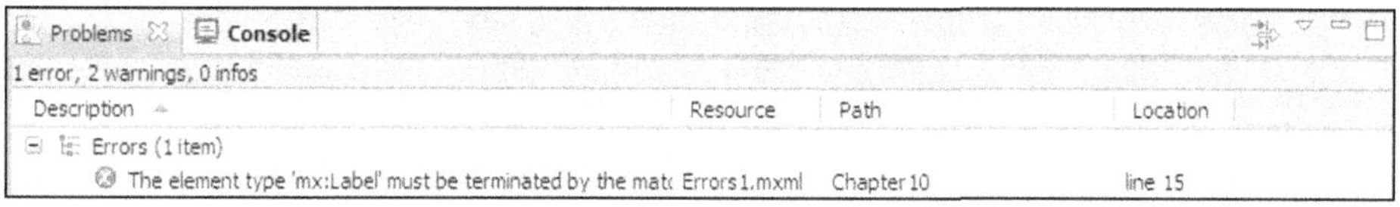

Figure 10-4. A compiler error displayed in the Problems panel

The error is produced by the following application, saved as Errors1.mxml with your resources:

```
<?xml version="1.0" encoding="utf-8"?>
<mx:Application xmlns:mx="http://www.adobe.com/2006/mxml"
  layout="absolute" creationComplete="loadLabel(event)">
  <mx:Script>
    <![CDATA[
      import mx.events.FlexEvent;
      private var myText = "Hello world";
      private function loadLabel(e:FlexEvent):void {
        lblMessage.text = myText;
```

```
        }
      ]]>
    </mx:Script>
    <mx:VBox x="10" y="10">
      <mx:Label id="lblMessage">
    </mx:VBox>
  </mx:Application>
```

The compiler error occurs because there is a missing ending tag in this line:

```
    <mx:Label id="lblMessage">
```

Luckily, the description included in this error makes it easy to track down and fix.

This type of error would also create problems when working in Design view, and Figure 10-5 shows you the associated error that you'd see.

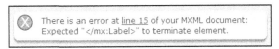

There is an error at line 15 of your MXML document: Expected "</mx:Label>" to terminate element.

Figure 10-5. A compiler error displayed in Design view

You can find a list of compiler error messages at http://livedocs.adobe.com/flex/201/langref/compilerErrors.html.

Run-time errors are more serious and occur in Flash Player 9 when a user tries to run or interact with an application.

Run-time errors

Run-time errors occur when you actually try to run the application. You may have seen them in a pop-up box when you run the application in the web browser, as shown in Figure 10-6.

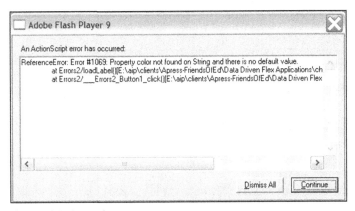

Figure 10-6. A run-time error

317

In this case, the error is caused in the following application because we are trying to access a nonexistent property color in the myArray object. The offending line appears in bold:

```
<?xml version="1.0" encoding="utf-8"?>
<mx:Application xmlns:mx="http://www.adobe.com/2006/mxml"
  layout="absolute">
  <mx:Script>
    <![CDATA[
      private var myArray:Array = ["one", "two", "three"];
      private function loadLabel(e:MouseEvent):void {
        lblMessage.text = myArray[0].color;
      }
    ]]>
  </mx:Script>
  <mx:VBox x="10" y="10">
    <mx:Label id="lblMessage"/>
    <mx:Button label="Click me!" click="loadLabel(event)"/>
  </mx:VBox>
</mx:Application>
```

Note that this problem doesn't generate a compiler error because the syntax is correct. The example is saved as Errors2.mxml with your resources.

The Adobe web site includes a list of run-time errors that you may encounter at http://livedocs. adobe.com/flex/2/langref/runtimeErrors.html.

Run-time errors are unsightly and may appear a little frightening to application users. Best practice dictates that we try to use ActionScript to deal with them.

Using ActionScript to catch run-time errors

As you can see in Figure 10-6, run-time errors are likely to be disruptive for users of a Flex application. Instead of allowing these errors to display in a web browser, you can intercept them and display more appropriate messages in the application interface or take alternative action using ActionScript.

The main tool for developers is the try catch block.

Working with try catch blocks

Using try catch statements allows you to respond to, or **catch**, an error caused by code within a try block. In ActionScript 3.0, they work like this:

```
try {
  // code that may cause an error
}
catch (e:ErrorType) {
  //code to deal with errors
}
```

The catch statement references an argument containing an Error object. You can respond by displaying the name property of the error or a message associated with the error object. You might also write alternative ActionScript code to deal with the situation. If you're not sure about which type of error you may encounter or you want to track any error in the application, use the generic type Error. This is the base class for all error types.

In addition, you can track down the cause of the error when debugging by using the getStackTrace method to return a string representation of the call stack. You can even display a string representation of the Error object using the toString method.

We could rewrite the code block containing the run-time error in the following way (you can find the complete file with your resources under the name Errors3.mxml):

```
private var myArray:Array = ["one", "two", "three"];
private function loadLabel(e:MouseEvent):void {
  try {
    lblMessage.text = myArray[0].color;
    }
  catch (e:Error) {
    trace ("Name is: " + e.name);
    trace ("Message is: " + e.message);
    trace ("Stack trace: " + e.getStackTrace());
    trace ("To string: " + e.toString());
  }
}
```

We've added the line that might cause an error in a try block:

```
lblMessage.text = myArray[0].color;
```

If we encounter an error, the catch block includes a number of trace statements to help us to track down the problem.

Running the application shows all the details associated with the run-time error in the Console view of Flex Builder. You can see this output in Figure 10-7.

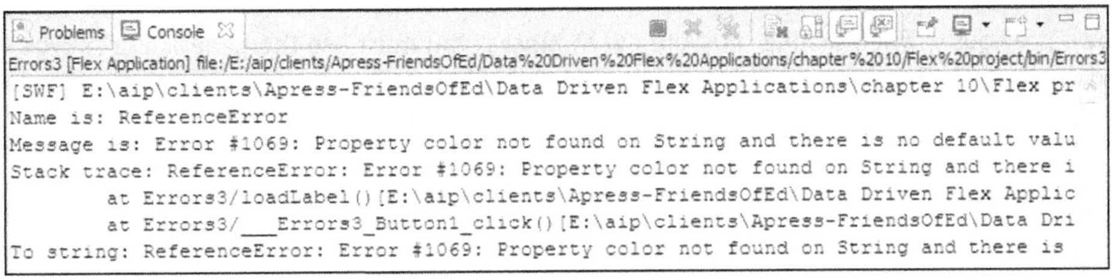

Figure 10-7. Displaying an error using a try catch block

In this case, we've caught a ReferenceError, and the error message is very descriptive, saying Property color not found on String and there is no default value. The getStackTrace method provides information from the stack about the method calls made in the script. We can see that the error arose from a button click.

If the code that you write has the potential to generate more than one type of error, you can include multiple catch blocks.

Including more than one catch block

You can include multiple catch blocks in your code if you want to respond to different types of errors that might arise from a single code block. You can find out about the error types recognized in Flex at http://livedocs.adobe.com/flex/201/langref/Error.html. For example, we could specifically target the ReferenceError type that occurred in the previous example using the following approach:

```
private var myArray:Array = ["one", "two", "three"];
private function loadLabel(e:MouseEvent):void {
  try {
    lblMessage.text = myArray[0].color;
  }
  catch (e:ReferenceError) {
    trace ("ReferenceError message is: " + e.message);
  }
  catch (e:Error) {
    trace ("Error message is: " + e.message);
  }
}
```

You can find the complete code for this example saved as Errors4.mxml with the other resources.

When you use multiple catch blocks, only one catch block will execute and it will be the first one with a matching error. This means you can't respond to all errors that might be raised within the block of code contained in the try section.

In the preceding example, we'll get a match with the first catch block, and debugging the application will display the text ReferenceError message is before the error message.

As shown previously, when writing multiple catch blocks, you must use the generic Error type in the last block. Using the Error type will create a match with all other errors because it is the base class for all error types. This will prevent any further catch blocks from being executed.

There's one more enhancement available to try catch blocks: the finally block.

Adding a finally block

You can use a finally block after the last catch block to execute code that will run regardless of whether or not an error was thrown by the code in the try block:

```
try {
  // code that may cause an error
}
catch (e:ErrorType) {
  //code to deal with errors
}
finally {
  //code that will always run after either the try or catch block
}
```

The following code block, illustrating the finally statement, appears in the resource file Errors5.mxml:

```
private function loadLabel(e:MouseEvent):void {
  try {
    lblMessage.text = myArray[0].color;
  }
  catch (e:ReferenceError) {
    trace ("ReferenceError message is: " + e.message);
  }
  catch (e:Error) {
    trace ("Error message is: " + e.message);
  }
  finally {
    trace ("Finally got to end of the try-catch statement!");
  }
}
```

Flex allows many different types of error tracking. It's also possible for developers to generate their own custom errors.

Throwing custom errors

As mentioned, there are many different types of errors that can be thrown and all are based on the top-level Error class. Developers can also create their own errors using the throw statement. This approach allows developers to word their own error messages and respond appropriately. For example, you could create custom errors to respond to messages encountered when loading external content.

You can see an example of a custom error in the following code block:

```
private var myArray:Array = ["one", "two", "three"];
private function loadLabel(e:MouseEvent):void {
  try {
    throw new Error("This is a custom error");
  }
  catch (e:Error) {
    trace ("Error message is: " + e.message);
  }
}
```

Running this simple application would display the message Error message is: This is a custom error. This example is very simplistic, but you get the general idea and you can find it saved in the Errors6.mxml file.

Developers can also create custom error classes.

Creating custom errors

Errors specific to an application might be best handled using a custom error class. For example, if you use the same server-side error messages when loading external content, you could develop a range of custom error classes to respond to each of the standard error messages.

All custom error classes must extend the top level Error class. The constructor function must call the super method, passing the error message and code as shown in the following code block:

```
package com.aip {
  public class MyCustomError extends Error {
    public function MyCustomError(message:String, errorCode: int) {
      super(message, errorCode);
    }
  }
}
```

You can use this custom error class by adding an import statement:

```
import com.aip.MyCustomError;
```

and calling it with the throw statement:

```
<?xml version="1.0" encoding="utf-8"?>
<mx:Application xmlns:mx="http://www.adobe.com/2006/mxml"
  layout="absolute">
  <mx:Script>
    <![CDATA[
      import com.aip.MyCustomError;
      private var myArray:Array = ["one", "two", "three"];
      private function loadLabel(e:MouseEvent):void {
        try {
```

```
          throw new MyCustomError("This is a custom error message",➥
            999);
        }
        catch (e:Error) {
          trace ("Error message is: " + e.message);
        }
      }
    }
  ]]>
  </mx:Script>
  <mx:VBox x="10" y="10">
    <mx:Label id="lblMessage"/>
    <mx:Button label="Click me!" click="loadLabel(event)"/>
  </mx:VBox>
</mx:Application>
```

You can find the Errors7.mxml and MyCustomError.as files with your resources.

In the preceding line, we'd be able to use the standard message property as well as the customCode property to display information about the error.

Some applications require more detailed analysis to determine errors, and that's where the Flex debugger tools come in.

Using the debugger

When you click the Debug button in Flex Builder, the application runs using the debug Flash player in the web browser. Any trace methods that you've included will display in the Console view back in Flex Builder. If you've included a number of trace statements, you may want to switch between the browser and Flex Builder as you interact with your application.

You can use breakpoints to pause the application at certain stages so you can track what's happening more closely. In debugging mode, when the application reaches a breakpoint, Flex Builder activates the Flex Debugging perspective. Unless you've clicked the Remember my decision option, you'll see the message shown in Figure 10-8.

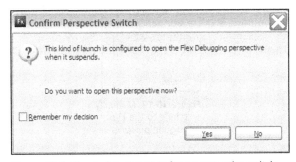

Figure 10-8. Flex Builder prompts for a perspective switch.

323

The focus will automatically switch from the web browser back to Flex Builder. If you say Yes to the message in Figure 10-8, you'll see the Flex Debugging perspective, as shown in Figure 10-9.

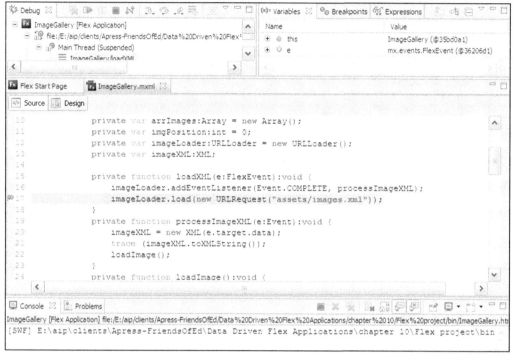

Figure 10-9. The Flex Debugger perspective

Notice that the screen layout appears quite different from the normal development environment. You can see the Debug view at the top left along with a toolbar containing debugging tools. You can also access the Variables, Breakpoints, and Expressions views at the top right.

You can manually switch to the Flex Debugging perspective at any time using the Perspective bar at the top right of the Flex Builder IDE, as shown in Figure 10-10.

Figure 10-10. Manually switching to the Flex Debugging perspective

You'll notice that three perspectives are available in Flex Builder, the others being the Flex Development and Flex Profiling perspectives. While debugging code, you might find it easier to use the Perspective bar to switch between the perspectives. Remember, though, that you might want to end the debugging session before you switch back to the Development perspective.

You can manage the debugging process in the Debug view, shown at the top left of the screen in Figure 10-10. The view contains a toolbar with buttons that are useful for debugging your code. Figure 10-11 shows this toolbar.

Figure 10-11. Debugging tools

Table 10-1 explains the buttons in the toolbar and their actions, describing each left to right.

Table 10-1. The buttons available in Debug view

Button	Purpose
Remove All Terminated Launches	Clears all terminated debugging sessions
Resume	Resumes a suspended application
Suspend	Suspends an application
Terminate	Stops the debugging session
Disconnect	Disconnects the debugger when using remote debugging
Step Into	Steps into a function, stopping at the first line
Step Over	Runs the current line of code
Step Return	Continues running the current function
Drop to Frame	An Eclipse function not supported in Flex Builder
Use Step Filters/Step Debug	An Eclipse function not supported in Flex Builder

Adding breakpoints

Developers use breakpoints to control how an application runs within the debug Flash Player. They add breakpoints so they can stop the application at a predetermined position. You can add breakpoints at any of the following locations:

- Where there is an event handler in an MXML tag
- On an executable line of ActionScript in a script block
- On an executable line of code in an ActionScript file

To add a breakpoint, switch to Source view and double-click to the left of the line number wherever you want the application to stop. You can also right-click and choose Toggle Breakpoint. Whichever method you choose, you should see a blue dot at the appropriate point, as seen in Figure 10-12.

Figure 10-12. A breakpoint at line 22 in the application

You can remove the breakpoint by double-clicking again, and there is no limit to the number of breakpoints that you can add.

If you try to set a breakpoint in a location other than the three mentioned previously, Flex Builder will try to find the next valid location in the next ten lines and move the breakpoint when debugging. If no valid location exists, the breakpoint won't be moved and will be ignored.

When the application hits a breakpoint, it will automatically stop. You can then control the flow of the application using the Resume, Terminate, Step Into, Step Over, and Step Return buttons. You can also add more breakpoints during the debugging process.

Managing breakpoints

The Breakpoints view allows you to manage your breakpoints. You can see this view in Figure 10-13.

Figure 10-13. The Breakpoints view

You can see that the view shows all breakpoints in the application. You can skip an individual breakpoint during debugging by unchecking the check box within this view. You can remove a single breakpoint by clicking the single cross button on the toolbar. You can remove all breakpoints using the double cross button.

Viewing variable values

Once you hit a breakpoint, you may want to look at the value of variables in your application. You can do this using the Variables view. Variables will appear in the context of the current object, located in the this reference. You will probably want to expand this reference by clicking the plus sign to the left.

Simple variables appear as a single line in the panel, while variables that are more complicated appear over several lines. Figure 10-14 shows the value of a variable in the Variables view. Note that I first had to expand this and imageXML before I could access the variable details.

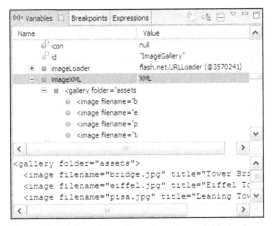

Figure 10-14. Examining the value of a variable in the Variables view

The imageXML variable contains the XML content shown at the bottom of the Variables view.

If a breakpoint appears within a function, you'll also be able to see the local variables defined in that function. These variables appear with an L icon, as shown in Figure 10-15.

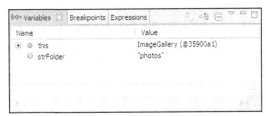

Figure 10-15. Local variable strFolder appears with an L icon.

In this case, we can see the local variable strFolder with a value of "photos".

You can find a variable by name by right-clicking in the list of variables and choosing the Find option from the shortcut menu. Make sure you expand any sections that you want to search within before you do so.

Figure 10-16 shows how you can use the Find dialog box to find a variable starting with the text image.

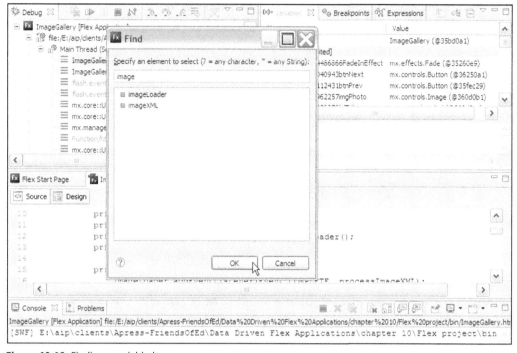

Figure 10-16. Finding a variable by name

If you have a lot of variables in your application, you might find this function very useful!

Changing the value of a variable

You can change the value of a variable during a debugging session. Change the value by right-clicking the variable in the Variables view and choosing Change Value. You can see this process in Figure 10-17.

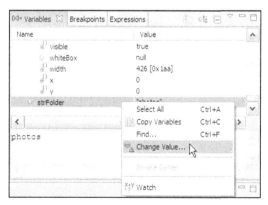

Figure 10-17. Changing the value of a variable

You can then enter a temporary value for the variable. This might be useful if you are going to continue debugging and want to use a new value for your variable. You can make the change and continue testing without permanently changing your application code.

Watching a variable

To watch a variable as you work through an application, right-click it in the Variables view and choose the Create Watch Expression option, as shown in Figure 10-18.

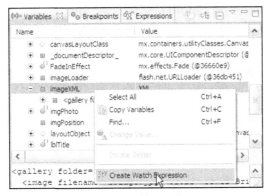

Figure 10-18. Adding a variable watch

You can also right-click the Expressions view and choose Create Watch Expression. Type in the variable name and click OK. Either approach will add the variable to the Expressions view, as shown in Figure 10-19. You can keep track of the values of these variables as you interact with the application while debugging. You can also use Create Watch Expression to add an expression rather than a variable.

You can see variables that you're watching in the Expressions view, shown in Figure 10-19.

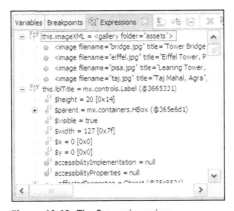

Figure 10-19. The Expressions view

Figure 10-19 shows a variable imageXML and a control. You can see the value of the variable. When you expand the lblTitle reference, you can see a list of all properties of the control. If you are watching many variables, you can right-click the Expressions view and choose Find to locate a specific variable name.

Summary

You can see that there are many different approaches that you can use to work with application errors in Flex Builder. From the use of the global trace method right through to setting breakpoints, stepping through code, and watching variables, there are tools available for every level of developer and for every type of application error.

This chapter ends Part 1 of the book. In the second section, we'll work through some simple applications, showing how you can include server-side logic to create working Flex applications. We'll work with XML, ColdFusion, ASP .NET 2.0, and PHP case studies in Part 2.

PART 2

DATA-DRIVEN APPLICATIONS

In the second part of this book, we show a number of different Flex applications. We start with a look at an XML application without server-side interaction. Then we work through ColdFusion, ASP.NET, and PHP case studies.

Chapter 11

XML CASE STUDY

We'll start Part 2 of the book by looking at an XML case study. The application we'll cover is a simple photo gallery application created using Flex Builder 3. You've probably seen several photo gallery applications in action, and that's why I've chosen it as the first case study. If you've built something similar in Flash, working through an example in Flex Builder will help you to understand how you can structure the application and take advantage of some of the Flex-specific features.

The application will allow users to choose a photo gallery containing a collection of images. They'll be able to view all images in that section or choose a different photo gallery. Each photo has a caption that will display at the same time as the image. We'll add a fade-in effect to the image as it appears.

In this application, the details of the galleries and photos come from an XML document that can be edited in any text or XHTML editor. Users won't be able to update the gallery details or add new photographs or captions from within the application.

The application will consist of the following parts:

- An assets folder containing the XML document describing the photo gallery and the related JPEG images
- A custom ActionScript class that handles the loading of the external XML document and the content within
- A custom component containing a Text and Image control for displaying the relevant caption and photo
- An application file that creates the interface, references the custom class and custom component, and handles the user interaction

You can download the resources for this chapter from the friends of ED website at www. friendsofed.com. It contains a zipped file with the finished project as well as the resource files for the application. You can also use your own images if you prefer.

We'll start by examining the application in a little more detail.

Understanding the application

Before we create the application, it's important to understand how it works and how the data source is structured. I'll walk you through the interface and the XML document.

The application interface

The application starts with a ComboBox control that displays a list of different gallery names, as shown in Figure 11-1. Each gallery corresponds to a folder of a different name that contains a number of photos.

Figure 11-1. The user can select a gallery from a ComboBox control.

Once the user has chosen a gallery, the Choose gallery prompt will disappear from the ComboBox, and the first image from the selected gallery will display in the interface. You can see this in Figure 11-2, in which we've chosen the Central Australia gallery.

Figure 11-2. Choosing a gallery displays the first image within that gallery.

The photo fades in, and a caption displays above the image. For the first image, a button appears at the top right, allowing the user to progress to the next image.

Once the user moves to the second image by clicking the next image button, they'll see both a next and previous button, as shown in Figure 11-3.

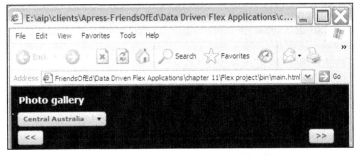

Figure 11-3. The interface, showing previous and next buttons

Users can click the buttons to navigate through the photographs in each gallery. The next button will not appear when they reach the last image in a gallery.

The application data source

The application is powered by a simple XML document. The file that I'll use for the application is saved as photos.xml with the resources download. The structure is as follows:

```
<?xml version="1.0" encoding="UTF-8"?>
<photoGallery>
  <gallery gName="" gFolder="">
    <photo file="">
      <caption></caption>
    </photo>
  </gallery>
</photoGallery>
```

For simplicity, I haven't shown the complete file here, but feel free to open photos.xml in your favorite text editor if you want to have a look while you read about its structure.

The XML document has a root element, <photoGallery>, which contains a number of <gallery> elements. Each <gallery> element has two attributes: gName indicates the name of the gallery for display as the label in the ComboBox control, and gFolder stores the name of the folder containing the photos for that gallery. Each gallery will be represented by a separate folder containing photographs within the Flex application.

Within the <gallery> element, details of each image appear inside a <photo> element. Each photo has a file attribute that stores the file name for the image. Inside the <photo> element, the caption appears in a child <caption> element. I could have added a description for the photo as an element here as well, but I wanted to keep things relatively simple.

The assets

I've provided a number of sample photos with the resources download, but you can easily use your own images. If you do this, you'll need to update the XML document to reference your own files and to structure them into galleries using folders as described here.

The photos appear within a folder called photos that I'll add to the assets folder in the Flex application. Each gallery appears as a separate folder inside that folder. For this example, I've created three galleries: African animals, Central Australia, and India. They are included in the folders Africa, Australia, and India, respectively, within the photos folder in the assets folder.

For simplicity, I've chosen images that are all landscape and sized them identically to 500 pixels wide. They vary slightly in height. You could extend the application so that the images size themselves appropriately, and I'll leave you to explore that option on your own.

Structuring the application

For this case study, you'll need to create a new Flex project, specifying the name and location of your choice. I set the root folder as the location for my source files. If you want to work through the steps with the chapter, add an assets folder and copy across the photos.xml file and the photos folder from the resources download.

Otherwise, if you want to import the completed application, you can use File ➤ Import and select the Archive file option. Navigate to the xmlCaseStudy.zip file with the downloaded resources and select the Flex project as the destination. When you click Finish, the relevant files will be added to the project.

Assuming that you're going to work through the steps to create the application from scratch, let's get started.

Creating the application structure

We'll need to create the interface, the custom class, and the custom component as parts of the application. During the process, I'll be moving between each of the different files rather than dealing with each one separately, so you can follow through the logical steps that you might follow in a similar situation.

I'll work through the following steps:

1. Creating the files and starting file structures
2. Structuring the custom class to load the XML document
3. Creating the custom object in the application
4. Processing the loaded XML content
5. Populating the ComboBox control with the XML content
6. Building the custom component interface and configuring it with ActionScript
7. Displaying the first image when a gallery is selected
8. Displaying the other images in a selected gallery

We'll start by creating the basic files that we'll need for the application.

Creating the interface

We'll start off by creating the interface for the application in the main application file. I've called my file main.mxml. Modify the application file so that the MXML tags appear as follows:

```
<?xml version="1.0" encoding="utf-8"?>
<mx:Application xmlns:mx="http://www.adobe.com/2006/mxml"
  layout="absolute" backgroundGradientColors="[#000000, #000000]">
  <mx:VBox x="10" y="10">
    <mx:Label text="Photo gallery" color="#ffffff" fontWeight="bold"
      fontSize="14"/>
    <mx:HBox>
      <mx:ComboBox id="cboGalleries"
        fillColors="[#e6e6e6, #c0c0c0]" fillAlphas="[1.0, 1.0]"
        prompt="Choose gallery"/>
    </mx:HBox>
```

```
        <mx:HBox width="100%">
          <mx:Button id="btnPrev" width="40" label="&lt;&lt;"
            fillColors="[#e6e6e6, #c0c0c0]" fillAlphas="[1.0, 1.0]"/>
          <mx:Spacer width="100%"/>
          <mx:Button id="btnNext" width="40" label="&gt;&gt;"
            fillColors="[#e6e6e6, #c0c0c0]" fillAlphas="[1.0, 1.0]"/>
        </mx:HBox>
      </mx:VBox>
    </mx:Application>
```

The interface contains a label for the title, a ComboBox control that we'll eventually populate with gallery names from the XML document, and next and previous buttons. Notice that I've changed the background to a black color because I think the photos look better that way. I've also lightened the gradient in the ComboBox and button controls to make the text easier to read. If you don't like how the interface appears, feel free to choose your own styling options.

If you run the application at this point, you should see an interface that looks the same as the one appearing in Figure 11-4.

Figure 11-4. The interface for
the application

We'll need to write some ActionScript in this file to make the application work, but first let's create the structure for the custom class file.

Creating the custom class

We'll handle the loading and processing of data in a custom class that we'll call GalleryLoader.as. Create this file using File ➤ New ➤ ActionScript Class. Enter the package name com.aip and the class name GalleryLoader into the dialog box. When you press the Finish button, the class file should contain the following code:

```
package com.aip
{
  public class GalleryLoader
  {
  }
}
```

We have a package and class declaration. Notice that by convention the package name appears in lowercase, while the class name uses an uppercase first letter.

The package corresponds to a folder hierarchy. If you look in the Navigator view, you should see that Flex Builder has also created the com and aip folders for the package structure. As I've mentioned previously, best practice requires that all classes are packaged in folders rather than in the top-level package at the root of the project. You should always make sure that your package keyword is followed by the folder path.

In addition to the custom class, we'll need a custom component to display the image and caption.

Creating the custom component

The custom component that we'll use will contain a Text control for the photo caption and an Image control into which we'll load the external image file. We'll also include a fade in effect when we show each image. We'll pass in the information for which photo to display from the application file.

Again, best practice indicates that we should store our component files in a subfolder rather than in the root directory. This approach helps us to organize the Flex Builder projects more effectively. They also allow us to reuse custom components in different applications.

Create a new folder in the com.aip package called components. Within this folder, create a new custom component using File ➤ New ➤ MXML Component. Give the custom component the name GalleryImage.mxml and base it on the VBox control. Remove the default values for width and height to leave the fields blank. We don't need to specify these properties.

When you click Finish, Flex Builder will create an MXML document containing the following code:

```
<?xml version="1.0" encoding="utf-8"?>
<mx:VBox xmlns="*" xmlns:mx="http://www.adobe.com/2006/mxml">
</mx:VBox>
```

We've built the document structures that we'll need. We're ready to get started on creating the application, so we'll switch back to the custom class file, GalleryLoader.as, and we'll start by loading the external XML document.

Writing the custom class

The custom class file will need to load the external XML document from the assets folder. We'll pass in the name and path of the XML document we want to load so that the class can be used with different documents.

After we've loaded the content, we'll dispatch an event to the application file, indicating that the content is available for display in the interface. The application will respond to the event and display the appropriate information in the interface.

We'll need to make the class bindable so that we can dispatch the event correctly. Add the following metatag above the class declaration, as shown here in bold:

```
[Bindable]
public class GalleryLoader {
```

Declaring private variables

The next step is to add the variables or properties that we'll need for the class file. Best practice indicates that we shouldn't allow an instance of the class to interact directly with these properties, so we'll make them private and then use getter and setter methods to access their values.

We'll use the following variables, so add them underneath the class declaration:

```
private var xmlGalleryContent:XML;
private var xmlLoader:URLLoader;
private var allGalleries:XMLList;
```

The first variable, xmlGalleryContent, will store the loaded content from the external XML document. It is of type XML because it will contain the complete document tree. We'll use the xmlLoader URLLoader object with a URLRequest object to load the file, and the final variable allGalleries is an XMLList that will store all the <gallery> nodes from the loaded content.

When you add the previous variables, Flex Builder should also add the following import statement automatically. If it doesn't, enter the statement yourself:

```
import flash.net.URLLoader;
```

Add another two import statements beneath this one:

```
import flash.net.URLRequest;
import flash.events.Event;
```

The first statement imports the URLRequest class that we'll need to specify the location of the external XML document for the URLLoader. We'll also use the Event class a little later.

I could also have changed the initial import statement as follows to import all classes from the package:

```
import.flash.net.*;
```

However, I prefer to see exactly which classes I'm using with my class files, so I choose to use separate import statements.

Creating the constructor method

All classes need a constructor method and it is good practice to add one, even if the method doesn't contain any code. However, in our case, the constructor will create the URLLoader object and add an event listener to process the loaded content.

Add the following method to the class file:

```
public function GalleryLoader() {
  xmlLoader = new URLLoader();
  xmlLoader.addEventListener(Event.COMPLETE, completeHandler);
}
```

We create a new URLLoader object and add an event listener that responds to the complete event. This event is dispatched when the content from the external XML document has finished loading. We'll need to add the completeHandler method a little later. The name of this method isn't significant, but it is common practice to name it in this way, using the name of the event and the word Handler.

We'll create an instance of this class using the constructor method in an ActionScript block within the application file shortly.

Loading the XML document

We need a public method in the class file to load the external XML document. We'll pass the name of the document to this method from the application so that we can use the class with more than one gallery application.

Add the public load method to the class file now:

```
public function load(xmlFile:String):void {
  try {
    xmlLoader.load(new URLRequest(xmlFile));
  }
  catch (e:Error) {
    trace ("Can't load exernal XML document");
  }
}
```

The method is very simple, taking a single parameter. It calls the load method of the URLLoader object, passing a URLRequest object that references the external file name. Notice that we've wrapped the load method in a try-catch block. For simplicity, we'll initially display the simple error message using the trace method when debugging, but we could also have added more robust error handling.

We added an event handler called completeHandler to the previous URLLoader that responds when the content is received, so we need to add it now as a private method:

```
private function completeHandler(e:Event):void {
  xmlGalleryContent = XML(e.target.data);
  trace (xmlGalleryContent.toXMLString());
}
```

To start with, we cast the loaded content, found using e.target.data, as an XML type object and assign it to the xmlGalleryContent variable. We need to do this because the data property returns a string. As we're going to use E4X expressions to locate specific data, we need to cast the value as an XML object. You can find out more about the URLLoader in Chapter 8 if you need a refresher. We'll use the global trace method to display the loaded content as part of the testing process.

Before we go on any further, it's a good idea to test that we can create an instance of the class within the application and successfully load the external XML content.

Creating the GalleryLoader object

Switch to the application file and add the following code block at the top, below the opening `<mx:Application>` tag:

```
<mx:Script>
  <![CDATA[
    import com.aip.GalleryLoader;
    import mx.events.FlexEvent;
    private var photoGalleryLoader:GalleryLoader = ➥
      new GalleryLoader();
    private function loadGalleryXML(e:FlexEvent):void {
      photoGalleryLoader.load("assets/photos.xml");
    }
    private function completeHandler(e:Event):void{
    }
  ]]>
</mx:Script>
```

The code block starts by importing the GalleryLoader class from the com.aip package. We need to do this so we can create an instance of the custom class in our application. The code block also imports the FlexEvent class. We'll load the external XML content after the interface is created, which we can capture with the creationComplete event of the application. A creationComplete handler function always receives a FlexEvent as an argument.

We create an object called photoGalleryLoader, which is an instance of the new custom class GalleryLoader. Notice that we use the new keyword to call the constructor method:

```
private var photoGalleryLoader:GalleryLoader = new GalleryLoader();
```

We also create a function called loadGalleryXML that we'll call when we create the application. The function will grab the content from the external XML document by calling the load public method of the GalleryLoader object. The function call passes the location of the XML document as an argument. In this case, we'll include the full path to the file, as well as the file name, using the following:

```
photoGalleryLoader.load("assets/photos.xml");
```

As I mentioned, we'll call the loadGalleryXML function in the creationComplete event of the `<mx:Application>` tag. Modify the tag as shown here in bold:

```
<mx:Application xmlns:mx="http://www.adobe.com/2006/mxml"
  layout="absolute" backgroundGradientColors="[#000000, #000000]"
  creationComplete="loadGalleryXML(event)">
```

A creationComplete handler function always passes an event of the type FlexEvent. Even if you don't use the passed event object in the handler function, best practice indicates that we should still pass the argument with the function call.

At this point, we'll test the application and check that it can display the content in the Console view using a trace statement. Click the Debug button and you should see the XML content from the external document display, as shown in Figure 11-5.

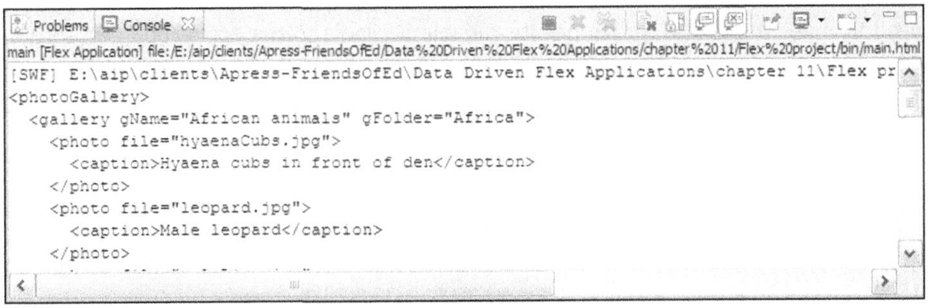

```
Problems   Console

main [Flex Application] file:/E:/aip/clients/Apress-FriendsOfEd/Data%20Driven%20Flex%20Applications/chapter%2011/Flex%20project/bin/main.html
[SWF] E:\aip\clients\Apress-FriendsOfEd\Data Driven Flex Applications\chapter 11\Flex pr
<photoGallery>
  <gallery gName="African animals" gFolder="Africa">
    <photo file="hyaenaCubs.jpg">
      <caption>Hyaena cubs in front of den</caption>
    </photo>
    <photo file="leopard.jpg">
      <caption>Male leopard</caption>
    </photo>
```

Figure 11-5. The loaded content appears in the Console view of the application.

Obviously if you've used your own images, you'll see different content.

We'll need to know when the external XML document has finished loading so the application can respond. It's only after the document finishes loading that the content becomes available and we can display the images in the gallery. The application will use the <gallery> nodes from the loaded content to populate the ComboBox so the user can choose which gallery to view. The custom class file will need to identify these nodes and dispatch an event to let the application know that the content is available for the interface.

Processing the loaded XML content

We'll work on the custom class file, so switch back to it now. The complete event handler for the URLLoader will need to access the loaded content, casting it as an XML object. It will also need to locate the <gallery> nodes from this object.

When it has finished processing the loaded content, the method will need to dispatch a complete event to the application. It will also need to make the <gallery> nodes available to the application.

Start by modifying the completeHandler function, as shown in bold here:

```
private function completeHandler(e:Event):void {
  xmlGalleryContent = XML(e.target.data);
  //trace (xmlGalleryContent.toXMLString());
  allGalleries = xmlGalleryContent.gallery;
  dispatchEvent(new Event(Event.COMPLETE));
}
```

We've commented out the trace method. We've also populated the allGalleries XMLList object with all the <gallery> nodes from the loaded content. To do this, we used the E4X expression xmlGalleryContent.gallery. Remember that xmlGalleryContent corresponds to the root node of the loaded content: <photoGallery>.

The function finishes by calling the dispatchEvent method to dispatch a complete event to the application. We could dispatch a custom event that passed the gallery content back to the application but, for simplicity, I haven't chosen this approach.

We'll need to make the allGalleries private variable available to the application and we'll do this with the getGalleryXML public method. Add this to the class file now:

```
public function getGalleryXML():XMLList {
  return allGalleries;
}
```

The function returns an XMLList containing all the <gallery> nodes. We can set this XMLList object directly as the dataProvider for the ComboBox control. When we do this, we'll need to specify which part of the object contains the label for the ComboBox.

We've now finished working with the custom class file. The complete code for this file follows, so you can check that you've got it set up in the same way as mine:

```
package com.aip {
  import flash.net.URLLoader;
  import flash.net.URLRequest;
  import flash.events.Event;
  [Bindable]
  public class GalleryLoader {
    private var xmlGalleryContent:XML;
    private var xmlLoader:URLLoader;
    private var allGalleries:XMLList;
    public function GalleryLoader() {
      xmlLoader = new URLLoader();
      xmlLoader.addEventListener(Event.COMPLETE, completeHandler);
    }
    public function load(xmlFile:String):void {
      try {
        xmlLoader.load(new URLRequest(xmlFile));
      }
      catch (e:Error) {
        trace ("Can't load exernal XML document");
      }
    }
    public function getGalleryXML():XMLList {
      return allGalleries;
    }
    private function completeHandler(e:Event):void {
      xmlGalleryContent = XML(e.target.data);
      //trace (xmlGalleryContent.toXMLString());
```

```
        allGalleries = xmlGalleryContent.gallery;
        dispatchEvent(new Event(Event.COMPLETE));
      }
    }
  }
```

The application file will need to respond to the dispatched complete event and populate the ComboBox control, so we'll need to add an event listener to the class file instance. Switch to the application file and modify the loadGalleryXML function as shown here in bold:

```
private function loadGalleryXML(e:FlexEvent):void {
  photoGalleryLoader.addEventListener(Event.COMPLETE, ➡
    completeHandler);
  photoGalleryLoader.load ("assets/photos.xml");
}
```

Again, I've named the handler function completeHandler to follow our standard naming convention and I'll add this function soon.

We'll use the event handler to store the returned XMLList in a bindable variable. That way we can use curly braces notation to bind the variable directly to the dataProvider property of the ComboBox control.

Add the following bindable variable at the top of the script block:

```
[Bindable]
private var galleryXML:XMLList;
```

We can now refer to this variable in the completeHandler function, so add it to the script block now:

```
private function completeHandler(e:Event):void{
  galleryXML = photoGalleryLoader.getGalleryXML();
}
```

The function sets the galleryXML variable to the returned XMLList object from the class file. We access the XMLList using the public getGalleryXML method of the photoGalleryLoader.

We'll use the galleryXML variable to populate the ComboBox control with a list of gallery names. We'll also set a change handler for the control to respond each time we choose a new gallery from the ComboBox.

Populating the ComboBox with galleries

We can start to populate the application interface by adding the gallery names to the ComboBox control. The gallery names are stored within the gName attribute of each <gallery> element. We'll bind the dataProvider of the ComboBox control to the galleryXML variable and set the labelField property to display this attribute.

Modify the ComboBox control as shown in bold:

```
<mx:ComboBox id="cboGalleries"
  fillColors="[#e6e6e6, #c0c0c0]" fillAlphas="[1.0, 1.0]"
  prompt="Choose gallery"
  dataProvider="{galleryXML}" labelField="@gName"/>
```

Because the data provider comes from an XMLList object, we can use the E4X expression @gName to target the gName attribute.

Figure 11-6 shows what happens when you run the application at this point.

Figure 11-6. The loaded ComboBox control

You should see the names of all galleries displaying in the ComboBox control. We now need to make the application respond when we choose a value from this control.

We'll do this by adding a change handler to the ComboBox control. The function will need to retrieve the value of the selected gallery folder and use it to display the first image and caption in the interface. That means we need to add these display elements to the custom component and reference them within the application file.

Building the custom component

We need to create the interface for the custom component, displaying a caption in a Text control and an image in an Image control. We also need to configure the component so we can pass values from the application to set the caption text and image source.

Let's start with the interface.

Creating the interface

Switch to the custom component file GalleryImage.mxml and modify the file as shown in bold to create the interface:

```xml
<?xml version="1.0" encoding="utf-8"?>
<mx:VBox xmlns="*" xmlns:mx="http://www.adobe.com/2006/mxml">
  <mx:Fade id="FadeInEffect" duration="1500"
    alphaFrom="0" alphaTo="1.0"/>
  <mx:Text id="txtCaption" color="#ffffff"
    fontWeight="bold" fontSize="12"/>
  <mx:HBox id="imageBorderBox"
    borderStyle="solid" borderThickness="1" borderColor="#ffffff"
    showEffect="FadeInEffect">
    <mx:Image id="imgPhoto" width="500" showEffect="FadeInEffect"/>
  </mx:HBox>
</mx:VBox>
```

The component is based on a VBox container. It contains a Fade effect that lasts for 1.5 seconds, fading in from an alpha value of 0 to 1.0. The component also includes a Text control with the id of txtCaption. We'll use this to display the caption from the loaded XML document.

The imagePhoto control displays the image and assigns the fade in effect to the showEffect property. In order to trigger this effect, we'll need to change the visible property of this control from false to true so it shows in the interface. We'll deal with that by using ActionScript.

Notice that I've added the Image control inside an HBox container. I've done this so I can display a 1-pixel white border around each image, as the Image control doesn't have these display properties. I've also added the showEffect property to the HBox so it fades in with the Image control. Feel free to leave out this HBox if you don't want the border.

If you switch to Design view to look at this component, you will see a missing image icon in the Image control. We will set the image source programmatically after we've accessed the XML content within the application.

Configuring the component

The next step is to add ActionScript that allows us to accept values passed from the application file. We'll use private variables in the component to keep track of the caption and image source, and create setter methods to set the values for these variables.

Add the following script block to the component:

```actionscript
<mx:Script>
  <![CDATA[
    private var photoCaption:String;
    private var imageSource:String;
    public function set caption(theCaption:String):void {
      photoCaption = theCaption;
      txtCaption.text = photoCaption;
    }
    public function set image(theImageFile:String):void {
      showControls(false);
      imageSource = theImageFile;
      imgPhoto.source = imageSource;
```

347

```
            showControls(true);
        }
        private function showControls(show:Boolean):void {
            imageBorderBox.visible = show;
            imgPhoto.visible = show;
        }
    ]]>
  </mx:Script>
```

The code creates the private string variables photoCaption and imageSource. It includes a setter method called caption to set the value of this variable. The caption method receives the caption as a string argument from the application file and uses it to set the value of the private variable. It then displays this variable in the text property of the txtCaption control.

The code also includes the image setter method, which receives the path and name of the photo file as an argument. It starts by hiding both the Image and HBox controls, so we can trigger the fade in effect. Notice that we use the private function showControls to handle the display of the two controls.

The image method sets the value of the imageSource variable to that passed from the application and uses it to set the source property for the Image control. It finishes by showing both the Image and HBox controls to trigger the fade in effect.

As mentioned, the showControls function shows and hides the HBox and Image controls. It receives a Boolean value that it uses to set the visible property of both controls.

We need to do one more thing to modify this component file. We will need to start with the Image and HBox controls hidden. We'll do this by calling the showControls method in the creationComplete event of the root VBox control, passing a value of false.

Modify the control as shown here in bold:

```
<mx:VBox xmlns="*" xmlns:mx="http://www.adobe.com/2006/mxml"
    creationComplete="showControls(false)">
```

That's it for the custom component file. The complete code for this file follows, so you can check what you've done:

```
<?xml version="1.0" encoding="utf-8"?>
<mx:VBox xmlns="*" xmlns:mx="http://www.adobe.com/2006/mxml"
  creationComplete="showControls(false)">
  <mx:Script>
    <![CDATA[
      private var photoCaption:String;
      private var imageSource:String;
      public function set caption(theCaption:String):void {
        photoCaption = theCaption;
        txtCaption.text = photoCaption;
      }
      public function set image(theImageFile:String):void {
        showControls(false);
```

```
      imageSource = theImageFile;
      imgPhoto.source = imageSource;
      showControls(true);
    }
    private function showControls(show:Boolean):void {
      imageBorderBox.visible = show;
      imgPhoto.visible = show;
    }
  ]]>
</mx:Script>
<mx:Fade id="FadeInEffect" duration="1500"
  alphaFrom="0" alphaTo="1.0"/>
<mx:Text id="txtCaption" color="#ffffff"
  fontWeight="bold" fontSize="12"/>
<mx:HBox id="imageBorderBox"
  borderStyle="solid" borderThickness="1" borderColor="#ffffff"
  showEffect="FadeInEffect">
  <mx:Image id="imgPhoto" width="500" showEffect="FadeInEffect"/>
</mx:HBox>
</mx:VBox>
```

We need to include this component within the application before we can display any of the images in the interface.

Displaying the first image

When we select a gallery name from the ComboBox control, we will need to display the first image from that gallery in the custom component. We'll do that using a change handler function for the ComboBox control, but we don't yet have any way to display the image.

The first step of including the custom component file is to add a namespace that refers to the custom component as an attribute in the <mx:Application> tag. Modify the tag as shown here in bold:

```
<mx:Application xmlns:mx="http://www.adobe.com/2006/mxml"
  xmlns:comp="com.aip.components.*"
  layout="absolute" backgroundGradientColors="[#000000, #000000]"
  creationComplete="loadGalleryXML(event)">
```

The namespace refers to the components folder in the com/aip folder. The application can use the namespace to access any component files stored within that folder by using the prefix comp. Remember that the name isn't significant.

We'll add the component to the application interface above the closing VBox control. Switch to the application file and add the following line shown in bold:

```
<comp:GalleryImage id="imgGallery"/>
</mx:VBox>
```

We are using this line to reference the file GalleryImage.mxml in the comp namespace. I've also given the custom component an id property so I can work with it programmatically. Because the component is based on a VBox control, it inherits the properties of that class including the id.

We need to pass the caption and image details to this custom component when we choose a new gallery from the ComboBox. We'll also need to change these details when we click the next and previous buttons.

We'll use a variable called imgCounter to keep track of which image we should display from the XMLList. Add the following line with the other variable declarations at the top of the script block:

```
private var imgCounter:int;
```

Initially, the value of this variable will be set to 0 to indicate the first item in the collection of photos for the selected gallery.

We'll load the images using a function called showImage. We'll create a changeHandler function to respond to the change event in the ComboBox and call showImage within that function.

Modify the ComboBox tag as shown in bold here:

```
<mx:ComboBox id="cboGalleries"
  fillColors="[#e6e6e6, #c0c0c0]" fillAlphas="[1.0, 1.0]"
  prompt="Choose gallery"
  dataProvider="{galleryXML}" labelField="@gName"
  change="changeHandler(event)"/>
```

Each time we choose a new value from the ComboBox we'll call the changeHandler function, passing an Event object. You'll now need to add the changeHandler function to the script block:

```
private function changeHandler(e:Event):void {
  imgCounter = 0;
  showImage();
}
```

This function sets the imgCounter variable to 0, so we can display the first photo in the gallery. Remember that XMLList objects are zero-based. The function also calls the showImage function, which we need to add now:

```
private function showImage():void {
  var imageCaption:String;
  var imagePath:String;
  imageCaption = cboGalleries.selectedItem.photo[imgCounter].caption;
  imagePath = "assets/photos/" + cboGalleries.selectedItem.@gFolder ➥
  + "/" + cboGalleries.selectedItem.photo[imgCounter].@file;
  imgGallery.caption = imageCaption;
  imgGallery.image = imagePath;
}
```

The showImage function sets string variables for the caption and location of the image called imageCaption and imagePath, respectively. The function then sets the values for these variables using the selectedItem from the ComboBox control. Because the ComboBox has the complete XMLList of galleries assigned as the data provider, we can use E4X expressions to target specific portions of the object. The starting point for each expression is cboGalleries.selectedItem, which represents the chosen <gallery> node.

In the case of the image caption, we use the imgCounter variable, currently set to 0, to select the first <photo> node from the chosen <gallery> element in the dataProvider. We then access the <caption> node within this element. To find the full path for each image, we have to use the string assets/photos/ with the gFolder attribute of the selected <gallery> node. We can then concatenate this value with the file attribute of the first <photo> element.

We set the appropriate properties in the custom component imgGallery using the setter methods caption and image.

Run the application now and you should be able to select a gallery and view the first photo, as shown in Figure 11-7.

Figure 11-7. Selecting a gallery name displays the first image in the interface.

Notice that the image fades in when you select a gallery. You'll also notice that both the previous and next buttons display in the interface and that nothing happens when you click them. It's time to deal with the display of the buttons and their functionality.

Displaying the other images

We can display the other images in each gallery by clicking the previous and next buttons. The previous button shouldn't display when we're at the first image, and the next button shouldn't display when we're showing the last image in a gallery. We'll set up a function to handle the showing and hiding of these buttons.

Add the following function to the script block in the application file:

```
private function showButtons(showPrev:Boolean, showNext:Boolean)➡
  :void {
  btnPrev.visible = showPrev;
  btnNext.visible = showNext;
}
```

The showButtons function takes two arguments, both Boolean. The first argument determines whether to display the previous button while the second argument deals with the display of the next button. We show and hide the buttons using the visible property.

Because we want to start with no buttons displayed, we'll hide them both in the loadGalleryXML function. Modify it as shown in bold here:

```
private function loadGalleryXML(e:FlexEvent):void {
  photoGalleryLoader.addEventListener(Event.COMPLETE, ➡
    completeHandler);
  photoGalleryLoader.load ("assets/photos.xml");
  showButtons(false, false);
}
```

We also want to display only the next button when we load the first image in the changeHandler function. Modify the function to call showButtons, as shown here in bold:

```
private function changeHandler(e:Event):void {
  imgCounter = 0;
  showImage();
  showButtons(false,true);
}
```

The last job is to add the click handler function for both buttons. We'll use the same handler function to set the value of the imgCounter variable appropriately, incrementing it for the next button and decrementing it for the previous button. We'll be able to tell which button was clicked as the id will be accessible through the target property of the MouseClick event object passed to the handler function.

Modify the button controls as shown here in bold:

```
<mx:Button id="btnPrev" width="40" label="&lt;&lt;"
  fillColors="[#e6e6e6, #c0c0c0]" fillAlphas="[1.0, 1.0]"
  click="clickHandler(event)"/>
<mx:Spacer width="100%"/>
<mx:Button id="btnNext" width="40" label="&gt;&gt;"
  fillColors="[#e6e6e6, #c0c0c0]" fillAlphas="[1.0, 1.0]"
  click="clickHandler(event)"/>
```

Now we'll need to add the clickHandler function shown here to the script block:

```
private function clickHandler(e:MouseEvent):void {
  var btnName:String = e.target.id;
  if (btnName == "btnPrev") {
    imgCounter --;
  }
  else if (btnName == "btnNext") {
    imgCounter ++;
  }
  showImage();
  if (imgCounter == 0) {
    showButtons(false, true);
  }
  else if (imgCounter == cboGalleries.selectedItem.photo.length() -1) {
    showButtons(true, false);
  }
  else {
    showButtons (true, true);
  }
}
```

The code block starts by identifying which button the user clicked using e.target.id. If the user clicked the button with the id btnPrev, the code decrements the imgCounter variable. Otherwise, if the user clicked btnNext, the variable increments. As the previous button doesn't display when imgCounter equals 0, we don't need to worry that we'll decrement to a negative value. The same applies to the next button, which hides when we get to the last image.

After setting the imgCounter variable appropriately, the clickHandler function then calls the showImage function to display the appropriate image. The function also handles the display of the buttons by determining our position in the list of photographs. If we're showing the first image, that is, the imgCounter variable has a value of 0, we hide the previous button and only show the next button using the showButtons function.

We can tell if we're at the last photo because the imgCounter variable will be the same number as one fewer than the total length of all photos. We find that number using the E4X expression cboGalleries.selectedItem.photo.length(). The length method returns the number of <photo> elements in the selected gallery. If we're at the last photo, we want to show the previous button but hide the next button. In all other cases, we want to display both buttons.

If you run the application, you should see the list of galleries within the ComboBox. When you select a gallery, you'll see the first image display in the interface with a caption. You should be able to navigate between images in a gallery using the next and previous buttons.

The application file is now finished, and the complete code for this file follows:

```
<?xml version="1.0" encoding="utf-8"?>
<mx:Application xmlns:mx="http://www.adobe.com/2006/mxml"
  xmlns:comp="com.aip.components.*"
  layout="absolute" backgroundGradientColors="[#000000, #000000]"
  creationComplete="loadGalleryXML(event)">
```

353

```
<mx:Script>
 <![CDATA[
   import com.aip.GalleryLoader;
   import mx.events.FlexEvent;
   private var photoGalleryLoader:GalleryLoader ➥
     = new GalleryLoader();
   [Bindable]
   private var galleryXML:XMLList;
   private var imgCounter:int;
   private function loadGalleryXML(e:FlexEvent):void {
     photoGalleryLoader.addEventListener(Event.COMPLETE, ➥
       completeHandler);
     photoGalleryLoader.load ("assets/photos.xml");
     showButtons(false, false);
   }
   private function completeHandler(e:Event):void{
     galleryXML = photoGalleryLoader.getGalleryXML();
   }
   private function changeHandler(e:Event):void {
     imgCounter = 0;
     showImage();
     showButtons(false,true);
   }
   private function showImage():void {
     var imageCaption:String;
     var imagePath:String;
     imageCaption = cboGalleries.selectedItem.photo[imgCounter] ➥
       caption;
     imagePath = "assets/photos/" + cboGalleries.selectedItem.➥
       @gFolder + "/" + cboGalleries.selectedItem.➥
       photo[imgCounter].@file;
     imgGallery.caption = imageCaption;
     imgGallery.image = imagePath;
   }
   private function showButtons(showPrev:Boolean, ➥
     showNext:Boolean):void {
     btnPrev.visible = showPrev;
     btnNext.visible = showNext;
   }
   private function clickHandler(e:MouseEvent):void {
     var btnName:String = e.target.id;
     if (btnName == "btnPrev") {
       imgCounter --;
     }
     else if (btnName == "btnNext") {
       imgCounter ++;
     }
     showImage();
     if (imgCounter == 0) {
```

```
          showButtons(false, true);
        }
        else if (imgCounter == cboGalleries.selectedItem.photo.➥
          length() -1) {
          showButtons(true, false);
        }
        else {
          showButtons (true, true);
        }
      }
    }
  ]]>
</mx:Script>
<mx:VBox x="10" y="10">
  <mx:Label text="Photo gallery" color="#ffffff" fontWeight="bold"
    fontSize="14"/>
  <mx:HBox>
    <mx:ComboBox id="cboGalleries"
      fillColors="[#e6e6e6, #c0c0c0]" fillAlphas="[1.0, 1.0]"
      prompt="Choose gallery"
      dataProvider="{galleryXML}" labelField="@gName"
      change="changeHandler(event)"/>
  </mx:HBox>
  <mx:HBox width="100%">
    <mx:Button id="btnPrev" label="&lt;&lt;"
      fillColors="[#e6e6e6, #c0c0c0]" fillAlphas="[1.0, 1.0]"
      width="40" click="clickHandler(event)"/>
    <mx:Spacer width="100%"/>
    <mx:Button id="btnNext" label="&gt;&gt;"
      fillColors="[#e6e6e6, #c0c0c0]" fillAlphas="[1.0, 1.0]"
      width="40" click="clickHandler(event)"/>
  </mx:HBox>
  <comp:GalleryImage id="imgGallery"/>
</mx:VBox>
</mx:Application>
```

You can find the zipped file containing the completed application files saved with the resources as xmlCaseStudy.zip.

Summary

In this chapter, we worked through an XML case study in which we populated a simple photo gallery application from an external file. We used a custom class file to handle the loading and manipulation of data for the application. We also used a custom component to display the image and related caption. This component included a fade in effect for the photos. The application file included this component in the application interface.

In the next chapter, we'll look at a simple ColdFusion application. We'll create a message board that stores its content in an Access database.

Chapter 12

COLDFUSION PROJECT

In the last chapter, we created a Flex application that used an XML data source. In the remaining chapters of this section, we'll see how to integrate Flex applications with other server-side technologies. In this chapter, we'll work with ColdFusion 8 and see how to integrate it with an Access database in a Flex application.

In Chapter 1, I explained that most web applications use something called n-tier, or multi-tier, architecture. These applications include a presentation tier made up of the user interface, and Flex provides this functionality. The data tier consists of content stored in a database. Between the two tiers is the business logic tier, also known as the middleware tier. This tier requests data from the database tier and provides it to the presentation tier. It also adds any business logic required to control the way data is accessed and flows through the application.

In this chapter, ColdFusion will serve as the business logic tier of our application. In the next two chapters, ASP.NET and PHP will provide that functionality. I've started with ColdFusion 8 because it integrates so well with Flex Builder 3.

We'll build a simple message board application that will allow a user to view existing messages and post new messages. To keep things simple, we'll use a Microsoft Access database with one table, a single ColdFusion file, and a single Flex application file. The application is very simple and uses a minimum of code. However, you will learn enough from the concepts shown here to apply it in situations that are more complex.

Flex Builder includes a number of wizards to help with the ColdFusion-Flex integration, but we won't use them in this example for the following reasons:

- It is important to understand how ColdFusion and Flex integrate. Using wizards makes this process happen automatically. It is easy to integrate the two products without understanding the underlying process.

- If you are creating projects without using Flex Builder, you won't have access to the wizards.

- We will use ColdFusion in the same way that we'll use the ASP.NET and PHP in the next two chapters, so you can compare the approaches.

You can download the finished project files for this chapter from the friends of ED web site at www.friendsofed.com. You can work through these files as you read through the chapter or create the application from scratch, as described here.

We'll start with a walk-through of the application.

Understanding the application

The application that we'll create in this chapter is very simple. It will allow a user to view and contribute to a message board.

When users first view the application, they'll see a list of existing messages from the database in a DataGrid component, as shown in Figure 12-1.

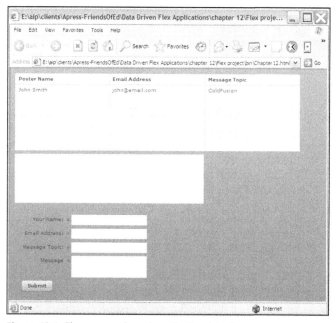

Figure 12-1. The message board application interface

Users can then click a row to view the message details in a TextArea control, as shown in Figure 12-2.

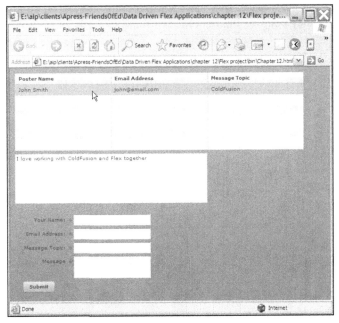

Figure 12-2. Clicking a row displays the message in a `TextArea` control.

The users can add a new message by filling in the form details underneath the `TextArea` and clicking the Submit button. When they do this, the `DataGrid` will automatically update to include the new entry, as shown in Figure 12-3.

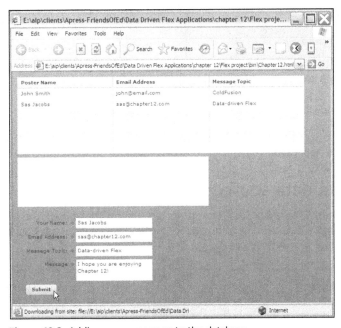

Figure 12-3. Adding a new message to the database

If users leave any of the fields blank, they can't add the entry. They'll see a red border around the blank field and when they point to the relevant control, they'll see an error message, as shown in Figure 12-4.

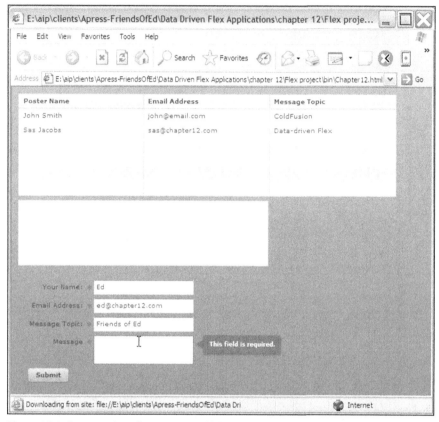

Figure 12-4. A user can't update an entry with blank fields.

It's a very simple application, but it will help to understand some key points in Flex and server-side integration.

The messages for the application come from an Access database, so we'll turn our attention there next.

The application data source

This application works with content stored in an Access database. The database is called MessageData.mdb, and you can find it with your resources. The database has a single table, messages, and Table 12-1 summarizes its structure.

Table 12-1. The structure of the messages table in the MessageData.mdb database

Field	Field type	Comments
ID	Autonumber	The primary key field
postername	Text(255)	Contains the name of the person making the post
emailaddress	Text(255)	Contains the e-mail address of the person making the post
messagetopic	Text(255)	Contains the topic for the message
message	Memo	Contains the content of the message

The database contains one test record. Feel free to add additional records for your own testing purposes if you'd like.

Structuring the application

For this exercise, I'll assume that you have installed the Developer's edition of the ColdFusion server and that you're using the web server included with ColdFusion. I'll also assume that ColdFusion is running on localhost:8500. If not, you'll need to make the appropriate changes as we work through the example.

Unzip the resource files and save the database to any location on your computer. We'll create the Flex project later.

Creating the application

To complete the application we'll need to do the following:

- Connect the database to the ColdFusion server
- Create a ColdFusion page to generate XML content from the database and handle updates
- Create the Flex application file to display the data and update

One advantage of working with ColdFusion is that you don't need to do much coding to connect to the database and generate XML content. The code you write is also relatively easy to understand.

We'll start by connecting to the ColdFusion server.

Connecting to the ColdFusion server

Our first step is to work with the ColdFusion administrator to set up the data source. You can use this feature to carry out administrative tasks such as configuring the server and adding data sources. We'll do the latter here so we can use our database in the application.

Start by opening the ColdFusion administrator at `http://localhost:8500/CFIDE/administrator/index.cfm`. Click the Data Sources link on the left side of the page. You'll find the link located under the DATA & SERVICES category.

If you just installed ColdFusion, you might see some practice databases, as shown in Figure 12-5. You don't need to do anything with these databases because they won't interfere with the project. After you've added the Access database, it will appear as another data source in the list.

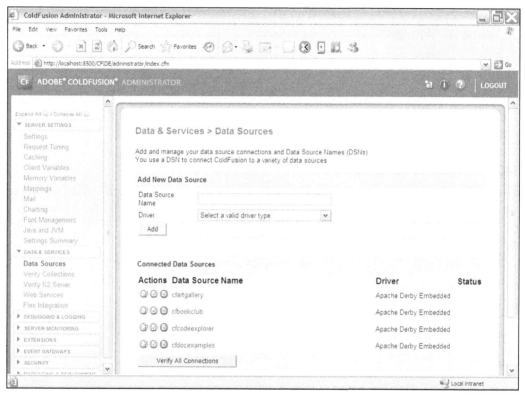

Figure 12-5. The ColdFusion administrator, showing data sources

We'll use the ColdFusion administrator to create a new data source connecting to our Access database. We need to provide a name for the data source and a driver for the database.

Enter the name messageConnection in the Data Source Name field. Expand the Driver drop-down menu and choose Microsoft Access with Unicode.

ColdFusion is built around the Java programming environment and uses Java Database Connectivity (JDBC). You can see the JDBC connectors in the drop-down menu, and there is a connector for the major database servers. There are two potential connectors for Access: Microsoft Access and Microsoft Access with Unicode.

Without getting into detail, the first driver, Microsoft Access, takes advantage of the Microsoft Windows internal ODBC connector. The second connector, Microsoft Access with Unicode, is more generic and better suited for non-Windows environments. I find that Microsoft Access with Unicode works a little more efficiently, so we'll choose that driver.

Once you've selected these options, click the Add button and you'll see the database connection screen shown in Figure 12-6.

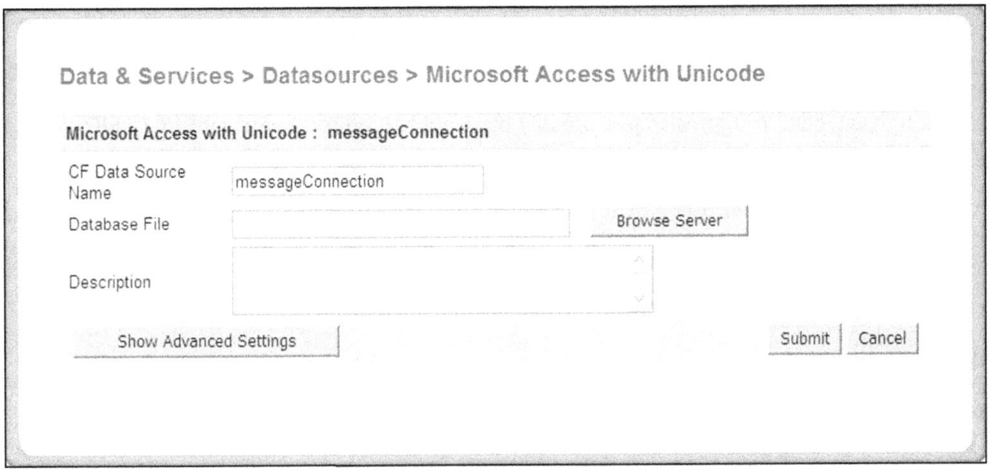

Figure 12-6. The Database connection screen

You'll use this screen to provide the location of the database file. Click the Browse Server button and choose the folder containing the database file that you downloaded for this chapter. Select the folder from the list and click Apply. You'll return to the database connection screen. You can enter a description for the database if you want.

When you've finished, click the Submit button. If all went well, the ColdFusion administrator should show the data source and display an OK message in the Status column, as shown in Figure 12-7.

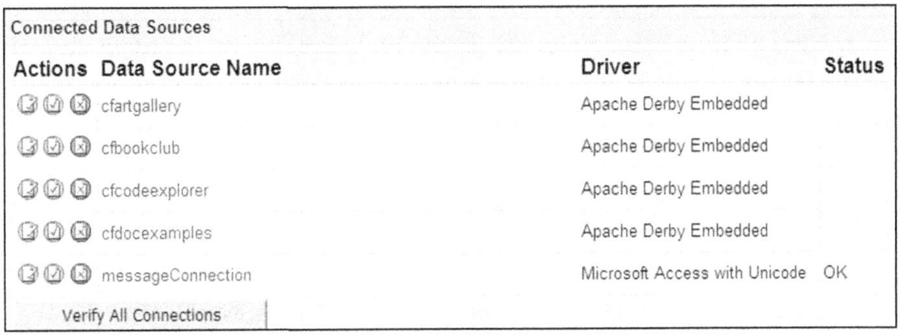

Figure 12-7. The ColdFusion administrator, reporting that messageConnection is OK

If you are new to ColdFusion, you may be surprised to learn that this process is all that is involved with connecting to a data source.

The next step is to build the ColdFusion page to generate the XML content for Flex.

Creating the ColdFusion page

The application includes a ColdFusion page that creates XML content from the database and processes any updates to the database. Flex has to consume the XML document supplied by ColdFusion because it cannot connect directly to a database. As this book is about Flex rather than ColdFusion, I'm going to present you with the finished code for the page and explain it instead of creating it with you step by step.

You can create the ColdFusion page using Adobe Dreamweaver CS3 or use the free CFEclipse plug-in found at www.cfeclipse.org. Bear in mind, though, that the latter option is better for experienced ColdFusion developers. You can also just use any plain old text editor if you want to. ColdFusion does not need a special editor.

If you're using Dreamweaver, you'll need to create a new site to set up an application workspace for the ColdFusion code. This process is similar to what you would do in Flex Builder. Rather than take you through the process step by step, in Table 12-2 I'll summarize the settings that you should enter during the site definition process.

Table 12-2. Dreamweaver site settings for the new site

Option	Setting
Site name	You can enter any option here to identify the site
Site URL	Enter http://localhost:8500/myMessageBoard
Server technology	Select Yes and choose the ColdFusion option
Editing and testing	Choose Edit and test locally (my testing server is on this computer)
Location for files	Enter C:\ColdFusion8\wwwroot\myMessageBoard\
Remote server	No

Make sure that you click the Test URL button as part of the site definition process. You'll need to edit the URL first to read http://localhost:8500/myMessageBoard before clicking this button. After you've clicked the button, you should see a success message.

The code for the ColdFusion page messageBoardConnector.cfm follows:

```
<cfprocessingdirective suppresswhitespace="yes" pageencoding="utf-8">
  <cfif isDefined("emailaddress") AND isDefined("message")
    AND isDefined("messageTopic") AND isDefined("postername") AND
    emailAddress NEQ "" AND message NEQ "" AND messageTopic NEQ ""
    AND postername NEQ "">
    <cfquery name="addInfo" datasource="messageConnection">
      INSERT INTO messages(emailaddress, message, messagetopic,
        postername) VALUES("#emailaddress#"," #message#",
```

```
              " #messagetopic#"," #postername#")
          </cfquery>
      </cfif>
      <cfquery name="allInfo" datasource="messageConnection">
        SELECT ID, emailaddress, message, messagetopic, postername
          FROM messages
      </cfquery>
      <cfxml variable="messageXML">
        <posters>
          <cfloop query="allInfo">
            <cfoutput>
              <posting>
                <id>#id#</id>
                <emailaddress>#emailaddress#</emailaddress>
                <message>#message#</message>
                <messagetopic>#messagetopic#</messagetopic>
                <postername>#postername#</postername>
              </posting>
            </cfoutput>
          </cfloop>
        </posters>
      </cfxml>
      <cfoutput>#messageXML#</cfoutput>
    </cfprocessingdirective>
```

This page serves two purposes. First, it adds new messages to the database; second, it generates an XML document containing details of all messages. The first functionality is only called when the Flex application sends new message details to the ColdFusion page.

Like MXML files, ColdFusion pages use an XML vocabulary for their code. The page starts with a <cfprocessingdirective> root tag that tells ColdFusion how to process the page. It contains two attributes, pageencoding and suppresswhitespace, which are just formalities. In nearly all cases, you would use the settings shown in the following code:

```
<cfprocessingdirective suppresswhitespace="yes" pageencoding="utf-8">
```

The remaining code for the page appears between the opening and closing <cfprocessingdirective> and </cfprocessingdirective> tags.

The database will only be updated if the ColdFusion page receives message details from the Flex application. For that reason, the code needs to test that the emailaddress, message, messagetopic, and postername fields are not blank before adding content to the database. We can do this using a <cfif> tag and the function isDefined. The isDefined function tests to see whether a variable exists. The <cfif> tag checks that the variables are not empty using NEQ "".

365

SQL code is always placed within opening and closing <cfquery> tags. The opening tag must include a name and a datasource attribute. The first <cfquery> element uses the name addInfo and specifies messageConnection as the data source:

```
<cfquery name="addInfo" datasource="messageConnection">
```

An INSERT statement appears inside the <cfquery> tag:

```
INSERT INTO messages(emailaddress, message, messagetopic,
    postername) VALUES("#emailaddress#"," #message#",
    " #messagetopic#"," #postername#")
```

Notice that ColdFusion reads variables sent from Flex using the # # symbols around the variable name. These variables will be passed from Flex when it requests this page.

After the closing </cfif> tag, the ColdFusion page includes a second <cfquery> called allInfo that uses the same data source: messageConnection. This tag includes a SELECT SQL statement that reads all the information from the message database table:

```
SELECT ID, emailaddress, message, messagetopic, postername
    FROM messages
```

The ColdFusion page also creates an XML document containing the values from the SELECT query using the <cfxml> tag. This tag has a variable attribute with a value of messageXML. We'll be able to output messageXML to generate the XML document.

The <cfxml> tags include the structure for the XML document. The code starts with the root element <posters>. It uses the <cfloop> to add the results from the SELECT query allInfo. Each variable appears delimited by # # symbols inside a <cfoutput> element. Every new message appears inside a <posting> element.

The final step in the ColdFusion file is the line outputting the messageXML variable so that is can be read by the Flex application:

```
<cfoutput>#messageXML#</cfoutput>
```

That's it for the ColdFusion side of things. Now it's time to switch to Flex Builder to work on the Flex application.

Creating the Flex application

Create a new project in Flex Builder and set the project location to C:\ColdFusion8\ wwwroot\myMessageBoard. That's the same location as the ColdFusion file. In fact, you don't need to store the files in the same place, but it makes it easier when you want to move the application to its production environment.

We'll work in Source view and add an <mx:HTTPService> tag to the application to connect to the XML data returned by the ColdFusion page. We'll set the url property to the ColdFusion page that you saw in the previous section: messageConnector.cfm. Because we need this page to be processed correctly by the web server, we'll need to reference it using the full URL: http://localhost:8500/ myMessageBoard/messageConnector.cfm.

Add the following tags between the opening and closing <mx:Application> tags of your application:

```
<mx:HTTPService id="messageRequest" method="POST" resultFormat="e4x"
  url="http://localhost:8500/myMessageBoard/messageBoardConnector.cfm">
</mx:HTTPService>
```

Notice that we've set the method to POST the variables to the ColdFusion page. I've set the resultFormat to e4x so I can use E4X expressions with the loaded XML document. Turn to Chapter 8 if you need a refresher on these expressions. I've also used both an opening and closing <mx:HTTPService> tag so that I can send variables with the request a little later.

We need to call the send method of the HTTPService element to make the request. This request will call the messageConnector.cfm page, which will run the database queries and return the relevant XML document. When the page runs, it will provide the contents of the message table in the database in XML format. If the request does not send data, the ColdFusion page will not process the INSERT statement in the first <cfquery> function.

We'll call the send function when the Flex application first opens, using the creationComplete attribute of the opening <mx:Application> tag. Modify the opening <mx:Application> tag as follows. The new attribute appears in bold:

```
<mx:Application xmlns:mx="http://www.adobe.com/2006/mxml"
  layout="absolute" creationComplete="messageRequest.send()">
```

You can test the application at this point, even though we've done no processing. If you run the application and see an empty browser window with no errors reported, you know you've made the request successfully. If you do get an error, you may need to check either the URL or the contents of the ColdFusion file.

Once you've successfully tested the application, you're ready to start on the interface.

Creating the Flex interface

If a user adds a new post, the Flex application needs to be able to send the new message to the ColdFusion page with the HTTPService request. It will do this using the <mx:request> element inside the <mx:HTTPService> opening and closing tags. That element will contain child elements corresponding to the variables that are to be sent. We'll use data binding to populate these elements from TextInput and TextArea controls that we'll add a little later.

Add the following content, shown in bold between your <mx:HTTPService> tags:

```
<mx:HTTPService id="messageRequest" method="POST" resultFormat="e4x"
  url="http://localhost:8500/myMessageBoard/messageBoardConnector.cfm">
  <mx:request xmlns="">
  <emailaddress>{emailaddress.text}</emailaddress>
  <message>{message.text}</message>
  <messagetopic>{messagetopic.text}</messagetopic>
  <postername>{postername.text}</postername>
  </mx:request>
</mx:HTTPService>
```

Note that Flex Builder will add the empty xmlns attribute of the `<mx:request>` tag automatically. You'll also notice that I deleted the extra lines that Flex Builder created when closing the XML tags. White space is ignored in MXML files, so it doesn't matter if we remove it from the code.

The new lines create an XML structure inside the `<mx:request>` element. The content for each element comes from a binding expression using the text property of TextInput and TextArea controls. We've yet to create the controls emailaddress, message, messagetopic, and postername, so if you save the file now, you'll see some error messages. You can ignore them for now.

We'll finish the Flex application by creating the user interface. All our elements will be laid out using a VBox container.

Add the following code block after the closing `</mx:HTTPService>` element. Notice that the id properties for TextInput and TextArea objects match the names used in the bindings within the `<mx:request>` element:

```
<mx:VBox x="10" y="10">
  <mx:Form x="25" y="10" width="500">
    <mx:FormItem label="Your Name:">
      <mx:TextInput id="postername" />
    </mx:FormItem>
    <mx:FormItem label="Email Address:">
      <mx:TextInput id="emailaddress" />
    </mx:FormItem>
    <mx:FormItem label="Message Topic:">
      <mx:TextInput id="messagetopic" />
    </mx:FormItem>
    <mx:FormItem label="Message">
      <mx:TextArea id="message" />
    </mx:FormItem>
    <mx:Button id="btnSubmit" label="Submit"/>
  </mx:Form>
</mx:VBox>
```

In order to make the application work, we need to add a click attribute to the button element. The value for the attribute will be messageRequest.send() so that we request the ColdFusion page when the button is clicked. The first query in the ColdFusion page checks for any sent variables and inserts the content into the database. When we POST data to the ColdFusion page, it will use the INSERT SQL statement to add the new message.

Modify the button as shown here in bold:

```
<mx:Button id="btnSubmit" label="Submit"
  click="messageRequest.send()"/>
```

When we click the button, we'll request the ColdFusion page again, this time posting values from the bound controls.

Although we can fill in and submit the form, we still don't have any way of seeing the current messages in the database. We'll show them in a DataGrid control. If you need a refresher on this control, please have a look at Chapter 9.

Add the following DataGrid control to the application interface above the opening <mx:Form> element, after the opening <mx:VBox> tag:

```
<mx:DataGrid id="dgMessage" x="25" y="200"
  dataProvider="{messageRequest.lastResult.posting}">
  <mx:columns>
    <mx:DataGridColumn headerText="Poster Name"
      dataField="postername" width="200"/>
    <mx:DataGridColumn headerText="Email Address"
      dataField="emailaddress" width="200"/>
    <mx:DataGridColumn headerText="Message Topic"
      dataField="messagetopic" width="200" />
  </mx:columns>
</mx:DataGrid>
```

The dataProvider property of the DataGrid is bound to the lastResult property of the messageRequest HTTPService element. It is set to an XMLList of all <posting> elements from the XML document returned by the ColdFusion page. As we discussed earlier in the book, messageRequest.lastResult is equivalent to the root element in the XML document.

The code block adds three columns to the DataGrid, setting the column header and identifying the XML node containing the data within the dataField attribute. For convenience, the width of all columns is set to 200. Notice that we don't display the message in the DataGrid.

The database supplied with the resource file contains one record that you'll see when you run the application. Unless you've added extra messages, when you run the application you should see the result shown in Figure 12-8.

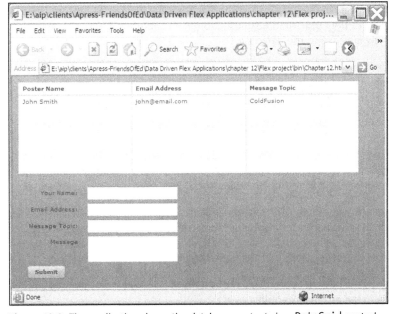

Figure 12-8. The application shows the database contents in a DataGrid control.

Notice that the DataGrid displays the name of the poster, the e-mail address, and the message topic. We'll display the message contents in a separate TextArea shortly.

You should be able to enter details in the form and see them added to the DataGrid when you click the Submit button, as shown in Figure 12-9.

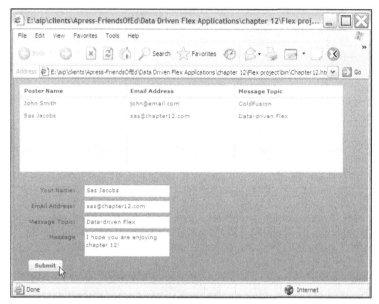

Figure 12-9. Adding a new post to the database

The new record appears in the DataGrid as soon as you click the Submit button. The user entries from the fields are sent to the ColdFusion page using the POST method. That page creates an INSERT query and adds the new message to the database.

The second query in the ColdFusion page then extracts all content from the database and generates an XML document for Flex. The HTTPService element receives this XML document, including the newly added record. The DataGrid updates as it is bound to the lastResult property of the HTTPService element.

You'll notice that the form fields don't clear when you submit the values. Other than the updating of the DataGrid, we don't know whether the update has been successful. In a real-world application, you'd probably clear the form, display a success message in the browser, and add some error handling. However, I'll leave you to extend this example in your own time.

Try adding a record where one of the fields is blank. You should notice that if you leave any fields blank and click the Submit button, nothing happens. The ColdFusion page only proceeds with the INSERT query if we have entries in all fields. We'll add some simple validation to the Flex application to make sure that users are aware that they need to fill in all fields.

Start by adding a required attribute to each of the four <mx:FormItem> elements. I've shown the first element here with the attribute in bold:

```
<mx:FormItem label="Your Name:"
    required="true">
```

Make the same change to the other form items.

From Chapter 4, you'll remember that adding the required attribute displays a red asterisk next to the field label, but it doesn't actually add validation to the relevant field. We'll need to add four StringValidator elements to make that happen, one for each element that needs validating. Note that you could also create a custom validator to validate all fields at the same time, but that's beyond the scope of this simple example.

Add the following elements below the closing </mx:HTTPService> element:

```
<mx:StringValidator id="nameSV" source="{postername}"
    property="text" trigger="{btnSubmit}" triggerEvent="click"/>
<mx:StringValidator id="emailSV" source="{emailaddress}"
    property="text" trigger="{btnSubmit}" triggerEvent="click"/>
<mx:StringValidator id="topicSV" source="{messagetopic}"
    property="text" trigger="{btnSubmit}" triggerEvent="click"/>
<mx:StringValidator id="messageSV" source="{message}"
    property="text" trigger="{btnSubmit}" triggerEvent="click"/>
```

These validators ensure that entries are made in each of the TextInput and TextArea fields. The default value for the required attribute for each validator is true. We've left out the attribute, so the default value applies and ensures that entry in the relevant control is required.

If users leave a field blank, they'll see a red border around that control after clicking the Submit button. When they move their mouse over an element, they'll see an error message, as shown in Figure 12-10. This figure shows that all fields have been left blank.

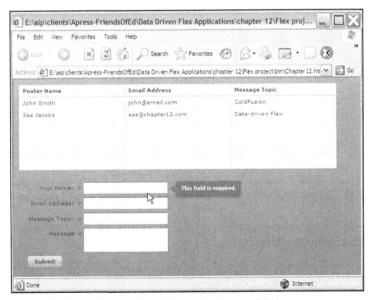

Figure 12-10. Pointing at an invalid entry displays a validation message.

As I mentioned earlier, the DataGrid control doesn't display the details of the message. We'll show the message details in a TextArea control, which we'll populate when the user clicks a row in the DataGrid control. We can do this by binding the message property of the selectedItem of the DataGrid to the text property of the TextArea. We can still access the message property associated with each row, even if it isn't displayed in the DataGrid.

Add the following TextArea control underneath the DataGrid:

```
<mx:TextArea height="100" width="400"
  text="{dgMessage.selectedItem.message}"/>
```

When you run the application and click a row, you should see the message in the TextArea, as shown in Figure 12-11.

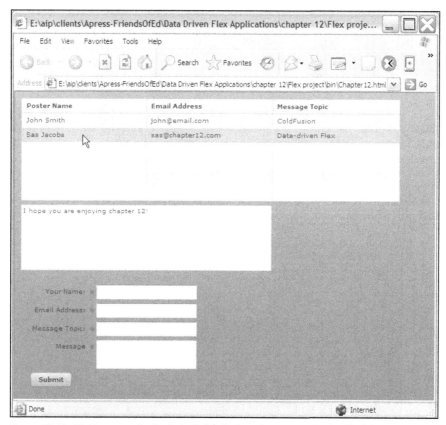

Figure 12-11. Clicking a row in the DataGrid displays the message in the TextArea.

We've now finished our simple message board application. You can find the completed files in the resources download file for the chapter.

Summary

By working through this application, you saw how easy it was to use ColdFusion to provide database content to a Flex application. A single ColdFusion page returned an XML document for use in the Flex application and provided the mechanism for adding content to the database.

This application was purposely simplistic—it only covered adding and viewing content from a database. As an exercise, you might want to see how you could add the functionality to edit and delete messages.

If you are an experienced ColdFusion programmer, you would probably use ColdFusion components (CFCs) to handle the database changes. However, we didn't use that approach because we could devote an entire book to the topic of CFCs.

In the next chapter, we'll work through a more detailed application, using ASP.NET as the middleware tier.

Chapter 13

ASP.NET CASE STUDY

In this chapter, we'll look at a Flex application that uses ASP.NET to interact with an Access database. The Flex application is a simple event booking system. It allows a user to select a date and view any relevant events. The user can update the details of the event as well as add a new event or delete an existing one.

The ASP.NET side of the application is written in VB 2008 and provides content to the SWF file in XML format. It includes pages that query the database for events on a specific day, a list of event categories and locations, a page that updates the details of an event, and one that deletes an event.

The application consists of the following parts:

- An Access database
- ASP.NET pages that interact with the database and generate XML content
- A custom ActionScript class to handle the loading and processing of XML content
- A custom component to display either the details of a selected event or a blank form for entering a new event
- An application file containing the interface, which handles the user interaction and interaction with other MXML and ActionScript files

You can download the finished project files for this chapter from the friends of ED web site at www.friendsofed.com. You can work through these files as you read through the chapter or create the application from scratch as described here.

Before we get started, let's learn a little more about the application.

Understanding the application

Before we build the application, I'd like to walk you through the interface and show you how the various parts of the application fit together. Bear in mind that I haven't spent any time styling the interface as the emphasis here is on its functionality.

The application interface

The application starts with a DateChooser control displaying today's date, as shown in Figure 13-1. As you can see, there are no events on the current day, so we see a message to that effect as well as an Add event button.

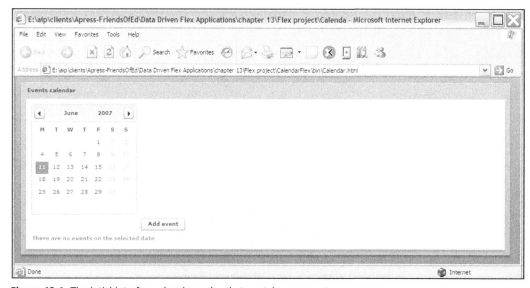

Figure 13-1. The intial interface, showing a day that contains no events

We can use the DateChooser control to navigate to a different date. Figure 13-2 shows what happens when we choose a day that has events scheduled.

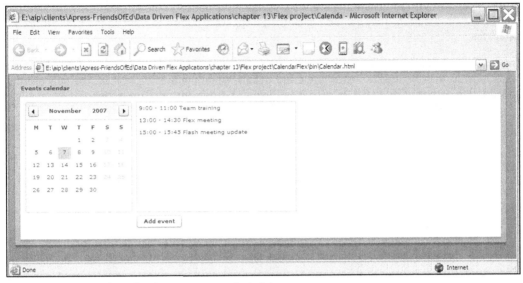

Figure 13-2. The interface, showing events on a selected day

We see a list of event start and finish times as well as the event titles. They are ordered by their start times.

The user can click one of the titles to find out further information about the event. When they do this, they'll see a form containing further details of the event, as shown in Figure 13-3.

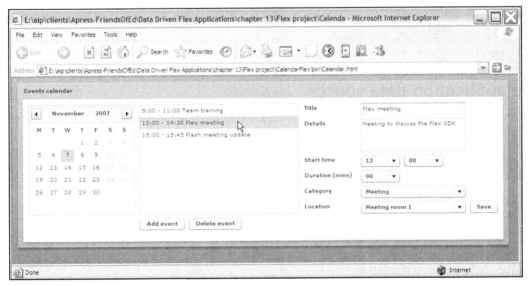

Figure 13-3. Displaying the details of an event

At this time, the user can update the event by changing the details in the form on the right side and clicking the Save button. They can also click the Delete event button to remove the event from the database.

The final option is to add a new event for the selected date. Clicking the Add event button displays a blank form so that the user can enter the event details. When the user clicks Save, the new event is added to the date selected in the DateChooser. Figure 13-4 demonstrates this action.

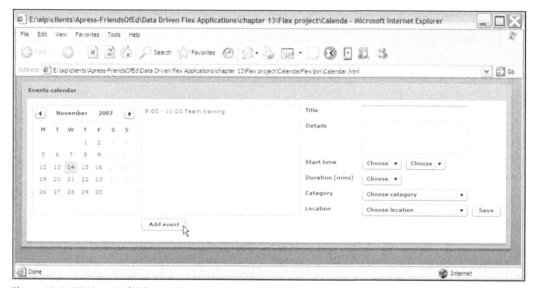

Figure 13-4. Clicking the Add event button displays a blank form allowing entry of event details.

That's it for the Flex side of the application. The content displayed in the interface comes from an Access database, and we'll find out more about that now.

The application data source

The application takes its data from an Access database with the file name events.mdb. The sample database provided with the resources includes some entries for 2007: November 7, 14, 16, 20, and 21. Feel free to add your own entries on different dates if you want to experiment. The database also provides a list of event categories and event locations. Again, you can expand this list by adding to the database if you'd like.

The database works with ASP.NET pages to deliver this content in XML format to the Flex application. Let's start with a look at the database structure and then look at the structure of the generated XML content.

The database structure

The database consists of three tables: events, categories, and locations. Figure 13-5 shows the Access Relationships window for this database.

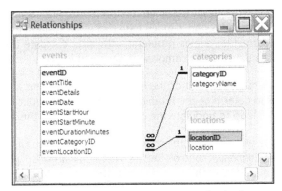

Figure 13-5. The relationships of the events database

The details of each event are stored within a table called events. Table 13-1 shows the structure of the events table. Note that all fields in this table are required.

Table 13-1. The structure of the events table in the events.mdb database.

Field	Field Type	Comments
eventID	Autonumber	The primary key field.
eventTitle	Text (100)	Contains the title for the event.
eventDetails	Memo	Contains the details of the event.
eventDate	Text (10)	A string representation of the event date in *YYYY-MM-DD* format.
eventStartHour	Number (Byte)	The starting hour of the event. The Flex application limits this field to values between 7 and 18.
eventStartMinute	Number (Byte)	The starting time of the event in minutes. The Flex application limits this field to values of 00, 15, 30, and 45.
eventDurationMinutes	Number (Integer)	The duration of the event in minutes. The Flex application limits this field to values from 15 to 480 minutes in increments of 15 minutes.
eventCategoryID	Number (Long integer)	A foreign key field. The relevant categoryID from the categories table.
eventLocationID	Number (Long integer)	A foreign key field. The relevant locationID from the locations table.

Access has data types that are specifically designed to store dates, but because XML content is passed backward and forward using strings, I find it much easier to use a string representation of the date in *YYYY-MM-DD* format. This structure avoids problems with different date formats around the world and easily allows us to split a date into its component parts within Flex.

I've stored the hours and minutes for each of the events as numbers. This approach makes it easy for me to do time calculations to determine the finishing time in the Flex application. In addition, it allows me to use numbers within a loop to populate the ComboBox controls in the interface.

The database also contains two lookup tables to normalize the data: categories and locations. These tables will populate ComboBox controls in the Flex application so that we can restrict users to choosing from a list of values. Each table consists of an autonumber primary key field and a 50-character-long text field containing the descriptive data.

The content from the database is provided to the Flex application using an XML format generated by ASP.NET pages.

The XML content

All content returned to the Flex application by ASP.NET pages uses an XML format. When requesting this content, Flex supplies any parameters to the ASP.NET pages using the form POST method. We'll start with a look at the structure of the XML document describing a list of events. Figure 13-6 shows the structure of this document displayed within a web browser. For simplicity, I've chosen a date with a single event.

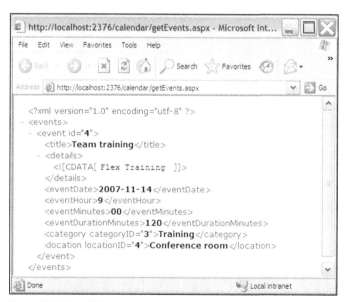

Figure 13-6. The XML structure used to describe events on a specific day

The root node of the document is the <events> element. This element contains one or more <event> elements that each equate to a single event. These events can be identified by their primary key from the database, which appears as an id attribute in the <event> element.

All of the event details appear within child elements of the `<event>` element. These include both `<category>` and `<location>` elements, which contain the relevant primary key values as attributes.

The list of categories is provided to the Flex application using the following structure:

```xml
<?xml version="1.0" encoding="utf-8" ?>
<categories>
  <category id="1">Meeting</category>
  <category id="2">Seminar</category>
  <category id="3">Training</category>
<categories>
```

The locations list uses the following XML structure:

```xml
<?xml version="1.0" encoding="utf-8" ?>
<locations>
  <location id="3">Board room</location>
  <location id="4">Conference room</location>
  <location id="1">Meeting room 1</location>
  <location id="2">Meeting room 2</location>
</locations>
```

Finally, when an event is updated or added, Flex receives XML content from the server-side page after the action is carried out. In the case of an update, the text Update: is joined with the event date in *YYYY-MM-DD* format, as shown here:

```xml
<?xml version="1.0" encoding="utf-8" ?>
<response>
  <message>Update:2007-11-14</message>
</response>
```

The add version of the same XML content is slightly different:

```xml
<?xml version="1.0" encoding="utf-8" ?>
<response>
  <message>Add:2007-11-14</message>
</response>
```

Structuring the application

For this case study, you'll need to create a new Flex project, specifying the name and location of your choice. Locate the files in the root directory of the project. Choose the Server type of Other/None rather than ASP.NET. While the locations of the Flex and ASP.NET applications could be the same, I find it easier to keep them in separate folders. This allows me to reuse the Flex application with different ASP.NET projects if needed. The other small point is that Flex and ASP.NET projects both reference a bin folder, so I'd have to rename one of these folders if I used the same location for all code. It isn't a problem to rename a folder, but I'd have to remember to do that each time I reused the code.

If you want to work through the steps in the chapter, you'll need a web server running Internet Information Services (IIS) or another web server capable of serving ASP.NET applications. For home users, IIS is available in Windows XP Professional and on all versions of Windows Vista, excluding

Windows Vista Starter and Home Basic. Note that IIS isn't installed by default, so you'll need to install it yourself (using Start ➤ Settings ➤ Control Panel ➤ Add or Remove Programs ➤ Add/Remove Windows Components in Windows XP or Start ➤ Control Panel ➤ Programs ➤ Turn on or off Windows features in Windows Vista).

I'll assume that you're using either Visual Studio or Visual Studio Express to manage your ASP.NET pages (available from http://msdn2.microsoft.com/en-us/vstudio/default.aspx). Set up a web application, calling it any name of your choosing. You can import the existing pages from the calendar_ASP.NETfiles.zip file or create your own by following the instructions in this chapter.

If you want to import the completed application files into Flex Builder, set up a new Flex project and import the files from the resource files available with the chapter. You can do this by right-clicking the project and choosing Import. You can use the File ➤ Import command. Select the Archive file option from the General category, as shown in Figure 13-7.

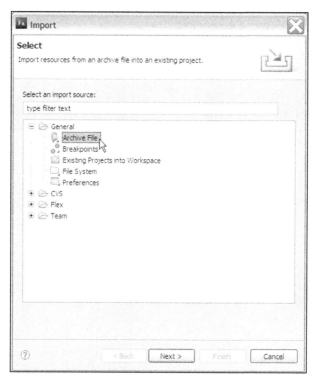

Figure 13-7. Selecting the Archive File option when importing resources

Click Next and use the Browse button to navigate to the CalendarFlexFiles.zip file included with the resources for the chapter. Select the Flex project as the destination, as shown in Figure 13-8.

When you click Finish, the relevant files will be added to the project.

For those of you who are going to work through the steps to create the application from scratch, let's get started.

Figure 13-8. Importing the resources into an existing Flex project

Creating the application

We'll need to create the interface, the custom class, and the custom component within the Flex application. We'll also need to create the ASP.NET pages for processing and returning content to the Flex application. As we work through the case study, I will take you through the building process, so we'll be skipping backward and forward between the various files so you can work through the logical steps that you might follow in a similar situation.

To finish the application, I'll work through the following steps:

1. Creating the Flex application interface
2. Creating the ASP.NET pages to generate XML content for the application
3. Creating the custom ActionScript class
4. Loading the events for a specific date
5. Populating the interface with the events
6. Creating a custom component for event details
7. Showing details of the selected event
8. Updating the selected event
9. Adding a new event
10. Deleting an existing event

We'll start by creating the application interface in Flex Builder.

Creating the Flex application interface

Within your main application file, add the following MXML tags to the Flex application, after the opening <mx:Application> tag:

```
<mx:Panel x="10" y="10" title="Events calendar"
  paddingTop="10" paddingLeft="10" paddingRight="10"
  paddingBottom="10">
  <mx:VBox>
    <mx:HBox>
      <mx:DateChooser id="dtSelector" width="200" height="200"/>
      <mx:VBox>
        <mx:List id="lstEvents" height="200" width="300"/>
        <mx:HBox width="300">
          <mx:Button id="btnAdd" label="Add event"/>
          <mx:Button id="btnDelete" label="Delete event"
            visible="false"/>
        </mx:HBox>
      </mx:VBox>
    </mx:HBox>
    <mx:Text id="txtMessage" color="#FF0000" fontWeight="bold"/>
  </mx:VBox>
</mx:Panel>
```

We've used VBox and HBox controls to automate the layout of the components. Figure 13-9 shows the interface that these tags will create.

Figure 13-9. The Flex application interface

We have a DateChooser control on the left showing the current date. Next to it, we have a List control with an Add event button below. The List control will display a list of events for the currently selected date.

The interface also includes a Delete event button, but it isn't visible as we've hidden the control. We'll only show this button when an event has been selected within the List.

Below the DateChooser, there is a Text control that we'll use to display messages to the user. You can't see it as it doesn't currently contain any text. We'll add the custom component to display event details to the right of the List control once we've created it a little later.

You might notice that in the finished application I configured the DateChooser so that the first date displayed is a Monday. I also disabled Saturday and Sunday, so it's not possible to add weekend events. To do this, add the following script block below the opening <mx:Application> tag:

```
<mx:Script>
  <![CDATA[
    import mx.events.FlexEvent;
    private function initApp(e:FlexEvent):void {
      setupDateChooser();
    }
    private function setupDateChooser():void {
      dtSelector.disabledDays = [0,6];
      dtSelector.firstDayOfWeek = 1;
    }
  ]]>
</mx:Script>
```

The script block creates two functions: initApp and setupDateChooser. I'll use the first function to set up the entire application. It will add event listeners and call the relevant setup functions, one of which is the setupDateChooser function. I find it useful to separate my functionality into separate functions to make the file easier to follow. There's an old adage in programming that a single function should achieve one thing!

The import statement should add itself automatically when you enter the FlexEvent argument in the initApp function. If not, you'll need to type it yourself.

We'll call the initApp function in the initialize event of the application. In other words, we'll set up the application after it has had any initialization properties set. This occurs before the application is drawn and before the creationComplete event fires.

I've purposely chosen the initialize event rather than the creationComplete event because I'll want to set a variable inside the custom component before it is drawn within the application. You'll understand it a little better later on when we set up the custom component.

Modify the opening <mx:Application> tag to call the initApp function as shown here in bold:

```
<mx:Application xmlns:mx="http://www.adobe.com/2006/mxml"
layout="absolute" initialize="initApp(event)">
```

If you run the application, it will look much the same as the interface shown in Figure 13-9. The only difference is that the first day of the week will be Monday and that Saturday and Sunday will appear grayed-out.

The next stage will be to generate the XML content from the database using ASP.NET pages.

Creating the ASP.NET pages to generate XML content for the application

We'll need to create three ASP.NET pages to generate XML content for populating the Flex application:

- getEvents.aspx: Displays events for a selected date
- getCategories.aspx: Displays a list of event categories
- getLocations.aspx: Displays a list of event locations

Create the files in Visual Studio by right-clicking the web project and choosing Add New Item ➤ Web Form. Enter the relevant name for each page and choose the Place code in separate file option. We'll use code-behind pages in this application. You won't need to choose a master page for any of the files as they won't be displaying the content visually within a web browser. The pages exist solely to provide data to the Flex application.

We'll also need to set the path for the database as a connection string in the web.config file for the web project. Add the database to the App_Data folder of the web project by copying it from the resources and pasting it into the folder in the Solution Explorer or in Windows Explorer. You will need to refresh the Solution Explorer to see the database.

Select the relevant section of the <configuration> element of my web.config file and add the following database connection string:

```
<connectionStrings>
  <add name="events" connectionString="Provider=Microsoft.Jet.OLEDB.
    4.0;Data Source=C:\Documents and Settings\Administrator\
    My Documents\Visual Studio 2008\Projects\Calendar\Calendar\
    App_Data\events.mdb;" providerName="System.Data.OledbClient"/>
</connectionStrings>
```

You can see the path to my application in the connectionString attribute of the <add> tag. You'll need to modify this to the full path in your computer to your own copy of this database.

The following sections use code-behind pages to keep my VB code separate from the interface. Each ASP.NET page consists only of a page declaration, so you'll need to delete all other content from the pages. There are no other elements as I don't need to generate XHTML content to display in a web browser. I've shown the declaration for the getEvents.aspx page here:

```
<%@ Page Language="VB" AutoEventWireup="false"
  CodeFile="getEvents.aspx.vb" Inherits="getEvents"%>
```

You'll need to compile the application to make the pages work correctly. You can do this using the command Build ➤ Build Solution or by publishing the web project with Build ➤ Publish [Project Name]. You'll choose the second option when you have finalized the files and are ready to copy them to their final location. I'll show you the declarative code used to generate the XML content from the database. We'll start with the code behind the getEvents.aspx page.

Displaying a list of events

The getEvents.aspx page will take a date as a parameter from the SWF movie and query the database for events occurring on that date. It will then generate an XML document containing the details of each event. Because the focus of this book is on Flex, I'll show the entire code for the code-behind ASP.NET page getEvents.aspx.vb and explain it afterward rather than creating it from scratch. You can view the code by right-clicking in the getEvents.aspx page and choosing View Code:

```
Imports System.IO
Imports System.Xml
Imports System.Data
Imports System.Data.OleDb

Partial Class getEvents
  Inherits System.Web.UI.Page
  Protected Sub Page_Load(ByVal sender As Object, ➥
      ByVal e As System.EventArgs) Handles Me.Load
    Dim selectedDate As String
    Dim dbConnString As String = ConfigurationManager. ➥
      ConnectionStrings("events").ConnectionString
    Dim dbConn As New OleDbConnection(dbConnString)
    Dim strSQL As String, objCommand As OleDbCommand
    Dim objDataReader As OleDbDataReader
    Dim eventsXMLDoc As XmlTextWriter = ➥
      New XmlTextWriter(Response.OutputStream, Encoding.UTF8)
    Dim strMinutes As String
    If Len(Request.Form("newDate")) > 0 Then
      selectedDate = Request.Form("newDate")
    Else
      selectedDate = formatDate(DateTime.Today)
    End If
    strSQL = "SELECT * FROM selAllEvents " _
      & " WHERE eventDate = '" & selectedDate & "'"
    dbConn.Open()
    objCommand = New OleDbCommand(strSQL, dbConn)
    objDataReader = objCommand.ExecuteReader()
    eventsXMLDoc.Formatting = Formatting.Indented
    Response.ContentType = "text/xml"
    eventsXMLDoc.WriteStartDocument()
    eventsXMLDoc.WriteStartElement("events")
    While objDataReader.Read()
      If objDataReader("eventStartMinute") = 0 Then
        strMinutes = "00"
      Else
        strMinutes = CStr(objDataReader("eventStartMinute"))
      End If
      eventsXMLDoc.WriteStartElement("event")
      eventsXMLDoc.WriteAttributeString("id", ➥
        objDataReader("eventID"))
      eventsXMLDoc.WriteStartElement("title")
```

```
              eventsXMLDoc.WriteValue(objDataReader("eventTitle"))
              eventsXMLDoc.WriteEndElement()
              eventsXMLDoc.WriteStartElement("details")
              eventsXMLDoc.WriteCData(objDataReader("eventDetails"))
              eventsXMLDoc.WriteEndElement()
              eventsXMLDoc.WriteStartElement("eventDate")
              eventsXMLDoc.WriteValue(formatDate(objDataReader("eventDate")))
              eventsXMLDoc.WriteEndElement()
              eventsXMLDoc.WriteStartElement("eventHour")
              eventsXMLDoc.WriteValue(objDataReader("eventStartHour"))
              eventsXMLDoc.WriteEndElement()
              eventsXMLDoc.WriteStartElement("eventMinutes")
              eventsXMLDoc.WriteValue(strMinutes)
              eventsXMLDoc.WriteEndElement()
              eventsXMLDoc.WriteStartElement("eventDurationMinutes")
              eventsXMLDoc.WriteValue( ➡
                objDataReader("eventDurationMinutes"))
              eventsXMLDoc.WriteEndElement()
              eventsXMLDoc.WriteStartElement("category")
              eventsXMLDoc.WriteAttributeString("categoryID", ➡
                objDataReader("categoryID"))
              eventsXMLDoc.WriteValue(objDataReader("categoryName"))
              eventsXMLDoc.WriteEndElement()
              eventsXMLDoc.WriteStartElement("location")
              eventsXMLDoc.WriteAttributeString("locationID", ➡
                objDataReader("locationID"))
              eventsXMLDoc.WriteValue(objDataReader("location"))
              eventsXMLDoc.WriteEndElement()
              eventsXMLDoc.WriteEndElement()
            End While
            eventsXMLDoc.WriteEndElement()
            eventsXMLDoc.Flush()
            eventsXMLDoc.Close()
            objDataReader.Close()
            dbConn.Close()
          End Sub

          Protected Function formatDate(ByVal theDate As Date) As String
            Dim strConvertedDate As String, strMonth As String
            Dim strDay As String
            If Month(theDate) < 10 Then
              strMonth = "0" & CStr(Month(theDate))
            Else
              strMonth = CStr(Month(theDate))
            End If
            If Day(theDate) < 10 Then
              strDay = "0" & CStr(Day(theDate))
            Else
              strDay = CStr(Day(theDate))
```

```
      End If
      strConvertedDate = Year(theDate) & "-" & strMonth & ➥
        "-" & strDay
      formatDate = strConvertedDate
    End Function
  End Class
```

The page starts by referencing the relevant namespaces that we'll need. We use the Page_Load event to create the XML document and start by declaring the relevant variables. We'll use an XmlTextWriter object to compose the XML document.

After the variables are declared, the sub checks whether a variable called newDate was posted to the page. If not, it creates a string from the current date, using the formatDate function that appears at the bottom of the code block. I'll get to that function shortly. It's useful to use this default variable so that I can test the page in a web browser independently of Flex.

The SQL statement used to query the database selects all of the events for the selected date using a DataReader. It references the selAllEvents query which joins the three database tables to extract all event information at once. An Access query is similar to a view in databases like SQL Server and Oracle. The page sets the content type of the document to text/xml and writes the start of the XML document using the WriteStartDocument method. It writes the root element using the following:

```
      eventsXMLDoc.WriteStartElement("events")
```

The code loops through the DataReader, creating the relevant XML nodes. We use the WriteStartElement, WriteEndElement, WriteAttributeString, WriteValue, and WriteCData methods to generate the XML content. Notice that the code rewrites the minutes as a string value so that we can represent 0 as 00.

After the loop finishes, the sub writes the closing root element and uses the Flush method to write the content to the XmlTextWriter. It then calls the relevant Close methods.

The formatDate function takes a Date object as an argument and returns a string formatted into *YYYY-MM-DD* format. As mentioned earlier, this is the date format I've chosen to work with in Flex.

Figure 13-6 earlier in the chapter shows the output from the page in a web browser. You can view the content by right-clicking the getEvents.aspx page and choosing View in Browser. You can also press F5 to view the page if you have allowed debugging in the web.config file or Ctrl+F5 if you have disabled debugging.

Displaying a list of categories and locations

The code behind the getCategories.aspx and getLocations.aspx pages is very similar, so I'll only show the first of those pages here. Again, you can view the relevant pages by right-clicking and choosing View Code:

```
      Imports System.IO
      Imports System.Xml
      Imports System.Data
      Imports System.Data.OleDb

      Partial Class getCategories
```

```
        Inherits System.Web.UI.Page
        Protected Sub Page_Load(ByVal sender As Object, ➥
          ByVal e As System.EventArgs) Handles Me.Load
          Dim dbConnString As String = ConfigurationManager. ➥
            ConnectionStrings("events").ConnectionString
          Dim dbConn As New OleDbConnection(dbConnString)
          Dim strSQL As String, objCommand As OleDbCommand
          Dim objDataReader As OleDbDataReader
          Dim eventsXMLDoc As XmlTextWriter = New XmlTextWriter(➥
            Response.OutputStream, Encoding.UTF8)
          strSQL = "SELECT * FROM categories " _
            & " ORDER BY categoryName"
          dbConn.Open()
          objCommand = New OleDbCommand(strSQL, dbConn)
          objDataReader = objCommand.ExecuteReader()
          eventsXMLDoc.Formatting = Formatting.Indented
          Response.ContentType = "text/xml"
          eventsXMLDoc.WriteStartDocument()
          eventsXMLDoc.WriteStartElement("categories")
          While objDataReader.Read()
            eventsXMLDoc.WriteStartElement("category")
            eventsXMLDoc.WriteAttributeString("id", ➥
              objDataReader("categoryID"))
            eventsXMLDoc.WriteValue(objDataReader("categoryName"))
            eventsXMLDoc.WriteEndElement()
          End While
          eventsXMLDoc.WriteEndElement()
          eventsXMLDoc.Flush()
          eventsXMLDoc.Close()
          objDataReader.Close()
          dbConn.Close()
        End Sub
      End Class
```

These pages start by importing the relevant namespaces. The code occurs within the Page_Load sub, which declares the relevant variables. The database query extracts a list of all categories and generates the XML content using the methods mentioned previously. The sub finishes by calling the Flush method of the XmlTextWriter and closing the relevant objects.

You can run the getCategories.aspx and getLocations.aspx pages in a web browser to see the output. Figure 13-10 shows the output from the getCategories.aspx page.

Now that we've successfully generated the XML content, we'll need to load it into the Flex application using a custom ActionScript class.

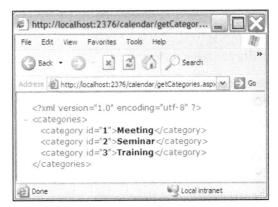

Figure 13-10. The getCategories.aspx page displayed in a web browser

Creating the custom class

We'll use a custom ActionScript class to handle the loading and processing of XML content into the Flex interface. The class will use the URLLoader class, and we'll make it generic so we can reuse it for each of the different ASP.NET files that we want to load.

Create a new ActionScript class called GenericLoader in the com.aip package. Flex Builder will create the folder structure com ➤ aip for you. The class doesn't extend any existing classes.

Add the following import statements below the package declaration:

```
import flash.net.URLLoader;
import flash.net.URLRequest;
import flash.events.Event;
import flash.net.URLVariables;
import flash.net.URLRequestMethod;
```

These statements represent the classes that we'll need to reference.

Modify the class file so that the class is bindable by adding the following metatag above the class declaration:

```
[Bindable]
public class GenericLoader {
```

We need to do this so that we can dispatch events to the application file.

Add the following private variables to the class file:

```
private var xmlContent:XML;
private var xmlLoader:URLLoader;
private var listNode:String;
private var allContent:XMLList;
```

These variables represent the loaded XML document, the URLLoader object, the relevant node to target in the XML document, and the returned content, respectively.

Add the GenericLoader constructor method shown here:

```
public function GenericLoader() {
  xmlLoader = new URLLoader();
  xmlLoader.addEventListener(Event.COMPLETE, completeHandler);
}
```

We use this method to create a new URLLoader object and add an event listener that responds when the call has been completed. Add the completeHandler event listener now:

```
private function completeHandler(e:Event):void {
  xmlContent = XML(e.target.data);
  trace (xmlContent.toXMLString());
}
```

This event listener casts the received data from the URLLoader as an XML object and assigns it to the xmlContent private variable. The function also traces the value of the variable, using the toXMLString method, so we can check what has been loaded. This technique is a useful step when loading external content.

The last thing we'll need to do is create a load method so we can make the request of the ASP.NET page. This method will take three parameters: the URL to load, the name of the node to locate in the loaded content, and the variables being passed with the request. Add the following public method to the class file:

```
public function load(xmlFile:String, node:String, vars:URLVariables)➥
  :void {
  var request:URLRequest = new URLRequest(xmlFile);
  request.method = URLRequestMethod.POST;
  listNode = node;
  try {
    if (vars != null) {
      request.data = vars;
    }
    xmlLoader.load(request);
  }
  catch (e:Error) {
    trace ("Can't load exernal XML document");
  }
}
```

This method starts by creating a new URLRequest for the file specified in the xmlFile parameter. We must make sure that this is the full server path to the ASP.NET page so that the content of the file is parsed correctly by the web server. You'll see what I mean shortly.

The function sets the request method to POST because we want to use that method to send any variables to the ASP.NET page. It assigns the node parameter to the private variable listNode. It uses a try-catch block to make the request. If a URLVariables object parameter is passed to the function, it assigns the object to the data property of the URLRequest. It then loads the URLRequest. In the case of an error, we trace a message to the console. Obviously, we could add some more stringent error handling if we chose.

We need to switch back to the main application file so we can create an object from this class to populate the interface.

Loading the events for a specific date

Before we start to populate the interface, let's add code to the main application file so we can check that we're loading the requested XML content correctly. Switch to this file and add the following import statement:

```
import com.aip.GenericLoader;
```

We need to import the class we just created before we can create a GenericLoader object.

Add the following private variable declarations to the script block:

```
private var serverPath:String = "http://localhost:2376/calendar/";
private var theEventsList:GenericLoader = new GenericLoader();
```

The first variable sets the path to the web server. I've set the path for my web server folder. You will undoubtedly need to change the value of this variable to suit your own development environment. You can find the correct URL when you view any ASP.NET page in a web browser. Look at the address bar and copy the path without the page name. The second variable creates a new GenericLoader object called theEventsList.

I find it very useful to set a single variable to the web server path and use it throughout the application. In that way, when I move the application to the production environment I can change the path in that location and update the entire application. I'll reference this variable later in the custom component file as well.

We'll make the request for the getEvents.aspx page in the initApp function. We'll do this using a new function called showEventsByDate. To start with, we'll hard-code the date to display events for 2007-11-07 because we know there is some data associated with that date in the database. Afterward, we'll set the application to display the events for the current date when it first loads and to send through the required date to the ASP.NET page.

Add the following function to the code block. It is a public function because eventually we'll need to call it from our custom component file:

```
public function showEventsByDate():void {
  var selectedDate:String
  var params:URLVariables;
  selectedDate = "2007-11-07";
  params = new URLVariables();
  params.newDate = selectedDate;
  theEventsList.load(serverPath + "getEvents.aspx", "event", params);
}
```

This function will change somewhat as we progress but it starts by requesting all events for the date November 7, 2007. Notice that I've written this in *YYYY-MM-DD* format as 2007-11-07.

The function creates a new URLVariables object that stores this date in the newDate property. It calls the public load method of the custom ActionScript class file. We pass the full path to the getEvents.aspx page as well as the <event> node from the XML document and the URLVariables object. The full path will look like the following for my application:

```
http://localhost:2376/calendar/getEvents.aspx
```

The details of each of the events for the selected date will be stored in the <event> nodes in the XML document. We pass the name of this node so we can generate the XMLList of events correctly in the class file.

Modify the initApp function to call the new showEventsByDate function:

```
private function initApp(e:FlexEvent):void {
    setupDateChooser();
    showEventsByDate();
}
```

We can test the application to this point by clicking the Debug button in Flex Builder. When you do this, you won't see any change in the interface as the trace statement only displays in the Console view. Switch back to Flex Builder and you should see the loaded XML content in the Console view, as shown in Figure 13-11.

Figure 13-11. Testing that the XML content successfully loads from the ASP.NET page

If all has gone according to plan, you should see the three events from the database displayed in XML format within the Console view. Once we've reached this stage, it's time to display the XML content in the List component.

Populating the interface with the events

We'll display the start and end times, and title for each event in the List component. When we click an item in the list, we'll eventually display the details in controls in the custom component, but we'll come to that a little later.

We'll use the complete event handler in the class file to create an XMLList of all events from the loaded XML content. We'll dispatch a complete event back to the application to let it know that the XMLList is available. The application file will then use the XMLList as the data provider for the List control.

Switch back to the class file and modify the completeHandler function, as shown in bold here:

```
private function completeHandler(e:Event):void {
  xmlContent = XML(e.target.data);
  //trace (xmlContent.toXMLString());
  allContent = xmlContent[listNode];
  dispatchEvent(new Event(Event.COMPLETE));
}
```

The first new line assigns the content from the required nodes to the private variable allContent. Notice that we've used xmlContent[listNode] to target the relevant nodes. We passed in the value of listNode with the load method. The last line dispatches the complete event so that the application file knows that the XML content is available to populate the List control.

We'll need to make the allContent private variable available to the application using a getter method, so add the following to the class file:

```
public function get targetNodes():XMLList {
  return allContent;
}
```

Switch back to the main application file and add the following private variable to the script block:

```
private var eventsXML:XMLList;
```

We'll use this variable as the data provider for the List control. We'll populate the variable when we receive notification that the URLLoader has completed loading the XML content; that is, in response to the dispatched complete event.

Add the complete event listener to the GenericLoader object in the initApp function:

```
private function initApp(e:FlexEvent):void {
  theEventsList.addEventListener(Event.COMPLETE, completeHandler);
  setupDateChooser();
  showEventsByDate();
}
```

By convention, I've given it the name completeHandler but you could use any other name for this function. We now need to add the completeHandler function to the application file:

```
private function completeHandler(e:Event):void{
  eventsXML = theEventsList.targetNodes;
  if (eventsXML.length() > 0) {
    lstEvents.dataProvider = eventsXML;
    lstEvents.labelFunction = showEventTitle;
    txtMessage.text = "";
    lstEvents.visible = true;
  }
  else {
    txtMessage.text = "There are no events on the selected date";
    lstEvents.visible = false;
    btnDelete.visible = false;
  }
}
```

This function assigns the results from the targetNodes getter method in the class file to the new eventsXML XMLList object. It checks to see whether there are any returned events using the length method. If so, we set the data provider for the List and call a label function named showEventTitle to create the label for the List. We'll add that function shortly. We also clear the message displayed in the txtMessage control and show the List control.

If there are no events returned from the database, we display a message in the txtMessage control and hide both the List control and delete button. Remember that we've currently hard-coded the date to 2007-11-07 in the showEventsByDate function, so there should be some events to display.

The next step is to add the label function showEventTitle to the code block. This is quite a long function because we're creating time strings from numbers and doing some time calculations with start times and durations. Add the following function to the script block:

```
private function showEventTitle(item:Object):String {
  var duration:int, hour:int, minutes:int;
  var hoursToAdd:int, leftOverMinutes:int;
  var finishHour:int, finishMinutes:int;
  var startMinutes:String, finishTime:String;
  var listLabel:String;
  duration = int(item.eventDurationMinutes);
  hour = int(item.eventHour);
  minutes = int(item.eventMinutes);
  if (minutes == 0) {
    startMinutes = "00";
  }
  else {
    startMinutes = String(minutes);
  }
```

```
      finishMinutes = duration + minutes;
      if (finishMinutes >= 60) {
        hoursToAdd = Math.floor(finishMinutes / 60);
        leftOverMinutes = finishMinutes - hoursToAdd * 60;
        finishHour = hour + hoursToAdd;
        finishMinutes = leftOverMinutes;
      }
      else {
        finishHour = hour;
      }
      if (finishMinutes == 0) {
        finishTime = String(finishHour) + ":00";
      }
      else {
        finishTime = String(finishHour) + ":" + String(finishMinutes);
      }
      listLabel = String(hour) + ":" + startMinutes + " - " + finishTime ➥
        + " " + item.title;
      return listLabel;
    }
```

The function receives an object as a parameter representing the current item in the data provider. It starts by declaring the variables we'll need, including variables for the duration, hour, and minutes of the event. It also creates other variables that we'll use to calculate the finishing times and create string representations of the numbers.

We populate the duration, hour, and minutes variables from the item argument, targeting the relevant properties of the XMLList. Notice that we cast them as the data type int because all XML content comes through as strings. We create the startMinutes string variable, using 00 as the display value for 0.

The function calculates the finishing minutes by adding the starting minutes and duration. If this figure is over 60, we calculate how many hours to add to the starting hours by finding the whole number of hours when we divide the calculated amount by 60. We then work out how many minutes are left over once we account for the hours. We create finishing hour and minutes values from the calculations. If our finishing minutes are less than 60, we can use the starting hour as the finishing hour.

We create the finishing time by displaying a 0 value as 00 and casting the relevant calculated finishing times as strings. Finally, we create a listLabel variable that shows the start and finish times as well as the title of the event and return this value.

Running the application shows the result seen in Figure 13-12.

Notice that I've chosen November 7, 2007 as the selected date in the DateChooser control to match the list of events. In fact, we'll see the same list of events regardless of the date chosen because we've hard-coded the date. Let's modify that approach now in the showEventsByDate function so we can pass in a date and see the relevant events.

Figure 13-12. Populating the List control from the loaded XML content

To start with, we'll need to modify the function signature so that it accepts a date parameter. We'll also hide the delete button and calculate the date string from the passed-in date. Make the modifications shown in bold to the showEventsByDate function:

```
public function showEventsByDate(theDate:Date):void {
  var monthString:String, dayString:String;
  var selectedDate:String;
  var params:URLVariables;
  lstEvents.dataProvider = [];
  btnDelete.visible = false;
  if (theDate.getMonth()+1 < 10) {
    monthString = "0" + String(theDate.getMonth()+1);
  }
  else {
    monthString = String(theDate.getMonth()+1);
  }
  if (theDate.getDate() < 10) {
    dayString = "0" + String(theDate.getDate());
  }
  else {
    dayString = String(theDate.getDate());
  }
  selectedDate = String(theDate.getFullYear()) + "-" + monthString + ➥
    "-" + dayString;
  params = new URLVariables();
  params.newDate = selectedDate;
  theEventsList.load (serverPath + "getEvents.aspx", "event", params);
}
```

The function uses the getFullYear, getMonth, and getDate methods to return the relevant portions of the passed-in date value. The getMonth method returns a zero-based value, so we need to compensate by adding 1 so that we can display the correct month number. We also add leading zeroes where the month and day are less than 10. We've created a string in the format *YYYY-MM-DD* from the date object.

We need to modify the call to this function in the initApp function. It needs to pass a date, and we'll use it to send through the current date as we want to display the current date's event when the application first loads. Modify this function as shown in bold here:

```
private function initApp(e:FlexEvent):void {
    theEventsList.addEventListener(Event.COMPLETE, completeHandler);
    setupDateChooser();
    showEventsByDate(newDate());
}
```

We'll also need to set up a function that responds when we choose a new date in the DateChooser control. Each time we choose a new date, we'll call the showEventsByDate function passing in the selected date. Add the following event listener to the DateChooser in the initApp function:

```
dtSelector.addEventListener(Event.CHANGE, dateChangeHandler);
```

Add the dateChangehandler function to the script block:

```
private function dateChangeHandler(e:CalendarLayoutChangeEvent)➥
    :void {
    showEventsByDate(e.newDate);
}
```

This function accepts a CalendarLayoutChangeEvent as an argument. We use this event to target the newDate property of the DateChooser. You'll also need to add the following import statement at the top of the script block if Flex Builder didn't add it automatically:

```
import mx.events.CalendarLayoutChangeEvent;
```

Now we're ready to run the application again. If you do this, you should be able to select a new date—for example, November 16, 2007—and see the relevant events in the List control. Where there are no events to display, you'll see an appropriate message in the interface.

We still need to be able to view the details of each event and we'll create a custom component to handle this functionality.

Creating a custom component for event details

We'll create a custom component that will show all of the details of each event, including the title, event details, start time and duration, event category, and location. We'll add the component to a folder called components in the com ➤ aip folder, so create that folder now.

Create a new MXML component inside the components folder called EventDetails based on a VBox component. Remove the width and height attributes. Add the following MXML tags to the interface:

```
<mx:HBox>
    <mx:Label text="Title" fontWeight="bold" width="100"/>
    <mx:TextInput id="txtTitle" width="200"/>
    <mx:Text id="txtSelectedDate" visible="false"/>
</mx:HBox>
<mx:HBox>
```

```
      <mx:Label text="Details" fontWeight="bold" width="100"/>
      <mx:TextArea id="txtDetails" width="200" height="60"/>
    </mx:HBox>
    <mx:HBox>
      <mx:Label text="Start time" fontWeight="bold" width="100"/>
      <mx:ComboBox id="cboStartHour" prompt="Choose" width="75"/>
      <mx:ComboBox id="cboStartMinute" prompt="Choose" width="75"/>
    </mx:HBox>
    <mx:HBox>
      <mx:Label text="Duration (mins)" fontWeight="bold" width="100"/>
      <mx:ComboBox id="cboDuration" prompt="Choose" width="75"/>
    </mx:HBox>
    <mx:HBox>
      <mx:Label text="Category" fontWeight="bold" width="100"/>
      <mx:ComboBox id="cboCategories" width="200"
        prompt="Choose category"/>
    </mx:HBox>
    <mx:HBox>
      <mx:Label text="Location" fontWeight="bold" width="100"/>
      <mx:ComboBox id="cboLocations" width="200"
        prompt="Choose location"/>
      <mx:Button id="btnUpdate" label="Save"/>
    </mx:HBox>
    <mx:Text id ="txtErrors" color="#FF0000" fontWeight="bold"/>
```

Figure 13-13 shows how the interface looks in Design view.

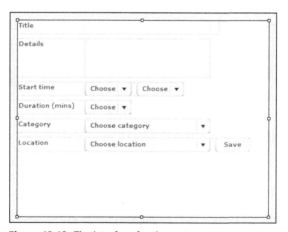

Figure 13-13. The interface for the custom component

We'll load the Category and Location ComboBox controls with the values from the categories and locations tables in the database. We have already created two ASP.NET pages, getCategories.aspx and getLocations.aspx, to provide us with XML content for these controls, so all we have to do is request their XML content.

We'll be able to use the GenericLoader class to access the XML content, so we need to add an appropriate import statement in a script block at the top of the component file:

```
<mx:Script>
  <![CDATA[
    import com.aip.GenericLoader;
  ]]>
</mx:Script>
```

We'll also need to create private variables for all of the properties that we'll want to access, as well as for the GenericLoader objects we'll need. Add the following declarations to the code block:

```
private var serverPath:String;
private var eventID:Number;
private var eventDate:String;
private var eventTitle:String;
private var eventDetails:String;
private var eventStartHour:int;
private var eventStartMinute:String;
private var eventDuration:String;
private var eventCategory:String;
private var eventLocation:String;
private var theCategoriesList:GenericLoader = new GenericLoader();
private var theLocationsList:GenericLoader = new GenericLoader();
private var updateDetails:GenericLoader = new GenericLoader();
private var categoriesXML:XMLList;
private var locationsXML:XMLList;
```

Notice that I've added a variable for the server path, which I'll populate from the main application file, as well as variables for the details of each event and for the XMLList objects that will populate the ComboBox controls. I've also added an extra GenericLoader object that we'll use when we update the event details. We'll use setter methods to set the values of the private variables and we'll come to that shortly. First, we'll load the list of categories and locations into the relevant ComboBox controls.

We'll start by adding an initComponent function that we'll call in the creationComplete event of the opening VBox tag. This function will assign the handlers for the first two GenericLoader objects and takes a FlexEvent as an argument. The function also calls another function, loadComboBoxes, which will call the load methods for the two GenericLoader objects:

```
private function initComponent(e:FlexEvent):void {
  theCategoriesList.addEventListener(Event.COMPLETE, ➥
    categoriesCompleteHandler);
  theLocationsList.addEventListener(Event.COMPLETE, ➥
    locationsCompleteHandler);
  loadComboBoxes();
}
```

Check that Flex Builder has added the following import statement, and if not, add it yourself:

```
import mx.events.FlexEvent;
```

Add the loadComboBoxes function now:

```
private function loadComboBoxes():void {
  theCategoriesList.load (serverPath + "getCategories.aspx", ➥
    "category", null);
  theLocationsList.load (serverPath + "getLocations.aspx", ➥
    "location", null);
}
```

You've seen the use of the load method in the main application file. We've used the serverPath variable with the page names to create the path to the ASP.NET files. We'll populate that variable soon from the main application file. We've also specified the node names that we want to use to target the loaded content. Because we're not sending parameters, we pass null as the third argument.

You'll also need to add the categoriesCompleteHandler and locationsCompleteHandler functions that follow:

```
private function categoriesCompleteHandler(e:Event):void {
  categoriesXML = e.target.targetNodes;
  cboCategories.dataProvider = categoriesXML;
}
private function locationsCompleteHandler(e:Event):void {
  locationsXML = e.target.targetNodes;
  cboLocations.dataProvider = locationsXML;
}
```

Again, these functions are similar to the ones we saw in the main application file. We call the targetNodes getter method to populate the XMLList and set this as the data provider for the relevant ComboBox.

Finally, we need to call the initComponent function in the root node, as shown in bold here:

```
<mx:VBox xmlns:mx="http://www.adobe.com/2006/mxml"
  creationComplete="initComponent(event)">
```

Before we add the component to the main application file, we'll need to create setter methods for all of the private variables. Add the following methods to the script block:

```
public function set server(theServerPath:String):void {
  serverPath = theServerPath;
}
public function set ID(theEventID:int):void{
  eventID = theEventID;
}
public function set date(theDate:String):void {
  eventDate = theDate;
```

```
    }
    public function set title(theTitle:String):void {
      eventTitle = theTitle;
      txtTitle.text = eventTitle;
    }
    public function set details(theDetails:String):void {
      eventDetails = theDetails;
      txtDetails.text = eventDetails;
    }
    public function set startHour(theStartHour:int):void {
      eventStartHour = theStartHour;
      cboStartHour.selectedItem = eventStartHour;
    }
    public function set startMinute(theStartMinute:String):void {
      eventStartMinute = theStartMinute;
      cboStartMinute.selectedItem = eventStartMinute;
    }
    public function set duration(theDuration:String):void {
      eventDuration = theDuration;
      cboDuration.selectedItem = eventDuration;
    }
    public function set category(theCategory:String):void {
      eventCategory = theCategory;
      cboCategories.selectedItem = eventCategory;
    }
    public function set location(theLocation:String):void {
      eventLocation = theLocation;
      cboLocations.selectedItem = eventLocation;
    }
```

These functions set the values of the relevant private variables. Where appropriate, they also populate the interface with this value. We'll need to set the value of the serverPath private variable immediately by calling the server setter method from the main application file so we can correctly identify the path to the web server in this component file.

Let's test that we've populated the ComboBox controls correctly by adding the component to the main application file. Switch to that file and modify the opening <mx:Application> tag to include a reference to the components namespace:

```
<mx:Application xmlns:mx="http://www.adobe.com/2006/mxml"
  layout="absolute"
  xmlns:comp="com.aip.components.*"
  initialize="initApp(event)">
```

We use the com.aip.components path to indicate the folders com ➤ aip ➤ components. We'll refer to any components inside this folder using the prefix comp.

Add the custom component to the interface just after the closing tag for the second VBox control:

```
<mx:VBox>
  <mx:List id="lstEvents" height="200" width="300"/>
  <mx:HBox width="300">
    <mx:Button id="btnAdd" label="Add event"/>
    <mx:Button id="btnDelete" label="Delete event"
      visible="false"/>
  </mx:HBox>
</mx:VBox>
<comp:EventDetails id="eventForm" visible="false"/>
```

We won't display the component until we have selected an event from the List control.

We need to set the web server path in the component within the initApp function using the following line:

```
eventForm.server = serverPath;
```

We call the server setter method of the eventForm component to set the value within the component. Note that I've done this within the initialize handler of the main application, so I can set the value before the creationComplete event of the custom component fires. That allows me to set the server path before I need to use it within the component.

I will need to make the custom component visible when I select an event in the List control, so I'll need to add an event listener that responds to the change event in this control. Add the following line to the initApp function:

```
lstEvents.addEventListener(ListEvent.CHANGE, listChangeHandler);
```

Check that Flex Builder has added the following import statement:

```
import mx.events.ListEvent;
```

Add the following listChangeHandler function:

```
private function listChangeHandler(e:ListEvent):void {
  eventForm.visible = true;
  btnDelete.visible = true;
}
```

This function makes both the custom component and delete button visible. A little later, we'll modify the function to call the relevant setter methods to pass values for display in the component, but for now, I just want to test that we can load the ComboBox controls in the component correctly.

Run the application, select a date that contains events, and click an item in the List control. You should see that the Category and Location ComboBox controls are populated, as shown in Figure 13-14.

Figure 13-14. Checking that the ComboBox controls are populated

We will also need to populate the other ComboBox controls showing the start time and duration, so switch back to the custom component file now. Add the following three functions:

```
private function populateHours():void {
  var dp:Array = [];
  for (var i:int=7; i< 19; i++){
    dp.push(i);
  }
  cboStartHour.dataProvider = dp;
}
private function populateMinutes():void {
  var dp:Array = ["00","15","30","45"];
  cboStartMinute.dataProvider = dp;
}
private function populateDuration():void{
  var dp:Array = [];
  for (var i:int=1;i<33;i++) {
    dp.push(i*15);
  }
  cboDuration.dataProvider = dp;
}
```

The first function, populateHours, loops through values from 7 to 18 and adds the number to an array called dp. It then assigns that array as the data provider for the cboStartHour control. These numbers will equate to the hours 7 AM to 6 PM.. You could choose other values for these hours if you like and you could also use a 12-hour format with an AM/PM indicator, but I haven't done that here to keep things simple.

The populateMinutes function adds the values 00, 15, 30, and 45 to the cboStartMinute control. Again, for simplicity, I've assumed that events can only occur at 15-minute intervals within an hour. The final function, populateDuration, adds duration values ranging from 15 minutes to 480 minutes (8 hours).

We need to call these functions in the initComponent function, so add the following lines now:

```
populateHours();
populateMinutes();
populateDuration();
```

You can test that these functions work correctly by switching to the main application file, running it, choosing a date containing events, and clicking an event title in the List control. You should see that all ComboBox controls are populated.

The next step is to show the details of the selected event in the controls contained within the custom component.

Showing details of the selected event

If you don't already have it open, switch to the main application file and locate the listChangeHandler function. We'll use this function to find the relevant event details and set the values inside the component. Remember that the data provider for the List component contains all items in the XMLList, so all we need to do is locate the relevant properties inside the XMLList to identify which values to use.

Modify the listChangeHandler function as shown in bold in the following code block:

```
private function listChangeHandler(e:ListEvent):void {
  var selectedEvent:Object = e.target.selectedItem;
  eventForm.visible = true;
  btnDelete.visible = true;
  eventForm.ID = selectedEvent.@id;
  eventForm.title = selectedEvent.title;
  eventForm.details = selectedEvent.details;
  eventForm.startHour = selectedEvent.eventHour;
  eventForm.startMinute = selectedEvent.eventMinutes;
  eventForm.duration = selectedEvent.eventDurationMinutes;
  eventForm.category = selectedEvent.category;
  eventForm.location = selectedEvent.location;
}
```

The new lines locate the selected event in the List control using the selectedItem property and store it in the selectedEvent object. We then target the properties of the selectedEvent object to locate the details and assign the values to the relevant setter methods of the eventForm control.

Figure 13-15 shows the effect of running this application and selecting an event in the List control.

The details of the selected event appear in the relevant controls within the custom component. Now that we can see the selected event details, we'll modify the custom component file so that we can update any of the details.

Figure 13-15. Populating the custom component to show details of the selected event

Updating the selected event

To add update functionality, we need to make changes to both the Flex application and add a new ASP.NET page to handle the database updates. We'll start by looking at the Flex changes.

Updating in Flex

We have already added a Save button to the custom component file. Now we need to configure the button to send the updated values to an ASP.NET page so that we can update the database. Before we do that, however, we'll add some validation to the form so we can make sure the user doesn't leave any important fields blank.

Switch to the custom component file and add the following validator controls below the script block:

```
<mx:StringValidator id="titleValidator"
  source="{txtTitle}" property="text"
  trigger="{btnUpdate}" triggerEvent="click"
  required="true" requiredFieldError="Enter a title for the event"/>
<mx:StringValidator id="detailsValidator"
  source="{txtDetails}" property="text"
  trigger="{btnUpdate}" triggerEvent="click"
  required="true" requiredFieldError="Enter the event details"/>
```

These string validators check that text has been entered in both the txtTitle and txtDetails controls. They perform the validation when the btnUpdate control is clicked.

We now need to add the click handler for the button control, so modify the initComponent function to include the following line:

```
btnUpdate.addEventListener(MouseEvent.CLICK, clickHandler);
```

The click handler needs to check the outcomes from the string validators as well as determine that we have a valid selection in the ComboBox controls. Add the clickHandler function to the script block. Note that we will still have to add some code to the else part of the if statement:

```
private function clickHandler(e:Event):void {
  var theValidationResult:ValidationResultEvent;
  var booValid:Boolean = true;
  var theResponse:String = "Errors:\n";
  theValidationResult = titleValidator.validate();
  if (theValidationResult.type == ValidationResultEvent.INVALID) {
    theResponse += "- " + theValidationResult.message + "\n";
    booValid = false;
  }
  theValidationResult = detailsValidator.validate();
  if (theValidationResult.type == ValidationResultEvent.INVALID) {
    theResponse += "- " + theValidationResult.message + "\n";
    booValid = false;
  }
  if (cboStartHour.selectedIndex == -1) {
    theResponse += "- Choose a start time\n";
    booValid = false;
  }
  if (cboStartMinute.selectedIndex == -1) {
    theResponse += "- Choose a start time\n";
    booValid = false;
  }
  if (cboDuration.selectedIndex == -1) {
    theResponse += "- Choose a duration\n";
    booValid = false;
  }
  if (cboCategories.selectedIndex == -1) {
    theResponse += "- Choose a category\n";
    booValid = false;
  }
  if (cboLocations.selectedIndex == -1) {
    theResponse += "- Choose a location\n";
    booValid = false;
  }
  if (!booValid) {
    txtErrors.htmlText = theResponse;
  }
  else {
  }
}
```

We'll need to extend this function a little later to carry out the updates within the else block, but to start with, we'll just include the validation of the controls. The function starts by declaring a ValidationResultEvent that will indicate whether or not validation succeeded. Check that Flex Builder adds the following import statement, and if necessary, add it yourself:

```
import mx.events.ValidationResultEvent;
```

We also declare a Boolean variable called booValid, which indicates whether the form is valid. We set the starting value of this variable to true. The final variable, theResponse, will contain a list of validation errors that we can display in the custom component's interface.

After declaring the variables, we call the validate method of the titleValidator control and check for an invalid result. If we have one, we add the validation error message and set the booValid flag to false. We repeat the process for the detailsValidator.

We use ActionScript to check that we haven't left any of the ComboBox controls unpopulated. We do this by checking for a value of -1. We add appropriate error messages for any unpopulated controls and set the booValid flag to false. In the case of an update, this isn't required, because the user can't select anything other than a valid value from the ComboBox controls. However, we'll need it when we use the form to add a new event because the user could leave the ComboBox prompt selected.

Finally, we check the booValid flag, and, if it is set to false, we display the error messages in the txtErrors control. We haven't added processing for a valid set of entries. We'll do that by adding code to the else section in the function a little later.

We can run the application to check that the validation works. Select an event and clear either the Title or Details entry. You won't be able to reset the ComboBox controls. Clicking the Save button should display an error message like the one shown in Figure 13-16.

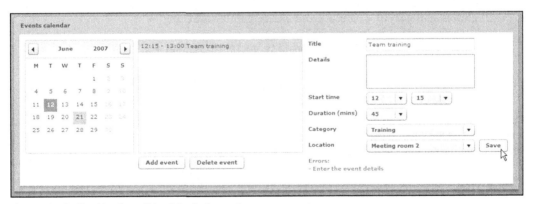

Figure 13-16. Checking for valid entries in the custom component

We must now modify the clickHandler function to pass the values to an ASP.NET page for updating. Start by adding the following new variable declarations at the top of the function:

```
var theValidationResult:ValidationResultEvent;
var booValid:Boolean = true;
var booAdd:Boolean = false;
var theResponse:String = "Errors:\n";
var params:URLVariables;
```

We've created another Boolean variable that we'll use to distinguish between adding and updating an entry. You'll see that this becomes important a little later on. The function also declares a URLVariables object that will contain the updated values.

Add the following code between the opening and closing else braces of the function:

```
else {
  txtErrors.htmlText = "";
  params = new URLVariables();
  if (isNaN(eventID)) {
    eventID = -1
    booAdd = true;
  }
  params.id = eventID;
  params.date = eventDate;
  params.title = txtTitle.text;
  params.details = txtDetails.text;
  params.startHour = cboStartHour.selectedLabel;
  params.startMinutes = cboStartMinute.selectedLabel;
  params.duration = cboDuration.selectedLabel;
  params.categoryID = theCategoriesList.getIDFromString(➥
    cboCategories.selectedLabel);
  params.locationID = theLocationsList.getIDFromString(➥
    cboLocations.selectedLabel);
  updateDetails.load(serverPath + "updateEvent.aspx", "message", params);
}
```

The code clears any existing message in the txtErrors control. It creates a new URLVariables object and checks that we have an eventID value set. We won't have one if we're adding a new event, so we'll set the eventID to -1 in that case and the booAdd flag to true.

We then set the value of the properties of the URLVariables object to the details in the relevant controls. The cboCategories and cboLocations controls only contain a selected label, so we'll call a public method called getIDFromString in the ActionScript class file. Of course, we'll need to create that method in the class file shortly.

The last line calls the load method of the GenericLoader class. It references the updateEvent.aspx page, which we still have to create. It locates the message node in the returned XML content and passes the URLVariables object.

Add the following getIDFromString public method to the GenericLoader class file:

```
public function getIDFromString(nodeValue:String):int {
  var matched:Boolean, selectedID:int;
  for (var i:int=0;i<allContent.length();i++) {
    if (allContent[i] == nodeValue) {
      matched = true;
      selectedID = allContent[i].@id;
      break;
    }
  }
  if (matched) {
    return selectedID;
  }
  else {
    return -1;
  }
}
```

This is the last modification to the class file. The function receives a string value and returns the related id. It loops through the XMLList variable and checks for a matching value. If it finds one, it locates the relevant id attribute and breaks out of the loop. The function returns either the selectedID value or a value of -1 if no match is found.

We now need to process the updates entered into the application interface using an ASP.NET file so that we can modify the database.

Updating in ASP.NET

We'll need to create a page called updateEvent.aspx to process the updated values from the SWF file. We'll use this page to process both updates to the database and the addition of new events. Again, this page won't have an XHTML interface as it will return XML content. I'll add the code to a code-behind page so the page itself will contain only the following declaration:

```
<%@ Page Language="VB" AutoEventWireup="false" ➥
  CodeFile="updateEvent.aspx.vb" Inherits="updateEvent" %>
```

The code-behind page contains the following VB statements. Again, I'll work through the file only briefly because our focus is really on the Flex side of the application:

```
Imports System.IO
Imports System.Xml
Imports System.Data
Imports System.Data.OleDb

Partial Class updateEvent
  Inherits System.Web.UI.Page
  Protected Sub Page_Load(ByVal sender As Object, ByVal e As ➥
      System.EventArgs) Handles Me.Load
    Dim intEventID As Integer, selectedDate As String
```

```
Dim strTitle As String, strDetails As String
Dim intStartHour As Integer, intStartMinutes As Integer
Dim intDuration As Integer
Dim intCategoryID As Integer, intLocationID As Integer
Dim dbConnString As String = ConfigurationManager.➥
  ConnectionStrings("events").ConnectionString
Dim dbConn As New OleDbConnection(dbConnString)
Dim strSQL As String
Dim objDA As OleDbDataAdapter
Dim autogen As OleDbCommandBuilder
Dim dSet As DataSet, dt As DataTable, drow As DataRow
Dim returnXMLDoc As XmlTextWriter = New XmlTextWriter(➥
  Response.OutputStream, Encoding.UTF8)
intEventID = CInt(Request.Form("id"))
selectedDate = Request.Form("date")
strTitle = Request.Form("title")
strDetails = Request.Form("details")
intStartHour = CInt(Request.Form("startHour"))
intStartMinutes = CInt(Request.Form("startMinutes"))
intDuration = CInt(Request.Form("duration"))
intCategoryID = CInt(Request.Form("categoryID"))
intLocationID = CInt(Request.Form("locationID"))
strSQL = "SELECT * FROM events " _
  & " WHERE eventID = " & intEventID
objDA = New OleDbDataAdapter(strSQL, dbConn)
autogen = New OleDbCommandBuilder(objDA)
dSet = New DataSet()
objDA.Fill(dSet, "events")
dt = dSet.Tables(0)
If intEventID = -1 Then
  drow = dt.NewRow()
Else
  drow = dt.Rows(0)
End If
drow("eventTitle") = strTitle
drow("eventDetails") = strDetails
drow("eventDate") = selectedDate
drow("eventStartHour") = intStartHour
drow("eventStartMinute") = intStartMinutes
drow("eventDurationMinutes") = intDuration
drow("eventCategoryID") = intCategoryID
drow("eventLocationID") = intLocationID
If intEventID = -1 Then
  dt.Rows.Add(drow)
End If
objDA.Update(dSet, "events")
dbConn.Close()
returnXMLDoc.Formatting = Formatting.Indented
Response.ContentType = "text/xml"
```

```
        returnXMLDoc.WriteStartDocument()
        returnXMLDoc.WriteStartElement("response")
        returnXMLDoc.WriteStartElement("message")
        If intEventID = -1 Then
          returnXMLDoc.WriteValue("Add:" + selectedDate)
        Else
          returnXMLDoc.WriteValue("Update:" + selectedDate)
        End If
        returnXMLDoc.WriteEndElement()
        returnXMLDoc.WriteEndElement()
        returnXMLDoc.Flush()
        returnXMLDoc.Close()
      End Sub
    End Class
```

The page starts by importing the relevant namespaces, and the processing code is contained in the sub that processes the Page_Load event. This sub declares the variables that we'll need and assigns the values from the Flex application using Request.Form. It casts the values correctly to integers as required.

The processing will be handled with a SELECT statement rather than an UPDATE SQL statement. This will allow me to use the same processing file for both additions and updates to the database. The SQL statement either identifies the ID for the current event or one with an ID of -1, in the case of an addition.

The remainder of the code loads a dataset and identifies the appropriate row of the data table for updating. In the case of an addition, we create a new row rather than take the first row in the data table as in updates. The sub sets the values for each field in the row and adds the row if we're processing an addition. It updates the dataset with the new values.

The sub finishes by generating an XML response. The XML document contains a <response> root element with a <message> child element. This child element either contains the word Add: or Update: with the value of the selectedDate variable. We'll use the returned date value to repopulate the data provider for the List control with events for the selected date. This allows us to see the updated details immediately.

Testing the update

We can't test the updating until we respond to the returned XML content from the ASP.NET page in the component file. Switch to this file and add the following event handler to the initComponent function:

```
        updateDetails.addEventListener(Event.COMPLETE, ➡
          updateCompleteHandler);
```

When the updateDetails object receives a response, it will call the updateCompleteHandler function, which you need to add now:

```
        private function updateCompleteHandler(e:Event):void {
          var strMessage:String = e.target.targetNodes;
          var selectedDateString:String, selectedDate:Date;
          var tempArray:Array;
          if (strMessage.substr(0,4) == "Add:") {
```

```
      selectedDateString = strMessage.substr(4, 10);
    }
    else {
      selectedDateString = strMessage.substr(7, 10);
    }
    tempArray = selectedDateString.split("-");
    selectedDate = new Date(tempArray[0], tempArray[1]-1, ➥
      tempArray[2]);
    Application.application.showEventsByDate(selectedDate);
  }
```

This function identifies the returned string from the <message> node and assigns it to the strMessage variable. It also declares some other variables that we'll need, including an array that we'll use to identify parts of the string date value.

We determine whether we're adding or updating the event by looking at the first four letters of the returned message. They'll say Add: if we've just added a new event. We choose the relevant part of the strMessage variable to identify the returned date string using the substr method.

We use the split method to separate the year, month, and day elements from the date string. We can then use the Date constructor to generate a new date object that we'll store in the selectedDate variable. Notice that we have to subtract one from the month value as months in ActionScript are zero-based, whereas we've used a one-based month value in the DateChooser control.

Finally, we call the showEventsByDate public method in the main application file, passing the selectedDate as a parameter. We'll need to add the following import statement in order to be able to reference the main application file:

```
import mx.core.Application;
```

We need to make a couple of modifications to the showEventsByDate function before we test the application. First, we need to clear the values in the form by creating and calling a public clear method in the custom component file. Switch to the component file and add the following clear function:

```
public function clear():void {
  txtTitle.text = "";
  txtDetails.text = "";
  cboStartHour.selectedIndex = -1;
  cboStartMinute.selectedIndex = -1;
  cboDuration.selectedIndex = -1;
  cboCategories.selectedIndex = -1;
  cboLocations.selectedIndex = -1;
}
```

The function simply clears all of the values in the form and resets the ComboBox controls to their prompt.

Switch back to the main application file and modify the showEventsByDate function to hide the custom component and call the clear method:

```
lstEvents.dataProvider = [];
eventForm.visible = false;
eventForm.clear();
```

Add the new lines below the line that clears the data provider.

We also need to call the date setter method in the component file by adding the following line, shown in bold:

```
eventForm.date = selectedDate;
params = new URLVariables();
```

This allows the component to keep track of the selected date so it can send it to the ASP.NET file.

We can test the update functionality by running the application and selecting a date containing events. Choose an event, enter a new title for it in the custom component, and click Save. You should see the List control update the title, and the custom component should no longer be visible, as shown in Figure 13-17.

Figure 13-17. The interface after updating an event

You can select the event in the List control to see the updated details. You should test that you can update all details of the selected event.

We'll use the functionality we just built to add a new event.

Adding a new event

We can use the same functionality for both updating and adding a new event. We need to start by configuring the click handler for the Add event button.

Switch to the main application file and add the following event listener to the initApp function:

```
btnAdd.addEventListener(MouseEvent.CLICK, addClickHandler);
```

Now add the addClickHandler function that follows:

```
private function addClickHandler(e:MouseEvent):void {
  lstEvents.visible = true;
  eventForm.visible = true;
  eventForm.ID = -1;
  eventForm.clear();
}
```

This function shows the List and custom components. It sets the ID property of the eventForm to -1 and clears any values from the custom component. The user can then add the details of the new event to the custom component and click the Save button to process the addition.

Try out the functionality by running the application, choosing a date, and clicking the Add event button. Enter details for the event and click Save. You should see the List control update with the new event, and clicking it should show the details in the custom component. If you forget to enter any values, you should see an appropriate error message underneath the custom component.

The last task remaining is allowing the user to delete an event from the database.

Deleting an event

We'll complete the application by allowing the user to delete a selected event. Again, this will require functionality in Flex as well as an ASP.NET page to handle the deletion from the database. We'll start by looking at the changes to the Flex application.

Deleting in Flex

The id of the event for deletion will be passed to an ASP.NET file with another GenericLoader object. Add the following declaration to the code block:

```
private var deleteEvent:GenericLoader = new GenericLoader();
```

We'll need to add a click handler for the Delete event button that deletes the event selected in the List control. We'll confirm the deletion with the user before we do the processing using an Alert.

Add the following event handler to the initApp function in the main application file to deal with the clicking of the Delete event button:

```
btnDelete.addEventListener(MouseEvent.CLICK, deleteClickHandler);
```

Add the deleteClickHandler function to the script block:

```
private function deleteClickHandler(e:MouseEvent):void {
  Alert.show("Are you sure you want to delete this event?", ➥
  "Question", (Alert.YES|Alert.NO),null,alertClickHandler);
}
```

You'll also need to add the following import statement:

```
import mx.controls.Alert;
```

The function shows an Alert containing the text Are you sure you want to delete this event? and Yes and No buttons. When the user clicks either button in the Alert, the alertClickHandler function will deal with processing, so add the function now:

```
private function alertClickHandler(e:CloseEvent):void {
  if (e.detail == Alert.YES) {
    var selectedEventIndex:Number = lstEvents.selectedIndex;
    var eventID:Number = lstEvents.dataProvider[selectedEventIndex]➡
      .@id;
    var params:URLVariables;
    params = new URLVariables();
    params.id = eventID;
    deleteEvent.load (serverPath + "deleteEvent.aspx", "message", ➡
      params);
  }
}
```

This function only needs to deal with the case where the user clicks the Yes button. In that case, the Flex application needs to call the relevant ASP.NET file to delete the record, passing the id of the event to delete.

You'll need to check that Flex Builder has added the following import statement:

```
import mx.events.CloseEvent;
```

You'll also need to add a complete event listener for the deleteEvent object. Add the following line to the initApp function:

```
deleteEvent.addEventListener(Event.COMPLETE, deleteCompleteHandler);
```

You'll now need to add this function:

```
private function deleteCompleteHandler(e:Event):void {
  var selDate:Date = dtSelector.selectedDate;
  if (selDate == null) {
    selDate = new Date();
  }
  showEventsByDate(selDate);
}
```

The function identifies the selected date and passes it to the showEventsByDate function. This will display the new list of events for the selected date, excluding the event that has just been deleted. Notice that we had to use today's date if there was no selection in the DateChooser. This would occur when the DateChooser first loads.

Before we can test the delete functionality, we need to create the ASP.NET page to remove the event from the database.

Deleting in ASP.NET

We can finish the ASP.NET side of things by creating the deleteEvent.aspx page. As with the other pages, the content is contained in a code-behind page, and the page itself looks like this:

```
<%@ Page Language="VB" AutoEventWireup="false" ➡
  CodeFile="deleteEvent.aspx.vb" Inherits="deleteEvent" %>
```

The code-behind page deleteEvent.aspx.vb contains the following content:

```
Imports System.IO
Imports System.Xml
Imports System.Data
Imports System.Data.OleDb

Partial Class deleteEvent
  Inherits System.Web.UI.Page
  Protected Sub Page_Load(ByVal sender As Object, ByVal e As ➡
      System.EventArgs) Handles Me.Load
    Dim intEventID As Integer
    Dim dbConnString As String = ConfigurationManager.➡
      ConnectionStrings("events").ConnectionString
    Dim dbConn As New OleDbConnection(dbConnString)
    Dim objCmd As OleDbCommand
    Dim strSQL As String
    Dim returnXMLDoc As XmlTextWriter = New XmlTextWriter(➡
      Response.OutputStream, Encoding.UTF8)
    intEventID = CInt(Request.Form("id"))
    strSQL = "DELETE FROM events WHERE eventID = " & intEventID
    dbConn.Open()
    objCmd = New OleDbCommand(strSQL, dbConn)
    objCmd.ExecuteNonQuery()
    dbConn.Close()
    returnXMLDoc.Formatting = Formatting.Indented
    Response.ContentType = "text/xml"
    returnXMLDoc.WriteStartDocument()
    returnXMLDoc.WriteStartElement("response")
    returnXMLDoc.WriteStartElement("message")
    returnXMLDoc.WriteValue("Deleted event with ID " & intEventID)
    returnXMLDoc.WriteEndElement()
    returnXMLDoc.WriteEndElement()
    returnXMLDoc.Flush()
    returnXMLDoc.Close()
  End Sub
End Class
```

After importing the relevant namespaces, the sub called Page_Load handles the processing. It creates the variables that it needs and then requests the id variable from the Flex application. The sub creates a DELETE SQL statement, processes it, and writes XML content.

Switch back to the Flex application. Run the application and test that you can delete an event. Figure 13-18 shows the confirmation required before deleting takes place.

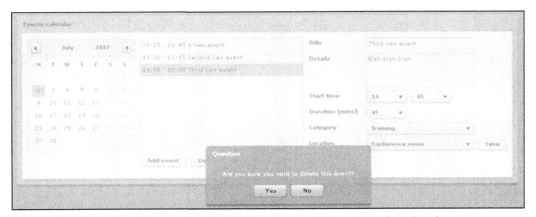

Figure 13-18. The user is asked to confirm the deletion of an event before processing takes place.

That completes the Flex application. You can find the completed files for both the Flex and ASP.NET application in the resources download file for the chapter.

Summary

In this chapter, we worked through a Flex application powered by ASP.NET. The application allowed us to view events by choosing a date from a DateChooser control. We could view a list of events and select one to see the associated details. We could also update the details of a selected event. Finally, the application allowed us to add a new event and delete an existing event from the database.

The content was stored in an Access database. It was passed between the database and the Flex application using ASP.NET pages written in VB 2008. These pages generated XML content that Flex could access using a custom ActionScript class and the built-in URLLoader class.

The next chapter provides the final case study for this section. In that chapter we'll look at a PHP 5 application that works with a MySQL database.

Chapter 14

PHP CASE STUDY

The final case study in this section is a Flex-PHP application. In this chapter, we'll work through an application with a PHP 5 back end and MySQL database, and a SWF interface. The application allows a user to manage a simple blog.

When the user first loads the application, they'll see a list of posts for the current month. They can also view archive posts from previous months. After users log in, they can add a new post, and edit or delete an existing post. The application is purposely simplistic because I want to focus on the interaction between PHP and Flex rather than add complicated functionality. I also want to keep the chapter relatively short.

The content for the application is held in a MySQL database. It is provided to the Flex application using PHP 5. The PHP pages include a page

- to get the details of the current post or the archives posts
- to add a new post or edit an existing one
- to delete a post

All pages generate XML content using a structure that is consistent with the RSS 2.0 specification. If you want to see the details of this specification, you can find out more at http://cyber.law.harvard.edu/rss/rss.html.

The application consists of the following:

- A MySQL database
- PHP pages that interact with the database and generate XML documents
- An MXML application file containing the interface
- ActionScript files containing the code to work with the interface
- A custom ActionScript class to handle the loading and processing of XML content
- ActionScript classes that create custom events
- An ActionScript class to store details of a selected post
- A custom component to display a form for either editing or adding a post
- A utilities class providing date-conversion functions

You can download the finished case study files from the friends of ED web site at www. friendsofed.com. You can either work through these files as you read through the chapter or create the application from scratch as I've described here.

Before we start coding, let's explore the application in further detail.

Understanding the application

It's important to understand more about the application that we're building before we get started. In this section, I'll show you how the application works. As with the other case studies, I haven't spent time adding styling to the application as the focus here is on functionality. Feel free to add as much or as little styling as you want.

The application interface

The application starts with a TabNavigator control that displays two tabs, one for a list of posts and another containing a login form, as shown in Figure 14-1. The Posts tab allows the user to view either the posts for the current month or archive posts. When the user views the current posts, the View current posts button is disabled. The application disables the View archives button when viewing archive posts.

If we know the username and password, we can log in using the form in the Login tab. This will give access to Administrator functionality. You can see this form in Figure 14-2.

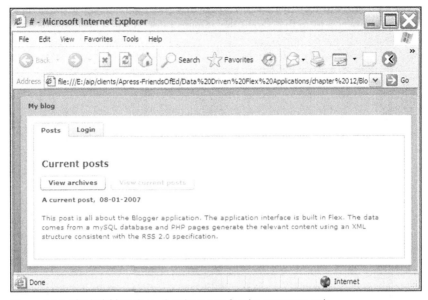

Figure 14-1. The intial interface, showing posts for the current month

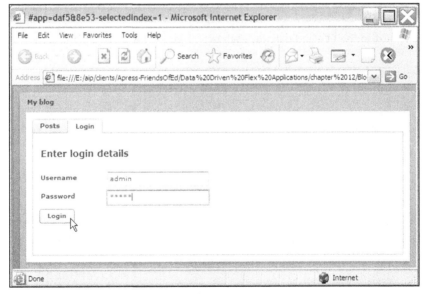

Figure 14-2. The Login form

Once we've logged in successfully, we'll see a message and an additional tab, as shown in Figure 14-3. The additional tab contains a form that allows the administrator to add a new post or edit an existing post.

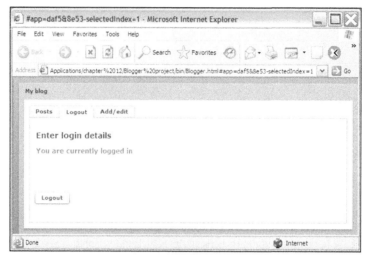

Figure 14-3. The interface after logging in

After successfully logging in, the Posts tab will display an Add new post button as well as Edit and Delete buttons next to the title and date for each post. Figure 14-4 shows the interface in this state.

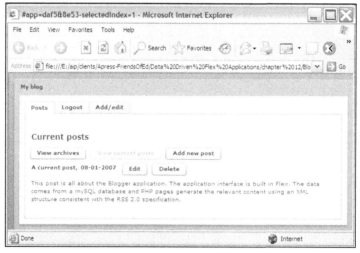

Figure 14-4. The Posts tab after logging in

Clicking the Add new post button shows the Add/edit tab without an entry. The administrator could also click the tab to display the form. You can see this tab in Figure 14-5.

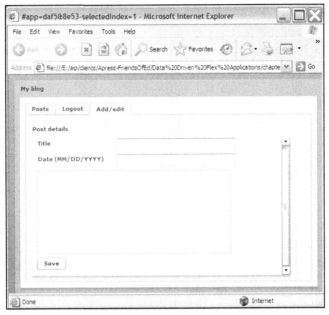

Figure 14-5. The Add/edit tab as it appears when adding a new post

Clicking the Edit button next to a post displays the same tab populated with the details of that post, as shown in Figure 14-6.

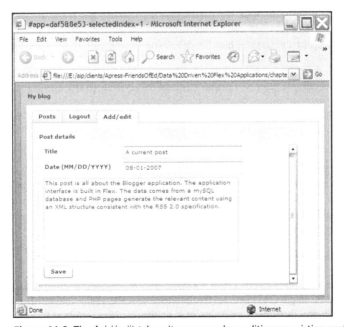

Figure 14-6. The Add/edit tab as it appears when editing an existing post

The user can then make changes to the title, date, or content and then click the Save button to update the database.

The posts displayed in the application are stored in a single table in a MySQL database. The next section describes the structure of the database.

The application data source

The application uses data stored in a MySQL database, although you could use any other type of database. I called my database blogger, but you're welcome to use any name. The structure of this database is very simple with only one table, posts, containing the blog entries. Table 14-1 shows the structure of the posts table.

Table 14-1. The structure of the posts table

Field	Field Type	Comments
postID	int(11)	Primary key. Not null. Auto-incrementing field.
postDate	date	Not null.
postTitle	varchar(100)	Not null.
postContent	text	Not null.

The resources for the chapter include the SQL script file used to generate the database and add two sample posts. Feel free to add your own content or to change the dates of the sample posts. I won't work through the setup of the database as I'm assuming you're able to complete this task yourself.

In the real world, we may want to classify posts by topic area and provide users with options to view different topics. However, for brevity, I haven't added this option to the application.

PHP pages access the database and provide the content to the Flex application as an XML document. Let's look at the structure of the generated XML content.

Viewing the XML content

The PHP pages provide XML documents to the Flex application that use a format consistent with the RSS 2.0 specification. RSS is an XML vocabulary that shares web site content. It is often used for blogs and news-oriented sites. I've added one element to the XML structure that isn't included in the specification <message> to allow me to pass messages to the Flex application.

Figure 14-7 shows the structure of this XML document.

The root node of the document is the <rss> element, which contains a single <channel> child element. This element contains single <title>, <link>, and <description> elements. These are required elements. In addition, the document contains one or more <item> elements. Each <item> element is equivalent to a post and contains the <guid> element that contains the primary key from the database.

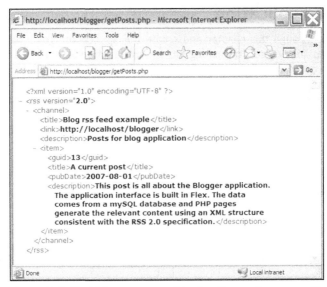

Figure 14-7. The XML structure used to describe events on a specific day

The other details for the post are contained within the <title>, <pubDate>, and <description> elements. The specification allows for other optional elements, but I haven't included them here. Notice that the <pubDate> element contains the date in *YYYY-MM-DD* format. This is the format used by the MySQL database. We'll convert this date format as required in the Flex application.

When a user adds, edits, or deletes a post, the PHP page processing the change will notify the Flex application of the outcome using an XML document. This document is consistent with the RSS 2.0 specification, but includes an additional element, <message>. Figure 14-8 shows the XML document generated by a successful addition or update to the database.

Note the <message> element, which notifies the SWF file of the page outcome. If there were an error processing the update, the relevant error message would appear in the <message> element. In the case of a deletion, the <message> element contains the text You have successfully deleted the post.

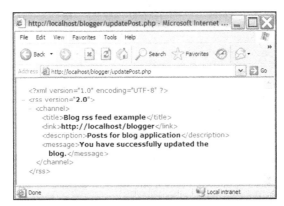

Figure 14-8. The XML content notifies of a successful update
to the database.

Structuring the application

If you want to work through this chapter and create the application, you'll need a web server to process the PHP pages. In my case, I'm running Internet Information Services (IIS) with PHP 5 installed. I've created a folder called blogger in the web server in the location C:\Inetpub\wwwroot. When I want to view the application in a web browser, I'll enter the URL http://localhost/blogger/. For Apache, set up a folder called blogger in the htdocs directory of your Apache installation. You will be able to view the site with the same URL as on IIS. However, we'll use an IIS server in this example, so just use the values for the Apache server in place of those shown (there's no difference in the steps).

For this case study, you'll need to create a new Flex project, choosing your own name and location. Choose the Application server type of PHP and enter the appropriate settings for the Folder field. Figure 14-9 shows the settings that I've used in my project.

Figure 14-9. The settings for the Flex project

When you click Next, you need to enter the Web root and Root URL for the application. My settings are shown in Figure 14-10. You must click the Validate Configuration button to check that your entries are correct. The screenshot in Figure 14-10 shows the message that you'll receive if you've entered the values correctly.

You can import the completed application files from the downloaded resources. Choose File ➤ Import and select the Archive file option. Navigate to the BloggerFiles.zip file and select the Flex project as the destination. When you click Finish, the relevant files will be added to the project.

You can also work through the steps in the rest of the chapter to create the application from the beginning.

Figure 14-10. The PHP server settings

Creating the application

We'll need to create the interface, the ActionScript files, the custom component, and the custom class files within Flex Builder. We'll also need to create the PHP pages that will provide content and process database updates.

I'll be building the application from scratch, so we'll be switching between the different application files so you can see how we approach building this application. I'll work through the following steps:

1. Creating the Flex application interface

2. Creating the PHP pages to generate the XML content

3. Creating the custom ActionScript class to load the content

4. Loading the XML content

5. Creating custom events

6. Displaying the current posts

7. Displaying the archive posts

8. Disabling administrator functions

9. Coding the login form

10. Creating a custom component for post details

11. Updating the selected post

12. Adding a new post

13. Deleting an existing post

We'll start by creating the application interface in Flex Builder.

Creating the Flex application interface

The interface consists of a TabNavigator container with three tabs: Posts, Login, and Add/edit. Only the first two of these tabs will be initially visible. The Add/edit tab appears after the user successfully logs into the application.

The TabNavigator container creates tabs from child container elements. In our case, we'll use VBox controls to store the content for each tab. Each VBox will contain the components for that tab. In the case of the Posts tab, we'll show the content from the database using a Repeater component.

Within your main application file, add the following MXML tags after the opening <mx:Application> tag:

```
<mx:Panel title="My blog" x="10" y="10" width="100%" height="100%"
  paddingTop="10" paddingLeft="10" paddingRight="10"
  paddingBottom="10">
<mx:TabNavigator id="navigator" width="100%" height="100%">
  <mx:VBox id="postContainer" paddingTop="10" paddingLeft="10"
    paddingRight="10" paddingBottom="10">
    <mx:Text id="txtMessage" fontSize="12" fontWeight="bold"
      color="#FF0000"/>
    <mx:Label id="postsLabel" fontWeight="bold" fontSize="14"
      text="Current posts" />
    <mx:HBox>
      <mx:Button id="btnArchives" label="View archives"/>
      <mx:Button id="btnCurrent" label="View current posts"/>
      <mx:Button id="btnAdd" label="Add new post"/>
    </mx:HBox>
    <mx:Repeater id="rptPosts">
      <mx:HBox>
        <mx:Text id="txtTitleAndDate" fontWeight="bold"/>
        <mx:Button id="btnEdit" label="Edit" />
        <mx:Button id="btnDelete" label="Delete"/>
      </mx:HBox>
      <mx:Text id="txtContent" width="100%"/>
    </mx:Repeater>
  </mx:VBox>
```

```
            <mx:VBox id="loginContainer" width="100%" paddingTop="10"
              paddingLeft="10" paddingRight="10" paddingBottom="10">
              <mx:Label id="loginLabel" fontWeight="bold" fontSize="14"
                text="Enter login details" />
              <mx:Text id="txtLoginMessage" color="#FF0000" fontWeight="bold"
                fontSize="12"/>
              <mx:HBox>
                <mx:Label text="Username" fontWeight="bold" width="100"/>
                <mx:TextInput id="txtUsername"/>
              </mx:HBox>
              <mx:HBox>
                <mx:Label text="Password" fontWeight="bold" width="100"/>
                <mx:TextInput id="txtPassword" displayAsPassword="true"/>
              </mx:HBox>
              <mx:Button id="btnDoLogin" label="Login"
                includeInLayout="false"/>
              <mx:Button id="btnDoLogout" label="Logout"
                includeInLayout="false" visible="false"/>
            </mx:VBox>
          </mx:TabNavigator>
        </mx:Panel>
```

The TabNavigator has two child VBox elements that correspond to the first two tabs. These have the IDs postContainer and loginContainer, respectively. We'll create the third tab using a custom component that we'll add a little later.

The postContainer element has a child <mx:Repeater> element that will display the title, date, and content, and an Edit and a Delete button for each post from the database. We'll hide the buttons until the user logs in to the application. Similarly, we'll hide the Add new post button unless the user is logged in.

You'll notice that the loginContainer element contains both a Login and Logout button. Depending on the user's status, we'll hide one of the buttons each time. We start by hiding the Logout button as users will only be able to log out once they've logged in. So that the hidden button doesn't affect the layout, we've set the includeInLayout attribute to false.

Figure 14-11 shows the interface for the application at this point.

We need to add labels for the tabs and disable the View current posts button using ActionScript. We're disabling this button as users will be presented with a list of current posts when the application first loads. Clicking the View current posts button at this point wouldn't make sense.

We'll place the ActionScript for the application in an external file called BlogCode.as. Create this file now using File ➤ New ➤ ActionScript File. Enter the name for the file and click Finish.

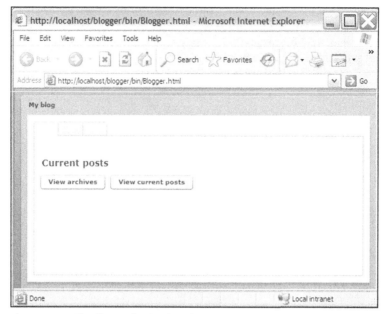

Figure 14-11. The Flex application interface

Add the following code to the file:

```
private var serverPath:String = "http://localhost/blogger/";
private var arrTabLabels:Array = ["Posts","Login", "Add/edit"];

private function initApp(e:FlexEvent):void{
  navigator.getTabAt(0).label = arrTabLabels[0];
  navigator.getTabAt(1).label = arrTabLabels[1];
  //navigator.getTabAt(2).label = arrTabLabels[2];
  //navigator.getTabAt(2).visible = false;
  btnCurrent.enabled = false;
}
```

These lines set up the variables that we'll need. The first variable is the path to the folder containing the application on the web server. You may need to change this line to reflect your own settings. The second variable contains the labels for the three tabs stored in an Array.

I find it useful to store the web server path in a variable within the application. I can then use the variable in any page, class, or component, and I can easily change its value from a central location.

The code block also contains the `initApp` function that assigns the labels from the `arrTabLabels` array to each tab. Notice that I've commented out the references to the third tab as we haven't yet added it to the TabNavigator. If we didn't comment out the lines, we'd get an error when running the application. The final line disables the `btnCurrent` button.

The function takes a FlexEvent as an argument because we'll call it in the `creationComplete` attribute of the `<mx:Application>` element.

Make sure that the file contains the following import statement. Flex Builder should add it automatically; if not, enter it yourself:

```
import mx.events.FlexEvent;
```

Switch to the MXML file now and add the following `<mx:Script>` element to reference the external ActionScript file:

```
<mx:Script source="BlogCode.as"/>
```

Modify the opening `<mx:Application>` tag as shown here in bold:

```
<mx:Application xmlns:mx="http://www.adobe.com/2006/mxml"
    layout="absolute" creationComplete="initApp(event)">
```

The application will call the initApp function after it finishes creating the interface. Run the application and you should see that the two visible tabs have the labels Posts and Login.

We now need to populate the first tab with the posts from the database using XML generated by a PHP page.

Creating the PHP pages to generate the XML content

The next task in creating this application is to write the PHP page that will generate the XML content containing the list of posts. I've named this page getPosts.php. In this book, we're focusing on Flex applications, so I'll show the entire code for each page and explain it rather than building it up step by step.

> As we're creating XML files with PHP, we need to be careful about using the shorthand opening tag `<?` for PHP code blocks. These two characters are the same as the beginning of the XML declaration:
>
> ```
> <?xml version="1.0"?>
> ```
>
> Turning on the short_open_tag *directive in the* php.ini *file can cause problems as the XML declaration may be interpreted as PHP code. You'll notice that I've used the full* `<?php` *opening characters in my pages.*

We'll call the getPosts.php page in one of two ways. First, we'll call it to display a list of posts for the current month, and second, we'll display a list of archive posts. We could extend the application to show the archives for a selected month, but I won't do that so that I can keep the application simple. That might be a topic for you to research yourself.

We'll take a parameter from the SWF movie to determine whether to display archive posts. The SWF movie will send the querystring parameter archive with a value of true. We'll achieve this by adding ?archive=true to the getPosts.php page when we request it within the Flex application. If the parameter is not present, we'll request posts from the current month; otherwise, we'll request posts from every month except the current one.

This page needs to communicate with the MySQL database. Because I'll want to create other PHP pages to update this database, I'll create a separate page that handles the database connection called dbConn.php. This page follows:

```php
<?php
$db_host = 'localhost';
$db_user = 'user_blogger';
$db_pass = 'blogme';
$db_name = 'blogger';
mysql_connect($db_host, $db_user, $db_pass);
mysql_select_db($db_name);
?>
```

The code specifies the name for the web server (localhost) as well as the username (user_blogger) and password (blogme). The code also sets the database name as blogger. You will probably need to change the settings to reflect your own MySQL configuration. We use mysql_connect to create the connection and specify the database using mysql_select_db.

We're using the RSS 2.0 specification for the XML structure. This means that the elements at the beginning of each XML document will be the same. All the XML documents in the application start with the following elements:

```xml
<?xml version="1.0" encoding="UTF-8" ?>
<rss version="2.0">
  <channel>
    <title>Blog rss feed example</title>
    <link>http://localhost/blogger</link>
    <description>Posts for blog application</description>
```

I've created those elements in a separate PHP page called writeIntroXML.php that we'll include at the top of the other PHP pages within the application. The writeIntroXML.php page contains the following code:

```php
<?php
$xml = new DomDocument('1.0', 'UTF-8');
$root = $xml->createElement('rss');
$root->setAttribute('version', '2.0');
$root = $xml->appendChild($root);
$channelElement = $xml->createElement('channel');
$channelElement = $root->appendChild($channelElement);
$titleElement = $xml->createElement('title','Blog rss feed example');
$titleElement = $channelElement->appendChild($titleElement);
$linkElement = $xml->createElement('link','http://localhost/blogger');
$linkElement = $channelElement->appendChild($linkElement);
$descriptionElement = $xml->createElement('description',➥
  'Posts for blog application');
$descriptionElement = $channelElement->appendChild(➥
  $descriptionElement);
?>
```

The code starts by creating a new version 1.0 DomDocument object with UTF-8 encoding. It uses the createElement, setAttribute, and appendChild methods to create the structure for the start of the XML document. The createElement method requires the name of the element as the first argument and has an optional second argument that indicates the content for the element.

We add the version attribute to the root element using setAttribute and passing the attribute name and value. Notice that each element has no position in the XML tree until we assign it using the appendChild method of the relevant element. We pass an argument that is the element to append.

Finally, the code for the getPosts.php page follows:

```php
<?php
header('Content-Type: text/xml');
include 'dbConn.php';
include 'writeIntroXML.php';
if (isset($_GET['archive'])) {
  $sql = 'SELECT posts.* FROM posts WHERE MONTH(posts.postDate) <> ➥
    MONTH(CURDATE()) ORDER BY postDate DESC, postTitle';
  $response = ' for the previous months';
}
else {
  $sql = 'SELECT posts.*FROM posts WHERE MONTH(posts.postDate) = ➥
    MONTH(CURDATE()) ORDER BY postDate DESC, postTitle';
  $response = ' for the current month';
}
$result = mysql_query($sql);
if ($result) {
  if (mysql_num_rows($result) > 0) {
    while ($row = mysql_fetch_array($result)) {
      $postID = $row['postID'];
      $postDate = $row['postDate'];
      $postTitle = $row['postTitle'];
      $content = $row['postContent'];
      $itemElement = $xml->createElement('item');
      $itemElement = $channelElement->appendChild($itemElement);
      $idElement = $xml->createElement('guid',$postID);
      $idElement = $itemElement->appendChild($idElement);
      $titleElement = $xml->createElement('title', $postTitle);
      $titleElement = $itemElement->appendChild($titleElement);
      $dateElement = $xml->createElement('pubDate', $postDate);
      $dateElement = $itemElement->appendChild($dateElement);
      $itemDescriptionElement = $xml->createElement('description', ➥
        $content);
      $itemDescriptionElement = $itemElement->appendChild(➥
        $itemDescriptionElement);
    }
  }
  else {
    $messageElement = $xml->createElement('message','There are no ➥
      posts' . $response . '.');
```

```
        $messageElement = $channelElement->appendChild($messageElement);
      }
    }
    else {
      $messageElement = $xml->createElement('message',mysql_error());
      $messageElement = $channelElement->appendChild($messageElement);
    }
    echo $xml->saveXML();
    ?>
```

The page starts by setting the content type to text/xml so that the content can be interpreted cor-rectly by the Flex application. It then includes the dbConn.php and writeIntroXML.php pages.

The next lines deal with constructing the SQL statement. If a querystring parameter archive is sent from the application, the SQL statement selects all posts, excluding those for the current month. Otherwise, only the posts from the current month are included. The lines also set the value of the response variable. We'll use this variable in the message returned to the SWF file.

The page then queries the database. If the query returns records, the page loops through them, retrieving the postID, postDate, postTitle, and postContent. The code then creates the relevant XML elements and creates the remainder of the XML document. It creates one <item> element per record.

If no records are returned when the query executes, the page creates a <message> element containing the message There are no posts for the current month or the message There are no posts for the previous months.

As I mentioned earlier, the <message> element is not part of the RSS 2.0 specification, but it does pro-vide a useful way for us to return content to the SWF file. In the case of a MySQL error, the <message> element returns the relevant error message.

Finally, the page finishes by writing the XML document using saveXML. If you viewed the page through a web browser, you'd see the screenshot shown in Figure 14-8. Don't forget to enter the full HTTP path for the page address so that the PHP code is parsed correctly. In my case, this path is http://localhost/blogger/getPosts.php.

Now that we've generated content for the application, we need to create a custom ActionScript class to handle the page requests.

Creating the custom ActionScript class to load the content

We'll use a custom ActionScript class to load the XML content for the Flex interface. The class will use the URLLoader class and will dispatch two custom events. The first event is dispatched when the data-base returns posts, while the second occurs when a message is sent from the PHP page.

Create a new ActionScript class called BlogLoader in the com.aip package. This class doesn't extend any existing classes. Flex Builder will create the folder structure com ➤ aip automatically when you cre-ate the class.

Enter the following import statements below the package declaration:

```
import flash.net.URLLoader;
import flash.net.URLRequest;
import flash.net.URLVariables;
import flash.net.URLRequestMethod;
import flash.events.Event;
```

The import statements represent the classes that we'll use in this file. If you'd rather, you can wait for Flex Builder to enter them automatically, but you'll need to check that all class references are in the file.

Modify the class declaration so that the BlogLoader class is bindable:

```
[Bindable]
public class BlogLoader {
```

Adding this metatag will allow us to dispatch custom events to the application file.

We need to create the following private variables in the class file:

```
private var xmlContent:XML;
private var xmlLoader:URLLoader;
```

The first variable represents the loaded XML document, while the second will store the URLLoader object used to request the PHP page.

The class file must include a constructor function. In our case, this function creates a new URLLoader object and adds an event listener that responds when the complete event is dispatched; that is, when the request finishes processing.

We need to add a function to respond to the complete event, and I've called this function completeHandler. You can call it anything that you like, but it's a common convention to use the name of the event and the suffix Handler. In our case, this convention gives us the name completeHandler.

Add the following constructor function to the class file:

```
public function BlogLoader() {
  xmlLoader = new URLLoader();
  xmlLoader.addEventListener(Event.COMPLETE, completeHandler);
}
```

We must also add the following completeHandler:

```
private function completeHandler(e:Event):void {
  xmlContent = XML(e.target.data);
  trace (xmlContent.toXMLString());
}
```

This function receives the event that it handles as an argument. It identifies the loaded XML content using e.target.data and casts it as an XML object, assigning it to the xmlContent private variable. The function also traces the value of the variable using toXMLString. This approach allows us to check that we are loading the XML data correctly.

We'll create a load method so we can actually make the request for the XML document generated by the PHP page. The method will take two parameters: the URL to load and the variables being passed with the request. If no URLVariables are passed, the default value for the vars variable is null. Add the following public method to the class file:

```
public function load(xmlFile:String, vars:URLVariables=null):void {
  var request:URLRequest = new URLRequest(xmlFile);
  request.method = URLRequestMethod.POST;
  try {
    if (vars != null) {
      request.data = vars;
    }
    xmlLoader.load(request);
  }
  catch (e:Error) {
    trace ("Can't load exernal XML document");
  }
}
```

This method starts by creating a new URLRequest for the file specified in the xmlFile parameter. We must make sure that this is the full server path to the PHP page; for example, http://localhost/blogger/getPosts.php.

The function sets the request method to POST as if we were sending form field entries to the PHP page. The function uses a try-catch block to make the request. If we have a URLVariables object, the method assigns the object to the data property of the URLRequest. The try section finishes by loading the URLRequest with the load method. If there is an error, we display a message to the Console. In a real-world application, you might want to add some more stringent error handling.

We need to switch back to the BlogCode.as file to test the application so far.

Loading the XML content

Now is a good time to test what we've done to make sure that we're loading the XML content generated by the getPosts.php page successfully. Add the following import statement to the BlogCode.as file to reference the custom class:

```
import com.aip.BlogLoader;
```

Add a private variable declaration to create an instance of the BlogLoader class:

```
private var postLoader:BlogLoader = new BlogLoader();
```

We'll make the request for the XML content in the getPosts.php page within the initApp function in BlogCode.as. Add the following line at the end of the function, after assigning event listeners:

```
postLoader.load (serverPath + "getPosts.php");
```

The line calls the load method of the BlogLoader class, passing the page reference. We don't pass anything for the second parameter, so the default value of null will apply.

Let's test the application by clicking the Debug button in Flex Builder. The interface in the web browser won't change, but you should see the output from the trace statement in the Console view in Flex Builder. Switch back to Flex Builder, and you should see the loaded XML content as shown in Figure 14-12.

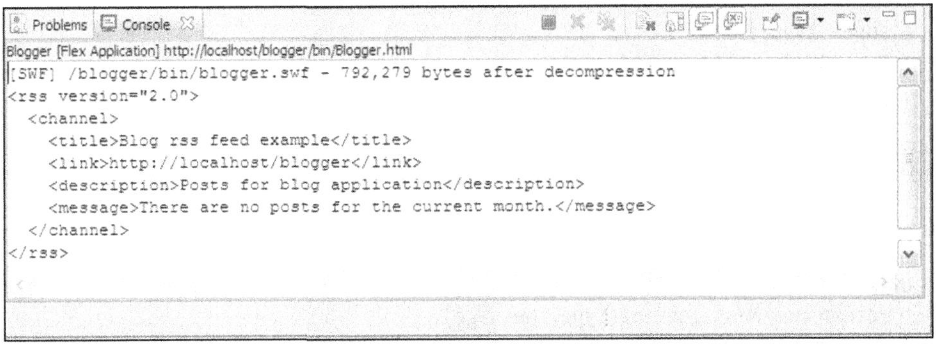

Figure 14-12. The loaded XML content displays in the Console view

You should see the XML content, starting with the root <rss> element. We can now display the details of all posts using the Repeater component. The first step is to create two custom events so we can notify the application about the returned XML.

Creating custom events

When we receive the XML document, one of two things can happen. We can either have posts to display in the interface or the document can notify us that there are currently no posts to display in a <message> element. The BlogLoader class will notify us of either outcome in custom events. We'll create two custom event classes: PostsEvent and MessageEvent. Both classes will extend the Event class.

Let's start with the MessageEvent class.

Creating the MessageEvent class

The MessageEvent class will notify the Flex application that a message has been received. Initially, it will respond when there is a message that there are no posts to display. Later, we'll use the class to inform the application about the outcome of database updates and deletions. The event will provide the relevant message to the application as a property of the event object.

Start by creating a new ActionScript class called MessageEvent in the com.aip package. Enter the superclass flash.events.Event because all custom event classes must extend this built-in class.

We need to add a public variable called message that will store the message from the PHP page. We'll return this value with the event object. We will also create a constant called MESSAGE that indicates the type of event, message.

Add the following code below the class declaration to create the variable and constant:

```
public var message:String;
public static const MESSAGE:String ="message";
```

The constructor for the custom event needs two parameters, the type of event and the message passed from the PHP page, as shown in the following code:

```
public function MessageEvent(type:String, theMessage:String) {
  super(type);
  message = String(theMessage);
}
```

We'll use this constructor method when we dispatch a new MessageEvent event. Notice that we needed to call the constructor of the base class, Event, with the super method, passing the event type.

We also need to override the clone method from the base class, so add the following code now:

```
override public function clone():Event{
  return new MessageEvent(type, message);
}
```

This override ensures that we can return a new instance of the MessageEvent class.

The BlogLoader class will dispatch the MessageEvent event when it detects that there is a <message> element in the returned XML content. We'll dispatch the event from the completeHandler function in the class file, and you'll see that shortly.

Creating the PostsEvent class

The BlogLoader object will dispatch the PostsEvent event when it receives an XML document containing at least one <item> element. It will include an XMLList of posts as a property of the event.

Create a new custom class called PostsEvent in the com.aip package that extends the Event class. Again, the class needs a variable to store the XMLList of posts from the loaded XML document. It also needs a constant to represent the event type POSTS. Add the following lines below the class declaration:

```
public var postsContent:XMLList;
public static const POSTS:String ="posts";
```

The constructor method receives as arguments the event type and an XMLList of all <item> elements. Add this method to the PostsEvent class:

```
public function PostsEvent(type:String, theXMLList:XMLList) {
  super(type);
  postsContent = theXMLList;
}
```

The method works in the same way as explained in the MessageEvent class. We also need to override the clone method from the base class, so add the following method:

```
override public function clone():Event{
  return new PostsEvent(type, postsContent);
}
```

We need to dispatch both custom events from the BlogLoader class, so switch to that file now.

Dispatching events from the completeHandler function

The BlogLoader class will dispatch either a PostsEvent or the MessageEvent event, depending on the content of the received XML document. The relevant event will be dispatched in the completeHandler function in the class file. Modify the function as shown in bold in the following code block:

```
private function completeHandler(e:Event):void {
  xmlContent = XML(e.target.data);
  var message:String = xmlContent.channel.message;
  if (message.length > 0) {
    var messageEventObj:MessageEvent = new MessageEvent(➥
      MessageEvent.MESSAGE, message);
    dispatchEvent(messageEventObj);
  }
  else {
    var posts:XMLList = xmlContent.channel.item;
    var postsEventObj:PostsEvent = new PostsEvent(➥
      PostsEvent.POSTS, posts);
    dispatchEvent(postsEventObj);
  }
}
```

The new lines start by locating the <message> element in the loaded XML document. The element is a child of the <channel> element, which is a child of the root element, so we can find the value using the E4X expression xmlContent.channel.message.

The function checks the length of the text within the <message> element. If the length is greater than zero, we have a <message> element; otherwise, there is no message, only <item> elements. In the first case, we dispatch a new MessageEvent object, passing the message string variable. Otherwise, we dispatch a new PostsEvent object, passing an XMLList of all <item> elements. We find the XMLList using the E4X expression xmlContent.channel.item.

The custom events will be dispatched to the main application file. We can test which event is dispatched by adding event handlers for the two custom events in the ActionScript associated with the MXML file. Switch to BlogCode.as and add the following import statements:

```
import com.aip.PostsEvent;
import com.aip.MessageEvent;
```

These lines reference the two new custom events in the com.aip package.

Add the two event listeners to the initApp function, before the call to the load method of the BlogLoader object:

```
postLoader.addEventListener(PostsEvent.POSTS, postsHandler);
postLoader.addEventListener(MessageEvent.MESSAGE, messageHandler);
```

These lines add event listeners that respond when either of the two new custom events is dispatched. Add the event listener functions now:

```
private function postsHandler(e:PostsEvent):void {
  trace ("PostsEvent received");
}
private function messageHandler(e:MessageEvent):void {
  trace ("MessageEvent received");
}
```

Initially, these functions just display a message indicating which event was dispatched. We'll eventually modify them to display content in the interface.

Click the Debug button to test the application. When you look at the Console view in the application, you should see the appropriate message. You may want to change the dates of items in the database so you can check that both events are dispatched correctly.

We now need to add the values from the custom event objects to the interface.

Displaying the current posts

We'll display the current posts in the first tab of the TabNavigator container when a PostsEvent event is dispatched. We can add code to deal with this outcome in the postsHandler function. The posts will display in the Repeater control. As the PostsEvent passes an XMLList of all posts, we can assign this to the dataProvider property of the Repeater.

Modify the postsHandler function in the BlogCode.as file as shown here in bold:

```
private function postsHandler(e:PostsEvent):void {
  rptPosts.dataProvider = e.postsContent;
}
```

If you ran the application now, all you would see is a set of Edit and Delete buttons, one for each post in the XML document. We need to add functions that return the relevant content to display in each control in the Repeater.

Displaying the title and date

We'll display the title and date of each post together in the txtTitleAndDate control. We'll create the text for the control in a function.

Add the following creationComplete attribute to the txtTitleAndDate control in the main application file:

```
<mx:Text id="txtTitleAndDate" fontWeight="bold"
  creationComplete="populateTitleAndDate(event.currentTarget, ➥
  event.currentTarget.getRepeaterItem())"/>
```

We'll populate the Text control using the populateTitleAndDate function. This function passes a reference to the current component, using event.currentTarget, and a reference to the current item in the data provider, using event.currentTarget.getRepeaterItem. We can use the second argument to retrieve the <title> and <pubDate> elements for each post from the loaded XML document. Add the populateTitleAndDate function now to the BlogCode.as file:

```
private function populateTitleAndDate(control:Object, post:Object)➥
  :void {
  var postXML:XML = XML(post);
  control.text = postXML.title + ",  " + postXML.pubDate;
}
```

The function creates an XML object from the <item> element passed into the function through the post argument. It then sets the text property of the relevant txtTitleAndDate control to a string made up of the <title> and <pubDate> elements.

Run the application now and you should see the title and date of each post from the database in the interface, as shown in Figure 14-13.

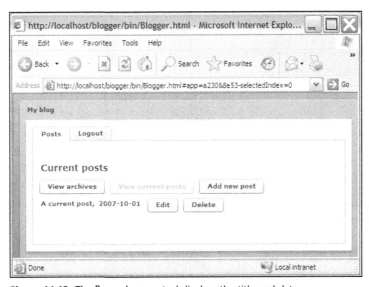

Figure 14-13. The Repeater control displays the title and date.

Notice that the date appears in the database format *YYYY-MM-DD*. We'll fix the date display a little later after we load the content of the post into the txtContent Text control.

Displaying the content

Again, we'll use a function to display the content of each post in the Repeater, so modify the tag as shown here in bold:

```
mx:Text id="txtContent" width="100%"
  creationComplete="populateContent(event.currentTarget, ➡
  event.currentTarget.getRepeaterItem())"/>
```

As before, the function passes a reference to the current control as well as the current <item> element. Add the following populateContent function to the BlogCode.as file:

```
private function populateContent(control:Object, post:Object):void {
  var postXML:XML = XML(post);
  control.text = postXML.description;
}
```

This function works in the same way as the populateTitleAndDate function, so I won't explain it again. Run the file and you should see the content below the title and date, as shown in Figure 14-14.

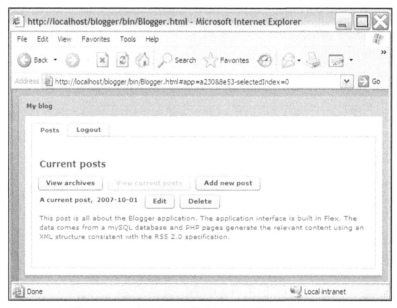

Figure 14-14. The content of each post displays in the Repeater control.

It's now time to fix the date display.

Changing the date format

We need to change the way the date displays so it uses a *MM-DD-YYYY* format. It's not usual to use *YYYY-MM-DD* to indicate a date.

Because we may want to convert more than one date string in the application, we'll create a Utilities class containing a static function to handle the conversion. Using a static function means that we don't have to instantiate a Utilities object each time we want to call the function.

Create a new ActionScript class in the com.aip package called Utilities. Add the following convertDateString to handle the date conversion:

```
package com.aip {
  public class Utilities {
    public static function convertDateStringMMDDYYYY(theDate:String)➥
      :String{
      var arrDate:Array = theDate.split("-");
      return arrDate[1] + "-" + arrDate[2] + "-" + arrDate[0];
    }
  }
}
```

This function takes a date in the *YYYY-MM-DD* format and uses the split function to create an array by separating out the elements between the hyphen characters. It then joins the array elements and hyphens in a different order to create the *MM-DD-YYYY* format.

We can reference this static function in the BlogCode.as file after adding the following import statement:

```
import com.aip.Utilities;
```

Modify the populateTitleAndDate function, as shown here in bold, to call the function:

```
private function populateTitleAndDate(control:Object, post:Object):➥
  void {
  var postXML:XML = XML(post);
  control.text = postXML.title + ",  " + ➥
    Utilities.convertDateStringMMDDYYYY(postXML.pubDate);
}
```

If you run the application, you should see the date in the correct format.

Displaying the archive posts

At the moment, we don't have any way to distinguish between current and archive posts, so that's the next task. We'll use the same Repeater to show archive posts, but we need to keep track of which type of post we're showing using a Boolean variable.

Add the following variable declaration to the BlogCode.as file:

```
private var isCurrent:Boolean = true;
```

Because we start by showing the posts for the current month, the initial value of the variable is true.

We need to add a function that responds when we click the View archives button. Modify the btnArchives element in the main application file as shown here:

```
<mx:Button id="btnArchives" label="View archives"
  click="viewArchives(event)"/>
```

Note that the click attribute passes a MouseClick event to the handler function.

Now add the viewArchives function to the BlogCode.as file. The function needs to clear the interface and make a call to the getPosts.php page passing the querystring archive=true, as we discussed earlier:

```
private function viewArchives(e:MouseEvent):void {
  isCurrent = false;
  clearInterface();
  postLoader.load (serverPath + "getPosts.php?archive=true");
  setUpInterface(isCurrent, "Archive posts");
}
```

This function starts by setting the value of the isCurrent variable to false and then calls a function called clearInterface, which we'll add shortly. It then calls the load method of the BlogLoader object, appending a querystring to the page name. Finally, we call the setUpInterface function, passing the value of the isCurrent variable and the text for the label.

You should add the following clearInterface function:

```
private function clearInterface():void {
  rptPosts.dataProvider = [];
  txtMessage.text = "";
}
```

The function clears the data provider for the Repeater and any text displaying in the txtMessage control.

Add the setUpInterface function:

```
private function setUpInterface(showCurrent:Boolean, theLabel:String)➥
  :void {
  btnArchives.enabled = showCurrent;
  btnCurrent.enabled = !showCurrent;
  postsLabel.text = theLabel;
}
```

This function uses a Boolean value to determine which buttons to enable and disable. If we're showing current posts, we enable btnCurrent and disable btnArchives. The converse happens with archive posts. The function also changes the label text.

We'll also need to add a click attribute and the supporting handler function for the View current posts function. Modify the relevant <mx:Button> tag in the main application file, as shown here:

```
<mx:Button id="btnCurrent" label="View current posts"
    click="viewCurrentPosts(event)"/>
```

Add the viewCurrentPosts function to the BlogCode.as file:

```
private function viewCurrentPosts(e:MouseEvent):void{
    isCurrent = true;
    clearInterface();
    postLoader.load (serverPath + "getPosts.php");
    setUpInterface(isCurrent, "Current posts");
}
```

This function works in the same way as the previous viewArchives function.

Run the application and check that you can switch between current and archive posts. Figure 14-15 shows how archive posts will appear in the interface.

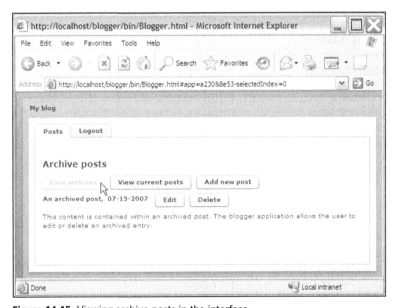

Figure 14-15. Viewing archive posts in the interface

You'll notice that while you can see both archive and current posts, you can also see all of the buttons that provide administrator functionality. The next step is to hide the buttons so that they only appear once the user has logged in.

Disabling administrator functions

We need to hide any buttons that provide administrative functionality in the application. This includes the Add new post, Edit, and Delete buttons. We'll do this by using a Boolean variable to track whether or not we're logged into the application.

Add the following variable declaration to the BlogCode.as file:

```
[Bindable]
private var isAdmin:Boolean = false;
```

You'll notice that I've made the variable bindable. I've done this so I can bind the value of the variable directly to the visible property of any control that I want to show or hide. I've also set the initial value to false as the application first loads without the user logged in. This means that the buttons will be hidden initially.

Modify the following elements in the main application file to add a visible property. Note that these elements don't appear next to each other in the file:

```
<mx:Button id="btnAdd" label="Add new post"
  visible="{isAdmin}"/>
<mx:Button id="btnEdit" label="Edit"
  visible="{isAdmin}"/>
<mx:Button id="btnDelete" label="Delete"
  visible="{isAdmin}"/>
```

These elements contain a visible property that is bound to the value of the isAdmin variable. As the variable starts with the value false, all controls are hidden when the application first loads. Once the user logs in, the value of this variable will change to true, and the buttons will be visible. You can test this binding by running the application.

Coding the login form

The second tab in the application displays a login form requiring the user to enter a username and password. Once the user has successfully logged in, the interface in the Posts tab will update to show the buttons enabling administrator functions.

I could have stored the username and password in the database. However, for simplicity, I've made them constants within the BlogLoader file. This method is not very secure and not appropriate in real-world applications.

Modify the BlogLoader class to add the following constants:

```
private const ADMINUSERNAME:String = "admin";
private const ADMINPASSWORD:String = "admin";
```

We'll test whether the user has entered the correct username and password in the isUserAdmin public method of the class. This method returns a Boolean value, indicating whether the user has successfully logged in:

```
public function isUserAdmin(username:String, password:String):Boolean {
  if (username == ADMINUSERNAME && password == ADMINPASSWORD) {
    return true;
  }
  else {
    return false;
  }
}
```

The function compares a passed-in username and password with the values of the ADMINUSERNAME and ADMINPASSWORD constants. If they are identical, the function returns true; otherwise, it returns false.

The application calls this function when the user enters login details and clicks the Login button. Add the following click attribute for this button in the main application file:

```
<mx:Button id="btnDoLogin" label="Login" includeInLayout="false"
  click="doLogin(event)"/>
```

Create the doLogin function in the BlogCode.as file:

```
private function doLogin(e:MouseEvent):void {
  if (txtUsername.text.length > 0 && txtPassword.text.length > 0) {
    isAdmin = postLoader.isUserAdmin(txtUsername.text, ➥
      txtPassword.text);
    if (isAdmin) {
      txtLoginMessage.text = "You are currently logged in";
      //navigator.getTabAt(2).visible = true;
      navigator.getTabAt(1).label = "Logout";
    }
    else {
      txtLoginMessage.text = "You could not be logged in. ➥
        Please try again.";
    }
    txtUsername.text = "";
    txtPassword.text = "";
  }
}
```

This function tests for an entry in both the txtUsername and txtPassword controls, and if it finds them, it passes the values to the isUserAdmin method of the BlogLoader object. The function assigns the returned Boolean value to the isAdmin variable. Users then see a message that varies depending on whether they have logged in successfully. Whatever the outcome, the values in the two TextInput controls are cleared.

Finally, if users log in successfully, they will see the third tab, which we have yet to add. I've added the appropriate line of code, but commented it out for the time being so we don't get an error message. The label for the second tab changes to Logout.

449

Run the application and test that you are able to log in successfully. Figure 14-16 shows the screen after a successful login.

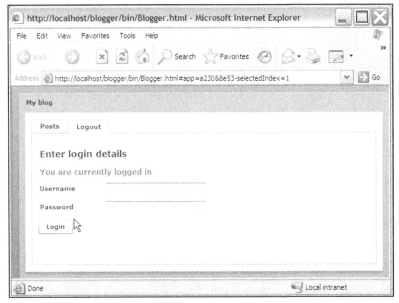

Figure 14-16. The interface after a successful login

Figure 14-17 shows what happens after an unsuccessful login attempt.

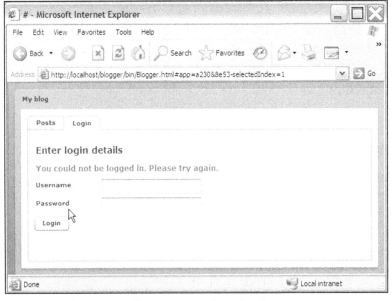

Figure 14-17. The interface after an unsuccessful login attempt

We still need to deal with the display of the user interface components in this tab. We can use the value of the isAdmin variable to control the display of these components. For example, we can set the visibility to the opposite of the value of the variable. If the user is an administrator, the Login button should hide. The value of isAdmin will be true, while the value of the visible property will be false.

Switch to the main application file and modify the user interface components in the second tab, as shown here in bold. Note that the elements don't appear next to each other in the main application file:

```
<mx:Label text="Username" fontWeight="bold" width="100"
   visible="{!isAdmin}"/>
<mx:TextInput id="txtUsername"
   visible="{!isAdmin}"/>
<mx:Label text="Password" fontWeight="bold" width="100"
   visible="{!isAdmin}"/>
<mx:TextInput id="txtPassword" displayAsPassword="true"
   visible="{!isAdmin}"/>
<mx:Button id="btnDoLogin" label="Login" includeInLayout="false"
   click="doLogin(event)"
   visible="{!isAdmin}"/>
<mx:Button id="btnDoLogout" label="Logout" includeInLayout="false"
   visible="{isAdmin}"/>
```

We have found the opposite of the value of the isAdmin variable using !isAdmin.

When a user has logged in successfully, the interface for the Login tab should change as shown in Figure 14-18.

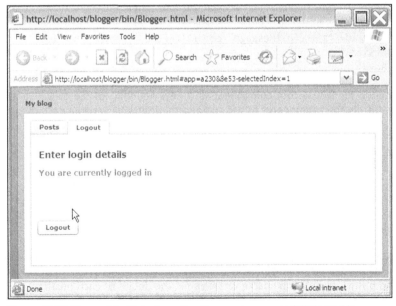

Figure 14-18. The updated interface after the user has successfully logged in

The user interface components change. The Logout button is visible, and the form fields and associated labels are hidden. I'll leave you to add logout functionality to the application yourself. Logging out will need to set the value of the isAdmin variable to false.

So far in the application, we haven't dealt with adding a new post or editing an existing post. That's the topic for the next section.

Creating a custom component for post details

We'll display the details of each post in a form that we'll create in a custom component. When editing, we'll populate the form using content from the XML document and use a blank form to add a new post. You can see what the form looks like in Figure 14-5.

Start by creating a new folder called components in the com ➤ aip folder. Create a new custom component in this folder by choosing File ➤ New ➤ MXML Component. Give the component the name Contents, base it on a TitleWindow, and give it the dimensions 500 wide and 350 high.

Add the following interface elements to the component:

```
<mx:VBox x="10" y="10">
  <mx:HBox>
    <mx:Text fontWeight="bold" text="Title" width="140"/>
    <mx:TextInput id="txtTitle" width="220"/>
  </mx:HBox>
  <mx:HBox>
    <mx:Text fontWeight="bold" text="Date (MM/DD/YYYY)" width="140"/>
    <mx:TextInput id="txtDate" width="220"/>
  </mx:HBox>
  <mx:TextArea id="txtContent" width="360" height="150"/>
  <mx:Button id="btnUpdateContent" label="Save"/>
  <mx:Text id="txtAddEditMessage" color="#FF0000" fontWeight="bold"
    fontSize="12"/>
</mx:VBox>
```

We'll add the code for the custom component to a new ActionScript file called ContentsCode.as. Create this file now in the components folder and add the following variable declarations:

```
public var server:String;
public var postID:String;
[Bindable]
public var postTitle:String;
[Bindable]
public var postDate:String;
[Bindable]
public var postContent:String;
```

We'll populate all of these variables from the container application file. We've created variables for the server path and postID, as well as bindable variables for the details of each post that we'll be editing. These variables will be bound to the relevant controls in the custom component.

Open the Contents.mxml file and modify the elements as shown in bold. Note that these elements don't appear next to each other in the component file:

```
<mx:TextInput id="txtTitle" width="220"
   text="{postTitle}"/>
<mx:TextInput id="txtDate" width="220"
   text="{postDate}"/>
<mx:TextArea id="txtContent" width="360" height="150"
   text="{postContent}"/>
```

When we set the values of the public variables from the main application file, the contents will update in the custom component due to these bindings.

We will also need to add a reference to the external ActionScript file below the opening <mx:Application> tag:

```
<mx:Script source="ContentsCode.as"/>
```

Switch to the main application file so we can add the custom component to the interface. Modify the opening <mx:Application> tag to add the following namespace, shown in bold:

```
<mx:Application xmlns:mx="http://www.adobe.com/2006/mxml"
   xmlns:comp="com.aip.components.*"
   layout="absolute" creationComplete="initApp(event)">
```

We'll use the prefix comp to refer to the custom component. Add a tag for the custom component after the last <mx:VBox> component, as shown here:

```
</mx:VBox>
<comp:Contents id="postDetails"/>
</mx:TabNavigator>
```

This line will display the custom component in the third tab in the TabNavigator. We can refer to the public variables in the component file as properties of the postDetails component.

Switch to the BlogCode.as file and uncomment the following line in the doLogin function:

```
navigator.getTabAt(2).visible = true;
```

As we now have a third tab, we can set the visible property after we've logged in successfully. We also need to add the following two lines to the initApp function:

```
navigator.getTabAt(2).label = arrTabLabels[2];
navigator.getTabAt(2).visible = false;
```

These lines set the label for the third tab and hide it when the application first loads. Run the application and log in. You should see the third tab, Add/edit, appear in the interface.

Let's configure the Edit button now so we can update a post using the custom component.

Updating the selected post

We need to add a click attribute to the Edit button so that users can change details of any existing post, current or archive. We'll do this with the editPost function. This function needs the details of the selected item from the data provider for the Repeater. It will set the value of the public variables in the custom component from this item and switch the TabNavigator to the third tab.

Because we're using the component for both adding and editing, we'll need to keep track of which action we're performing in a Boolean variable. Add the following variable to the BlogCode.as file:

```
private var isAdding:Boolean;
```

We'll set its value when we either add or edit a post.

Once we've clicked the Edit button, we'll store the details of the selected post using an ActionScript custom class.

Creating the custom class to store post values

We'll use a SelectedPost custom class to store the values of the post selected for editing. Create this new ActionScript class in the com.aip package. It doesn't extend any existing class.

The class needs to store the postID, title, date, and contents for the selected post. We'll set all of these values in the constructor for the class, storing them in private variables that we'll access with getter methods. The full class follows:

```
package com.aip {
  public class SelectedPost {
    private var selectedPostID:String;
    private var selectedPostTitle:String;
    private var selectedPostDate:String;
    private var selectedPostContents:String;
    public function get postID():String {
      return selectedPostID;
    }
    public function get postTitle():String {
      return selectedPostTitle;
    }
    public function get postDate():String {
      return selectedPostDate;
    }
    public function get postContents():String {
      return selectedPostContents;
    }
    public function SelectedPost(theID:String,theTitle:String,➥
      theDate:String,theContents:String) {
      selectedPostID = thetID;
      selectedPostTitle = theTitle;
      selectedPostDate = theDate;
      selectedPostContents = theContents;
    }
```

```
    }
}
```

The code is straightforward. We create several private variables, all using the String data type. The class includes the getter methods postID, postTitle, postDate, and postContents. The constructor, SelectedPost, takes values for all of the private variables as parameters.

We'll need a variable in the BlogCode.as file to store the SelectedPost object. Add the following import statement to reference the custom class:

```
import com.aip.SelectedPost;
```

Declare a variable called currentPost of the type SelectedPost:

```
private var currentPost:SelectedPost;
```

We'll use this object in the editPost function.

Creating the editPost function

The editPost function creates a new SelectedPost object to store the values from the clicked item. Add this function to the BlogCode.as file:

```
private function editPost(post:Object):void{
    var postXML:XML = XML(post);
    var postID:String = postXML.guid;
    var postTitle:String = postXML.title;
    var postDate:String = Utilities.convertDateStringMMDDYYYY(➥
      postXML.pubDate);
    var postContents:String = postXML.description;
    currentPost = new SelectedPost(postID, postTitle, postDate, ➥
      postContents);
    isAdding = false;
    navigator.selectedIndex = 2;
}
```

The function takes the post object as an argument. This object contains the XML for the selected post, so the first step is to cast the value to an XML data type. We then create variables for each of the properties of the SelectedPost object. Notice that we call the convertDateStringMMDDYYYY static function to change the date format.

Finally, we create a new SelectedPost object, passing the variable values in the call to the constructor method. We finish the function by setting the value of the isAdding Boolean variable to false and display the third tab in the TabNavigator container.

We'll call the editPost function in the click attribute of the btnEdit button. Modify it as shown here in bold:

```
<mx:Button id="btnEdit" label="Edit" visible="{isAdmin}"
  click="editPost(event.currentTarget.getRepeaterItem())"/>
```

Notice that we pass the current <item> element to the editPost function using event. currentTarget.getRepeaterItem.

So far, we've set up code to create a new SelectedPost object and display the third tab. However, we haven't yet populated any of the components in the tab.

Handling the edit

When the view changes to the third tab, we want to populate the custom component with the values from the SelectedPost object. We can do that by listening for an IndexChangedEvent in the TabNavigator. If we changed the index to a value of 2, representing the third tab, we want to populate the form from the SelectedPost object.

Add an event listener listening for the IndexChangedEvent event in the initApp function in the BlogCode.as file:

```
navigator.addEventListener(IndexChangedEvent.CHANGE, ➥
  indexChangedHandler);
```

Make sure that Flex Builder adds the following import statement or, if necessary, add it yourself:

```
import mx.events.IndexChangedEvent;
```

Now we'll add the indexChangedHandler function. This function will test which tab caused the change and respond appropriately in the case of the tab with an index of 2:

```
private function indexChangedHandler(e:IndexChangedEvent):void{
  if (e.newIndex == 2) {
    postDetails.txtAddEditMessage.text = "";
    postDetails.server = serverPath;
    postDetails.postID = currentPost.postID;
    postDetails.txtTitle.text = currentPost.postTitle;
    postDetails.txtDate.text = currentPost.postDate;
    postDetails.txtContent.text = currentPost.postContents;
  }
}
```

The function only responds if the third tab displays. It clears the txtAddEditMessage control, which we'll use to display messages. It also sets the values of the relevant custom component properties using the getter methods of the SelectedPost class.

Run the application and log in. Click the Edit button next to one of the posts. Figure 14-19 shows the result.

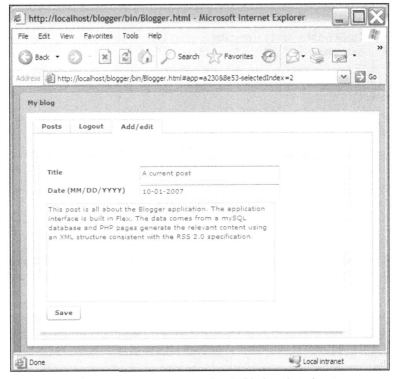

Figure 14-19. The custom component populated with the selected post

Now that we've populated the form, we still need to carry out the updates in the database.

Processing the updates

We'll use the page updatePost.php to process the updates to the database. The page will also process new entries. It will be able to distinguish between posts that we're adding and those that we're editing because we'll set the value of the postID variable to 0 when we add a new post. The Flex application will use the POST method to send the values to the PHP page. Again, I'll show the PHP page in its entirety and explain it afterward:

```php
<?php
header('Content-Type: text/xml');
include 'dbConn.php';
include 'writeIntroXML.php';
$postID = $_POST['postID'];
$postTitle = $_POST['postTitle'];
$postDate = $_POST['postDate'];
$content = $_POST['content'];
if (intval($postID) > 0) {
  $sql = 'UPDATE posts SET postDate = "' . $postDate . '", postTitle ➥
    = "' . $postTitle . '", postContent = "' . $content . '" ➥
    WHERE postID = ' . $postID;
```

```
        }
        else {
          $sql = 'INSERT into posts (postDate, postTitle, postContent) VALUES➡
            ("' . $postDate . '", "' . $postTitle .'", "' . $content .'")';
        }
        $result = mysql_query($sql);
        if ($result) {
          $message = 'You have successfully updated the blog.';
        }
        else {
          $message='There was an error updating the blog. ' . mysql_error();
        }
        $msgElement = $xml->createElement('message', $message);
        $msgElement = $channelElement->appendChild($msgElement);
        echo $xml->saveXML();
        ?>
```

The page starts by declaring its content type as text/xml. As with the previous PHP page, we include the dbConn.php page to make the database connection and the writeIntroXML.php page to write the initial XML elements.

The page requests the relevant variables from the Flex application using the POST method. It checks to see if the postID is greater than zero as this indicates an edit. The page uses this comparison to write the correct SQL statement, either an UPDATE statement for edits or an INSERT statement for additions.

The next code block processes the query and adds an appropriate message to the XML document, either one of success or one reporting an error. The page finishes by writing the XML content.

The Flex application needs to request the PHP page, using the POST method to send the values for the update. We'll do this in the custom component, but first we need to validate the form contents to make sure we have entries in each component.

Validating the form contents

Before we process the updates, we need to make sure that all of the entries are valid. We'll do this using validators. We need to check for a valid date, a title, and some content.

Switch to the Contents.mxml file and add the following validators underneath the <mx:Script> opening tag:

```
        <mx:DateValidator id="postDateValidator"
          source="{txtDate}" property="text" required="true"
          trigger="{btnUpdateContent}" triggerEvent="click"
          formatError= "Enter the date in MM-DD-YYYY format"
          requiredFieldError = "The date is required" />
        <mx:StringValidator id="postTitleValidator"
          source="{txtTitle}" property="text" required="true"
          trigger="{btnUpdateContent}" triggerEvent="click"
          requiredFieldError = "The title is required" />
          <mx:StringValidator id="postContentValidator"
```

458

```
source="{txtContent}" property="text" required="true"
trigger="{btnUpdateContent}" triggerEvent="click"
requiredFieldError = "Some post content is required" />
```

The postDateValidator checks for the existence of a string date value in the *MM-DD-YYYY* format. I didn't need to specify this format as it is the default setting for the validator. The DateValidator carries out the validation in response to clicking the btnUpdateContent button. I have specified errors to display in the case of an incorrect format or if the field is left blank.

Both StringValidator controls check to see that content has been entered in the txtTitle and txtContent controls using the attribute required=true. Again, they carry out the validation in response to the button click and provide custom error messages where the value is left blank.

We'll add a click attribute to the btnUpdateContent control to process the validation and respond appropriately:

```
<mx:Button id="btnUpdateContent" label="Save"
click="doValidation(event)"/>
```

When the user clicks the button, the application will call the doValidation function. This function will process the update, sending the values to the PHP page using the POST method. This means we'll need to create a new instance of the BlogLoader class first.

Add the following private variable to the ContentsCode.as file:

```
private var updatePostLoader:BlogLoader = new BlogLoader();
```

Check that the following import statement has been added to the file as well. You may need to enter it yourself:

```
import com.aip.BlogLoader;
```

We'll assign an event listener to the BlogLoader object when we've created the custom component. The event handler will process the message returned by the PHP page.

Add the initComponent function to the ContentsCode.as file:

```
private function initComponent(e:FlexEvent):void {
    updatePostLoader.addEventListener(MessageEvent.MESSAGE, ➡
        messageHandler);
}
```

Make sure that the FlexEvent class has been imported. If not, add the following import statement yourself. We also need to add the messageHandler function listed in the previous code block, but we'll do that a little later.

Modify the opening <mx:Application> tag in the Contents.mxml file to call the initComponent method in the creationComplete attribute:

```
<mx:TitleWindow xmlns:mx="http://www.adobe.com/2006/mxml"
    layout="absolute" width="500" height="350"
    creationComplete="initComponent(event)">
```

459

Now that we've created the BlogLoader and related functionality, we need to add the doValidation function to carry out the updating:

```
private function doValidation(e:MouseEvent):void {
  txtAddEditMessage.text = "";
  var theValidationResult:ValidationResultEvent;
  theValidationResult = postDateValidator.validate();
  if (theValidationResult.type == ValidationResultEvent.INVALID) {
    txtAddEditMessage.text = theValidationResult.message + "\n";
  }
  theValidationResult = postTitleValidator.validate();
  if (theValidationResult.type == ValidationResultEvent.INVALID) {
    txtAddEditMessage.text += theValidationResult.message + "\n";
  }
  theValidationResult = postContentValidator.validate();
  if (theValidationResult.type == ValidationResultEvent.INVALID) {
    txtAddEditMessage.text += theValidationResult.message;
  }
  if (txtAddEditMessage.text.length == 0) {
    var params:URLVariables;
    params = new URLVariables();
    params.postID = postID;
    params.postTitle = txtTitle.text;
    params.postDate = Utilities.convertDateStringYYYYMMDD(➡
      txtDate.text);
    params.content = txtContent.text;
    updatePostLoader.load (server + "updatePost.php", params);
  }
}
```

The function clears any message displayed in the txtAddEditMessage control. It then checks for valid entries using the validate method of the three validators. If an entry is not valid, the error message is appended to the txtAddEditMessage control and displays in the interface. Figure 14-20 shows how these error messages appear.

After checking all entries, the function tests the length of the text in the txtAddEditMessage control. If it is equal to zero—that is, there are no validation error messages—the update processing occurs. The function creates a new URLVariables object and adds the values to POST to the PHP page. It finishes by calling the load method of the updatePostLoader control.

Notice that we've called a static function named convertDateStringYYYYMMDD when we process the post date. This function will convert the date to a *YYYY-MM-DD* format ready for insertion into the MySQL database. Switch to the Utilities.as class file and add the function now:

```
public static function convertDateStringYYYYMMDD(theDate:String)➡
  :String{
  var arrDate:Array = theDate.split("-");
  return arrDate[2] + "-" + arrDate[0] + "-" + arrDate[1];
}
```

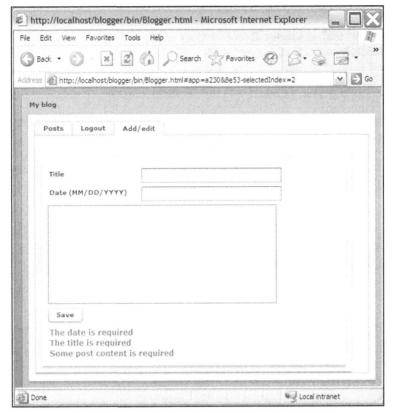

Figure 14-20. The error messages produced by the validators

The function works the same way as the other date-conversion function, using the split method. It reassembles the split portions of the date to produce the required MySQL *YYYY-MM-DD* date format.

Because we created a BlogLoader object, a URLVariables object, and called a static function in the Utilities class, we need to add the following import statements to the ContentsCode.as file:

```
import flash.net.URLVariables;
import com.aip.Utilities;
import com.aip.BlogLoader;
import com.aip.MessageEvent;
```

I've included the custom MessageEvent class because we'll need to be able to respond to the returned message from the PHP page.

Responding to the returned message

Earlier, we added an event listener in the initComponent function within the ContentsCode.as file. This event listener called a function called messageHandler that we now need to create. This function responds to the returned message from the PHP page by listening for the MessageEvent event.

Add this function to the ContentsCode.as file:

```
private function messageHandler(e:MessageEvent):void {
  txtAddEditMessage.text = e.message;
}
```

The function displays the returned message in the txtAddEditMessage control.

Run the application, log in, and edit an existing post. Figure 14-21 shows the update success message displayed in the custom component.

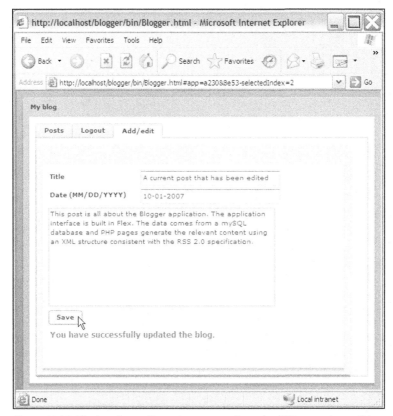

Figure 14-21. The interface reflects the message from the PHP page when editing a post.

That works well, but if you switch back to the Posts tab, you'll see that the updated post doesn't appear in the interface. We can fix this problem by reloading the Repeater component from the database.

Refreshing the data provider for the Repeater

In order to refresh the data provider for the Repeater control, we'll need to modify the indexChangedHandler function in BlogCode.as to request the getPosts.php page when the TabNavigator changes to display the Posts tab. We also need to check whether we were viewing current or archive posts prior to the update so we can refresh the interface with the correct data.

Modify the indexChangedHandler function as shown in bold here:

```
private function indexChangedHandler(e:IndexChangedEvent):void{
  if (e.newIndex == 0) {
    if (isCurrent) {
      postLoader.load (serverPath + "getPosts.php", null);
    }
    else {
      postLoader.load(serverPath + "getPosts.php?archive=true", null);
    }
  }
  else if (e.newIndex == 2) {
    postDetails.txtAddEditMessage.text = "";
    postDetails.server = serverPath;
    postDetails.postID = currentPost.postID;
    postDetails.txtTitle.text = currentPost.postTitle;
    postDetails.txtDate.text = currentPost.postDate;
    postDetails.txtContent.text = currentPost.postContents;
    }
}
```

When we switch to the first tab, we check our previous view to determine whether to load current or archive posts. We then call the load method of the postLoader to request the latest data and use it to refresh the data provider for the Repeater. Now if you run the application and edit a post, switching back to the first tab will reflect any changes that you have made.

Adding a new post

We can use much of the same code to process additions to the database. We need to start by enabling the Add new post button in the main application file. We'll call a function called addPost so modify the following <mx:Button> element in the main application file to call this function as shown here:

```
<mx:Button id="btnAdd" label="Add new post"
  visible="{isAdmin}" click="addPost(event)"/>
```

Create the following addPost function in the BlogCode.as file:

```
private function addPost(e:MouseEvent):void {
  currentPost = new SelectedPost("0","","","");
  isAdding = true;
  navigator.selectedIndex = 2;
}
```

This function creates a new SelectedPost object, assigning a value of zero for the postID and zero length strings for the remaining properties. It sets the variable isAdding to true, and displays the third tab in the TabNavigator. The indexChangedHandler function responds to this change and populates the relevant values in the custom component.

463

Run the application, log in, and click the Add new post button. You should see an empty form in the third tab, as shown in Figure 14-5. Because we already added the relevant functionality when editing a post, you should be able to add a new post and see it display when you switch to the first tab.

The last task is to add delete functionality to the application.

Deleting an existing post

The deletePost.php page handles deleting a post. This page requires the postID of the post to delete. We'll send this through in the querystring when we request the deletePost.php page from the SWF file. The full PHP page follows:

```php
<?php
header('Content-Type: text/xml');
include 'dbConn.php';
include 'writeIntroXML.php';
$postID = $_GET['postID'];
if (intval($postID) > 0) {
  $sql = 'DELETE FROM posts WHERE postID = ' . $postID;
  $result = mysql_query($sql);
  if ($result) {
  $message = 'You have successfully deleted the post';
  }
  else {
    $message = 'There was an error deleting the post. ' . ➥
      mysql_error();
  }
}
else {
  $message = 'Could not determine which post to delete';
}
$msgElement = $xml->createElement('message', $message);
$msgElement = $channelElement->appendChild($msgElement);
echo $xml->saveXML();
?>
```

As with the others, this page starts by declaring the content type and including the dbConn.php and writeIntroXML.php files. It determines the postID and checks that the value is greater than zero. If this is the case, the page creates a DELETE SQL statement and processes the delete, sending back an appropriate message in the <message> element of the XML document.

We need to request this page when we click the Delete button in the application. Modify the button in the main application file as shown here in bold.

```
<mx:Button id="btnDelete" label="Delete" visible="{isAdmin}"
  click="deletePost(event.currentTarget.getRepeaterItem())"/>
```

We'll create a Boolean variable to indicate whether we're currently deleting a post. You'll see why we need to do this shortly. Add the following variable declaration to the BlogCode.as file:

```
private var isDelete:Boolean = false;
```

We set the value of this variable to false initially as the application first loads before we can delete posts when logged in.

The deletePost function call passes the selected <item> element as an argument. Add this function now:

```
private function deletePost(post:Object):void {
  isDelete = true;
  var postXML:XML = XML(post);
  var postID:String = postXML.guid;
  postLoader.load (serverPath + "deletePost.php?postID=" + postID);
}
```

This function sets the value of the isDelete variable to true and casts the post object to the data type XML. It finds the value of the postID and calls the load method of the postLoader, appending the postID to the page URL.

When processed, the deletion will dispatch a MessageEvent that is handled by the messageHandler function in the BlogCode.as file. At the moment, that function only includes a trace statement.

In addition, the messageHandler function will also handle a MessageEvent dispatched when we request the posts. This message might occur because of a database error or because there are no posts to display. We'll use the isDelete Boolean variable to handle messages associated with deletion differently from the other messages.

The messageHandler will clear the data provider for the Repeater. In the case of a deletion, it will either request the current or archive posts, depending on what view was displayed prior to the deletion. Modify the messageHandler function in BlogCode.as, as shown here in bold:

```
private function messageHandler(e:MessageEvent):void {
  txtMessage.text = e.message;
  rptPosts.dataProvider = [];
  if (isDelete) {
    if (isCurrent) {
      postLoader.load (serverPath + "getPosts.php", null);
    }
    else {
      postLoader.load (serverPath + "getPosts.php?archive=true", null);
    }
    isDelete = false;
  }
}
```

The function now clears the txtMessage control and the dataProvider property for the Repeater. If deleting, it checks whether we're viewing current or archive posts, and requests the relevant PHP page to refresh the Repeater. It finishes by setting the isDelete variable to false.

Run the application, log in, and delete one of the posts. You should see the message shown in Figure 14-22, and the content in the Repeater control should refresh.

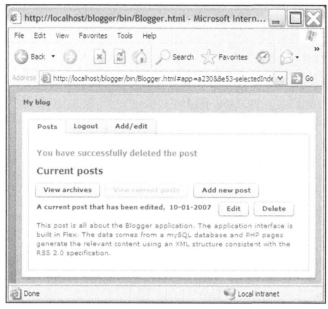

Figure 14-22. The interface after deleting a post

That completes the Flex application. You can view, add, edit, and delete posts from the database. The completed files for both the Flex and PHP application are in the resources download file for the chapter in the zip file called BloggerFiles.zip.

Summary

In this chapter, we created a Flex application powered by PHP pages and a MySQL database. The application allowed us to view and manage posts in a blog. We worked with custom ActionScript classes, custom events, and a custom component, and saw how to use the Repeater control. We were able to add, edit, and delete posts from the database using the Flex application.

That's the final case study in this part of the book. The next section looks at LiveCycle Data Services as an alternate means of loading data into a Flex application.

Part 3

LIVECYCLE DATA SERVICES

In this part of the book, we introduce the LiveCycle Data Services (LCDS). By using LCDS you can extend the capabilities of the Flex 3 framework. Extending means that you will be able to access and synchronize data across one or more applications built in Flex.

In Chapter 15, we will look at the different services involved in LCDS. In Chapter 16, we will build a fully managed and scalable application using the LiveCycle Data Services Data Management Services.

Chapter 15

INTRODUCTION TO LIVECYCLE DATA SERVICES

LiveCycle Data Services (formerly Flex Data Services) is the server software that extends the capabilities of the Flex client framework by providing additional services. These additional services are the remote procedure call (RPC) services, the Message Service, and the Data Management Services.

- RPC services: These services allow you to create Flex applications that make requests to remote services and let you access external data.

- Message Service: This service gives you the possibility to create Flex applications that can send messages to and receive messages from other Flex applications.

- Data Management Services: These services let you create Flex applications that are always using up-to-date data. The services provide data synchronization between server and client(s).

This chapter goes into more detail about LiveCycle Data Services.

Because LiveCycle Data Services is a J2EE server application, we need to have an application web server that can run J2EE applications. J2EE is a widely used platform for programming server-side applications in the Java programming language.

Specific J2EE application servers that can run LiveCycle Data Services include the following:

- JRun 4 Updater 6 (included in the integrated installation option)
- Apache Tomcat
- BEA WebLogic 8.1 (SP 2 or higher) and 9
- IBM WebSphere 5.x or 6.x
- JBoss 4.0.3 SP 1 and 4.0.4
- Oracle 10G AS (10.1.3)
- SAP web application server 6.40
- Fujitsu Internstage 7
- Hitachi Cosminexus 6

The two application servers are the servers we will use in this chapter for the exercises. The first one, JRun, comes with the LiveCycle Data Services installed. This means that the JRun server is automatically installed and configured so it can run Flex applications that use LCDS.

The second indicated server, Apache Tomcat, is not integrated, and we will have to manually download and install this server to get some exercises to work. We will go through the installation process later on. We'll also discuss the situations in which you'd choose one over the other.

After completing this chapter, you will be able to do the following:

- Install and run LiveCycle Data Services on JRun and Tomcat servers
- Set up a Flex application that uses LiveCycle Data Services
- Build a basic chat application that uses the Message Service
- Consume a web service using the Proxy Service
- Connect to a remote Java object using the remote object service
- Build an application that uses the Data Management Service

LiveCycle Data Services features

The following list gives an overview of the supported features in LiveCycle Data Services:

- The Message Service supports real-time chat and collaboration applications
- The Data Management Service supports real-time data synchronization between a Flex client application and data (for example, a database)
- The Flex Proxy Service routes requests to remote web and HTTP services from Flex applications without needing a cross-domain policy file on the remote server
- Remote object service management makes server-side custom Java classes accessible to Flex client applications

When we use those features provided by LiveCycle Data Services ES, we can deliver an application that provides a richer, more satisfying experience for users.

Sounds interesting! So let's get started with the installation of LiveCycle Data Services ES.

Installing LiveCycle Data Services ES

Before you dive into our first LiveCycle Data Services ES project, we want to briefly explain how to install the LiveCycle Data Services ES. It is important that you read this section first if you are planning to follow along with the example projects.

You can install LiveCycle Data Services ES using two different models:

- LiveCycle Data Services ES with integrated JRun
- LiveCycle Data Services ES J2EE web application

Both installations are the same and put the same files on your hard disk; the only difference is that in the first case a web server (JRun) is also installed, which is handy if you do not already have a server running on your machine.

For development and testing environments, you can select either option. For production environments in which you already have Java applications running, you can select the J2EE web application because then you do not need to install JRun. Therefore, the choice depends on what you already have at your disposal.

Both options create a J2EE web application archive file inside the install directory (the default is C:\lcds) called flex.war (.war stands for Web ARchive). This file is an industry standard .zip-formatted file that can be opened and viewed with WinZip or any other zip-compatible utility, and can be placed on any of the application servers listed previously. It contains a complete copy of LiveCycle Data Services. In other words, this file is a compressed version of the LiveCycle Data Services application that Java application servers can expand and host for you.

In the next part we will install LiveCycle Data Services first with integrated JRun and then on a Tomcat server. If you want to be able to run all the examples, both installs must be done as explained in the following two topics.

The first thing you must do is download the installer for LiveCycle Data Services. Download the installer lcds251-win.exe (Windows installer) from www.adobe.com/go/trylivecycle_dataservices.

There are also downloads for operating systems other than Windows available on the Adobe web site. Unfortunately, LiveCycle Data Services does not support Mac OS X at the time of writing. So to complete the exercises you need to work on a Windows computer. Run the installer and follow the install wizard:

1. Accept the license agreement. Click Next.
2. To install the express version of LCDS, leave the serial number blank. Click Next.
3. Enter an installation path. We chose the default folder C:\lcds. Click Next again.
4. Now you have to choose the installation option discussed before. Choose the LiveCycle Data Services with integrated JRun. Click Next and then click Install.

Your chosen install directory will be created. Now we are ready to start the integrated JRun server. We'll cover Tomcat in the following section.

LCDS with integrated JRUN

When you choose to install LiveCycle Data Services ES with integrated JRun there will be an extra /jrun4 directory installed. This directory contains a custom installation of JRun that includes flex, samples, and flex-admin web applications expanded and deployed in the default server. The JRun application server runs on port 8700 and can be started by navigating into Start Menu ➤ Programs ➤ Adobe ➤ LiveCycle Data Services ES and choosing Start Integrated LiveCycle Data Services Server.

You can also start the JRun application server with a command. To do so, start the server with these steps:

1. Open a command window.

2. Change to the directory in which jrun.exe is located (for instance, C:\lcds\jrun4\bin\ jrun.exe).

3. Enter the command jrun -start default to execute the jrun.exe file.

> *Since JRun is running as an application, you must keep the command window open to keep the server running. You can just minimize the command window on your desktop during development.*

When JRun is started, you can test the LiveCycle Data Services ES installation under http://localhost:8700. You should see the LiveCycle Data Services ES welcome screen.

At the welcome screen you can have a look at the samples provided by Adobe to see what is possible with LiveCycle Data Services ES. If you navigate to http://localhost:8700/flex/ you see a template of an empty application.

To stop JRun at any time on Windows, go to the command window that is hosting the server and press Ctrl+C.

LCDS J2EE application

When you have a look at your LCDS install directory (C:\lcds) you will recognize the flex.war file inside the install directory. As we saw earlier, this file is created at installation time so you can deploy the LCDS application on another web server and then on JRun (which is mostly the case in a production environment). The flex.war file is actually a zip-formatted file that can be opened with WinZip and contains a full copy of LCDS.

We already have installed LCDS on JRun, but in order to be able to complete some of the next exercises and to show you how it usually works in real-life situations, we are also going to install the LCDS application on an Apache Tomcat. Before we can dive into the process of installing the flex.war file, we first must install Tomcat.

First you have to download and install Apache Tomcat 6.0 from http://tomcat.apache.org. By default on Windows machines, Tomcat is installed in C:\Program Files\Apache Software Foundation\Tomcat 6.0 and runs on port 8080. At the end of the installation, the Apache Tomcat server will be started as a Windows service.

The following steps need to be followed in order to successfully deploy and install the flex.war file on the Tomcat application server.

1. If Tomcat is running, stop it.

2. Go to the Tomcat install directory: /webapps.

3. You can do one of two things next (both have the same outcome, although the first requires you to restart Tomcat only once). Removing the .war file once it has been unzipped will prevent it from being unzipped again and potentially overwriting any file you may have changed. This will happen only if the .war file is newer than the unzipped directories, so it's rare that you'll need to delete the .war file and do the double restart.

   - Create a /webapps/flex directory and copy flex.war there. Unzip the .war file by typing the following command in a command window (make sure you are in the same directory as the .war file): jar -xvf flex.war. You can also use an application such as WinZip; just be sure to unzip into the webapps/flex directory. Then delete the .war file or move it elsewhere.

   - Copy the .war file to the webapps directory. Start Tomcat and it will automatically unzip the .war file. Then stop Tomcat and delete the .war file or copy it elsewhere. This is the optional step; you don't often need to do this.

4. Start Tomcat.

5. Enter the following URL to test the LiveCycle Data Services ES installation under Tomcat: http://localhost:8080/flex. You should see the LiveCycle Data Services ES welcome screen. LiveCycle Data Services ES is deployed now under Tomcat.

So now we have set up two working configurations: one deployed on a Tomcat server (running on http://localhost:8080/flex) and one deployed on the JRun server (running on http://localhost:8700).

We will use both configurations in the exercises in this chapter, so make sure both configurations are working properly.

LiveCycle Data Services ES directory structure

LiveCycle Data Services ES uses a directory structure that follows the standard model for all J2EE web applications.

In a standard J2EE web application, the application root is known as a context root, under which you will always find a directory called WEB-INF. This directory contains all the directories and files that configure the behavior of a J2EE application.

LiveCycle Data Services ES is a J2EE web application, and the name of the web application is flex, so that is our context root. It is located at C:\lcds\jrun4\servers\default\flex or C:\Program Files\Apache Software Foundation\Tomcat 6.0\webapps\flex, depending on the deployment server.

Notice that the resources placed inside the /flex directory are publicly available. The WEB-INF directory is private to the web application, so any attempt to directly access this directory or the resources inside will result in a 404 Not Found error.

Inside the WEB-INF directory you will find directories and files that configure the behavior of the Flex web application, as shown in Figure 15-1, and described in the next few sections.

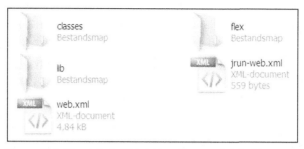

Figure 15-1. The default C:\lcds\jrun4\servers\default\ flex\WEB-INF directory

- **web application deployment descriptor**: An XML file named web.xml. It describes the configuration information for the entire web application.

- **flex directory**: Contains all libraries and configuration files required by LiveCycle Data Services ES.

- **classes directory**: The preferred directory for compiled Java classes that will be called by LiveCycle Data Services ES at run time. You need this when working with Java server classes (discussed later on).

- **lib directory**: The preferred location for .jar files that contain compiled Java classes that will be called by LiveCycle Data Services ES at run time (.jar files are simply zipped files with a different extension, Java ARchive, to distinguish them from regular zipped files). In this directory you can place extra resources to be called from the Flex application, such as a database driver. We will look at this directory later when installing a database on our server.

Set up a Flex application for use with LiveCycle Data Services ES

When you create a new Flex project, you can create the project so the files are placed within the LiveCycle Data Services ES application and compiled upon request from the browser. Alternatively, you can compile the files beforehand—you'll look at this in the setup process. This is just a sample setup; we won't be placing any functionality in it.

1. Select File ➤ New ➤ Flex Project.

2. In the New Flex Project dialog box, choose LiveCycle Data Services as Server type. Give the project the name CH15_LCDS_01.

3. Select Compile application on the server when the page is viewed. For applications that compile on the server, MXML files are saved on the server. No HTML wrapper file is generated and saved when the application is compiled. For applications that compile locally, Flex Builder saves MXML files in the local Flex Builder project directory, and saves SWF files and HTML wrapper files on the server. Creating a project that compiles locally is a good idea if you plan to deploy your finished application with an HTML wrapper file rather than an MXML file. (Users see an .mxml extension when files are compiled on the server and .html when compiled locally.) Server-side compilation has the advantage that the files stay up to date. Every time users navigate to the application, they see the latest compiled version, although there may be a slight drop in performance as the application compiles.

The next step is to choose the server's root folder, root URL, and context root. These differ depending on whether you are using JRun or Tomcat.

Using JRun

To set up a Flex project that uses the integrated JRun as application server, you can accept the defaults:

1. Because projects with integrated JRun are the default in Flex, you can just check the box that indicates Use default location for local LiveCycle Data Services server. The root folder and the root URL are filled in automatically with the correct values.

2. Again, the next steps are the same as for creating a regular Flex project (enter project name and location). Choose the default location to save the project.

3. Click Finish to make a new Flex project. Here you can test your application by clicking the Run button. You'll see a blank Flex application.

Let's see how to use Tomcat now.

Using Tomcat

When you choose the default location for the LiveCycle Data Services ES server location, it will be pointed to the integrated JRun server's Flex context root. However, Tomcat uses a different context root. Also notice that the port is different when you work with Tomcat instead of the integrated JRun server. Default Tomcat uses port 8080, and JRun uses 8700.

To set up a project with Tomcat:

1. Enter the Root directory pointing to the Flex context root of the Tomcat server As noted previously, this context root is located at C:\Program Files\Apache Software Foundation\Tomcat 6.0\webapps\flex.

2. Enter the Root URL. Use port 8080 (this is the port Tomcat is running on).

The rest of the steps are the same as for creating a regular Flex project.

3. Keep the project name (CH15_LCDS_01).

4. Click Next and set the main application file and the default location for your project.

Click Finish and click the Run button inside Flex Builder if you want to test. At this moment there is not much to see except a blank Flex application with the default background because we haven't written any code at all.

Using LiveCycle Data Services

Now that we know how to set up a project for use with LiveCycle Data Services ES, we can finally start to examine it. There are three major parts of LiveCycle Data Services ES:

- Message Service
- RPC services
- Data Management Services

Let's start with the Message Service.

Message Service

The LiveCycle Data Services ES messaging framework is the basis for all data services. By using the Message Service, you can communicate from your Flex client application to the LiveCycle Data Services ES services on the server. This functionality gives the possibility to deliver a whole new kind of application: peer-to-peer chat applications, gaming applications, or other collaborative innovative applications.

The model used when building collaborative applications is called **publish-subscribe messaging**. The Flex client applications can subscribe to one or more topics; when a client or the server publishes a message to one of these topics, it is received by all clients who have subscribed to that topic.

Of course, when every client or server is sending messages, there must be some management involved to make sure everything is delivered well. This is done by a messaging adapter.

On the client side, we have two components that we can use to publish or subscribe to a topic:

- Producer
- Consumer

The three most important things to remember concerning publish-subscribe messaging on the Flex client side are these:

- To subscribe to a topic, use the subscribe method of the Consumer object.
- When a message is published to a topic you subscribed to, the message event is triggered on the Consumer object.
- To send a message to a topic, use the send method of the Producer object.

Message channels actually take care of the transportation of the messages. You can configure your Flex clients to use either real-time channels or channels that retrieve messages from the server using polling. (**Polling** is the term used to describe an application making continuous requests for data.) You provide a list of channels to connect to, and the Flex client will use the first channel that succeeds in connecting to the server.

Let's put those concepts into practice by building one of the simplest real-time messaging applications: a basic chat application.

Building a basic chat application

The first thing we have to do is to create a new Flex project that uses the LiveCycle Data Services ES called CH15_LCDS_SimpleChat.

In this example, we will be using Tomcat as our application server, so be sure to set the server location as described earlier. If you want to use JRun, you can, but make sure to set up the Flex project in the appropriate way.

We are going to create a foed directory, in which we will place the exercises for this chapter. Therefore, when you select the project location, choose the C:\Program Files\Apache Software Foundation\Tomcat 6.0\webapps\flex\foed directory (keep the server settings the same).

Open CH15_LCDS_SimpleChat.mxml and add some basic UI components:

```
<?xml version="1.0" encoding="utf-8"?>
<mx:Application xmlns:mx="http://www.adobe.com/2006/mxml"
    layout="absolute">
  <mx:Panel title="Simple Chat using Message Services">
    <mx:TextArea id="chatBody" width="300" height="300"/>
    <mx:HBox width="300" >
      <mx:TextInput id="messageToSend" width="100%"/>
      <mx:Button id="sendMessage" label="SEND"/>
    </mx:HBox>
  </mx:Panel>
</mx:Application>
```

Now we are ready to set up the serious stuff. We must define a configuration so our Flex client application knows where to find the necessary services. Let's set up the message destination.

Setting up the message destination

Before we can actually use the Message Services, we have to configure our message destination. This is done in a configuration file called messaging-config.xml. To make it easier within the Flex environment to edit this file, we will set up a link to it:

1. Right-click your Flex project and select New ➤ File.

2. Open the Advanced options and select the Link to file in the file system check box.

3. Browse to the WEB-INF/flex directory of the LCDS context root. Because we are working with Tomcat, our context root is C:\Program Files\Apache Software Foundation\Tomcat 6.0\webapps\flex.

4. Select the messaging-config.xml file inside the WEB-INF/flex directory. This is a file that is installed with LCDS, but we are going to edit it

5. Click Finish and you should see the XML file appear in your project linked to its physical location on your hard drive.

When you set up a destination in this XML file, follow two steps:

1. Define a message adapter. This is actually the server part taking care of the sending and receiving classes that will be used. This determines which client applications will be able to participate in the messaging application. Two adapters are already defined in the configuration file:

   ■ ActionScript adapter: Flex clients can participate in the messaging.

   ■ JMS adapter: JMS-based clients can participate in the messaging. The Java Message Service (JMS) API is a messaging standard that allows application components based on J2EE to create, send, receive, and read messages. Use of this adapter is outside the scope of this book.

2. Define a protocol, called a **message channel**, to be used for messaging. There are two predefined message protocols you can use:

- my-rtmp protocol for real-time data pushed to clients. RTMP is a real-time protocol built on
top of TCP/IP for the purposes of media streaming. It contains interleaved audio, video, and
data content. Flex uses only the data portion of RTMP, and performs no audio or video
streaming.

- my-polling-amf protocol for data pushed to clients based on polling.

Because we are working only with Flex clients and want to have real-time data pushed to these clients,
it is obvious which protocol and adapter we want to use. Now we can write our destination:

1. Locate the <adapters> element in the messaging-config.xml file.

2. Directly under this element, create the following destination:

```
<destination id="simpleChatDest">
  <channels>
    <channel ref="my-rtmp" />
  </channels>
</destination>
```

We are not defining an adapter in our destination because the ActionScript adapter is the default
adapter to be used in a Flex application. Now we can go to our Flex application to set up a <producer>
element that will be responsible for sending messages to the application server.

Sending messages to the server

A producer in the messaging flow will be responsible for sending the data to the destination using the
configured channel (as declared in the messaging-config.xml file).

To declare a <producer> element in your Flex applications, add the following MXML code just after
your Application opening tag. Give it an id and set the destination to point toward the
simpleChatDest defined in the configuration:

```
<mx:Producer id="simpleChatProducer" destination="simpleChatDest"/>
```

We want the text from our TextInput component to be sent to the server when we click the SEND
button. To do this, we must configure an event handler on the button:

```
<mx:Button id="sendMessage" label="SEND" click="sendMyMessage()"/>
```

Write the sendMyMessage function in a Script block just after your Application opening tag:

```
<mx:Script >
  <![CDATA[
    private function sendMyMessage():void{
    }
  ]]>
</mx:Script>
```

Before we can actually write the sendMyMessage function we must know how the data is formatted when sent to the server. This is done by using AsyncMessage objects. These objects have two places where you can put data: a body and a headers property:

- The headers property is like a generic Object type in which you can store data using a key and a value, just like in a normal ActionScript object.

- The body property can be any ActionScript data type you want.

So now we can set up our AsyncMessage object and complete our sendMyMessage function with the following code:

```
<mx:Script >
  <![CDATA[
    import mx.messaging.messages.AsyncMessage;
    private function sendMyMessage():void{
      var msg:AsyncMessage= new AsyncMessage();
      msg.body = messageToSend.text;
      //send the data with the producer
      simpleChatProducer.send(msg);
      //empty textInput field after sending
      messageToSend.text = "";
      }
  ]]>
</mx:Script>
```

Now the message is actually sent to the server, but we still cannot receive the messages that are sent from any client. That is where the consumer comes in.

Receiving messages from the server

The messaging service destination will send data to a consumer in a client application using the configured channel. But the consumer is not automatically listening to receive data from the server. It must be explicitly told to start listening using the subscribe method.

When data arrives at the consumer, it will fire a message event that contains the data, which makes it extremely easy to react to the received data. So let's set up a consumer in our SimpleChat application.

Just after the Producer tag in your MXML code, create a Consumer tag as follows:

```
<mx:Consumer id="simpleChatConsumer" destination="simpleChatDest"/>
```

Add a callback function for the message event. This function will be executed when new data is received and will receive an event of type MessageEvent:

```
<mx:Consumer id="simpleChatConsumer" destination="simpleChatDest"
             message="showMessage(event)"/>
```

Just as when a message is sent, data is packaged as an AsyncMessage object. So our showMessage function can parse the headers and body properties directly from the MessageEvent.

Create the callback function directly after the sendMyMessage function in the Script block:

```
private function showMessage(evt:MessageEvent):void{
  chatBody.text+=evt.message.body+"\n";
}
```

We also need to import the MessageEvent class:

```
import mx.messaging.events.MessageEvent;
```

When we run the application now, we will still not see any messages in our application. As discussed before, you must explicitly tell the consumer to start listening for incoming messages by using the subscribe method. The best place to do this is when the client application has been created.

Add a creationComplete event to your Application MXML opening tag:

```
<mx:Application xmlns:mx="http://www.adobe.com/2006/mxml"
        layout="absolute"
        creationComplete="simpleChatConsumer.subscribe()">
```

You can now fully test the application by running the application in two browser windows and send messages between the two browser windows, as shown in Figure 15-2.

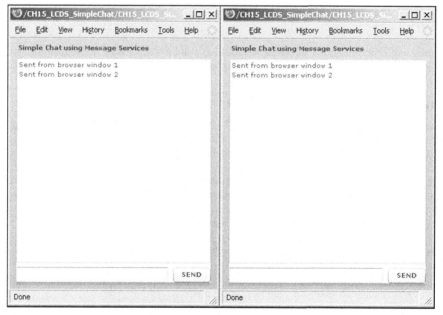

Figure 15-2. The final chat application in action

If your application is not running as expected, make sure you have restarted your server. When you edit the configuration files, it's always best to restart your application server.

RPC services

Sometimes RPC is referred to as **remote invocation** or **remote method invocation**. So our Flex application (client) will call a procedure or method on a remote machine (server), asking for some data. To accomplish this, the client must first send a request message (call message) that specifies the procedure to use. The client can also send arguments to pass into the remote procedure. The next step for the client is to wait for a reply message to be sent back from the remote server. When the reply message is finally sent to the client, the client can extract the information from the message and use it in some way.

But what is happening on the server? It is dormant, awaiting the arrival of a request message. And when the message arrives, the server will extract the information needed (the procedure's parameters), compute the result, and send a reply message to the client. Then the server waits for the next call message.

There are three RPC services available in LiveCycle Data Services ES:

- Web services
  - Aim: Call operations from web services using the SOAP protocol
  - RPC Flex component: WebService component

- HTTP services
  - Aim: Send and receive data using HTTP GET and POST
  - RPC Flex component: HTTPService component

- Remote object services
  - Aim: Call server-side Java objects using AMF3 protocol
  - RPC Flex component: RemoteObject component

All the messaging between clients and servers is handled in an asynchronous way. This means that you will have to configure a listener as part of your RPC client component to know when a reply message is returned from the server. When it has returned, you can extract the data and use it immediately in your Flex application.

We will explore these three services in detail by creating a simple example for every service. First we will start with the web service in combination with the Proxy Service. You will learn that using the Proxy Service gives you extra power concerning security.

Exploring web and HTTP services

You have probably already heard about web services. Actually it is an application that provides functionality, is published on the Internet, and provides a way for applications (for example, Flex applications) to communicate with each other. To enable them to communicate with each other, an XML-based protocol is used: the SOAP protocol. SOAP makes it possible to write messages to send and receive web service requests and responses over the Internet. Every web service provides functionality that is described in XML, including the available functions, accepted parameters, and results returned. That XML-based description, Web Services Description Language (WSDL—"whiz-dull") is made available online by the web service provider. This makes it easy to see what function you can call, what arguments you can send, and the data types your arguments need to have.

For example, Amazon provides a web service called AmazonSearch that makes it possible to search for keywords in its database. Amazon's WSDL file is located at http://soap.amazon.com/schemas2/AmazonWebServices.wsdl.

Suppose we want to consume the Amazon web service in Flex. We can access web services by using the <mx:WebService> component in Flex:

```
<mx:WebService id="amazonService"
        wsdl="http://soap.amazon.com/schemas2/AmazonWebServices.wsdl" />
```

But we have to keep something in mind. Some security issues are involved because we are reading information from another domain. We already know from an earlier chapter that it is possible to read data from another domain only when a crossdomain.xml (cross-domain policy) file that allows access from your application's domain is installed on the web server.

If we look to the cross-domain file specific for the web server that hosts the Amazon web services, we see that the cross-domain file (http://soap.amazon.com/crossdomain.xml) grants access to everybody. So we have permission to load data from that Amazon web server.

> If you are running a Flex application at http://localhost:8080/myFlexApp.mxml and you try to load a web service from http://127.0.0.1:8080/myWebservice, it will also look as if you are loading from a different domain.

But if we want to consume a web service located on a web server without a cross-domain file or with a cross-domain file that is not granting access, we have to consider another approach. This is where the LiveCycle Data Services ES proxy server comes in.

Understanding the Proxy Service

If we use the LiveCycle Data Services ES Proxy Service, our Flex application will not connect directly to the remote web server in which the web service resides. It will forward the requests to the Proxy Service, which provides the resource to the Flex application by connecting to the specified server and requesting the web service on behalf of the Flex application. In this way the Flex application is sending and receiving data from a local source, so no security restrictions are involved.

The Proxy Service can also be used with HTTP services, which we will discuss later in this chapter.

To show the power of the Proxy Service and to learn how it must be configured we will build a small application that consumes the ShortLynx web service.

Consuming a web service

There are lots of web services available online for use in your applications. We use the free web service delivered by ShortLynx.com that will turn a long URL into something itty-bitty that anyone can remember. This can be useful when integrating into a chat application in which very long URLs are not very comfortable to read, for example. At the time of writing, this ShortLynx web service is located at http://shortlynx.com/shortlynx.asmx?WSDL. This service is free to use for developers.

Take a look at the documentation at http://shortlynx.com/shortlynx.asmx and you will see that this web service has an operation name (method you can call), ShortLynx, which takes LongURL as a parameter.

Now that we have examined the web service we can start setting our Flex project.

Setting up the Flex project

The first thing we have to do is create a new Flex project that uses the LiveCycle Data Services ES called CH15_LCDS_ConsumingWebservice. In this example, we will be using Tomcat as our application server, so be sure to set the server location to point to the Tomcat's context root, as discussed earlier. We are compiling on the server side. Also specify the project's location as C:\Program Files\Apache Software Foundation\Tomcat 6.0\webapps\flex\foed.

Open CH15_LCDS_ConsumingWebservice.mxml. This code adds some basic layout for our Flex application:

```
<?xml version="1.0" encoding="utf-8"?>
<mx:Application xmlns:mx="http://www.adobe.com/2006/mxml"
        layout="absolute">
  <mx:Script >
    <![CDATA[
      //script comes here

    ]]>
  </mx:Script>
  <mx:Panel x="10" y="10" width="300" height="200" layout="vertical"
          title="ShortLynx">
    <mx:TextArea id="longURL" width="100%" height="100"/>
    <mx:HBox width="100%">
      <mx:Text id="shortURL" width="65%"  />
      <mx:Button id="MakeShort" label="Generate" />
    </mx:HBox>
  </mx:Panel>
</mx:Application>
```

Figure 15-3 shows the basic layout.

Figure 15-3. The basic layout of the application

The first thing we are going to do is create the WebService object in MXML code. Just after the closing Script tag, we instantiate a WebService object:

```
<mx:WebService id="shortlynxService"
                destination="shortlynxDestination" useProxy="true">
</mx:WebService>
```

As you can see, we tell our WebService object to use the Proxy Service by setting the Boolean useProxy to true. This is the only thing you must do on the Flex side to take advantage of the Proxy Service.

You also see that we have added a destination. The destination we are using here is called shortlynxDestination, but at the moment this destination cannot be resolved because we did not write it yet. So let's configure our destination in the proxy-config.xml configuration file.

Setting up the soap-proxy destination

To make it easier within the Flex environment to edit the proxy-config.xml configuration file, you set up a link to this file, as we did earlier. This is done in the same way as we did with the messaging-config.xml file in the previous exercise (proxy-config.xml is in the same location). We are going to add some functionality to the configuration file.

Look into the XML file and locate the adapters. You see there are two adapters preconfigured:

- http-proxy adapter: Used for an HTTP service (for example, loading RSS feed)
- soap-proxy adapter: Used for a web service

We have to reference these adapters in our destination so that the Proxy Service knows what classes to use. The http-proxy adapter is the default adapter when nothing is declared in a named or default destination.

The default destination typically looks like this:

```
<destination id="DefaultHTTP">
  <properties>
    <dynamic-url>http://www.onesite.com/*</dynamic-url>
    <dynamic-url>http://www.secondsite.com/*</dynamic-url>
    ...
  </properties>
</destination>
```

As you can see, there can be several <dynamic-url> patterns specified. This gives permission to use the proxy server and to communicate with remote servers when a URL matches the pattern specified.

We will not use the default destination; instead we will set up our own destination.

Just after the default destination in the proxy-config.xml file, specify the following destination:

```
<destination id="shortlynxDestination" adapter="soap-proxy">
  <properties>
    <wsdl>http://shortlynx.com/shortlynx.asmx?WSDL</wsdl>
```

```
        <soap>http://shortlynx.com/shortlynx.asmx</soap>
    </properties>
</destination>
```

We specify the WSDL location and allow the URL http://shortlynx.com/shortlynx.asmx as properties of the destination called shortlynxDestination. Now these locations can be used with the Proxy
Service. We also explicitly declare in the destination tag to use the soap-proxy adapter because otherwise the default http-proxy adapter will be used.

Now that we have our destination, we can get back to our MXML code to actually call an operation
from the web service.

Connecting to the web service and handling the result

To connect to the web service, we first must define the operation we want to call, and if there are
parameters to be sent with the call we have to put these parameters in a request object. We will also
define a result handler to do something when data is received.

Just after the opening tag of your WebService tag, we write the code to define that we want to call
ShortLynx method:

```
<mx:operation name="ShortLynx" result="handleShortLynxResult(event)">
</mx:operation>
```

But as we know from the ShortLynx web service documentation, this method needs a LongUrl parameter when called. That's where the request object comes in; we must define the parameters we want
to send in a request object. That request object is a child of the operation tag. So our final
WebService tag looks as follows:

```
<mx:WebService id="shortlynxService"
               destination="shortlynxDestination" useProxy="true">
  <mx:operation name="ShortLynx" result="handleShortLynxResult(event)">
    <mx:request>
      <LongUrl>{longURL.text}</LongUrl>
    </mx:request>
  </mx:operation>
</mx:WebService>
```

Now we are ready to handle the result when data is coming back from the web service. From the documentation we know that we get back a simple String (short URL). So we can define our
handleShortLynxResult function as follows:

```
private function handleShortLynxResult(evt:ResultEvent):void{
  shortURL.text = evt.result.toString();
}
```

The result property from the ResultEvent is pointing to the data that we cast to a String to avoid
type errors. We put the result in the text field named shortURL. We also need to import the
ResultEvent class:

```
import mx.rpc.events.ResultEvent;
```

To fully test your application, you only need to activate the web service component by using the send method from the operation you want at the moment you want (the click event of the button):

```
shortlynxService.ShortLynx.send();
```

Figure 15-4 shows an example run of the application.

Figure 15-4. The final ShortLynx application in action

Consuming an HTTP service

Another service that can contact an RPC service directly is HTTPService. Another common name for an HTTP service is a REST-style web service. (REST stands for Representational State Transfer and is an architectural style for distributed hypermedia systems.) For more information about REST, see www.ics.uci.edu/~fielding/pubs/dissertation/rest_arch_style.htm.

In this example, we will consume an RSS feed, which is accessible through the HTTPService Flex component. RSS feeds contain frequently updated content such as news headlines and blog entries. We will read the youTube RSS feed that contains the top-viewed videos from youTube.

Setting up the Flex project

The first thing we have to do is create a new Flex project that uses the LiveCycle Data Services ES called CH15_LCDS_YouTube. Again we use Tomcat as our application server and we compile on the server.

We want to use the foed directory as before, so the place where you will create your MXML files for this exercise would look like this: C:\Program Files\Apache Software Foundation\Tomcat 6.0\webapps\flex\foed\CH15_LCDS_YouTube.

We already wrote some code to get started. In the code there is an HTPPService component declared as follows:

```
<mx:HTTPService id="YTService"
                url="http://youtube.com/rss/global/top_viewed.rss"
                result="YTResultHandler(event)"
                fault="YTFaultHandler(event)"/>
```

You can see that the url property is pointing directly to the address where the RSS feed is located. There is also a result and fault handler defined, and the callback functions look like this:

```
import mx.collections.ArrayCollection;
import mx.controls.Alert;
import mx.rpc.events.ResultEvent;
import mx.rpc.events.FaultEvent;

[Bindable]
private var YTData:ArrayCollection = new ArrayCollection();

private function YTResultHandler(evt:ResultEvent):void{
        YTData = evt.result.rss.channel.item;
}
private function YTFaultHandler(evt:FaultEvent):void{
        Alert.show(evt.fault.faultString,evt.fault.name);
}
```

We are pushing all the item nodes in an ArrayCollection called YTData when the HTTP request succeeds. The YTData ArrayCollection is bound to a DataGrid as dataProvider. This all happens in the YTResultHandler method. If not, the YTFaultHandler method is called and shows an Alert box showing what exactly went wrong:

```
<mx:DataGrid dataProvider="{YTData}" width="350" >
  <mx:columns>
    <mx:DataGridColumn headerText="title" dataField="title"/>
  </mx:columns>
</mx:DataGrid>
```

Finally, we need to send the request for the RSS feed information:

```
<mx:Application xmlns:mx="http://www.adobe.com/2006/mxml"
                layout="absolute"
                applicationComplete="YTService.send()">
```

Not really difficult to understand. When you run the CH15_LCDS_YouTube.mxml file, you see the error shown in Figure 15-5.

Figure 15-5. Security error

We were expecting that our DataGrid would be filled with the titles of the most-viewed videos. But instead we get the security warning Security error accessing url. This is exactly the same problem we experienced when talking about web services and security.

You cannot access the youTube data because the RSS feed is on a domain different from the domain on which your Flex application is running (localhost). The solution is the same as with web services: Set up a proxy destination in the proxy-config.xml configuration file.

So again you see the importance of the LiveCycle Data Services ES Proxy Service.

Setting up the http-proxy destination

If you want, you can again set up a link to the proxy-config.xml file in your Flex project as you did earlier or you can open the file in your favorite text editor. This time we are not going to set up a custom destination but we are going to use the default destination.

At the moment the default destination looks like this:

```
<destination id="DefaultHTTP" />
```

You can extend the default destination by defining dynamic-url patterns as much as you want. We are going to configure a dynamic-url pattern for the youTube site. Because we want every URL that starts with http://youtube.com/ to be intercepted by the Proxy Service, we change the default destination to fulfill these requirements:

```
<destination id="DefaultHTTP">
        <properties>
            <dynamic-url>http://youtube.com/*</dynamic-url>
        </properties>
</destination>
```

We use the star at the end of the URL as a wildcard so that every URL that starts with http://youtube.com/ is accepted.

That is all we have to set up in the configuration. Let's get back to Flex.

Connecting to the RSS feed through Proxy Service

Now the magic starts. Because we are using the DefaultHTTP destination, we have to add only one small thing to our code to get it working. We have to say explicitly that we want to use the Proxy Service now:

```
<mx:HTTPService id="YTService"
                useProxy="true"
                url="http://youtube.com/rss/global/top_viewed.rss"
                result="YTResultHandler(event)"
                fault="YTFaultHandler(event)"
    />
```

If you now run the application you will see that the data is correctly loaded and the grid is populated with the top videos of YouTube, as shown in Figure 15-6.

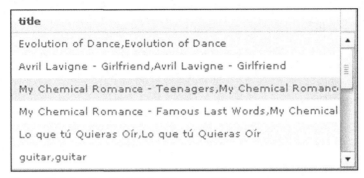

Figure 15-6. Reading the RSS feed from youTube

Exploring the remote object service

RemoteObject components let you access the methods of server-side Java objects. You can use a RemoteObject component instead of a WebService component when objects are not already published as web services, when web services are not used in your environment, or when you would rather use Java objects than web services. You can use a RemoteObject component to connect to a local Java object that is in the LiveCycle Data Services.

So the remote object service system is similar to accessing a web service, except that you are now communicating with a Java object instead of a web service.

Consuming a simple remote object service

In this exercise we will connect to a remote Java object on the server, so we need to write a plain old java object (POJO). If you are not familiar with Java, do not be scared. We will explain every step in detail, and if you are familiar with ActionScript, Java is not that difficult to understand.

We will create a loginPanel that verifies the login credentials on the server and then sends back the result to Flex. When we receive that result, we can set up the necessary actions (for example, to show a notification that the login was successful). Let's get started setting up our Flex project.

Setting up the Flex project

For this exercise we create a new Flex project that uses LiveCycle Data Services (called CH15_LCDS_REMOTEOBJECTS_LOGIN) and we will use Tomcat again as our application server. Remember to use the foed directory as well. In CH15_LCDS_REMOTEOBJECTS_LOGIN_Start.mxml, define a panel, two input textfields, two labels, and a button:

```
<?xml version="1.0" encoding="utf-8"?>
<mx:Application xmlns:mx="http://www.adobe.com/2006/mxml"
    layout="horizontal">
```

```
<mx:Script >
 <![CDATA[

 ]]>
</mx:Script>

<mx:Panel verticalCenter="0" horizontalCenter="0"
  title="Please log in">
  <mx:VBox>
    <mx:HBox>
        <mx:Label text="Name: " width="70"/>
        <mx:TextInput id="loginName" width="100%"/>
    </mx:HBox>
    <mx:HBox>
        <mx:Label text="Password: " width="70"/>
        <mx:TextInput id="pass" width="100%"
            displayAsPassword="true"/>
    </mx:HBox>
        <mx:HBox width="100%" horizontalAlign="right">
        <mx:Button id="loginBtn" label="LOGIN" />
    </mx:HBox>
  </mx:VBox>
</mx:Panel>
</mx:Application>
```

When we run this code we see the login panel shown in Figure 15-7, and nothing happens when we press the LOGIN button because there is still no click handler defined.

Figure 15-7. The login application
with remote objects

When we press the LOGIN button in our application a request will be sent to our remote Java object, and we will then pass the name and password of the user. On the server side, our Java object will examine whether the credentials are correct and send back a Boolean value representing the success of the login. Let's set up the Java class that checks the login data.

Setting up the Java project

Before we set up the Java project let's remember what the current WEB-INF directory looks like within your Flex context root (see Figure 15-8).

Figure 15-8. The WEB-INF directory in the context root (located at C:\Program Files\Apache Software Foundation\Tomcat 6.0\webapps\flex\WEB-INF)

We look at this structure because the Java project we will create will use this WEB-INF directory to store its files. A standard Java project needs a classes directory to store classes when compiled, and the LiveCycle Data Services ES must be able to find the classes you wrote. The most common strategy is thus to place your compiled classes in the classes directory.

But a standard Java project also wants a place to store its source files (.java files). Most often this directory is named src for neatness. But there is no src folder in our current directory structure, so we have to create one. When you have done that, your WEB-INF directory is ready to be used for a Java project and looks like Figure 15-9.

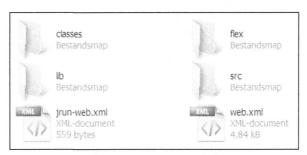

Figure 15-9. Adding an src directory to the WEB-INF directory

One last important thing to keep in mind when using LiveCycle Data Services ES with Java: make sure you always make one Java project that resides in your WEB-INF directory; otherwise, Flex builder might have problems accessing your files. But if you make your Java classes on another location, that is also okay, but do not forget to place your compiled classes in the WEB-INF/classes directory.

Now we are ready to set up our Java project. Follow these steps when setting up a Java project in Flex builder or in Eclipse when using the Flex plugin:

1. Select File ➤ New ➤ Other ➤ Java ➤ Java Project and click Next.

If you cannot select a new Java project it means you do not have the Java development tools installed. This is no problem—you can easily update your Flex Builder to have Java development support (in Flex Builder, go to Help ➤ Software Updates ➤ Find and Install).

    a. Choose Search for new features to install. Click Next.

    b. Choose Eclipse Project Updates and click Finish.

    c. Select Eclipse Java Development Tools; click Next.

    d. Accept the license agreement; click Next.

    e. Click Finish to start downloading. When the download is done, click Install all to install the Java Development Tools.

    f. Restart Flex Builder for changes to take effect.

    g. From now on, you can create a new Java project as we discussed.

2. Name the Java project CH15_LCDS_JAVAPROJECT and select Create project from existing source pointing to the WEB-INF directory inside your Flex context root. Click Next.

3. You should see your project workspace now, including the contents of the WEB-INF directory. Now we have to say what folder we want to use as the source folder and what our output folder is (the folder in which compiled classes will be stored). So we right-click on our src folder and choose Use as Source Folder. You see the icon change to indicate that it is a recognized source folder now (see Figure 15-10). Also set <projectname>/classes as the default output folder. Click Finish.

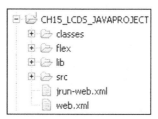

Figure 15-10. Use the src folder as source folder

Normally Flex Builder will ask you if you want to open the associated perspective because you just made a Java project. Click Yes to open the Java project in the Java perspective.

Now we are fully settled to start writing our first Java class.

Writing the LoginPojo.java class

Just like ActionScript, Java also uses packages. To make types easier to find and use, to avoid naming conflicts, and to control access, most programmers bundle groups of related types into packages. We will bundle all our Java classes in the package named foed.

1. Create a package in the src folder by right-clicking on the src folder in the Flex Builder navigator and choose New ➤ Package. Give the package the name of foed. You will see that the same structure is immediately created in the classes directory.

2. Right-click now on the foed package in the src folder and select New ➤ Class. Fill in the Name with LoginPojo and leave all the other settings as they are. Click Finish.

3. Your first class, called LoginPojo, is now created and looks like this:

```
package foed;

public class LoginPojo {

}
```

The package is declared at the top of the Java document. Note the many similarities with ActionScript. Each Java class that you want to expose to your Flex application must be written as a plain old java object (POJO), which is a simple Java class with public methods. In this example we will write one public method called login. Before we do this, however, we must write a constructor as we do in ActionScript.

There must be at least one constructor defined in order to get this Java class working with LiveCycle Data Services ES. "At least one constructor" might sound strange, but in Java it is possible to write multiple constructors. We are just going to set up an empty constructor like this:

```
package foed;

public class LoginPojo {
//make a constructor; we need at least an empty constructor
        public void LoginPoJo(){
            //empty
        }
}
```

As you see, the constructor has the same name as the class definition. This is the same as in ActionScript, except we do not write the function keyword when defining a constructor or method.

Now we are going to add the method that will handle the logic. As discussed, this method must be public; otherwise, LiveCycle Data Services ES cannot call this method.

Underneath the constructor, write the following function that is passed two parameters and then uses a standard if statement to compare each incoming String with the predefined value. The method also returns a Boolean (true or false) back to the Flex application to say whether the userName and passWord were correct:

```
public boolean login(String userName,String passWord){
    if((userName.equals("koen")) && (passWord.equals("friendsofed"))){
        return true;
    }else{
        return false;
    }
}
```

Unlike ActionScript, Java has another way to compare a String: by using the equals method of the String class. The equals method applied to a String performs a character-by-character comparison. What also might look strange is that data types are declared in front of the variables. So in Java we say String name (instead of name:String in ActionScript).

> *When you are working on the Java side of a LiveCycle Data Services ES project or editing LiveCycle Data Services ES configuration files, keep in mind that you always have to restart your application server for changes to take effect.*

Good. Now we are ready to set up our Java class so it executes the functionality we want. We need a way to couple this Java class to our Flex project. This is done by defining a destination.

Setting up the remote object destination

To configure your class so it can be used by the Flex application, you must set up a destination in the remoting-config.xml file that is located in the WEB-INF/flex directory of your Flex context root. For each class that you want to expose to your Flex application, you need to set up such a destination. Each destination also has a unique identifier.

If you want, you can link the remoting-config.xml file, as we did earlier with the other configuration files, to make it easier to access it inside Flex Builder. You can also open it in your favorite text editor.

We are going to add a destination just as we did earlier, but there are other properties to be set. Write the following destination under the <default-channels> node in the XML file:

```
<destination id="loginService">
      <properties>
            <source>foed.LoginPojo</source>
            <scope>application</scope>
      </properties>
</destination>
```

The id is the name that will be used to call the remote object service from the Flex application. The source property describes the full name (including the package foed) of the class that needs to be called when Flex invokes the loginService. The scope property gives you the possibility to do some memory management by creating the LoginPojo class, one for each application. You can also set this property to session if you want to create the class for every browser session. The last possible setting is request. Then the Java class will be created for every request that is done. For all the examples, we will choose application as our scope.

Now that we have defined our destination, we are ready to call the Java class from our Flex application. We will do this by using the RemoteObject class.

Connecting to the destination and handling the result

Now we finally can go back to our Flex project. Now that we have configured our destination, we can use the RemoteObject MXML tag to connect to that destination.

Just after the Script block, create a RemoteObject tag as follows:

```
<mx:RemoteObject id="loginRO"
        destination="loginService"
        result="loginResultHandler(event)"
        fault="loginFaultHandler(event)"
/>
```

You can now clearly see the relationship between the Flex application, the destination, and the server-side Java class. Our RemoteObject tag points to the destination, and the destination points to the Java class to be called. In this way, we are able to communicate with the Java class.

We also have result and fault events, just as with the WebService and HTTPService. They are calling callback functions that we now have to write. The loginResultHandler takes a resultEvent object as a parameter. In the Script block, write the following loginResultHandler callback method.

Also write the following loginFaulthandler callback method that takes a faultEvent as parameter. You can access the returned result by using the ResultEvent.result property. Your Script block now looks like this:

```
<mx:Script >
    <![CDATA[
        import mx.controls.Alert;
        import mx.rpc.events.FaultEvent;
        import mx.rpc.events.ResultEvent;

        private function loginResultHandler(evt:ResultEvent):void{
            Alert.show(evt.result.toString());
        }
        private function loginFaultHandler(evt:FaultEvent):void{
            Alert.show(evt.fault.faultString)
        }
    ]]>
</mx:Script>
```

As you see, I also added a simple Alert to show what value will be returned from the Java class. But before something will be returned, we actually need to call the remote login method. In general, you can call a remote method like this:

```
myRemoteObject.remoteMethod(arg1,arg2,arg3)
```

Always be sure that you pass the arguments in the same order as they are accepted in the remote method. In our case, it should be the following:

```
loginRO.login("koen","friendsofed")
```

Let's try this out. The first thing we have to do is define a click handler for the button component:

```
<mx:Button id="loginBtn" label="LOGIN" click="sendMessage(event)" />
```

Inside your Script block, define the sendMessage function that will be called when the loginBtn is clicked:

```
private function sendMessage(evt:MouseEvent):void{
    var name:String = loginName.text;
    var pass:String = pass.text;
    loginRO.login(name,pass);
}
```

We take the values from the text input fields and pass them as explicit parameters to the remote login method.

When you run the application, you should see that it is all working fine. But imagine the situation in which there are different remote methods in the remote class, instead of only one. Then we want an easy-to-use way to react differently to each response we get back from a specific remote method. However, the way we declared our remoteObject means we cannot really do that. All methods that are called will use the same result and fault handler.

The solution for this is to use a <method> tag as a child of the RemoteObject tag. Because the <method> tag can have its own fault and result handlers, our problem is solved. We use the <method> tag like this:

```
<mx:RemoteObject id="loginRO"
        destination="loginService"
        fault = "loginFaultHandler(event)" >
    <mx:method name="login"
        result="loginResultHandler(event)" />
</mx:RemoteObject>
```

Make sure that the name property of the <method> tag matches the name of the remote method to be called.

When you define the remote method using the <method> tag, you can also send arguments in a slightly different way by using parameter binding. Parameter binding allows you to predefine the source of data that will be passed as arguments. The arguments must be passed in correct order. You can use the arguments tag to wrap one or more bound parameters:

```
<mx:RemoteObject id="loginRO"
        destination="loginService"
        fault = "loginFaultHandler(event)" >
    <mx:method name="login"
        result="loginResultHandler(event)" >
        <mx:arguments>
                <arg1>{loginName.text}</arg1>
                <arg2>{pass.text}</arg2>
        </mx:arguments>
    </mx:method>
</mx:RemoteObject>
```

The names arg1 and arg2 are not necessary. You can call them what you want because the names are not important; only the order in which the parameters are defined matters.

The way you have to send your data request to the remote method is also slightly different because the arguments are now already known. So the only thing you have to do is call the send method of the RemoteObject in sendMessage:

```
loginRO.login.send();
```

When you run the application and fill in the right name and password, you can log in as shown in Figure 15-11. (Remember that you might have to restart the server to register the configuration changes.)

Figure 15-11. The login application in action

Data Management Services

The LiveCycle Data Services ES Data Management Services (DMS) give you the opportunity to make high-level functionality applications. It's easy to build an application that connects to a database. It is not the client that connects directly to the database; there is some application logic on the server that fulfills this task.

When the server has the data the client asked for, the data is sent back to the client. From then on, the client can manipulate the data or display it. If changes are made to the data on the client side, the changes will be automatically sent to the server. If other clients are also using the same data, their data will be updated. You do not have to send RPC requests to say that your data has changed; it is all synchronized automatically. This makes the data services very powerful as you can imagine, but it's also a bit dangerous because synchronization conflicts can occur. Imagine that a client tries to update data that has already been deleted from the server, or that a client commits changes but the data has already changed since the client received the data. You can handle those conflicts by defining an event handler that is executed when a DataConflictEvent occurs. The classes used for conflict management are situated in the mx.data.Conflicts, mx.data.Conflict, and mx.data.events.dataConflictEvent classes.

The steps to set up a data management application will sound familiar. The only difference is that you now have client- and server-side components.

- On the client side, the Flex application uses the DataService component to connect to a server-side destination.
- On the server side, you define that destination through which data will be synchronized. You also have to create and deploy server-side code that manages the transfer of the data to a database.

The three steps to set up a DMS application will always be the same:

1. Configure a DMS destination in the data-management-config.XML file.

2. Set up data adapters and assemblers.

3. Create a DataService component on the client side.

As discussed in earlier parts of this chapter, a **destination** is the place where you send data to and receive data from. The file where we configure a destination for use with LiveCycle Data Services ES DMS applications is located in the Flex directory from the WEB-INF directory in your context root.

You can configure a lot in the configuration file. You can set a specific network element to define, for example, how many messages the server can receive or send per second. We will discuss the destination configuration in depth later on.

The next step is to set a data adapter. The most commonly used adapter is the Java adapter, whose function is to pass changes that happen to your data (for example, an update of a specific field is done on the client side) to a method that is available on a Java class on the server. The class to which the Java adapter redirects is called an assembler class. It is this assembler class that will interact with the database. For example, imagine that we have a database filled with books. If our Flex application wanted to get a specific book from the book database, we will connect to our destination where the adapter to use is declared. That adapter will then redirect the call to the right assembler class. And finally, the assembler class will have a public method declared (for example, getBook) that accesses the database directly to get the right book. Using this approach (writing your own assembler class) means that you must have serious knowledge of Java server-side coding. But this is not always necessary, as you will see later in the SQLAssembler discussion.

Finally, the data goes the whole way back to the Flex client that accepts the response and can do something with the returned data. Important also to know is that the DMS automatically maps sent or received objects. To give an example, if we have a Java class Book on the server and an ActionScript class Book on the client, objects will be mapped if they have the same properties defined. In our example, we should get back a Book object in ActionScript. The mapping is automatically done by the DMS. To let the DMS recognize the ActionScript class that must be mapped, you have to define a metadata tag in your ActionScript class that says what class must be mapped:

```
[RemoteClass(alias="myPackage.Book")]
Public class Book{
      ...//rest of the actionscript class
}
```

> *Make sure that you use the fully qualified name of the Java class (including the package names).*

Writing custom assembler classes and server-side Java code is mostly used when you have sophisticated data models or if you have serious knowledge about Java server-side code. Although this Java approach is outside the scope of this book, if you want to know more about the Java integration for the DMS server side, feel free to have a look at the official documentation: www.adobe.com/go/lcds_javadoc/.

Happily, there is also a solution if you do not have knowledge about Java but want to make Flex applications that communicate with a back-end database and also have all those great data management advantages: You can use a predefined assembler called the SQL assembler. By using this assembler, you can expose your database to MXML without writing any Java server-side code. This is the assembler we will use to examine the possibilities of the Data Management Services through an example.

In the example we will also go in detail into how to set up the DataService component—the third step in setting up a data management application.

Using DMS with SQLAssembler

In this example, we will set up a small application that shows a DataGrid filled with content coming from a database. We will use the SQLAssembler Java class because then we do not have to write server-side components in Java. When using the SQL assembler we can just provide a series of SQL statements indicating how data should be retrieved and how changes should be persisted in the database. In this way we can easily make Flex CRUD applications that are able to create, read, update and delete (CRUD) data in the database.

Setting up the Flex project

This time we will use the default location for LiveCycle Data Services ES services, so we are going to use the built-in JRun server. We are using JRun because Tomcat asks for too much configuration to get started with the Data Management Services, and that would lead us too far. We already installed LiveCycle Data Services with integrated JRun in the beginning of this chapter, so we just have to switch to the appropriate location to save our project.

Create a foed directory in the JRun context root located at C:\lcds\jrun4\servers\default\flex. We'll place our CH15_LCDS_DMS_DB_DataGrid application here.

If you are curious about what we are going to make, Figure 15-12 shows the final project for this example.

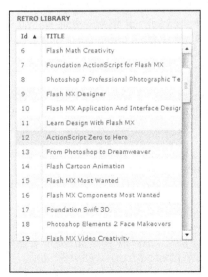

Figure 15-12. The RETRO library application in action

Create a new Flex project that uses LiveCycle Data Services ES and make sure the root folder, root URL, and context root are pointing to appropriate locations. Give your project the name CH15_LCDS_DMS_DB_DataGrid and click Next. Make sure that the foed folder is included in the project location and click Finish to open CH15_LCDS_DMS_DB_DataGrid.mxml inside Flex Builder.

Our application has a vertical layout, and we will use a DataGrid to represent the library data. So we add a DataGrid component to our stage and give it a libraryGrid identifier. We want to represent the DataGrid in a nice way, so we put in a Panel. We need only two columns: one to represent the id and one for the author. So the code for this application must look like this:

```
<?xml version="1.0" encoding="utf-8"?>
<mx:Application xmlns:mx="http://www.adobe.com/2006/mxml"
                layout="vertical">
    <mx:Style source="bookStyle.css"/>
    <mx:Panel width="300" height="400" title="RETRO LIBRARY"
            fontSize="9">
    <mx:DataGrid id="libraryGrid"
         width="100%" height="100%">
        <mx:columns >
            <mx:DataGridColumn width="40" headerText="Id"
                    editable="false"/>
            <mx:DataGridColumn headerText="Title"/>
        </mx:columns>
    </mx:DataGrid>
    </mx:Panel>
</mx:Application>
```

These are the only things we do now in the Flex application. We first have to make sure that there is some data available on the server side. So let's set up the database first.

Configuring the database for use in our Flex client application

There are several databases on the market. For this example we will use one of the simplest but most reliable databases in the world, which is based on simple text files: HSQLDB. It's a database that is written completely in Java. HSQLDB is a free open-source database that can be downloaded from http://hsqldb.sourceforge.net/.

You do not have to download the database because we include a compiled version in the source files provided with this book (in the database directory). We will use this database to get data in this exercise, and in Chapter 16 we will extend the functionality so we are also able to write to the database.

The only thing we need to do is make sure that our LiveCycle Data Services ES Data Management Services can connect to our database. Therefore we need to put the compiled version (which also includes the driver of the database) in our WEB-INF/lib directory. The file you have to place there is called hsqldb.jar.

> *Always make sure that the JDBC driver for your database is in the classpath of your web application (for example, in {context-root}\WEB-INF\lib).*

The placement of hsqldb.jar is very important because otherwise we will not be able to connect to the database because the driver won't be found (and it is the driver that tells the server how to connect to the database).

The other thing that is important to know about HSQLDB is how databases are represented. To understand how the database looks, open the database folder from the source files of this chapter. The database folder looks like Figure 15-13.

Figure 15-13. The HSQLDB is represented by simple TXT files

The .script file contains the database. This file is actually a simple text file containing a bunch of SQL statements to create the database in memory when a connection is made.

When you open the .script file in a text editor, we already made the database for you to use. (If you want to learn how to set up your own database, take a look at the HSQLDB web site at http://hsqldb.sourceforge.net/.) To be complete, we must say the .log file contains an overview of the changes that are made when the database was used by an application. The .log file is created or updated when connection with the database is made. The HSQLDB driver automatically takes care of the .script file, and when the connection is closed, the changes that are collected in the .log file are committed in the .script file.

Later on during the exercise we will use an absolute path to connect to the database, so it is very important to place the database in an easy-to-navigate-to location. I suggest you copy the database to the root directory of your computer. So the URL to access the database could be C:\database\FOEDBookArchive. You can, of course, choose another place, but just make sure that you have to fill in the right path to the database later on.

But what does our database look like? Figure 15-14 shows the structure of the table named BOOKS that we will use.

BOOK_ID	TITLE	ISBN	PUBDATE	AUTHOR	DESCRIPTION	IMAGEPATH
1	New Mas	1590592	October 200	Tomasz Jankov	New Masters of F	(null)
2	New Mas	1590592	June 2001	Hoss Gifford, Ma	Following on from	1590592069.jpg
3	New Mas	1590591	June 2001	Gavin Cromhou	friends of ED sco	(null)
4	Transitio	1590592	May 2002	Jerome Turner,	Transitions is a d	1590592050.jpg
5	50 Photc	1590592	June 2002	Scott Hamlin, Sc	Time and money	1590592026.jpg
6	Flash Ma	1590591	June 2002	Glen Rhodes, K	This is a book of	(null)
7	Foundati	1590591	June 2002	Sham Bhangal,	This book will tak	1590591666.jpg
8	Photosh	1590591	July 2002	Gavin Cromhou	Fully illustrated in	159059147X.jpg
9	Flash MX	(null)			2002	(null)
10	Flash MX	1590591	October 200	Glen Rhodes, K	In these amazing	1590591585.jpg
11	Learn De	1590591	October 200	Linda Goin, Kris	If you	(null)

Figure 15-14. The BOOKS table structure

What you clearly see is that we have seven columns: BOOK_ID, TITLE, ISBN, PUBDATE, AUTHOR, DESCRIPTION, and IMAGEPATH. It is important to know that each row in the table is uniquely identified by its BOOK_ID, which is known as the PRIMARY KEY for our table.

Now that we have installed the HSQLDB driver (hsqldb.jar) into our WEB-INF\lib directory and we placed our database itself in an easy-to-remember location, we can have a look at the Java server components involved. As we said earlier, because we are using the SQLAssembler as our assembler class we do not have to write one letter Java code on the server side. We can set up everything by simply configuring a destination. So let's go ahead.

Setting up the java-dao destination

Here we will set up the destination step by step to let you understand what everything you write means. We start by navigating to the data-management-config.xml file that is located in the WEB-INF/flex directory of your LiveCycle Data Services ES context root. When you open the file in a text editor, you see that there is only an <adapters> element defined like this within the <service> tag:

```
<adapters>
<adapter-definition id="actionscript" class="flex.data.adapters.ASObjectAdapter"
    default="true"/>
        <adapter-definition id="java-dao" class="flex.data.adapters.JavaAdapter"/>
</adapters>
```

These XML tags define the two standard adapters you can use. This statement is used to know what LiveCycle Data Services ES Java classes to call when you are referencing one of those two adapters.

Next, we have to define at least one channel. A channel is used to send messages to and from the server, just as with the other services in LiveCycle Data Services ES.

There is a configuration element called <default-channels>, in which we can define several channels to use in order of importance. We will be using the RTMP protocol as a channel to send and receive messages. You can also add a channels element specific to a destination. Define the <default-channel> element as child of the <service> element:

```
<default-channels>
        <channel ref="my-rtmp" />
</default-channels>
```

Now we are ready to set up our destination. Every destination has some properties that depend on the adapter you use. Most of the properties you can use are independent of the adapter you are using. We will start with this destination:

```
<destination id="sql-bookDest">
<adapter ref="java-dao" />
    <properties>
        <source>flex.data.assemblers.SQLAssembler</source>
        <scope>application</scope>
        <metadata>
            <identity property="BOOK_ID"/>
        </metadata>
```

```
        <network>
            <subscription-timeout-minutes>20
            <subscription-timeout-minutes>
            <paging enabled="false" pageSize="10" />
            <throttle-inbound policy="ERROR" max-frequency="500"/>
            <throttle-outbound policy="REPLACE" max-frequency="500"/>
        </network>
    </destination>
```

You can see that we defined inside our destination that we want to use the java-dao adapter. Inside the <properties> tag there are several settings. Let's go through them one by one:

- <source> node: This node points to the assembler class that we will use. In this case, we are using the built-in SQLAssembler class (because we do not want to write Java classes), so we have to specify the fully qualified name of that class. If you are an experienced Java developer and you want to use your own assembler class, you have to point to your own class.

- <scope> node: This node refers to the way your application will be scoped, as in the other LiveCycle Data Services destination configuration.

- <metadata> node: Inside this node, you see that we define an <identity> element, which maps to a database field that is the primary key of that database. This can be one or more elements to make sure you can identify items in a unique way.

- <network> node: The <network> node gives you the possibility to configure some network settings, as follows:

    The <subscription-timeout-minutes> node defines the idle time in minutes before a client is unsubscribed.

    The <paging> node defines how data must be split when sent to the client. So if you want to send the database data per ten records, you can set this node value to 10. In our case, it is not enabled.

    <throttle-inbound> and <throttle-outbound> nodes define the number of messages that can be received and sent per second, respectively. You can return an ERROR when the limit is reached or you can REPLACE the previous message when the limit is reached.

Now the most interesting part of our destination configuration: we will set up the communication with the assembler and the database. Therefore, we define a <server> element under the <network> element:

```
<server> </server>
```

Within the <server> element we define how to connect to the database:

```
<database>
    <driver-class>org.hsqldb.jdbcDriver</driver-class>
    <url>jdbc:hsqldb:file:C:/database/FOEDBookArchive</url>
    <username>sa</username>
    <password></password>
    <login-timeout>15</login-timeout>
</database>
```

We have to define the driver for the database, which you can find in your database documentation. We are using the HSQLDB database, so we define the driver in the <driver-class> node accordingly. Most databases can be protected using a username and password. You can set the <username> and <password> nodes. HSQLDB has the default user set as sa and no password. You can also set a <login-timeout> to make it more secure.

If you need to connect to another database (for example, MySQL or SQL Server), you must fill in the appropriate data in the previous node. Also make sure that the driver of your database is in the class-path of your application.

The next thing we have to add is the ActionScript class that is used on the client to represent the data so that the necessary mapping can happen when communicating between the Java back end and the ActionScript Flex front end. The class (we will set up this class later on) will be named Book and will reside in the package vo (which stands for value object—a small object used widely throughout an application).

```
<actionscript-class>vo.Book</actionscript-class>
```

Now that the database connection configuration and the ActionScript mapping are set up, we are going to define the configuration for the SQL assembler. We will define different operations that can be executed. These operations (<fill>, <create-item>, <update-item>, <delete-item>, and <count>) are standard operations that need to be defined. Each method will have some SQL that will be executed by the assembler.

We start with defining a fill operation as follows:

```
<fill>
    <name>all</name>
    <sql>SELECT * FROM BOOKS ORDER BY TITLE</sql>
</fill>
```

You have to give the fill operation a name because you can define several fill operations, and by using another name every time, they are unique. But imagine that you want to write a search query in which you want to pass in a string the user typed on the Flex client side. You can write another fill method and send arguments like this example:

```
<fill>
    <name>search_ISBN</name>
    <sql>SELECT * FROM BOOKS WHERE ISBN LIKE CONCAT('%t',
        CONCAT(#searchStr#,'%'))</sql>
</fill>
```

The SQL code indicates the searchStr that is passed as an argument object as #argName#.

The next operation will make it possible to create a new Book in the database. The create-item operation indicates properties from the Book object to use with #propName#. But you see there is also a second special query defined called id-query. This element obtains the identity of the newly created object from the database. The SQL to get that identity depends on the database you are using. For the HSQLDB, the SQL to obtain the identity is CALL IDENTITY():

```
<create-item>
    <sql>INSERT INTO BOOKS
```

```
        (TITLE,ISBN,PUBDATE,AUTHOR,DESCRIPTION,IMAGEPATH)
        VALUES (#TITLE#, #ISBN#, #PUBDATE#, #AUTHOR#,
        #DESCRIPTION#, #IMAGEPATH#)</sql>
    <id-query>CALL IDENTITY()</id-query>
</create-item>
```

The update-item operation is very similar to the previous ones; only the SQL statement differs. Actually, the current value and the previous value from the client are compared. We declare the operation like this:

```
<update-item>
    <sql>UPDATE BOOKS SET TITLE=#TITLE#, ISBN=#ISBN#,
        PUBDATE=#PUBDATE#, AUTHOR=#AUTHOR#,
        DESCRIPTION=#DESCRIPTION#,IMAGEPATH=#IMAGEPATH#
        WHERE BOOK_ID=#_PREV.BOOK_ID#</sql>
</update-item>
```

Also the delete-item operation is easy to understand:

```
<delete-item>
    <sql>DELETE FROM BOOKS WHERE BOOK_ID=#BOOK_ID#</sql>
</delete-item>
```

Another operation you can define is the count operation. This returns the number of elements in the database:

```
<count>
    <name>all</name>
    <sql>SELECT COUNT(*) FROM BOOKS</sql>
</count>
```

That's all we had to set up for our destination. Now we can dive into Flex again to connect to that destination and get the result. Therefore, we will use the DataService component. We will start with creating our client-side Book ActionScript class so that the mapping we defined in our destination can occur.

Setting up the managed Book class

You can map client-side classes to the server-side equivalents using the [RemoteClass] metatag just above the class declaration. Because we are writing the SQL assembler, you do not have to write a server version yourself. But when data from the database is returned, it will be automatically formatted as an ActionScript object that you have declared with the metatag.

Our Book class does nothing more than define the same properties that are available in the database. You must use the same property names to ensure that the mapping can happen correctly. In this example, when we set up the destination we said that we were going to write our class in the package vo.

The last thing we must write in our client-side data object is the [Managed] metatag. This metatag ensures that the compiled object generates appropriate events and errors that are required by the client-side DataService component.

Create a new folder called vo in your Flex project and insert a new class in that folder (right-click Folder and choose New Actionscript Class). You can write the client-side vo.Book class so that it looks like this:

```
package vo
{
    [Managed]
    [RemoteClass]
    public class Book
    {
            public var BOOK_ID:int;
            public var ISBN:String="";
            public var TITLE:String="";
            public var PUBDATE:String="";
            public var AUTHOR:String="";
            public var DESCRIPTION:String="";
            public var IMAGEPATH:String="";
            //constructor
                public function Book(){

                }
    }
}
```

Now we can connect to the destination using the DataService component.

Connecting to the destination and handling the result

A DataService component manages the interaction with the server-side data management server destination. We write our DataService component with id bookDS just above the <Panel> tag in our MXML code:

```
<mx:DataService id="bookDS" destination="sql-bookDest" />
```

We declare the destination to connect to as the destination property of the component. In our case, the destination is with the id sql-bookDest.

Now we can connect to the destination, and when data is sent to the Flex application it will be stored in an ArrayCollection. So we must define an arrayCollection object to capture the sent data. Because we want to use that ArrayCollection as the dataProvider for our dataGrid, and data is sent asynchronously, we will make it Bindable. So we declare a Script block in which we define the Bindable ArrayCollection myBooks:

```
<mx:Script >
    <![CDATA[
            import mx.collections.ArrayCollection;
            [Bindable]
            private var myBooks:ArrayCollection;
    ]]>
</mx:Script>
```

Bind the dataProvider of our DataGrid libraryGrid to our myBooks ArrayCollection. Also set the right dataField to be used for every column. Because we are getting an ArrayCollection with Book objects, we can refer to the properties of a Book object to be used as a dataField in the column. The final DataGrid component looks like this now:

```
<mx:DataGrid id="libraryGrid"
    dataProvider="{myBooks}"
    width="100%" height="100%" >
    <mx:columns >
        <mx:DataGridColumn dataField="BOOK_ID" width="40"
            headerText="Id"
            editable="false"/>
        <mx:DataGridColumn dataField="TITLE"
            headerText="Title"/>
    </mx:columns>
</mx:DataGrid>
```

Start the integrated LiveCycle Data Services server and run the application. The DataGrid is not populated at all because we are not calling any operation in our destination at all now. But are we already connected to the destination? The answer is yes. You can check this by using the TraceTarget debug method, as explained earlier in this book.

We can generally call any specific operation in the destination like this:

```
dataService.operation(arrayCollection, param1,param2,param3…)
```

We would like to call the fill method with the name 'all'. That specific fill method will select all records from the database and order them by title. We want to call that operation on application startup, so we are going to add an applicationComplete event in the application openings tag that calls the fill operation identified with the name 'all'.

```
<mx:Application xmlns:mx="http://www.adobe.com/2006/mxml"
        layout="vertical"
        applicationComplete="bookDS.fill(myBooks,'all')">
```

Run the application again, but this time in debug mode using the <TraceTarget> with the debug level set to level 2. Again we see no data appearing in the DataGrid. But we clearly see what the problem is in our console: Caught error initializing metadata for datastore: null error: ArgumentError: Collection argument must have a non null value.

We get this error because we try to store the result in an ArrayCollection myBooks that is not initialized. Because we have used ActionScript to declare myBooks, we have to explicitly create a new instance of the ArrayCollection class. If we had declared myBooks using MXML, we would not run into this issue because when you define an MXML tag, the object is also automatically initialized.

We will do this in an initApp function that is called when the applicationComplete event is fired. So change the Application tag like this:

```
<mx:Application xmlns:mx="http://www.adobe.com/2006/mxml"
        layout="vertical"
        applicationComplete="initApp()">
```

Write the initApp function in your Script block:

```
private function initApp():void{
    myBooks = new ArrayCollection();
    bookDS.fill(myBooks,'all');
}
```

Run the application again and you should see now how the DataGrid is finally populated with the data from the database.

To let you experience the data management and synchronization features of the LiveCycle Data Services ES Data Management Services, we will now do something very simple: simply set the editable property of the DataGrid control to true:

```
<mx:DataGrid id="libraryGrid"   editable="true" …
```

Run the application again and see that you can now manipulate the data and that changes are immediately sent to the server. This is because the autoCommit property of the DataService component is set to true. Your application should look like Figure 15-15.

Figure 15-15. The final application with synchronized and managed data

Another cool thing to try is opening the application in another browser window. You see that when you manipulate data in one browser window, the changes are immediately reflected to the other connected clients. This is because the autoSync property of the DataService component is set to true. The DMS can do this in real time because it is based on the LiveCycle Data Services ES Message Service.

In some applications, the autoSync and autoCommit features are not needed. In that case, you can easily set those properties to false in the DataService component:

```
<mx:DataService id="bookDS" destination="sql-bookDest"
        autoCommit="false"
        autoSyncEnabled="false"
/>
```

We will extend this exercise in Chapter 16 to build a fully featured book management system, so make sure to save your application.

Summary

In this chapter you learned how to set up a Flex application that uses the LiveCycle Data Services. You now know how to install it on an application server and use the Message Service, RPC services, and Data Management Services. The Message Service lets you create collaborative and real-time applications. The RPC services let you make asynchronous requests to remote services that process the requests and then return the data directly to our Flex application.

And—last but not least—we looked at the Data Management Services, which give you the opportunity to create applications that provide data synchronization, data replication, and on-demand data paging. We used the SQLAssembler class, which makes it easy to set up a data managed application by providing a series of SQL statements that indicate how data should be retrieved and how changes should be persisted in the database.

In the next chapter, we will extend the library application with extra functionality. We will make an application that lets users browse the books and a separate application in which books can be added and edited, or images can be uploaded.

Chapter 16

LIVECYCLE DATA SERVICES CASE STUDY

In this chapter, we will build a Flex application that uses the Data Management Services from LiveCycle Data Services (LCDS). The Data Management Service lets you create applications that work with distributed data. It can synchronize the client and server versions of data and do real-time data updates. The Data Management Service also gives you the power to do on-demand data paging and to work with occasionally connected clients. In our case study, we will use an HSQL database as the data source.

The Flex application is a sort of library management system. It allows the administrator to add books or edit the information from a particular book. Changes made on particular books are immediately processed on the server side and sent to other clients who are using the same data. In this way, those clients always have the latest data.

The application consists of the following parts:

- An HSQL database filled with book data
- An LCDS Data Management configuration file that declares the SQL statements to manipulate and retrieve the data in the database
- A managed client-side Book class
- A JSP file to handle the file upload of book images
- A Flex application containing the interface that handles the user interaction and communication with the LCDS Data Management Service on the server

JavaServer Pages (JSP) is a technology that, in the most basic sense, embeds Java code in web (HTML) pages. This way you can separate the dynamic part of your pages from your static HTML. The embedded Java code is executed on the server before the page is returned to the browser. JSP files have the extension `.jsp` and are placed on web servers that support JSP (for example, JRun, Tomcat, and WebSphere).

In this chapter we will use JSP server scripting to handle file uploads. You do not have to write the Java code inside the JSP page yourself because that is outside the scope of this book. We will explain later on in this chapter what the Java code does. (If you want to learn more about JSP, have a look at `http://java.sun.com/products/jsp/`.)

We will use the exercise from Chapter 15 as a starting point for this case study. If you want to create the application from scratch while you are reading, it is best to download the start files from the friends of ED web site at `www.friendsofed.com`. You can also download the finished case study at that location.

Before we start jumping into code it is important to understand the application structure and configuration, respectively, on the client and server side.

Understanding the case study

The case study actually consists of two applications that work together to deliver a fully manageable system:

- **book admin application**: This application makes it possible to manage (edit, add, delete) books. For example, only the administrator can interact with this admin application.
- **book viewer application**: This application is available for all the users who want to have a look to the books. Because we use LCDS Data Management Services, which automatically manages changes, this application will always have the latest information available.

Before we start building the application, let's examine both applications in a bit more in depth.

The book admin application

The book admin Flex application runs on the client side and uses LCDS to browse books that are in our database, to edit the details, to add new books, to delete books, and to upload new covers associated with the books.

This results in three panels that have the following structure (as shown in Figure 16-1):

- **Overview panel**: This panel consists of a DataGrid showing the books in our database. This is actually the part we already built during the last exercise in Chapter 15.
- **Detail view panel**: When a book is selected in the DataGrid, this panel shows the details from that currently selected book: Title, Author, ISBN, Publication date, and Description. The user can edit these details, and changes are saved when the user clicks the Save book changes button. The user can also cancel these changes, by clicking the Cancel book changes button.
- **Cover panel**: This little panel shows the associated cover image from the currently selected book. A user can upload a new cover to the server. For that we will use the built-in

FileReference class of Flex on the client, and also an upload script on the server that will process the actual file upload.

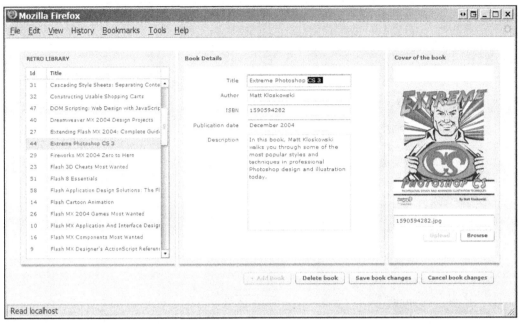

Figure 16-1. The book admin application interface

The book viewer application

The book viewer application is the application that will be visible to users who want to browse the available books and read the description or other details of the books. It is shown in Figure 16-2.

The Flex application structure consists of the following:

- **Application control bar**: Shows the friends of ED logo on top of the application. This is the branding of the application.
- **Left side of the catalog panel:** A TileList component with a custom itemRenderer that shows the book covers. The user can click on a cover in the list to see the details of that particular book.
- **Right side of the catalog panel**: A VBox component filled with several components to show the details of a book when a book cover is clicked in the TileList.

To make the Flex application as usable as possible, we will also add a horizontal divider container as a child of the catalog Panel. The user can drag the divider to resize the area as needed.

Now that we have a clear understanding of what we are going to build during this case study, it's time to also have a look what we have to configure on the server.

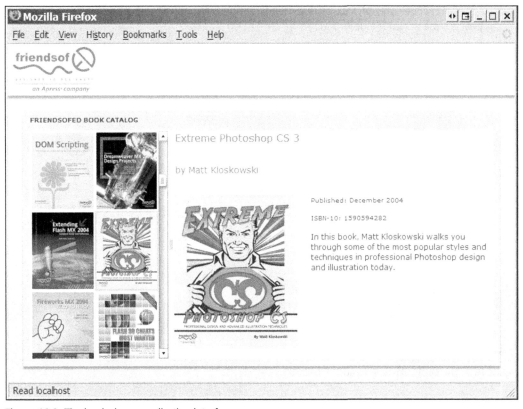

Figure 16-2. The book viewer application interface

The server-side configuration

As we already know from Chapter 15, we need to configure a destination if we want to use the Data Management Services. But because we are extending the functionality of the application, we can reuse our destination from Chapter 15. We will again use the destination called sql-bookDest.

I won't go over much of this again, so if you want more background on the configuration, take a look at Chapter 15, which discussed the server configuration when using SQLAssembler.

Our sql-book destination inside the data-management-config.xml file looks like this:

```
<destination id="sql-bookDest">
  <adapter ref="java-dao" />
  <properties>
    <use-transactions>true</use-transactions>
    <source>flex.data.assemblers.SQLAssembler</source>
    <scope>application</scope>
    <metadata>
      <identity property="BOOK_ID"/>
    </metadata>
```

```
    <network>
      <session-timeout>20</session-timeout>
      <paging enabled="false" pageSize="10" />
      <throttle-inbound policy="ERROR" max-frequency="500"/>
      <throttle-outbound policy="REPLACE" max-frequency="500"/>
    </network>
    <server>
      <database>
        <driver-class>org.hsqldb.jdbcDriver</driver-class>
        <url>jdbc:hsqldb:file:C:/database/FOEDBookArchive</url>
        <username>sa</username>
        <password></password>
        <login-timeout>15</login-timeout>
      </database>
      <actionscript-class>vo.Book</actionscript-class>
      <fill>
        <name>all</name>
        <sql>SELECT * FROM BOOKS ORDER BY TITLE</sql>
      </fill>

      <create-item>
        <sql>INSERT INTO BOOKS
          (TITLE,ISBN,PUBDATE,AUTHOR,DESCRIPTION,IMAGEPATH)
          VALUES (#TITLE#, #ISBN#, #PUBDATE#, #AUTHOR#,
          #DESCRIPTION#, #IMAGEPATH#)</sql>
        <id-query>CALL IDENTITY()</id-query>
      </create-item>

      <update-item>
        <sql>UPDATE BOOKS SET TITLE=#TITLE#, ISBN=#ISBN#,
          PUBDATE=#PUBDATE#, AUTHOR=#AUTHOR#,
          DESCRIPTION=#DESCRIPTION#,IMAGEPATH=#IMAGEPATH#
          WHERE BOOK_ID=#_PREV.BOOK_ID#</sql>
      </update-item>

      <delete-item>
        <sql>DELETE FROM BOOKS WHERE BOOK_ID=#BOOK_ID#</sql>
      </delete-item>

      <count>
        <name>all</name>
        <sql>SELECT count(*) FROM BOOKS</sql>
      </count>

    </server>
  </properties>
</destination>
```

Our destination references the java adapter and uses SQLAssembler that interacts directly with the data resource, our database. The SQLAssembler is a specialized assembler that provides a bridge from the Data Management Services to our database. We can use this assembler because we do not have a very complex database (only one table). The other possibility is (as discussed earlier in this book) to write your own assembler in Java.

When we are connected to this destination, we can call the fill method to get all the data in the database.

When updates or changes are made to the data on the client side, and changes are committed by the client-side DataService component, LCDS will execute the necessary SQL operations on the database as defined in your destination.

As you can see in the destination here, we are connecting to the same database as we did at the end of Chapter 15. We provide a driver for our database and a url to indicate where our database is stored. Let's get started building the two applications.

First, we will create the book admin application.

Creating the book admin application

To get started with this exercise, we open the start project for this case study. This is actually the last exercise we made in Chapter 15. If you do not have the exercise files from Chapter 15, you can use the start files for this chapter that you can download at the friends of ED web site.

Let's look at the code that is already in the start MXML file. When the application is fully loaded, we call the function initApp that communicates with our destination via the bookDS DataService object to call the fill method with the name 'all':

```
private function initApp():void{
  myBooks = new ArrayCollection();
  bookDS.fill(myBooks,'all');
}
```

The results are sent back from the server to the dataService component and are stored inside the ArrayCollection. The myBooks ArrayCollection is then used as the dataProvider for the DataGrid. The final code to visualize the books in the DataGrid looks like this:

```
<?xml version="1.0" encoding="utf-8"?>
<mx:Application xmlns:mx="http://www.adobe.com/2006/mxml"
                layout="vertical" applicationComplete="initApp()">
  <mx:Style source="bookStyle.css"/>
  <mx:Script >
    <![CDATA[
      import mx.collections.ArrayCollection;
      [Bindable]
      private var myBooks:ArrayCollection;

      private function initApp():void{
```

```
        myBooks = new ArrayCollection();
        bookDS.fill(myBooks,'all');
      }

    ]]>
  </mx:Script>
  <mx:DataService id="bookDS" destination="sql-bookDest"
                  autoCommit="false" autoSyncEnabled="false"/>
  <mx:TraceTarget level="2"/>

  <mx:Panel width="300" height="400" title="RETRO LIBRARY"
                  fontSize="9">
    <mx:DataGrid id="libraryGrid"  editable="true"
                  dataProvider="{myBooks}" width="100%" height="100%">
      <mx:columns>
        <mx:DataGridColumn dataField="BOOK_ID" width="40"
                            headerText="Id" editable="false"/>
        <mx:DataGridColumn dataField="TITLE" headerText="Title"/>
      </mx:columns>
    </mx:DataGrid>
  </mx:Panel>
</mx:Application>
```

If we want to edit the data, we can simply set the autoCommit and autoSyncEnabled properties to true in our DataService. The server will update the records in real time as they are changed (as shown in Chapter 15). Of course, we must also set the DataGridColumn editable="true" property to give the user permission to edit that specific column. If we set editable="false", we prevent the user from editing the data in that column.

The server will keep track of every item and collection managed on each client. However, we want the user to decide when changes are sent to the server. We will provide the user with a form in which they can view and edit the information.

Let's set up a form in a new panel.

Showing the selected book details

We want to show all the book details in a panel with a form that appears against the DataGrid. The best way to accomplish this is by putting all the panels in a horizontal box layout container.

The form for editing book details is as follows:

```
<mx:Panel width="400" height="400" title="Book Details">
  <mx:Form>
    <mx:FormItem label="Title" >
      <mx:TextInput id="txtTitle" text="" width="200"/>
    </mx:FormItem>
    <mx:FormItem label="Author">
      <mx:TextInput id="txtAuthor" text="" width="200"/>
    </mx:FormItem>
```

```
      <mx:FormItem label="ISBN">
        <mx:TextInput id="txtIsbn" text="" width="200"/>
      </mx:FormItem>
      <mx:FormItem label="Publication date">
        <mx:TextInput id="txtPubdate" text="" width="200"/>
      </mx:FormItem>
      <mx:FormItem label="Description">
        <mx:TextArea width="200" id="txtDescription"
                      text="" height="180"/>
      </mx:FormItem>
    </mx:Form>
  </mx:Panel>
```

We set the text properties of the TextInput fields to an empty String. Of course, this is not what we want; we actually want to show the content of the selected book in the DataGrid. Therefore, we need to set up a managed client-side Book class that then is mapped automatically to the server-side Book object from Chapter 15.

Creating the client-side Book class

One of the key features of the Data Management Services is that the data can be sent from server to client (and back the same way) as an object. If we have the same objects on the client and server, the LiveCycle Data Services will automatically map values between them. The server will send us an ArrayCollection filled with real ActionScript typed Book objects instead of general untyped objects. But there are a few things to do before we actually communicate with Book objects:

1. Set up an ActionScript version of the Book class object with all the necessary public properties. Those properties are the same properties that each Book record has in the database.

2. Write a [RemoteClass] metatag to tell the server that this class must be mapped to the server-side equivalent. By doing this, Book data can be serialized and deserialized by LiveCycle Data Services.

If we want LiveCycle Data Services to automatically manage our objects, we must also add the [Managed] metatag. The Book object (in our case) will then automatically trigger events when its properties are changed and these events are caught by the server.

We already made the Book class in Chapter 15, so we are going to reuse that class. That Book class is situated in the vo package and looks like this:

```
package vo
{
  [Managed]
  [RemoteClass]
  public class Book
  {
    public var BOOK_ID:int;
    public var ISBN:String="";
    public var TITLE:String="";
    public var PUBDATE:String="";
    public var AUTHOR:String="";
```

```
        public var DESCRIPTION:String="";
        public var IMAGEPATH:String="";
        //constructor
        public function Book(){
          //empty
        }
      }
    }
```

Now that we have a managed Book class, we can get the Book object as a result of the fill method call from our DataService.

In the next part we will set up a double binding between the TextInput fields and the selected Book object in the DataGrid. Every time the user clicks a record in the DataGrid, we will fill a Book object with the correct data and show that information in the corresponding text fields.

Populating the form with the book details

To set up a double binding between the Book object and the text fields, we first declare a Book object just after the Script block.

In this case, we are going to declare that Book object in MXML and immediately bind the value of each property of that object to the corresponding value of the text fields:

```
<vo:Book id="book"
        TITLE="{txtTitle.text}"
        AUTHOR="{txtAuthor.text}"
        DESCRIPTION="{txtDescription.text}"
        ISBN="{txtIsbn.text}"
        PUBDATE="{txtPubdate.text}"/>
```

By declaring the Book object in MXML, it is automatically instantiated. Make sure that you add the necessary namespace to the application tag because otherwise the Book object cannot be found. The namespace used here is the following:

```
xmlns:vo="vo.*"
```

This is the first part of the binding. The other part binds the text property of the TextInput fields to the corresponding properties of our Book object:

```
...
<mx:TextInput id="txtTitle" text="{book.TITLE}" width="200"/>
...
<mx:TextInput id="txtAuthor" text="{book.AUTHOR}" width="200"/>
...
<mx:TextInput id="txtIsbn" text="{book.ISBN}" width="200"/>
...
<mx:TextInput id="txtPubdate" text="{book.PUBDATE}" width="200"/>
...
<mx:TextArea width="200" text= "{book.DESCRIPTION}" id="txtDescription"
            height="180"/>
...
```

We have full Book objects available in the DataGrid. So the only thing we still have to do is assign the currently selected Book object in the DataGrid to the book variable. This will happen when the user clicks a record in the DataGrid, which corresponds with the change event of the DataGrid control.

Add the change event to the DataGrid control and fill our declared Book object with the data from the selected item:

```
<mx:DataGrid id="libraryGrid"  editable="false"
            change="{book=libraryGrid.selectedItem as Book;}"
            dataProvider="{myBooks}"
            width="100%" height="100%">
```

Run the application and you should see that the text fields are filled in with the correct Book data when you click on a row in the DataGrid, as shown in Figure 16-3.

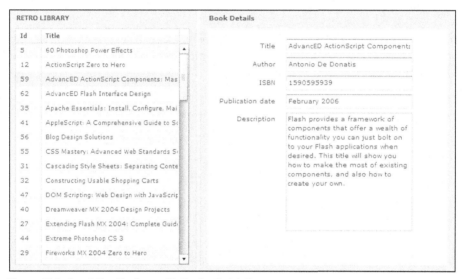

Figure 16-3. Populating the form with the book details

Showing the book cover image

We also want to show a cover for every book. There is a cover file name available for each book item in the database stored on the client side in the IMAGEPATH property of each Book object. Later on in this chapter, we will add the functionality to update a cover and upload a new cover image.

To show the image associated with a Book object, we will use an Image component. We create a new Panel with an image component inside:

```
<mx:Panel title="Cover of the book" horizontalAlign="center"
        verticalAlign="middle" height="400">
  <mx:VBox >
    <mx:Image id="theCover" width="200" height="245"
            source="covers/{book.IMAGEPATH}"/>
    <mx:TextInput id="txtPathToFile" text="{book.IMAGEPATH}"
```

```
                                       width="100%"/>
              </mx:VBox>
           </mx:Panel>
```

We bind the source attribute of the Image component to the Book object's IMAGEPATH property. We also bind the text property of the TextInput component in this way.

To make this work, we must extend our Book object and bind the IMAGEPATH property also to the text field:

```
<vo:Book id="book"
         TITLE="{txtTitle.text}"
         AUTHOR="{txtAuthor.text}"
         DESCRIPTION="{txtDescription.text}"
         ISBN="{txtIsbn.text}"
         PUBDATE="{txtPubdate.text}"
         IMAGEPATH="{txtPathToFile.text}"/>
```

The last thing we need to do is make sure that we can access the images.

The source path for the images now refers to the covers directory, which must be placed in the bin directory of your project so it can be accessed from within the Flex application. If you now run the application, you should see the image component showing the correct cover corresponding to each Book object.

We now have a basic version of our application. However, when we edit the book's details, changes are not saved, so let's go ahead and add that functionality.

Updating the selected book details

We are going to give the user the capability to edit book details. When changes are made, they will be able to save the changes or revert to the original version. You will see that this is extremely simple to implement because of the built-in methods of the DataService class:

- When changes are made to the book data, you can save the changes by calling the DataService.commit method.
- When you want to revert to the original version after you made changes to data, you can simply call the DataService.revertChanges method.

We place a ControlBar underneath the three panels that contain the two Buttons, as shown in Figure 16-4.

Our three panels are children of an HBox container. The HBox container is, together with the ControlBar, a child of the VBox container. So we need to add a VBox container and a ControlBar container:

```
<mx:ControlBar horizontalAlign="right" width="100%">
  <mx:Button label="Save book changes"
             enabled="{bookDS.commitRequired}"
             click="bookDS.commit()"/>
```

```
        <mx:Button label="Cancel book changes"
                   enabled="{bookDS.commitRequired}"
                   click="bookDS.revertChanges()"/>
    </mx:ControlBar>
```

The commit method will send the changes to the server. When changes are made to the data, the commitRequired property is automatically set to true and the Save book changes button is enabled. When you run the application now, you can edit book details and send the changes to the server or cancel the changes.

The user must also be able to delete and add a book. Let's have a look how to do that.

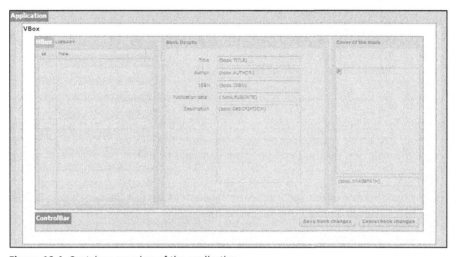

Figure 16-4. Container overview of the application

Deleting a Book object

We add an extra Button to the ControlBar component that has a callback function defined for the click event.

```
        <mx:Button label="Delete book" click="deleteBook()"/>
```

In the deleteBook function we are going to call the deleteItem method from the DataService component. This client-side method will contact the correct method on the server that will execute the necessary SQL operation to delete book data from the database.

The callback function to be added in your Script block looks like this:

```
    private function deleteBook():void{
      bookDS.deleteItem(libraryGrid.selectedItem)
      bookDS.commit();
    }
```

The deleteItem method asks the id as parameter, so only that specific record is deleted in the database. We also again need to call the commit function manually for changes to take effect. That's all we need to do to implement the delete functionality.

Adding a Book object

We also add an extra Button in our controlBar that has a callback function defined called newBook:

```
<mx:Button label="+ Add Book" click="newBook()"
           enabled="{!bookDS.commitRequired}"/>
```

When the user adds a new Book, we want to send that data also as a Book object to the server. So to add a new Book, we must start with an empty new Book object. We add that new Book instance to the ArrayCollection that is used as the dataProvider for the DataGrid and set the selectedIndex to the newly added book.

The newBook function looks like this:

```
private function newBook():void{
  myBooks.addItem(new Book());
  libraryGrid.selectedIndex = myBooks.length - 1;
}
```

When we run the application, we can add a new Book that is instantiated with BOOK_ID 0 and each empty String as a value for the other properties.

We can fill in the details and then click the Save book changes button to send the newly created Book object to the server. On the server, the correct BOOK_ID is given as described in the configuration of our destination.

Let's go a step further and give users the ability to upload a new cover.

Uploading a book cover to the server

In this part of the case study we are going to implement some file transfer basics. The steps to implement file transfer are the following:

1. Present a Browse button to the user.
2. Show a dialog box that allows the user to search the local file system for a file to upload.
3. Upload the file to the server.
4. Process the file upload using a server-side script.

To implement a file transfer in a Flex application we need to use the FileReference class. We can use the browse, upload, and cancel methods of the FileReference class to manage the upload process. So let's start by creating a FileReference object.

Creating a FileReference object

In the Script block of our application we create an instance of the FileReference class called imageFileRef. The code is as follows:

```
private var imageFileRef:FileReference = new FileReference();
```

The FileReference object refers to one file on the user's computer and is populated with all kinds of information about the file (for example: size, type, name, creation date, modification date, and creator).

Browsing the file system

The FileReference class has a browse method that shows a standard dialog box (to browse the local file system) and allows the user to select a file for upload. We are going to call that browse method when the user clicks a Browse button. When a file is selected in the dialog box, the user can upload the selected image file by pressing an Upload button.

We place the buttons just after our txtPathToFile TextInput field. So our structure for the image Panel will look like Figure 16-5.

Figure 16-5. Container structure
of the third panel

The highlighted VBox in Figure 16-5 is represented by the following code:

```
<mx:VBox horizontalAlign="right" width="200">
  <mx:TextInput id="txtPathToFile" text="{book.IMAGEPATH}" width="100%"/>
  <mx:HBox>
    <mx:Button id="uploadbtn" label="Upload" enabled="false"
               click="fileUpload()"/>
    <mx:Button id="browsebtn" label="Browse" click="fileBrowse()"/>
  </mx:HBox>
</mx:VBox>
```

As you can see, we define the two Buttons and we call a specific function when a Button is clicked.

We will first look at the callback function of the Browse Button. Inside your Script block write the following code for the fileBrowse callback function:

```
private function fileBrowse():void{
   imageFileRef.browse();
}
```

Also inside the fileBrowse method we are going to start listening for the Select event of the FileReference class. This way, the onSelect function will be executed when a file is selected.

Add the following eventListener inside the fileBrowse function:

```
imageFileRef.addEventListener(Event.SELECT,onSelect);
```

The onSelect function looks like this and must be added inside your Script block:

```
private function onSelect(evt:Event):void{
   txtPathToFile.text = imageFileRef.name;
   uploadbtn.enabled = true;
}
```

As you see, the only thing we do here is enable the uploadbtn so that the file can be uploaded when there is one selected. Also we read the name of the selected file and place it inside the txtPathToFile text field.

If you run the application and you click the browsebtn Button, you should see the Browse dialog box appear, in which you can select a file from your local file system.

Now that we know the selected file, we can start uploading the selected file.

Uploading the selected file

When the user clicks the Upload button, the FileReference upload method is called. It can take two parameters (the second is optional):

- URL: A URLRequest object that forms the link to the server-side upload script.
- UploadDataFieldName: By default, Flex assumes that the variable name used in the server-side script to reference the upload file name is Filedata. You can use this parameter to rename the variable. We will use the default name in our case study.

So we need a URLRequest object to be passed to the upload method of the FileReference class. Let's instantiate this object on top in our Script block as follows:

```
private var uploadTarget:URLRequest =
   new URLRequest("ProcessFileUpload.jsp");
```

We point to the JSP page called ProcessFileUpload.jsp. (You can find this JSP page in the upload folder of the start files for Chapter 16.) Place this JSP page in the same folder as your MXML application to make sure the application can access it. We will explain this JSP page in the next part. You can easily open the JSP page in a text editor of your choice.

Now we can write the `fileUpload` function. The code for the callback function looks like this:

```
private function fileUpload():void{
  imageFileRef.upload(uploadTarget);
}
```

We just need to call the upload method of the `FileReference` instance and pass the `URLRequest` instance as the parameter.

The actual processing of the uploaded file is done by our upload script on the server, so let's take a look at how that script works. We will work through the server script only briefly because our focus is really on the Flex side of the upload process.

Understanding the server-side script

We are using a script on our server to do the processing of the upload. In our case we are using a JSP page. You do not have to write the JSP page yourself. You can use the `ProcessFileUpload.jsp` file, which is included inside the upload folder of the start files for this chapter.

Before you can use this JSP page in the Flex application, we must first add some extra libraries to our application server because JSP does not have a built-in mechanism for handling file uploads. We are using the well-proven Apache Commons FileUpload library, which easily handles file uploads in JSP. (We included the necessary `commons-fileupload.jar` library in the upload\extra libraries folder of the start files for Chapter 16.)

If you want to know more about the FileUpload project or want to download the latest FileUpload library yourself, have a look at the Commons FileUpload project home page: `http://commons.apache.org/fileupload/`.

We also need another third-party library: `commons-io.jar`. We need the Commons IO library because the Commons FileUpload library uses it internally. The Commons IO library contains file input- output-specific classes.

So we have two extra libraries that we need to install on our web server. To do this, just copy the files `commons-fileupload.jar` and `commons-io.jar` to the WEB-INF/lib/ directory in the document root of your web application. The full path depends on where you have your LCDS installation but it will probably look like this: ..\jrun4\servers\default\flex\WEB-INF\lib.

Now that we made those extra libraries available, we can have a look at the JSP page that will handle the file upload.

The script is already built for you with the guidelines in the FileUpload package, which are available on the Apache Commons web site. Because we are not going to examine this script in much detail, you can find a lot more information in the user guide online: `http://commons.apache.org/fileupload/using.html`.

The total JSP page looks like the following:

```jsp
<%@ page contentType="text/html;charset=windows-1252"%>
<%@ page import="org.apache.commons.fileupload.*"%>
<%@ page import="org.apache.commons.fileupload.disk.*"%>
<%@ page import="org.apache.commons.fileupload.servlet.*"%>
<%@ page import="java.util.*"%>
<%@ page import="java.io.*"%>
<%
  DiskFileItemFactory factory = new DiskFileItemFactory();
  ServletFileUpload upload = new ServletFileUpload(factory);
  upload.setSizeMax(1000000);
  List fileItems = upload.parseRequest(request);
  Iterator itr = fileItems.iterator();
  String requestPath = request.getServletPath();
  int lastSlash = requestPath.lastIndexOf("/");
  String covers = application.getRealPath(requestPath.substring(0,
    lastSlash) +"/covers");

  while(itr.hasNext()) {
     FileItem fi = (FileItem)itr.next();

     if(!fi.isFormField()) {
       File fNew= new File(covers, fi.getName());
       fi.write(fNew);
       break;
     }
   }
%>
```

The first part of the script parses the data contained in the HTTP request coming from our Flex application. DiskFileItemFactory is a class contained in the fileupload.disk package:

```java
DiskFileItemFactory factory = new DiskFileItemFactory();
ServletFileUpload upload = new ServletFileUpload(factory);
upload.setSizeMax(1000000);
List fileItems = upload.parseRequest(request);
```

If everything works fine, fileItems will contain a list of file items that are instances of the FileItem class, which is part of the FileUpload library. The ServletFileUpload instance called upload will parse the request by calling the parseRequest method. If the file size of the data exceeds a particular value, the upload will not be executed.

Next we determine the current home directory and append the covers path to it in order to figure out where to place the file:

```
String requestPath = request.getServletPath();
int lastSlash = requestPath.lastIndexOf("/");
String covers = application.getRealPath(requestPath.substring(0,
    lastSlash) +"/covers");
```

Finally, we iterate through the file items and process each of them. We process the List of file items, which can be either a form field or a file. We determine each file item's type by calling the FileItem.isFormField method; if it returns false, it is a File. Requests generated by Flash Player's FileReference can contain only a single file, so we write only one file to disk:

```
while(itr.hasNext()) {
    FileItem fi = (FileItem)itr.next();

    if(!fi.isFormField()) {
      File fNew= new File(covers, fi.getName());
      fi.write(fNew);
      break;
    }
}
```

When we run the application now, we can search for an image on our local file system and upload that image to our server. The script processes that file and saves it in the covers directory.

In next part of this case study, we will build the viewer application that gives a user the ability to browse through the books, but editing is not possible. The viewer will always have the latest data to visualize because it is supported by the LiveCycle Data Services Data Management Services.

Creating the book viewer application

We will build a simple book viewer application that easily can be placed on the Web to give visitors the ability to browse books. When they click the book in the list, they see the details.

The users can easily see all the data on one page, making the user experience more enhanced. If they are browsing the books and at some point the data is changed by the admin application, changes are automatically reflected to all visitors who are using the book viewer application. This is all automatically done by LiveCycle Data Services Data Management Services.

Let's get started by building the Flex application.

Adding an application ControlBar

We will make this part of the application from scratch, so the first thing we need to do is add a new MXML application to our project:

1. Right-click on your project and choose New ➤ MXML application. Give it the name BookViewer and choose a vertical layout. Click Finish.

2. Now add an Image component inside an application ControlBar to the application:

```
<mx:ApplicationControlBar barColor="0xFFFFFF" width="100%" dock="true"
                          fillAlphas="[1.0, 1.0]"
                          fillColors="[#FFFFFF, #FFFFFF]">
  <mx:Image source="@Embed('friendsofed.gif')"  scaleContent="false"/>
</mx:ApplicationControlBar>
```

Make sure that the image of the logo is placed in the same directory of your MXML project. Now we will connect to the destination using a DataService component.

Setting up the Flex DataService

A DataService component manages the interaction with a server-side Data Management Services destination.

- Add a DataService component that connects to our sql-bookDest server-side destination and set the autoSyncEnabled property to true. The autoSyncEnabled property determines whether we should track changes for items returned from the server:

```
<mx:DataService id="bookDS" destination="sql-bookDest"
                autoSyncEnabled="true" />
```

- We want to call the remote fill method when the application is fully loaded, so we declare an applicationComplete event in the Application opening tag. The remote fill method wants an ArrayCollection as a parameter where it can map all the retuned objects. We declare an ArrayCollection object called theBooks inside our Script block and instantiate it inside the initApp function:

```
<mx:Application xmlns:mx="http://www.adobe.com/2006/mxml"
                layout="vertical"
                applicationComplete="initApp()">
  <mx:Script>
    <![CDATA[
      import mx.collections.ArrayCollection;
      [Bindable]
      private var theBooks:ArrayCollection;
      private function initApp():void{
        theBooks = new ArrayCollection();
        bookDS.fill(theBooks,'all');
      }
    ]]>
  </mx:Script>

  <mx:DataService id="bookDS" destination="sql-bookDest"
                  autoSyncEnabled="true"/>
  <mx:ApplicationControlBar barColor="0xFFFFFF"
                  width="100%" dock="true"
                  fillAlphas="[1.0, 1.0]"
                  fillColors="[#FFFFFF, #FFFFFF]">
```

529

```
        <mx:Image source="@Embed('friendsofed.gif')"
                        scaleContent="false"/>
    </mx:ApplicationControlBar>
</mx:Application>
```

Make sure that you set the ArrayCollection theBooks bindable by using the [Bindable] directive.

Now that we have the data from the database available, we are ready to visualize that data using a TileList component that will show all the covers of the books available in the ArrayCollection. As a best practice, we will use a custom itemRenderer for our TileList. This makes it easier to reuse and we can separate the code a bit. So let's set up that custom item renderer first.

Building the custom item renderer

You already built some custom components in Flex in earlier chapters, but let's review how it works.

- We already have a package called vo available where we stored our Book object. In this same package we will place our custom component. Right-click on the vo folder and choose File ➤ New ➤ MXML component. Give it the file name BookThumb, based on a Canvas and dimensions 100 × 120 pixels. Click Finish.

- Inside the Canvas opening tag we also set the horizontalScrollPolicy and verticalScrollPolicy to off, so no scrollbars will appear inside our item:

```
<?xml version="1.0" encoding="utf-8"?>
<mx:Canvas xmlns:mx="http://www.adobe.com/2006/mxml"
            width="100" height="120"
            verticalScrollPolicy="off"
            horizontalScrollPolicy="off">
</mx:Canvas>
```

Next we place an Image component between the Canvas tags to show the cover of the current item. We can access the current Book object's IMAGEPATH property inside our component by referring to data.IMAGEPATH. We also make it bindable to make sure that the image is shown when the data becomes available. Because our covers are located in a folder called covers, we concatenate that directory with the IMAGEPATH property:

```
<mx:Image source="covers/{data.IMAGEPATH}" width="100"
                height="120" horizontalCenter="0"/>
```

If you want, you can also show other information about the current book by just referencing the data.propertyName. For example, if you want to show the ISBN for each book element in the TileList, just add a text field inside your custom component that refers to the data.ISBN property.

Now we can actually use our custom component as an item renderer in a TileList. Let's add a TileList in our Bookviewer MXML application.

Showing the books in a TileList

To make things as user friendly as possible, we choose to work with a horizontal divided box container. Our TileList is a child of that HDividedBox container, and we will use our brand-new BookThumb component as the item renderer. The code looks like this, and we add this code after the DataService declaration:

```
<mx:HDividedBox width="100%" height="100%">
  <mx:TileList id="bookTiles" dataProvider="{theBooks}"
               width="30%" height="100%"
               itemRenderer="vo.BookThumb"
               columnWidth="105" rowHeight="125" borderStyle="none"/>
</mx:HDividedBox>
```

We bind the dataProvider property to the ArrayCollection we declared as bindable earlier. In this way, our TileList is filled with Book objects, presented by our itemRenderer. This happens when data becomes available from the server.

When we run the application now, we see a TileList filled with book covers, as shown in Figure 16-6.

Figure 16-6. The book viewer TileList filled with book covers

Now we are going to extend this application so that when an item is clicked in the list, we see all the details of the selected item.

Showing the details of each book

Just as in the first part of the application, we will write an event handler for the change event of the TileList component. When an item is selected in the list, we fill a Book object with the data from the selected item. If we then bind that Book object to our visual controls, our controls will always show the correct data. The only difference here is that there is no double binding because we do not want to let the user change the values of the Book object:

```
<mx:TileList id="bookTiles" dataProvider="{theBooks}"
            width="30%" height="100%"
            itemRenderer="vo.BookThumb"
            columnWidth="105" rowHeight="125" borderStyle="none"
            change="{book=bookTiles.selectedItem as Book;}"/>
```

If we want to use the Book component in MXML, we also must declare a namespace in our application tag before we can instantiate Book objects. We have built our client-side Book class already and it is located in the vo package, so inside the Application tag we can add xmlns:vo="vo.*" as an extra namespace, for example.

Now we can start with declaring an MXML Book object just after the Script block:

```
<vo:Book id="book"/>
```

We add a VBox component after the TileList component and inside the HDividedBox component. That VBox consists of several read-only TextArea controls. We bind the TextArea controls to the Book object we just declared. The total code is as follows:

```
<mx:VBox width="50%" height="100%" >
  <mx:TextArea styleName="titleStyle" id="txtTitle" text="{book.TITLE}"
              width="100%" borderStyle="none"
              editable="false"
              backgroundAlpha="0"/>
  <mx:TextArea styleName="authorStyle" id="txtAuthor"
              text="by {book.AUTHOR}"
              width="100%"  borderStyle="none"
              editable="false"
              backgroundAlpha="0"/>
  <mx:HBox width="100%" height="100%" horizontalGap="20">
    <mx:Image id="bookImage" source="covers/{book.IMAGEPATH}"/>
    <mx:VBox width="100%" height="100%" verticalGap="10">
      <mx:Text styleName="smallText" id="txtPubdate"
              text="Published: {book.PUBDATE}"/>
      <mx:Text styleName="smallText" id="txtIsbn"
              text="ISBN-10: {book.ISBN}"/>
      <mx:TextArea styleName="descText" borderStyle="none"
                  id="txtDescription" text="{book.DESCRIPTION}"
                  editable="false" width="100%" height="100%"
```

```
                                    backgroundAlpha="0"/>
                </mx:VBox>
            </mx:HBox>
        </mx:VBox>
```

The code shows that there are also some styles applied on the controls. The stylesheet used for this application is included in the start files, and you can simply apply the style to your application by writing a style declaration tag that points to the CSS file. Feel free to style your application as you want or use the included bookStyle.css stylesheet.

```
<mx:Style source="bookStyle.css"/>
```

As a finishing touch, we could place the whole HDividedBox in a Panel:

```
<mx:Panel title="FRIENDSOFED BOOK CATALOG" width="100%" height="100%"
          paddingTop="2" paddingLeft="2" paddingBottom="2"
          paddingRight="2">
    //the HDividedBox comes here
    ...
</mx:Panel>
```

Now our second application is also fully created. Let's have a look now how the two applications work together.

Testing both applications

By testing the applications, you will experience why LCDS Data Management Services are so powerful.

- Run both the book admin and one (or more) book viewer applications in separate browser windows. Arrange the windows so you can clearly see both applications.
- In both applications, search for a book you want to test with.
- Change some details in the data admin application and save the changes.
- You clearly see in the book viewer that the changes you made in the admin application are immediately reflected in the viewer application.

Summary

This chapter showed you how easy it is to set up an application that uses the basics of the Data Management Services. The data is synchronized between client and server without compromising the user experience, the integrity of the data, or the scalability and performance of the application.

We used the SQLAssembler class, which communicates with our database when changes are made, and the server side can propagate one client's changes to other clients to ensure that the client has the most up-to-date view of the data.

The LiveCycle Data Services, and especially the Data Management Services, have a lot more functionality then described here. We only showed you a small portion of its capabilities to let you learn the basics and to get started using those interesting services to build real-time collaborative applications.

INDEX

symbols
* asterisk, 101
== equality operator, 231
" " quotes, 218, 224
{ } curly braces notation, 20, 54, 185–190, 195, 244
@ symbol, 229, 274

A
Access databases
  ASP.NET and, 375
  as external data source, 360
ActionScript 3.0, 8, 17–44
ActionScript classes and, 10
  alerts and, 76
  best practices for, 43
  CDATA blocks and, 220
  complex data structures and, 179–187
  consuming web services and, 263
  creating projects and, 36
  data binding and, 42, 187 195–200
  data models and, 97
  errors and, 315–323
  event handling and, 40
  HTTPService class and, 148, 159, 164
  JavaScript and, 131, 135
  major changes in, 9, 17
  URLLoader class and, 153, 156
  user input validation and, 110
  working with in Flex applications, 18–40
  XML content and, 391, 436
ActionScript components
  creating, 63–67
  dispatching events from, 66
  vs. MXML components, 67
  values, passing to, 65
ActionScript functions, data binding and, 189
ActionScript Virtual Machine (AVM2), 17
ActionScript Virtual Machines (AVMs), 8
ActiveX, 130
AC_OETags.js file, 125
addEventListener method, 149, 258
addListener method, 40
aip prefix, 204

Ajax applications, 5
Alert control, 76, 78–84
alerts, 76–84
  modifying, 82
  parent for, 77
allow-access-from tag, 175
allowDomain method, 144
allowMultipleSelection property, 281
AMF content, Flex and, 12
Apache Commons FileUpload library, 526
Apache Tomcat servers, LiveCycle Data Services and,
    470, 475
appendChild method, 235
application (business logic) tier, 4, 357
application development process, list of steps for,
    13
Application tag, 7, 19–25, 216, 221
applications. *See* Flex applications
architecture, 4
ASP.NET, 167, 170, 375–419
ASP.NET pages, event booking system case study
    and, 386–390
asterisk (*), indicating required field, 101
attribute method, 234
attributes, 218, 224
attributes method, 234
automatic layouts, 269
AVM2 (ActionScript Virtual Machine), 17
AVMs (ActionScript Virtual Machines), 8

B
BEA WebLogic servers, LiveCycle Data Services and,
    470
best practices
  for ActionScript 3.0, 43
  validators and, 201
binary files, as external data source, 148
[Bindable] metatag, 268
binding expressions, 185
Binding tag, 187, 189–195, 245
bindProperty method, 195, 198
bindSetter method, 195, 197–200
blog (case study), 421–466

535

friendsofed.com/forums

Join the friends of ED forums to find out more about our books, discover useful technology tips and tricks, or get a helping hand on a challenging project. *Designer to Designer*™ is what it's all about—our community sharing ideas and inspiring each other. In the friends of ED forums, you'll find a wide range of topics to discuss, so look around, find a forum, and dive right in!

■ **Books and Information**

Chat about friends of ED books, gossip about the community, or even tell us some bad jokes!

■ **Flash**

Discuss design issues, ActionScript, dynamic content, and video and sound.

■ **Web Design**

From front-end frustrations to back-end blight, share your problems and your knowledge here.

■ **Site Check**

Show off your work or get new ideas.

■ **Digital Imagery**

Create eye candy with Photoshop, Fireworks, Illustrator, and FreeHand.

■ **ArchivED**

Browse through an archive of old questions and answers.

───────────── **HOW TO PARTICIPATE** ─────────────

Go to the friends of ED forums at **www.friendsofed.com/forums**.

1-59059-543-2 $39.99 [US]

1-59059-518-1 $39.99 [US]

1-59059-542-4 $36.99 [US]

1-59059-517-3 $39.99 [US]

1-59059-651-X $44.99 [US]

EXPERIENCE THE
DESIGNER TO DESIGNER™
DIFFERENCE

1-59059-558-0 $49.99 [US]

1-59059-314-6 $59.99 [US]

New Masters of Photoshop

1-59059-315-4 $59.99 [US]

1-59059-619-6 $44.99 [US]

1-59059-304-9 $49.99 [US]

1-59059-355-3 $24.99 [US]

1-59059-409-6 $39.99 [US]

1-59059-748-6 $49.99 [US]

1-59059-593-9 $49.99 [US]

1-59059-555-6 $44.99 [US]

DOM Scripting

1-59059-533-5 $34.99 [US]

Web Accessibility

1-59059-638-2 $49.99 [US]

HTML Mastery
Semantics, Standards, and Styling

Paul Haine

1-59059-765-6 $34.99 [US]

Blog Design
Solutions

1-59059-581-5 $39.99 [US]

CSS Mastery
Advanced Web Standards Solutions

1-59059-614-5 $34.99 [US]

Flash Application
Design Solutions
The Flash Usability Handbook

1-59059-594-7 $39.99 [US]

WEB STANDARDS SOLUTIONS

1-59059-381-2 $34.99 [US]

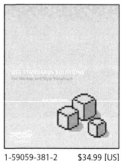

PODCAST
SOLUTIONS
The Complete Guide to Podcasting

1-59059-554-8 $24.99 [US]